CULTURE IN PROCESS

CULTURE IN PROCESS

Second Edition

Alan R. Beals
University of California, Riverside

George Spindler
Stanford University

Louise Spindler
Stanford University

HOLT, RINEHART AND WINSTON, INC.
New York   Chicago   San Francisco   Atlanta
Dallas   Montreal   Toronto   London   Sydney

Joe Edwin Hargrove, the illustrator of this book,
was born at El Campo, Texas, on May 30, 1937. He
studied art at Texas Southern University, San Jose
State College, California (under Professors Thomas Elsner
and Richard Sorby), and at the Oakland Institute of Art.
He is currently director of the art production department,
Stanford Press, Stanford, California.

COPYRIGHT ACKNOWLEDGMENTS

The authors wish to thank the following copyright holders for permission to reprint extracts from their listed works:

Appleton-Century-Crofts, for *The Study of Man,* by Ralph Linton, copyright © 1936. Reprinted by permission of Appleton-Century-Crofts, Educational Division, Meredith Corp.

The Beacon Press, for *We, the Tikopia: A Sociological Study of Kinship in Primitive Polynesia,* by Raymond Firth, 1963. (First published in 1936 by George Allen & Unwin Ltd.)

Columbia University Press, for "The Tanala of Madagascar," by Ralph Linton, in *The Individual and His Society,* ed. by Abraham Kardiner, 1939.

E. P. Dutton & Co., Inc., and Routledge & Kegan Paul Ltd., for *Argonauts of the Western Pacific,* by Bronislaw Malinowski, 1922.

Fawcett World Library, Premier Books, for *My Life as an Indian,* by Jessie W. Schultz, 1907, 1956.

Glydendal Publishers, for *The Intellectual Culture of the Iglulik Eskimos.* (Report of the 5th Thule Expedition, 1921–1924, Vol. VII, No. 1, W. Worster trans.), 1929.

Gregg International Publishers Ltd., for *Aboriginal Women: Sacred and Profane,* by Phyllis Kaberry, 1970.

Harper & Row, Publishers, Inc., for pp. 291–292 of "A Reformer of His People," by David G. Mandelbaum, in *In the Company of Man*, edited by Joseph B. Casagrande. By permission of Harper & Row, Publishers, Inc.

Holt, Rinehart and Winston, Inc., for *Being a Palauan*, by H. G. Barnett, 1960; *Bunyoro: An African Kingdom*, by John Beattie, 1960; *Yanomamö: The Fierce People*, by N. Chagnon, 1968; *The Eskimo of North Alaska*, by Norman A. Chance, 1966; *K'un Shen: A Taiwan Village*, by Norma Diamond, 1969; *Hano: A Tewa Indian Community in Arizona*, by Edward Dozier, 1966; *Growing Up in Two Worlds: Education and Transition among the Sisala of Northern Ghana*, by Bruce T. Grindal, 1972; *The Tiwi of North Australia*, by C. W. M. Hart and A. R. Pilling, 1960; *A Guadalcanal Society: The Kaoka Speakers*, by Ian Hogbin, 1964: *The Hutterites in North America*, by John A. Hostetler and Gertrude E. Huntington, 1967; *The School at Mopass: A Problem of Identity*, by Richard A. King, 1967; *The Swazi: A South African Kingdom*, by Hilda Kuper, 1963; *The Crow Indians*, by Robert H. Lowie, 1956; *The Lugbara of Uganda*, by John Middleton, 1965; *Changing Japan*, by Edward Norbeck, 1966; *Life in a Turkish Village*, by Joe E. Pierce, 1964; *Que Gitano! Gypsies of Southern Spain*, by Bertha B. Quintana and Lois Gray Floyd, 1972; *"Shut Those Thick Lips": A Study of Slum School Failure*, by Gerry Rosenfeld, 1971; *Them Children: A Study in Language Learning*, by Martha Coonfield Ward, 1971; and *The Dusun: A North Borneo Society*, by Thoman Rhys Williams, 1965.

Kroeber Anthropological Society, for "Deviancy and Social Control: What Makes Biboi Run?" by Robert Murphy, *Kroeber Anthropological Society Papers*, 24: 55–61.

Mouton and Co., for *Sociétés d'Initiation Bambara: le n'domo, leKorè*, by Dominique Zahan, 1960.

Martinus Nijhoff, for *Ngaju Religion: The Conception of God among a South Borneo People*, by Hans Schärer, 1963, Rodney Needham, trans.

Oxford University Press, for *The Religion of an Indian Tribe*, by Verrier Elwin, 1955.

Russell Sage Foundation, for "Technological and Social Institutions: Australia," by Lauriston Sharp, in *Human Problems in Technological Change*, ed. by Edward E. Spicer, 1952.

University of California Press, Los Angeles, California, for *Sociocultural and Psychological Process in Menomini Acculturation*, by George D. Spindler, 1955.

University of Minnesota Press, for *The People of Alor: A Social-Psychological Study of an East Indian Island*, by Cora Du Bois. University of Minnesota Press, Minneapolis: © 1944, University of Minnesota: © 1972, C. Du Bois; *The Makah Indians: A Study of an Indian Tribe in Modern American Society*, by Elizabeth Colson, 1953.

University of Nebraska Press, for *Son of Old Man Hat*, by Walter Dyk. Copyright © 1938 by Walter Dyk. Renewal copyright © 1966 by Walter Dyk. Reprinted by permission of University of Nebraska Press.

Weidenfeld and Nicolson, Publishers, for *The People of the Sierra*, by J. A. Pitt-Rivers, 1961.

Then, in those early times, in those far-off days, when mankind still lived in the jaws of the coiled Watersnake, Manyamei Limut Garing spoke with friendly words and tender voice to his children, and warned them in the following fashion:

"My white-coloured children, you three, be so good as to lend me your ears, ornamented with ear-hangers, listen to my speech, pay attention to my words that I have to address to you!"

Maharaja Buno, Maharaja Sangen, and Maharaja Sangiang fell silent immediately, there was no further word from them, and they made no more sound while they harkened to the words of their father, the hornbill (Schärer 1963:188)

ABOUT THE AUTHORS

Alan Beals

Alan Beals is a Professor of Anthropology at the University of California, Riverside, having moved there from Stanford University in 1968. He has spent four years engaged in field research in South Indian villages focusing on problems of ecology, demography, conflict, and cultural change. He is the author of *Gopalpur: A South Indian Village*, one of the Holt, Rinehart and Winston Case Studies in Cultural Anthropology. With Bernard J. Siegel, he is an author of *Divisiveness and Social Conflict*, published by the Stanford University Press. Currently he is a member of the Ethics Committee of the American Anthropological Association and an Associate Editor of the *Annual Review of Anthropology*.

George Spindler

George Spindler is Professor of Anthropology and Education at Stanford University, California, where he has been since 1950. His joint appointment accurately represents a lifetime interest in the application of anthropology to education. He is also interested in the psychology of culture change and urbanization. His writings include books on Menomini culture change and psychological adaptation, the transmission of American culture, education and anthropology, fieldwork in anthropology, and urbanization and identity in a German village.

Louise Spindler

Louise Spindler is Research Associate-Lecturer in Anthropology at Stanford. She is interested in the psychology of culture change and has co-authored writings on this subject with George Spindler. She has published a monograph on women's roles in culture change among the Menomini, and articles on witchcraft and culture change among the Menomini. She is recently co-author of *Dreamers without Power: The Menomini Indians*, a Case Study in Cultural Anthropology, and author of the chapter on the Menomini for the Bureau of American Ethnology Handbook on North American Indians. She is coeditor, with her husband, of the Case Studies in Cultural Anthropology, Studies in Anthropological Method, Case Studies in Education and Culture, and Basic Anthropology Units, published by Holt, Rinehart and Winston.

George and Louise Spindler edited the *American Anthropologist* from 1962 to 1966.

PREFACE

Cultural anthropology involves the systematic description and comparison of the ways of life of all the peoples of the world. Because the understanding of other ways of life is essential to the perception and understanding of our own way of life, cultural anthropology has fundamental implications for all of our humanistic and scientific understandings of the human condition and of the world around us. Because an understanding of other peoples provides a consciousness of the mythologies and prejudices of our own tribes and nations, it offers a special kind of intellectual liberation which should be the property of any educated person. All of our perception of the nature of things and of the problems which confront us are deeply conditioned by our own culture. In making available an understanding of other ways of life and of the solutions to human problems developed by other peoples, cultural anthropology offers new ways of looking at the nature of things and may lead, therefore, to new approaches to the solution of our own outstanding problems.

Cultural anthropology has existed as an organized scientific discipline for less than one hundred years. During much of this time the energies of anthropologists have been directed toward understanding and describing the ways of life of other peoples. In this process of discovering humanity, the discipline has gradually moved away from simplistic and culturally biased interpretations of the nature of humanity and reached a position where it is able to ask intelligent questions and apply reasonably sophisticated methods in solving them. The foundations of the house of anthropology have been laid, but the house itself exists only in the form of tentative plans and sketches. Although our completed descriptions of many of the peoples of the world constitute an important and useful body of data, which will someday permit the formulation of general propositions concerning the processes leading to the development of similarities and differences among the peoples of the world, the task of constructing a scientific cultural anthropology has only begun. We have identified a host of propositions about humanity that are false or only partly true and we have developed many intriguing perspectives concerning the nature of humanity. We do not yet possess the kind of hard and definitive findings that might characterize an older or more developed discipline.

On the basis of anthropology's control of a unique body of data concerning other cultures, *Culture in Process* sets forth a variety of useful perspectives concerning the nature of humanity. It does not and cannot provide a statement of the kinds of laws or generally accepted theories that might be found in a natural science textbook. Because most of the important breakthroughs and great discoveries of cultural anthropology have to do with ways of framing questions and collecting and interpreting data, *Culture in Process* emphasizes an inductive approach in which each section presents an important question, a selection of data relevant to the question, and a discussion of the possible conclusions that can be reached. We have followed the method of stating the facts first and the conclusions afterward because we feel that this pattern closely parallels the process actually used by anthropologists in approaching their subject matter.

Because it is not possible to supply completely adequate data in every case or to organize the data in such a way that it leads to one and only one definitive answer, we recognize that the student will often have to skip to the end of a section in order to find out what the selection of data presented at the beginning is supposed to illustrate. Against this minor inconvenience the fact must be considered that the process of puzzling about data and wondering what conclusions may be drawn from it creates the feeling of doing anthropology and being an anthropologist. It is the ability to ask anthropological questions and examine the details of human behavior from an anthropological perspective that constitutes the core of cultural anthropology and its chief value to those who study it. In order to help the student anticipate what is coming, we have provided summary statements at the beginning of each chapter.

In emphasizing the questions and approaches underlying the process of anthropological discovery our goal has been to provide glimpses of anthropological problems and illustrations of some of the ways in which those problems can be handled. Wherever possible direct quotations, reminiscences, and other primary materials have been used as a means of indicating the nature of anthropological reality and the richness of our data.

Culture in Process does not attempt to summarize all of the theoretical approaches or all of the subdisciplines of the field. Although it refers to many important anthropologists, it does not present a history of the discipline. It contains only a few paragraphs on human history and it lacks any summary of the peoples and cultures of the world. We have presented and defined a number of important words and concepts, but we have generally adhered to the principle that technical terms are best defined in the context of technical courses.

In preparing this second edition of *Culture in Process,* we have revised every chapter with a view toward bringing questions, data, and conclusions into a sharper and more focused relationship. We have continued the practice of suggesting progressively more refined methodological approaches in each of the chapters. We have also tried to center our discussion around such master concepts as adaptation, system, and process, perhaps more explicitly in some chapters than in others. Although the basic organization of the book remains the same, we have added two new chapters presenting background information concerning the nature of humanity and the carrying out of anthropological fieldwork. Where possible we have continued the practice of citing inexpensive paperback or other recent editions of the works referred to in the text.

Like most revisions, the present work is somewhat longer than its predecessor, yet we continue to hope that it will be used in conjunction with other textbooks, collections of ethnographic readings such as the Case Studies in Cultural Anthropology, studies in methodology, and theoretical essays such as those found in anthologies or in the Bobbs-Merrill reprints and Addison-Wesley modules. *Culture in Process,* as any textbook must, presents a particular and focused view of the discipline. A student who has the opportunity to read other material in addition to the textbook, has a greater opportunity for exposure to the confusion, excitement, disagreement, discourse, and movement characteristic of our embryonic discipline.

Although the reading of one or several books about anthropology is necessary for an understanding of anthropological methods and viewpoints, some experience with the practice of anthropology should be a part of any training program. This is best accomplished through field and laboratory work in which the student is presented with simple problems and exercises and asked to work them out. It is not necessary to go to Timbuctoo to collect a genealogy; rituals take place near at hand and every day; social control and conflict are everywhere; and all human beings entertain opinions and beliefs, and a desire to talk about them. Without having collected at least one genealogy, without doing at least one interview, without observing at least one activity, the student is in a poor position to understand either the results or the methods of anthropology. He begins to *know* anthropology only when he rings his first doorbell or addresses his first question to a potential informant. As a guide to this process of learning by doing, a selection of "Problems and Questions" follows each chapter. Because the projects we have suggested do not exhaust the range of possibilities, we hope that the ingenuity of students and instructors will result in the formulation of problems and questions not anticipated in the text.

In practicing anthropological fieldwork we believe that the student should enjoy the same privileges accorded to any other citizen. He or she should be free to observe or participate in any kind of public performance and to ask questions about the activities witnessed. Because students are not professional anthropologists and may therefore be unaware of their responsibilities in regard to the protection of the identity and privacy of their informants, or ill-informed concerning the sensitive nature of particular topics, it is important that students undertaking fieldwork projects work closely with their instructors. Students should be advised of the hazards involved in writing down confidential or private information, and the instructor should protect himself from the unscrupulous student by refusing to read papers that contain such information without the written permission of the informant(s) involved.

In preparing this second edition, we have maintained the same division of labor that characterized the first: George Spindler wrote Chapter 9; Louise Spindler wrote Chapter 11; and Alan Beals wrote the remaining chapters. We are indebted to each other for advice and assistance. More than in the previous edition, we are indebted to the many teachers and students of anthropology who have freely provided their comments and suggestions. If this edition is any improvement upon the first, much of the credit must go to the well-founded and constructive suggestions sent in by our colleagues. We can only hope that we have responded appropriately. We are especially grateful to Alan Fix, David Kronenfeld, Pell Fender, and Ernest Schusky for their extensive comments on the first draft of this edition. We owe a special debt to David Boynton of Holt, Rinehart and Winston, whose encouragement, concern for quality, and special understandings of anthropology made this book possible. We are grateful to Howard Johnston, a talented graduate student at UCR, for his assistance in correcting our bibliographies, preparing our indexes, and generally overseeing the preparation of the manuscript. To Joe E. Hargrove, who has once again graced our book with his sensitive and imaginative drawings, we acknowledge our special gratitude and affection.

March 1973

Alan R. Beals
Riverside, California

George Spindler
Louise Spindler
Stanford, California

CONTENTS

3. **Culture, System, and Process   55**

4. **Environment and Ecology   82**

5. **The Nature of Tradition   105**

CULTURE IN PROCESS

1

The human condition

Anthropology is the scientific discipline charged with the development of general propositions concerning the nature of the human species. This chapter deals with the problem of defining the origins and nature of humanity. The questions dealt with below include the problem of the similarities and differences between human beings and other animals, the nature of such characteristically human attributes as the posesssion of language and culture, the kinds of comparisons that can be made between human beings and their closest relatives, the primates, the circumstances and events that may have led to the development of the human species, and the significance of biological factors as explanations of the similarities and differences among human groups and human individuals.

How did you gain your advantage?

Far north, where the ice shelf rests on the waters of the Arctic Ocean, there are holes in the ice (blowholes) where seals rise up to breathe. In season, according to complex plans laid down by Ancestors, the hunter comes. Alone, wrapped in garments of fur, he waits with his harpoon beside the blowhole of a seal. A rising seal breaks the thin ice covering the blowhole. Now, drawing upon the advice of friends and kinsmen, basing his actions upon years of play and practice, the hunter casts his weapon. It strikes the seal, and the handle breaks away leaving a barbed hook embedded in the animal's flesh. The seal dives and the line attached to the hook burns across the gloved hands of the hunter. The harpoon handle bobs against the ice on the side of the blowhole. Centuries of experience have led to the perfection of the hunter's clothing, weapons, and hunting techniques; now, he has difficulty gaining a firm grip upon the harpoon line. He is half frozen and weak from hunger. The seal is bleeding and in need of oxygen.

Human and seal, highly evolved and intelligent mammals, struggle for survival, and both may die. The hunter's feet begin to slip. He is lost, alone. As his whole being cries out for help, he gives one last desperate pull upon the line. Suddenly, he feels behind him, helping him, the hands of father, grandfather, and all those who died before. In an invisible line the helping spirits of the ancestors stretch beyond the hunter toward the mist and blackness of the distant shore. With a wild burst of strength, the unlonely hunter heaves the seal from the water, cuts its throat, and drinks the outward pulsing blood.

Humans and seals are warm-blooded animals. The flesh and blood and bones of the seal are much like those of the human, but the seal is smaller and has slightly less brain tissue per pound of body weight. The seal is long adapted to the Arctic; humans are newcomers there. Humans learn from experience, so do seals. The seal observes the world around him and learns the basic tricks of survival, so do humans. Both animals learn complicated routines, do tricks, and appear in circuses. Neither the eye of the camera nor the knife of the surgeon can tell us precisely what it is that gives the human being his edge over the seal. The Eskimo hunter senses his kinship with the seal and honors him for yielding up his soul so other souls may live.

Questions about the similarities and differences between Eskimoes and seals lead to more general questions about the similarities and differences between human beings and all other animal species.

What is the difference?

The grand divide between human beings and all other animals is expressed in the Eskimo's harpoon, clothing, and brain—not just the shape of the brain, but what goes on inside it. The Eskimo built his harpoon following models furnished by other men. His wife stitched his clothing following patterns of her parents and her parent's parents. A traditional division of labor between old and young, male and female frees the man's time to wait beside the blowhole. A traditional pattern of hunting handed down from man to man explains the technique for handling a harpoon. More than anything else, the hunter's success rests upon the spirits of his ancestors represented as a body of tradition reaching back uncounted millennia and involving the accumulated experience of vast numbers of individuals.

The difference between humans and animals lies in the human's possession of a *cultural tradition*, a set of memories, recipes, procedures, definitions, beliefs, and values handed down from generations past. The seal learns by observation and experience and by imitating the behaviors of other seals, but when he dies, most of his accumulated wisdom and knowledge dies with him. The human being learns in all of the ways that a seal learns, but he also learns through the use of language. If we think of the brain of a seal or human being as a kind of computer which receives data from the environment and then acts upon it in terms of a program or set of instructions, both the seal and the human contain a set of "manufacturer's" specifications obtained through birth by the mechanisms of biological heredity.

In both the seal and the human being, the biological instructions are sufficiently broad to permit the modification of inherited patterns of behavior in the light of experience. Because a large part of the experience of the human being takes the form of verbal messages transmitted from other human beings, the human being has access to the wisdom and experience accumulated by other human beings. Because the seal lives in association with other seals, he too has access to a kind of culture transmitted within his own particular group of seals, but the quantity of information that can be transmitted within a group by observation alone is far less than the quantity of information that can be transmitted by means of language. Both seals and human beings are products of the interaction of messages transmitted by means of biological inheritance and life-time experience. Because human experience involves the use of language, human behavior comes to be strongly influenced by cultural messages that are largely transmitted by verbal means. Human behavior, then, arises out of a complicated and continuing relationship among biological, experiential, and cultural messages. The following section considers the nature of the genetic or biological message.

Genetics: what is the message?

The biologically inherited or genetic message is inscribed in code within molecules of a chemical called DNA (deoxyribonucleic acid). This chemical takes essentially the same form and plays essentially the same role in all living things. The differences among different plants and animals derive not so much from differences in the nature of biological inheritance as from differences in the messages inscribed within the molecules of DNA which they contain.

DNA consists of a chain of subunits called nucleotides. Each nucleotide consists of a phosphate ion, a sugar called deoxyribose, and one of four basic nitrogenous molecules called adenine, guanine, cytosine, and thymine. Because each nucleotide contains only one of the four basic molecules, four different kinds of nucleotide are possible. These can be represented by the letters A, G, C, and T, indicating the basic nitrogenous molecule characteristic of each kind of nucleotide. The nucleotides are arranged in groups of three within the chainlike molecule of DNA. The genetic code is expressed in terms of different arrangements of each group of three nucleotides. Thus, AAC (adenine, adenine, cytosine) means something different from CGT (cytosine, guanine, thymine). The difference in meaning has to do with the manufacture of particular amino acids used in the construction of protein molecules in the cell.

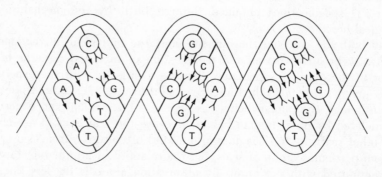

By controlling the production of protein by cells, DNA influences the form, development, and behavior of the particular plant or animal specified in the DNA message. The basic form of the DNA molecule is that of a helix or two strand piece of rope with the basic molecules on each strand being connected to complementary basic molecules on the opposite strand. A is always connected to T and G is always connected to C.

In the cell, DNA molecules are connected together to form chromosomes. In the process of cellular fission or *mitosis*, the chromosomes and other genetic materials replicate or copy themselves to produce two sets of identical or virtually identical hereditary materials. The problem of duplicating the genetic message is solved by unwinding the two strands of DNA and allowing each to re-form by adding basic molecules that are complementary to those present on each strand. The result, if all goes well, is two identical molecules of DNA.

In the process of germ cell formation or *meiosis*, the DNA molecules reproduce themselves in the same way, but the number of chromosomes in the two new cells is cut in half. The egg cell and the sperm cell each contain half the genetic materials of the ordinary cell. When the egg cell and the sperm cell are united, the resulting new organism contains the normal complement of genetic materials, half being derived from the male ancestor and half being derived from the female ancestor. Some of the things that can happen as the genetic message is transmitted from parents to offspring are considered in the following section.

Like Father, Like Son?

Because the function of the hereditary materials is to produce an individual of the same species as its parents, most of the hereditary materials received from the male parent and the female parent are identical and are shared by all members of the species. Individual variation occurs when the gene pool (the set of genes available for transmission from parents to offspring) contains a number of different genes or *alleles* which can occupy the same place or *locus* on the chromosome. When alleles are present there is a chance that the individual will receive a chromosome from his male parent containing one allele at a particular locus and a choromosome from his female parent containing a different allele at that locus. When this happens, one of the alleles may be dominant or partially dominant and the effect of the other, recessive, allele may be negligible. When both alleles have an impact upon the individual, the individual is likely to be partly like his mother and partly like his father in terms of the particular characteristics influenced by the genes at a given chromosome locus.

Without knowing for sure which genes occur in the form of alleles or which genes are dominant and recessive, it is impossible to estimate the extent to which the individual is likely to resemble or differ from his parents or the extent to which the genes of one parent or the other will influence his biological development. The situation is further complicated by the fact that genes at different locations may influence each other. Biologically, an individual resembles other individuals in the species in most ways; he resembles both parents in more ways; he resembles either parent in some ways; and he is completely unique in other ways. Although the average individual could be considered to be half like his mother and half like his father, any particular individual, depending upon the distribution of dominant and recessive genes, may be more similar to one parent than to the other.

Because the hereditary materials represent organizations of matter, they are subject to the general law that they will tend to decay unless energy is used to arrest the processes of disorganization. As a message is repeated, errors creep in. The collection of forces that create disorganization or errors in messages is called *noise*. When noise creates a change in the chemical structure of a gene, the altered gene is called a *mutation*. When mutations are transmitted during the process of biological reproduction, they contribute to the biological uniqueness of the resulting individuals.

In sum, the presence of several alleles at a single locus on the chromosome combined with the possibility that various kinds of noise may interfere with the transmission of the genetic message leads to the consequence that the *genotypes* or genetic constituents of different individuals, unless they happen to be identical or "one-egg" twins, are always different. Because the expression of particular genes and therefore of the individual's genotype depends upon the nature of environmental influences upon individual genes and upon the individual as a whole, each individual tends to develop a unique constitution or *phenotype*. The phenotype, which represents the individual as he actually is, is the product of an interaction between the genotype and the environment. Because individuals, even if they are identical twins, tend to be affected by the environment in different ways, it is theoretically impossible to find any pair of individuals who are exactly the same in every respect.

As the set of different individuals composing a population interact with the environment, some survive and some do not, some bear children and some do not. The survival of any particular individual depends upon his *fitness*, the capacity of his phenotype to survive the environmental challenges that it encounters. The process whereby some survive and some do not is called *selection*. Where selection is governed primarily by the "natural" environment, it is called *natural selection*, and where it is governed by the social or "artificial" environment, it is called *social or artificial selection*. This distinction is important but it should not be taken to imply that societies or the environments they construct are somehow unnatural, nor should "selection" imply that somebody is doing the selection.

As the forces of selection operate against those individuals who are in some way unfit to survive in any particular environment, the hopeful result is a gradual change in the genetic message leading to the presence of increasing numbers of individuals within the population who are fit to survive and reproduce. Individuals who survive but do not reproduce do not, of course, contribute to the transmission of the genetic message. The overall process of the development of individual genotypes and phenotypes that are increasingly fit to survive is called *adaptation*. We can think of populations or species as adapting to their environments as a consequence of selection.

When environments change or when populations enter new environments, they will tend to be less well adapted than they were before. Under such circumstances the rate of selection will increase and relatively small numbers of individuals will survive to produce children. The effect of this process on the genetic message is the elimination of genes that are no longer adaptive and an increase in those genes that are adaptive. Ultimately a population that has experienced environmental change or entered a new environment may come to be so different from more "conservative" populations of the species as to constitute a new species. The overall process by which one species develops out of another is called *biological evolution*.

The nature of the genetic message and the processes of biological evolution is discussed in detail in biology textbooks and in some of the works cited at the end of this chapter. The main point to be made here is that the genetic message changes relatively slowly over a number of generations, largely as a consequence of selection. Because the larger mammals, human beings included, tend to have relatively long periods of time between successive generations, their genetic messages can change only relatively slowly in response to environmental change.

This limitation upon the rapidity with which the mammalian species can evolve biologically goes hand in hand with the fact that many aspects of mammalian behavior are not specified in detail in the genetic code. Mammalian behavior is less likely to be "instinctive" or genetically programmed than is the behavior of other kinds of animals, and mammals are more likely to depend upon learned behavior as a means of adapting to short-run changes in their environments. The following section, with special reference to the behavior of our close relatives, the primates, considers the nature and special importance of the experiential message.

The experiential message: what happened to you?

Only a few years ago the central questions to be answered through the study of the behavior of nonhuman primates had to do with the identification of genetically controlled forms of behavior which might be characteristic of both human beings and primates. Although some of the outlines of what might be called a basic primate genetic message have been tentatively identified, one of the main discoveries of recent primate studies has been that the experiential message is far more important among primates than had been thought possible:

In 1952, workers from the Japan Monkey Center began feeding a troop of Japanese macaques on a beach on the island of Koshima. The feeding consisted of throwing sweet potatoes on the sand. After a year, a two year old female began carrying sweet potatoes to a nearby brook and holding them in the water while she brushed off the sand covering them. After five years, eighty percent of the monkeys in the group between two and seven years old had adopted the practice of carrying their potatoes to the ocean and washing them in salt water. When the monkeys were fed wheat, the same female innovator picked up handfuls of wheat and sand, threw them into the water and picked out the grains of wheat. This trait, too, was soon copied by other monkeys of the same age and younger. Lured to the water by the presence of food, some of the monkeys learned to swim and many commenced to bathe regularly in hot weather (Adapted from Kawai 1965:1–30).

In his studies of Hamadrayas baboons, Hans Kummer (1971:66–67) found that after the morning rest period different young adult males would lead small groups of monkeys short distances in different directions. These small groups or *pseudopods* would protrude and withdraw again until one of the older males in the center of the troop would move in the direction of a particular pseudopod. At this, the entire troop would move off in the same direction. When Kummer restudied the same group of baboons later, he found almost no trace of this pseudopod system. Now, instead of protruding and retracting pseudopods, the troop simply moved off in one direction or another.

Some years ago, when only a few kinds of primates had been studied, primatologists were inclined to think of most primate behavior as being governed by the genetic message. Now, when there have been opportunities to study different groups of the same species or to observe single troops over periods of time, it has become evident that not just man, but all of the primates rely heavily on learned behavior. Kummer (1971:37–38) suggests that primates lack the detailed genetic programs for complex behavioral sequences that occur in social insects or even in rodents. In other words, the primate genetic message focuses upon ways of learning to behave rather than upon precise instructions for behavior. Primates also lack the human ability to invent and transmit highly complicated techniques and behaviors by means of language. The unusual asset of the primates is their possession of a society in which the constant association of young and old over a long life span produces adults who have great experience. The old male, in some cases the old female, in the primate troop depends largely upon experience in providing a kind of leadership to the younger animals in the troop. Patterns learned by individuals are likely to spread horizontally through the age group and downward to younger individuals, eventually becoming characteristic of the troop.

The young primate may study the actions of the older primate, but he has no access to the actual experiences upon which those actions are based. When he follows his elder to a feeding site, he does so not because he shares the memories of his elder, but through a kind of blind faith. Because other primates are so similar to human beings, because human beings are primates, it is apparent that experiential learning is extremely important among human beings, but with a difference so vital as to justify a special importance for the category of verbal learning and cultural transmission. The following section discusses the nature of language and its vital contribution to the formation of the cultural message.

The cultural message: what did you say?

The human being is able to transmit his personal experience to other human beings through the use of language. Listening to what other people say is a form of experience, but the type of experience gained through language is sufficiently unique to justify regarding the verbal message as distinct from other forms of experiential messages. The transmission of information by means of language is as complicated as the transmission of information by means of DNA and involves a coding procedure not unlike that involved in the genetic message. Not surprisingly, in view of the biases of Western Civilization, no one ever received a Nobel prize for breaking the linguistic code.

Whereas the biological code is based upon four basic molecules, the linguistic code rests upon a series of individual types of sounds. While some of these types are found in a great many languages, others are not. All genetic messages are based upon the same four basic molecules, whereas each human language is based upon a unique set of basic types of sounds. The number of basic sound types required to form a language is variable, with no established upper or lower limit. At a guess, most natural languages involve between forty and sixty sound types.

The *phonemes* or basic types of sounds of a language are identified by searching for the smallest element of sound which can change the meaning of an utterance. Consider the contrasts between "pit" and "bit" or "pack" and "back" or "cap" and "cab." The difference in meaning between the two words in each pair is given by the contrast we symbolize as "b" and "p." Both "b" and "p" are formed by using the lips to stop a flow of air through the mouth. The sound "b" involves vocalization or the vibration of the vocal cords, while the sound "p" does not. In languages where vocalization is unimportant in this context, speakers might consider "b" and "p" to be the same sound. In a sense the "basic speech sounds" are not sounds so much as defined ways of producing sounds which are recognized as significant or meaningful by other speakers of the language.

When a linguist studies a language, he frequently pays someone, an informant, to work with him. When the informant talks, the linguist attempts to write down the sounds that are made in terms of the method of making them. The linguist then reads back the word or utterance to the informant to see if he has gotten it right. Eventually through experimentation and by searching for pairs of words that show the kinds of contrast inherent in "pit" and "bit," the linguist arrives at a list of the phonemes or basic sound types in the language. If you use this technique to establish the phonemes in English, you should come out with approximately forty-one different types of sounds, depending upon the dialect being spoken.

Schaller, in his study of mountain gorillas (1963:211), recorded over twenty-two different meaningful sounds or cries. Because chimpanzees rarely combine these sounds to produce longer utterances, the ability of chimpanzees to communicate verbally is limited. Human beings combine a small number of noises to form *morphemes* (words or parts of words) and they combine morphemes according to grammatical rules in order to produce longer phrases, sentences, and paragraphs. Three other characteristics of language are of the greatest importance to an understanding of human behavior: arbitrariness, displacement, and productivity.

Arbitrariness: Why Do "Bit" and "Pit"
Mean Different Things?
The difference between "bit" and "pit" lies in the fact that they contain different phonemes, but why should "bit" mean things like a "drill," a "tiny piece," or an act of biting carried out in the past? The explanation of this state of affairs lies in the fact that, consciously or unconsciously, human beings *arbitrarily* assigned these meanings to the combination of phonemes represented by "bit." As Humpty Dumpty said, "a word means what I want it to mean." Human beings do not, as a rule, meet in committees and invent languages. To do that they have to possess a language already. Languages usually grow through unspoken agreements, based on the fact that communication is possible only when people have, perhaps without thinking about it, arrived at some agreement as to what the words mean.

The ability to assign arbitrary meanings to various aspects of experience is essential to language and a great many other human endeavors. A game depends upon the presence of a set of arbitrary understandings, so does a system of mathematics or a theory about the nature of the universe. An agreement that each man should have only one wife or that peas should be eaten with a knife is equally arbitrary. Because most such arbitrary agreements were made long ago and handed down as a part of cultural traditions, we do not know precisely how such agreements were reached and are often unaware of their existence. The Pythagorean theorem in geometry assumes the existence of straight lines, yet there is no such thing as a perfectly straight line. Human beings who are aware of the Pythagorean theorem often believe that it reflects a "natural" law, when in fact it is a set of arbitrary conventions. Very often the arbitrary set of conventions by means of which human beings understand their universe and govern their behavior is regarded as reflecting the proper and natural state of things and not the "make believe" conception that it is. Understandings of the arbitrary basis of much of human behavior represent one of the great discoveries of cultural anthropology and linguistics; one which has revolutionary implications for daily life and for the development of our knowledge of reality.

Displacement: Does the Ape Know Tomorrow or Yonder?

According to Hans Kummer (1971:30–31), primates (excluding man) can communicate only about the here and now. A monkey can inform another monkey about the location of a distant stand of mushrooms only by leading him there. A monkey cannot say, "Let us meet at sunup by the old oak tree," or "There is a tree full of nuts three miles to the east." There is some recent evidence, however, that with intensive training chimpanzees can learn to communicate complicated messages by means of gestures or by the manipulation of tokens. Thus some of the differences between human beings and other primates may not be quite as revolutionary as they seem at first glance.

Human beings can speak about and think about things that are not present, things that will be present, or things that once were present. They can talk about objects displaced in time and space. The dreamy teenager who seems to be with us but is really sailing with Captain Bligh, the cultural anthropologist whose head is in the jungles of the Amazon, or the history teacher living in the fifteenth century are notorious examples of the human capacity for *displacement* carried to a point that threatens survival in the here and now. Displacement, like arbitrariness, presumably provides adaptive advantages sufficient to overcome the inevitable confusion among past, present, future, here and there. In particular, it provides a means of learning about things without actually experiencing them: The Eskimo brings to his first seal hunt a detailed knowledge of seal hunts carried out by others.

Productivity: Why the Green Man?

In the process of combining morphemes to produce utterances, human beings inevitably form expressions like "little green men," "flying island," or "time travel." These expressions appear to have meaning. They are grammatically correct, yet so far as we know they do not refer to nature. This feature of language is called *productivity* because the manipulation of morphemes can produce objects and entities that are not a part of experience. Although productivity can lead men to fruitless searches for hairy monsters, perpetual motion, or underground cities, it can also lead to the discovery of new continents or flying fish.

The coding of language in terms of *phonemes* and the properties of *arbitrariness, displacement,* and *productivity* permit the transmission of information between human beings and across generations on an enormous scale. A man has access to the genetic information handed down to him by his parents, and he also has access to the linguistic information handed down and across by all of the members of his group and by all of the speakers of his language. Whereas from a theoretical viewpoint almost any kind of message might be expressed in the genetic code and stored away in chromosomes, the genetic message represents a kind of accidental collection of information. It is a message without an author but one firmly edited by selection. Linguistic messages have authors. These authors work in terms of present experience but also use the faculties of arbitrariness, displacement, and productivity to place themselves outside of current reality and to develop poetry, religion, art, games, and cultural traditions. In the present state of the art, human beings can revise genetic messages only by a tedious process of induced mutation, breeding, and selection. Verbal messages can be revised instantly as developing situations warrant.

The human capacity to create and use language is fundamental to the emergence of the cultural message. Because a number of other animals, as various as dolphins, finches, wolves, and chimpanzees, are suspected of creating or learning to use subtle and sophisticated forms of communication, it is not clear whether the use of language makes human beings totally different or only slightly different from all other animals. So far, the vast complexity of all known human languages and their use in the transmission of even more complicated cultural messages have not been equaled by representatives of any other species.

Material culture: are these really artifacts?

Although the cultural message can be thought of as primarily transmitted by means of language, the impact of the cultural message upon human behavior results in the development of constructed environments that reflect culturally induced regularities of human behavior. These constructed environments, in turn, influence the quality of human experience and the nature of the human genetic message. The influence of the cultural message upon the material world is expressed in the term *material culture*. Because evidence of the past development of human cultures exists largely in the form of material culture, especially in the form of tools and artifacts preserved in archaeological sites, much of our knowledge of the early forms of humanity and culture rests upon our knowledge of material culture. This section considers the importance of material culture and especially the use of tools to an understanding of the nature of the human condition.

The sea otter floats upon his back, casually demolishing mussel shells by pounding them on a flat rock placed on his stomach. The chimpanzee builds a nest inferior to a good bird's nest, but he also pokes at insects with sticks that he has pruned with his teeth. In captivity he can learn to wear clothing, ride bicycles, and use a kind of nonverbal language. Ants plant gardens and regularly milk "domesticated" insects. A human being wearing nothing at all and carrying a crude stone knife seems hardly different from these other animals until his behavior or his productions are studied in detail.

Wherever the remains of definite human beings are found there is evidence of: (1) a wide variety of tools and tool uses, (2) premeditation in the assembling of materials and the construction of long-lasting tools and structures, and (3) a traditional patterning or stylistic form of tools and other materials. In Olduvai Gorge in Africa, Louis B. and Mary Leakey discovered the fossil remains of a proto-human creature that lived two million years ago. Excavations carried out elsewhere in Africa by F. Clark Howell have produced evidence that these proto-humans, called Australopithecines, may have lived as much as three and a half or five million years ago. At Olduvai Gorge, there is more than a suggestion that the Australopithecines possessed some kind of permanent campsite or "home base" and that they accumulated there a variety of stone and bone materials of different shapes and sizes.

Because the materials accumulated at Olduvai are crude, it is difficult to say whether they actually represent tools constructed in response to some definite cultural tradition. If they are tools, they are tools of several different kinds. This, and their presence in places where they are not normally found, suggests a measure of premeditation and might be taken to indicate a capacity for displacement normally associated with the use of language. At any rate, starting at least two million years ago at Olduvai Gorge, there has been progressive improvement in the quality of tools found in association with proto-human and human remains. Perhaps one and three quarter million years ago, according to most authorities, tool types and styles became sufficiently developed to confirm the presence of cultural traditions and therefore of beings who might be classified as human.

Although the evidence is sketchy and authorities disagree concerning what might constitute proof of humanity or the time periods at which such proofs are to be found, it seems reasonable to suppose that the presence of definite tool traditions is evidence that those who possessed them also possessed language or some early form of language. Most authorities believe that language and tool use and manufacture developed side-by-side with the gradual emergence of the human culture-building capacity.

Whether transmitted verbally by means of language or nonverbally by means of material culture, possession of a detailed and complicated cultural message appears to represent the most important dividing line between human beings and other animals. There are, however, some other important differences. These differences, especially as they pertain to differences between human beings and other primates, are the subject of the following section.

How else do we differ?

Human beings habitually walk erect. Closely related primates may walk erect from time to time, but they do not do so habitually. As a result of erect posture, or rather in connection with it, a number of other changes have occurred. The human head is balanced upon an "S" shaped spinal column, eliminating the need for large muscles necessary to support the head when traveling on all fours. The fact that the head is balanced rather than supported by muscles may have facilitated the progressive enlargement of the human brain. The human foot has become adapted to walking and has lost some of its ability to grasp and manipulate objects. Unlike primate infants, the human infant cannot use its feet to cling to its mother when she moves about. The human hand, no longer needed for locomotion, has developed a thumb which can be opposed to the fingers, thus permitting precise manipulation of objects. The human pelvis has changed its form and rotated so that the human birth canal is relatively small. The human mouth lacks the fangs or protruding canine teeth used by other primates for defense or for puncturing and slicing. Some authors think this may be connected with the use of tools for puncturing and slicing. Other changes in the shape of the human face and skull are connected with increases in the size of the human brain, and some of them may have taken place in response to the development of language.

Human beings share comparatively excellent vision with the other primates, but they appear to have even better eyesight in some respects and an even greater facility for eye-hand coordination. Comparatively large portions of the human brain are dedicated to the speech organs and to the hands and eyes, probably at the expense of the senses of smell and hearing. The human infant is carried in his mother's womb for a comparatively long period and has a longer life expectancy at birth than do other primates. Nevertheless, the human infant is born in a comparatively immature state. He cannot walk or cling to his mother and must be fed and cared for over a long period before he can take care of himself. This is one reason why the possibility that the Australopithecines possessed permanent campsites or home bases is so important. The immaturity of the human infant at birth can be related to the large size of the human brain and the relatively small size of the human birth canal. This opens up the fascinating possibility that erect posture and the accompanying small birth canal created such dreadful problems that human ancestors could survive only by the development of culture.

Human beings and other primates are born into well-organized social groups within which infant care takes place. The primate infant may be cared for by other members of the troop beside his mother and may continue to recognize his mother and his siblings (brothers and sisters) throughout his lifetime. The human being tends to recognize a wider circle of relatives including his father or a suitable substitute. It has been suggested that the helplessness of the human infant forces both mother and infant to depend on others for survival. The earliest human or humanlike groups may have possessed an organized division of labor among persons of different ages and sexes and a pattern for the exchange of food within and between family groups. That human females are sexually attractive throughout the year while primate females are sexually attractive only during brief periods has sometimes been related to the formation of human social groups, but it could also be related to the fact that human social arrangements made it possible to care for infants born at any time of the year.

Although groups formed by the different primate species differ from each other almost as much as they do from human groups, the basis of primate organization appears to lie in the prolonged association of younger primates with older and more experienced individuals. Primate adaptations often rest upon the wisdom and experience of older animals who assume leadership roles and are imitated and followed by younger animals. Although primate groups may have one or several "leaders" who are usually but not always males, and although these males may sometimes but not always have exclusive possession of particular females, adult male primates within a particular troop may often get along quite well together. There is a suggestion that these primate tendencies ultimately led to the more human situation in which teams of friendly and cooperative adult males assumed reponsibilities for hunting and defense. For many primates, peace and cooperation within the group, as well as leadership and dominance, form the basis of a society in which prolonged association permits younger animals to benefit from the experience of their elders.

Nonhuman primates, like human primates, differ in the extent to which they define or defend territory, and they differ in the degree of friendliness or hostility with which they greet outsiders of the same or different species. Fundamental to both human and primate societies is the ability to recognize group members and to enter into cooperative or at least relatively nonviolent relationships with them. All of these characteristics of nonhuman primates may be interpreted as fundamental to the emergence of humanity. Because groups of nonhuman primates base important aspects of their social organization and behavior upon experiential messages, troops of primates, even within the same species, may be quite different. As a result, it is difficult to point to specific adaptations having to do with territorial defense, group organization, aggression, cooperation, or love, which human beings share with all other primates. Rather there is a general similarity in the fields of group formation and experiential learning. It has been suggested that there is a kind of broadness in the genetic programming of all primates which permits a flexible adaptation to changing circumstances based upon the possession of large brains, good memories, curiosity, and a willingness to learn.

It appears likely that all primates share a comparatively developed ability to modify or override genetic instructions when such instructions come into conflict with learned instructions. Most markedly among human beings, but among other primates as well, biological urges toward sex, aggression, hunger, sleep, or thrist may be repressed, deferred, or rechanneled even to the point where the resulting strain upon the organism becomes almost unbearable. Where human behavior, in particular, is attributed to specific genetic mechanisms underlying war, love, or any other complicated behavior, we must always reflect that this runs counter to all that we know about the role of learning as an influence upon the behavior of human beings and other primates.

Due to the importance of experiential and cultural messages to the development of human behavior, it is unwise to base any conclusion about human beings solely upon studies of other animal species. The study of fruit flies, white rats, or primates provides important insights concerning the human condition only when it goes hand in hand with the study of human beings. By the same token no statement about human beings based upon the study of reprensentatives of a single human culture can be accepted until it has been validated by research carried out in a variety of cultures. Statements about human beings in general can only be confirmed through the study of human beings in general.

Comparisons of different groups of living human beings, the discovery of fossilized skeletal materials, the investigation of ancient archaeological sites, and comparisons of human beings with other animals, especially the primates, have led to a variety of speculations about the manner in which human beings developed.

Whence Came We?
Basically, the development or evolution of the human species has been governed by the progressive development of the cultural message, including language and material culture. Because our information concerning many aspects of this development is literally buried in the earth and because direct evidence of the use of language, the presence of particular

social arrangements, the development of particular ways of doing things, or the utilization of perishable materials is generally unavailable, we can know the broad outlines but not the specific details of human evolution. During the past several million years there must have been great cultural inventions and great changes in the nature of the human genetic message. We do not know exactly when such changes took place, and we cannot speak precisely of their causes or their nature. We are certain that the various qualities leading toward humanity developed over a long period of time following an intricate process of reciprocal rather than linear causation.

Under a pattern of linear causation, a "cause" is interpreted as leading to some particular "effect." Under a pattern of reciprocal causation, there is a relationship among a variety of factors such that a change in A leads to a change in B and a change in B leads to a change in A. Thus, the progressive development of the cultural message undoubtedly triggered changes in the form of the human body, while at the same time changes in the form of the human body triggered further development of the cultural message. Increasing use of tools must have facilitated the development of language, and the development of language must have facilitated the increasing use of tools.

If there was a single cause or a single beginning to the process of evolution in the human direction, it may well have been the movement of our ancestors from a forest to a grassland or savannah environment. In the new environment, with few trees to climb for safety, it appears likely that the proto-human had to rely upon vocalization, good eyesight, increasingly upright posture, and cooperation with his fellows for protection from predators. Because a developing ability to walk upright would have freed the hands for carrying things, it is possible to imagine proto-humans collecting small animals, roots, or nuts and carrying them to a safe place while using vocalizations to indicate the location of food, the presence of predators, and the direction of travel. Upright posture and increased use of the hands, eyes, and mouth presumably led to the enlargement and refinement of the brain and vice versa.

Carrying things around would contribute to the development of the human talent for thinking about things removed in time and space, a talent that is critical for the use of tools and the development of language. Upright posture combined with increasing brain size may well have led to the birth of progressively immature human infants and this must have gone hand in hand with the development of work-sharing and food-sharing human groups. The need for increased cooperation within such groups would have led to more vocalization, larger brain size, greater reliance on tools, and upright posture. Some anthropologists, perhaps more observant than others, suspect that tool use is related to the human habit of sitting upright, rather than to the habit of standing upright. If we ask which came first, increased brain size, tool use, upright posture, the beginnings of language, infant helplessness, or the development of food-sharing groups, we are at a loss to find an answer. Each small step toward humanity influenced other small steps by a process of reciprocal causation.

The development of language, the cultural message, and human social arrangements must have been quite critical to the evolution of humanity and it is therefore unfortunate that the archaeological record tells us so little about these things. Because the individual's survival and his capacity to bear viable offspring was dependent upon the capacity to cooperate with other group members, there may well have been strong social selection against individuals who were greedy, violent, uncooperative, nonverbal, or physically unattractive by whatever standards might have been in force.

Against the demonstrable necessity for love and cooperation must be placed the fact that human beings early began to kill large animals, perhaps other human beings as well, for food. At the same time that human beings were developing an improved capacity to cooperate, they were becoming the most ferocious predatory mammal on the planet. Because rules governing sexual and marital relationships, including rules forbidding sexual relationships with close relatives, are found in a wide variety of existing human cultures, it is tempting to conclude that the need to obtain sexual and marital partners outside the immediate family and often outside the immediate group might have created affiliations which served to restrict predation within the group and between the group and its immediate neighbors. The fact that human beings might well have been their own worst enemies might also have encouraged the development of defensive alliances among neighboring groups. The development of relationships both of enmity and alliance among neighboring groups of human beings could have been one of the factors in human evolution.

With the progressive refinement of the human capacity to use language and to build culture, the importance of "purely" biological factors and of adaptation to the "natural" environment in human evolution must have progressively declined. In other words, as human beings solved their adaptive problems by developing new patterns of culture or new kinds of tools and implements, their genetic message became progressively more insulated from direct effects of the natural environment. The survival and reproduction of the human individual came to depend increasingly upon his ability to function within a social environment and decreasingly upon his ability to cope individualistically with the problems of survival in nature. In modern urban societies, the "natural" environment practically disappears, although we forget it at our peril, and human biological and cultural evolution takes place almost entirely within a man-made environment. Human beings now tend to construct the forces that lead to their own biological evolution. Figuratively speaking, the automobile has replaced the tiger as an agent of natural selection.

What Was Our History?

The earliest written records hardly go back six thousand years, many human groups lacking written history even today. This leaves at least two million years of human prehistory to be painfully reconstructed on the basis of those human bones, tools, and other materials which have somehow survived the ravages of time. Partly on the basis of the fossil record and partly because it could have been no other way, the earliest proto-humans must have resembled in most respects the various other primate species that exist today. Presumably, proto-humans existed in small groups vaguely resembling existing troops of baboons, chimpanzees, or gorillas.

If, in fact, human evolution was triggered by the replacement of forests by grasslands, we can imagine groups of proto-humans dispersed over the savannah regions of Africa, Southern Europe, and South Asia. Each of these groups would have constituted a breeding population, sometimes mating with members of other groups, but for the most part mating and exchanging genes within the troop. Due to chance, and the success of some individuals in producing comparatively large numbers of offspring, there is a tendency for such small groups to diverge genetically. A human or proto-human who produces ten offspring who live to produce offspring of their own will have a far greater genetic impact than will an individual who produces no offspring or only one or two. The different groups of proto-humans must, then, have had a tendency to concentrate different genes from the pool of genes available to the species as a whole.

Some of the groups of proto-humans would have occupied environments that were relatively favorable; others would have had greater difficulty in surviving. Where survival is difficult, only the lucky or gifted few survive to produce offspring. Those who survive tend to be those who possess genes which equip them to survive. In groups under stress, the rate of selection is increased and evolution proceeds comparatively rapidly. If the rate of selection is too high, the group perishes. Certain groups of proto-humans presumably evolved more rapidly than others. Because the individuals in these groups were, at least, proto-humans, their adaptation to stress must have involved simultaneous change in both genetic and cultural messages. Proto-humans may have adapted biologically or through the invention of new forms of behavior to be transmitted within the group by learning. Because a useful invention has the effect of changing the odds of survival and because genetic change in the human direction would tend to increase the ability to invent things, genetic and cultural evolution must have taken place together.

Evolution, whether genetic or cultural, often increases rates of survival and reproduction, thus leading to population increase, that is, more children survive to become adults and to produce children. A new capacity, whether it is a better brain or a sharper rock, now spreads through two mechanisms. First, the more numerous group may begin to replace less numerous groups. Second, the new trait will begin to spread from group to group as a result of intergroup mating if it is a genetic trait and as a result of imitation if it is an invented trait. Because human beings who carry sharp stones are presumably better adapted than human beings who carry dull stones, it is likely that they will be more successful in obtaining mates and bearing offspring.

An invented trait diffusing from group to group is likely to have the effect of increasing the rate of genetic mixing between neighboring human populations. Once a new genetic or invented trait has diffused or spread over the environment within which it is advantageous, the different human or proto-human populations will again begin to diverge as a result of isolation.

The course of human prehistory suggests that periods of rapid genetic and cultural evolution led repeatedly to a kind of genetic homogenization of the species so that it is unlikely that proto-humans or humans ever developed into separate species. In particular, the different breeding populations never or rarely became so different as to preclude interbreeding. Alternatively, if separate species did develop, and there is little evidence one way or another, successive genetic or cultural revolutions appear to have driven the less progressive or less human species into extinction. Although the notion of more human creatures hunting down and exterminating less human creatures has a certain genocidal appeal, the most probable and most frequent case would appear to have been the overwhelming of the less progressive groups through interbreeding. The more human creatures got the girls or the boys, as the case may have been, and, even more important, produced the larger number of viable offspring. Love is a more important means of genocide than war.

Although biological and cultural evolution must inevitably take place together, the two types of evolution differ in important ways. Minor biological changes can take place quickly as human populations merge and diverge, but major biological changes such as might be involved in the formation of a new species appear to require many generations for their fulfillment. Recognizably manlike apes appeared some three to five million years ago. *Homo erectus*, the first indisputably human form, arose at least 750,000 years ago. The first forms of *Homo sapiens*, including *Homo sapiens neanderthalensis*, appeared between 100,000 and 300,000 years ago, and *Homo sapiens sapiens*, our own form of man, developed about 35,000 years ago and appeared in all parts of the world some 10,000 to 20,000 years ago. The major stages in the development of the genus *Homo* required at least three million years. If we assume five human generations in each period of one hundred years, ten thousand years only provides time for five hundred generations. Because five hundred or even one thousand generations do not provide much time for alteration of the genetic message, we would not expect great biological change since *Homo sapiens* first spread across the world. All varieties of modern man are pretty much the same from a biological standpoint.

Cultural evolution, which may proceed by changing the materials taught to children, can be far more rapid than biological evolution; it also appears to have built-in properties of acceleration as if each idea led to the development of a host of additional ideas. In the archaeological record, stone tools developed very slowly starting about two million years ago. By one and three quarter million years ago, there was a recognizable human tool kit. The earliest stone tools appear to have been manufactured by pounding one stone against another to produce flakes or cores which could then be shaped further by more delicate pounding. Later, flakes were trimmed by pressing them with a hard object (pressure flaking) and still later, presumably, by grinding and polishing them. The period during which the major part of the archaeological record consists of stone tools is called the *Paleolithic* or Stone Age. The *Lower Paleolithic*, lasting from perhaps 2 million to 35,000 years ago, and the *Upper Paleolithic*, dominated by *Homo sapiens* and lasting from 35,000 to 10,000 years ago, reveal progressive refinements in tool manufacture and the formation of a variety of separate cultural traditions. In the Upper Paleolithic, the development of clothing, art, systematic burial, and possibly religious ritual are major evidences of revolutionary change.

The archaeological record, particularly during the Lower Paleolithic, gives only the sketchiest indications of the cultural evolution that was undoubtedly taking place. We know nothing of the stages of evolution of language and precious little about the emergence of art, games, religion, drama, or ritual. We can only make guesses about the revolutionary advances in social organization which permitted the emergence of the various systems of marriage or the various techniques for organizing tribes and clans. While we might be able to document the first fish hook, the first stone bead, or the first stone figurine, it is practically impossible to find evidences of the first piece of twine, the first portable water container, the first fish net, or the first deadfall trap for animals.

During the Lower Paleolithic, human beings must have produced one great cultural revolution after the other. Imagine the survival advantage conferred by the first portable infant carrier. This would have freed the mother's hands for other work and would have protected the infant from falling or being dropped when the group moved from one place to another. Each such invention must have had radical effects on human survival and must have served as a means of breaking down developing genetic or cultural differences among human groups. Each successive development must have increased the number of environments within which man could survive, leading in the Upper Paleolithic to the occupation of every continent and grasslands, tropical rain forests, Arctic shorelines, deserts, and mountain slopes. These new environments would have exposed new populations to heavy selective pressures, triggering further genetic and cultural evolution.

These developments coincided with the emergence of *Homo sapiens sapiens*, a creature of great genetic and cultural variability, but at the same time a single, widespread biological species. Where animals of another species expanding into new environments might have developed unique and highly specialized races or varieties, *Homo sapiens sapiens* appears not to have done so. Presumably, this can be accounted for by the fact that tendencies toward the development of genetic uniqueness in local populations were continually confounded by the genetic consequences of the rapid spread of revolutionary new cultural traits. The following section considers the significance of existing biological differences within the human species.

What kinds of men?

Although biological differences between groups of human beings as compared with those characteristic of other species are essentially trivial, noticeable differences do exist. A man from a village in Nigeria presents an appearance or phenotype quite distinct from that presented by a man from a village in Sweden or China. The presence of such differences has impelled some students of human biology to divide the species into three major racial groups: Caucasoid, Mongoloid, and Negroid. Using various criteria, some human biologists or physical anthropologists have then defined a number of subraces or varieties within each of these "major races." Although many authorities would accept the validity of a division of the species into several geographical races, there is disagreement concerning the manner in which such races are to be defined, the geographical areas they might be supposed to occupy, and the importance of the differences thought to exist between them. Several authorities believe that the term *race* should not be applied to human beings.

The earliest racial classifications tended to be based upon *type* specimens and upon a series of *phenotypic* or constitutional traits which could be identified by measurements of such things as head shape, stature, skin color, eye color, and hair form. In these terms, a Negroid would be a person who resembled a type specimen, perhaps from a village in Nigeria, more than he resembled type specimens from villages in the Caucasus (Caucasoids or "whites") or type specimens from villages in China (Mongoloids).

If a racial classification were based upon a single trait, skin color, for example, it would be possible to divide the entire population of the world into two groups of equal size constituting a light race and a dark race. We could multiply the number of such races by using finer criteria: very dark, dark, middling, light, and very light. If there were easily defined human races, a second trait, such as hair form, would tend to reinforce the classification obtained by using skin color. In fact, the correlation between different traits is not that good. A great many people in Africa have dark skin and tightly curled hair, and a great many people in Europe have light skin and wavy hair. A great many people in China have an intermediate skin color and very straight hair. What now becomes of all the people in Northern Africa who have light skin and curly hair? All of this could be explained under certain circumstances, if we could avoid introducing further racial criteria. If we do so, we become more confused. We must either multiply the number of races in our classification endlessly or throw our hands up in disgust. Very often, using such a method of classification, it is necessary to place children in different "races" than their parents or brothers and sisters. Human beings are a mixed-up bunch of people and no one has found a system of measurements which would lead to a convincing demonstration of the existence of clear and definite human races, most of whose members share a variety of phenotypic traits that are rare or absent elsewhere.

In recent years, as advanced techniques have permitted the identification of a variety of human genes, attempts have been made to identify human races in terms of genes or frequencies of genes characteristic of particular populations. If anything, the distribution of human genes has proved to be more erratic than the distribution of phenotypic or constitutional factors. The gene for "rh negative" blood factors is fairly common in the British Isles. Moving away from this center, the gene becomes less and less frequent until it disappears somewhere in Russia. The genes underlying the "ABO" blood types are found almost everywhere, but in different percentages in different places. Philippine Negritos, a people of dark skin color and short stature, have been reported to possess almost the same frequencies of these genes as white hospital patients in New York.

A defined set of people such as "American Negroes" can be expected to differ in gene frequencies and in phenotypic characteristics from "American whites," but "American Negroes" would include numerous individuals who possessed all or some of the characteristics typical of "American whites." In general, any large set of people, whether defined geographically or in terms of social status or supposed "ethnic" background, will contain somewhat different frequencies of genetic or other characteristics from other such groups, but the group as a whole will be so variable as to make the classification of particular individuals difficult. Any large set of human beings will possess most of the same characteristics possessed by any other large set of human beings; a few of the characteristics will be more frequent and a few will be more infrequent than in other groups. The placing of particular individuals within one group or another will depend upon the selection of characteristics thought to be of "racial" significance. On the basis of a few carefully selected criteria, most individuals can be placed in one race or another. If other criteria are used or if the number of criteria used for classification is increased, the racial classification breaks down.

Small groups of people living in isolation and forming tightly closed breeding populations tend to be more homogeneous and may differ from other such populations in terms of the frequencies of comparatively large numbers of phenotypic and genotypic criteria. For such small populations, painstaking research might ultimately lead to demonstrations of some sort of concrete relationship between genetic factors and characteristic group behaviors. Although terms such as *race, strain,* and *variety* will probably continue to be used to describe differences between groups of human beings, they should never be used to conceal the fact that all human beings are closely related and quite similar from a biological standpoint. The evidence so far is that members of any group of human beings can learn any culture, language, or set of practices that can be learned by the members of any other group of human beings.

Within any group of human beings, particular individuals may differ considerably in terms of their abilities, and these differences may be partly of biological origin. The human species is characterized by substantial individual variation, presumably arising from the tremendous mixing-up of peoples caused by successive biological and cultural revolutions. These same revolutions have apparently prevented the geographical isolation and tight inbreeding which might result in the formation of easily identified or significantly different human races or varieties.

Like other people, anthropologists would be delighted if the behaviors of different groups of human beings could be explained in terms of such easily observed characteristics as skin color, eye color, nose shape, stature, or hair form. This is a case where wanting something to be so, just doesn't go quite far enough in making it so. There is always the hope that some obvious differences between groups or some genetic differences between groups will explain some of the other differences between them. When we think of such complex performances as speaking Chinese, hunting ducks, running fast, building automobiles, or inventing a new theory, we must expect that the contribution of biology to such performances is highly complicated and involves many physical and genetic characteristics most of which would be present, perhaps in different frequencies, in any two human groups chosen at random. Bluntly, racial discrimination or discrimination based upon biological differences between groups requires that we be able to define groups in biological terms, and that once we have done so it makes a difference. So far, biological explanations of the differences between human groups, like baloney, contain very little meat, and there is a gathering suspicion that they are false. The thrust of anthropological explanations of such similarities and differences has to do with the effects of different environments and cultural traditions. Biological explanations of human similarity and difference have much more to contribute to the explanation of similarities and differences between individual human beings, but even here there are problems.

In Whose Image?

Before birth, the expression of the biological message contained in the individual is influenced by his mother's psychological states, diet, and activities. After birth, the impact of experiential and cultural variables is dramatically increased. The individual who learns nothing and experiences nothing, like a child raised in a closet, will by default be a product of his biological heredity. The relative contribution of biology and environment or nature and nurture to the development of the individual depends very much upon the individual case. For normal individuals existing in normal human environments, a great many characteristics relevant, for example, to internal physiological processes are likely to reflect biological heredity almost entirely. Other characteristics, particularly the performance of those complex behaviors which are distinctively human, are likely to reflect experience and verbal learning almost entirely. In most cases, human abilities and performances are a complicated product of nature and nurture. Consider a simple behavior such as the lifting of objects weighing one hundred pounds or more.

The ability to lift such a weight can be tested and some sort of alternation of testing and training would probably make it possible to estimate an individual's potential weight-lifting capacity. In the United States, there are very few women who can lift weights of one hundred pounds, but there are quite a few men who can do so. From this fact one might guess that weight-lifting ability is biologically determined by genes located on the chromosomes that determine sex. Had we conducted our initial research among the Ona of Tierra del Fuego, we would have discovered that when it became necessary to move from one campsite to another, the women carried the two hundred pound leather tent.

Apparently weight lifting is influenced by training, and the poor weight-lifting ability of American women is the product of what Robert Merton called a self-fulfilling prophecy. The existence of the folk belief that women cannot lift weights results in a failure to train women to lift weights and in an incapacity to lift weights. After careful investigation, a prudent individual would reach the following conclusion about the inheritance of weight-lifting ability: "Among normal human beings perhaps 20 to 40 percent of weight-lifting ability is biologically determined." A statement that the average male is a better weight lifter than the average female, while quite possibly true, does not provide a basis for sexual discrimination because it leaves open the possibility that many females are better weight lifters than many males. Weight lifting is a simple and easily measured ability. What is the situation in regard to a more complicated and less easily measured ability?

Who Is the Cleverest of Them All?

It is widely believed that there is some sort of special human ability to learn things and to solve problems which might be defined as "intelligence."

Because people in different groups learn different things and solve different kinds of problems, anthropologists have encountered difficulty in finding any general measure of intelligence which could be universally applied. For example, how much weight should be given to an ability to make stone knives, to stalk kangaroos, or to skin kangaroos with stone knives?

In most modern societies, "intelligence" tests are constructed by discovering series of tasks which individuals considered intelligent by virtue of their grades in school, their income, or some other criterion can perform better than those who have lower grades, lower incomes, etc. The individual's score on an intelligence test is, in fact, a reflection of his similarity to the group of people considered intelligent by the person who constructed the test. Very often an individual's intelligence test score is correlated with his ability to perform other tasks and most particularly with his school grades, income, and social class position.

To obtain a score on a typical written intelligence test, the individual must be sufficiently capable from a biological viewpoint to hold a pencil in his hand and to see the test instructions, and he must be sufficiently well trained to make the proper marks with the pencil and to read the test instructions. Right away, then, we know that an intelligence test score is a measure of both inherited and acquired ability. We also know that nature and nurture will affect different individuals differently depending upon the amount of training that they have had. An illiterate "genius," depending solely upon his biological inheritance, will flunk the test, while an individual with a lot of training and not too much biological ability will do fairly well.

Despite these obvious facts there has been a good deal of passionate investigation directed at determining the relative importance of nature and nurture in influencing intelligence test scores. Because two individuals with substantially the same training will tend to differ as a result of biological differences, while two individuals with substantially the same biological inheritance will tend to differ as a result of training, the results of such investigations have generally depended upon biases built in by the investigator.

For example, one-egg twins raised in the same household show a mean difference in intelligence test scores of 5.9 points (Bodmer and Cavalli-Sforza 1970:25). Twins coming from different eggs show a mean difference in intelligence of approximately 10 points. Because twins are likely to be quite similar in terms of training and experience, the study of twins appears to show that biologically identical persons have similar test scores while biologically different persons have different test scores. On the other hand, the difference is not really great and could be interpreted as a demonstration that twins coming from different eggs are almost totally unaffected by the sizable biological differences between them. Because identical twins look the same, they may tend to be treated the same, and this might be sufficient to explain why their test scores are so similar.

This suggests a critical test. Why not look at identical twins who are raised apart? Of course there are not many such twins, nor are they likely to be raised very far apart, certainly not in different cultures. Twins raised apart tend to have quite similar intelligence test scores. Is this a proof of the overwhelming importance of heredity or is it simply the result of the fact that twins raised apart are often raised by relatives or by persons of similar social and economic status?

An alternative way of investigating the role of nature and nurture in determining intelligence test scores is to provide special training and see if it results in marked increases in test scores. It does. If an individual repeats an intelligence test after a period of years, his score may vary by 20 to 30 points, roughly twice the average difference between the scores of white and Negro Americans. Again, if an individual takes several different intelligence tests, his separate scores are likely to vary considerably. Finally, over the past several decades there has been a substantial average increase in intelligence test scores, suggesting that over the years people have become test-wiser, if not wiser. These examples all support the importance of training in influencing intelligence test scores.

While it is fairly clear that the individual's performance on an intelligence test is a result of nature and nurture working together, there appears to be no easy way of estimating the relative contribution of each component. Because the idea of an intelligence test rests upon the assumption that a test can be constructed which will measure an ability that may not even exist except as a convenient fiction, it may be somewhat premature to worry about the relative impact of nature and nurture upon intelligence tests or intelligence. Where an individual's abilities or disabilities can be treated as biological in origin, there is little that can be done about them. Where the individual's disabilities are the result of training, there is always the prospect of overcoming them. Under these circumstances, if we must guess wildly concerning the relative influence of nature and nurture in particular cases, it is more practical to err upon the side of nurture and attempt a cure, than to err upon the side of nature and assume that disabilities are incurable.

In general, then, when differences occur between individuals in the same group and there is no clear evidence that the differences are the result of biological inheritance, the first questions to ask have to do with differences in the training and experience of the individuals. If such differences cannot be found or if they do not fully explain the observed differences, then genetic evidence can be sought. Because genetic influence is easily identified only when the individual characteristic is inherited through simple mechanisms involving a very small number of genes, the search for proof positive of a relationship between individual behavior and genetic inheritance is often doomed to failure. By contrast, a great variety of individual variation within groups is easily explained in terms of such things as social position, access to resources, or the parts of the cultural message transmitted to and received by the individual.

Summary

Human beings differ from all other animals in that their behavior is powerfully influenced by cultural traditions transmitted through a combination of language and experience. Human behavior, like that of all other animals, is influenced by a biological or genetic message transmitted from parents to children by means of the genetic code. Because biological individuals are the result of a unique combination of the genes of both parents and because the genetic message may be distorted by noise, each individual differs in some respects from all other individuals. Because some individuals are better adapted to the conditions of life, processes of selection encourage their survival and reproduction and the transmission of their genes to future generations. In the mammalian species, most particularly among primates and most markedly among human beings, the genetic code tends not to specify behavior in detail, much of the individual's behavior being based upon information acquired through experience.

The human being derives a major part of his behavior from the information contained in verbal messages. Such verbal messages take the form of a language or code based upon phonemes and having such properties as arbitrariness, displacement, and productivity. Human beings also differ from other animals in their possession of material culture. These special properties of human beings are summed up in the phrase "*Homo sapiens* is a culture-building animal."

Human beings appear to be self-made creatures who developed as a result of reciprocal causation involving the interaction of a variety of environmental, biological, and cultural factors. Comparison of human beings and other primates indicates the existence of a series of differences consistent with an explanation of human evolution in terms of a pattern of reciprocal causation. Because human evolution proceeded rapidly, particularly in its later stages, and because human evolution was conditioned by human culture, the human species failed to develop any very distinct biological varieties, races, or subspecies. Biological variation within human groups tends to be greater than biological variation between human groups. Biological differences between groups usually take the form of average differences or differences in the frequencies of particular traits. Because variation around the averages creates overlap between groups and because differences in the frequency of traits are rarely great, individual members of groups often do not possess the traits supposed to differentiate the group from another group. Because different human genes tend to follow different patterns of distribution, there would appear to be little hope of developing a scientific or biologically meaningful classification of human races. Small groups forming isolated breeding populations may represent biologically meaningful units.

In accounting for the behavior and abilities of different individuals, difficulties lie in the way of evaluating the role of biological and environmental forces. A simple ability, such as the ability to lift weights, appears to be the outcome of complex interactions among a variety of factors. Because human beings tend to act as they are expected to act, much of human behavior may be the outcome of self-fulfilling prophecies concerning the nature of different kinds of people. For a more complicated and more hypothetical ability such as intelligence, problems of measurement and interpretation are infinitely complicated.

Examination of the nature of the human species as compared to other species, consideration of the nature of language, reflections upon human history and evolution, and investigation of the problems of measuring human abilities all lead to the conclusion that the differences between human groups find their primary explanation in terms of differences in training and experience within the context of culture. The discoveries that human beings are largely what other human beings have made them and that cultures are constructed by human beings have revolutionary implications for the understanding of human behavior and for the development of new and better planned ways of living.

Further readings

Different disciplines and subdisciplines use quite different approaches to reach understandings of the human condition. Biologists and, to a lesser extent, physical anthropologists tend to emphasize the importance of the human biological message, while cultural anthropologists and linguists tend to emphasize the cultural message. Even those who have deep knowledge of the disciplines concerned with the human condition have difficulty in forming any coherent or generally acceptable understanding of it.

The biological viewpoint is to be found in almost any textbook of general biology. A good, current summary of human biology is Lerner's *Heredity, Evolution and Society* (1968). Physical anthropology textbooks, such as those by Kelso (1970), Birdsell (1972), Hulse (1971), and Downs and Bleibtreu (1969) combine discussions of basic biology with more detailed information concerning human evolution and human biological variation. Alland (1971, 1972) considers human diversity from both biological and cultural viewpoints, while Bates (1958), a zoologist, stresses the importance of the cultural message in a light-hearted discussion of food and sex. A more poetic view of man, perhaps overstressing the uniqueness and unpredictability of things, is Eisley's *The Unexpected Universe* (1969).

A readable introduction to the world of the primates is Kummer's *Primate Societies* (1971). Convenient summaries of current research on particular species can be found in the works edited by Jay (1968) and DeVore (1965). Works by Schaller (1963), van Lawick-Goodall (1968), and Kummer (1968) are among the many excellent field studies of particular primate species. Kummer (1971) has an excellent annotated bibliography of primate studies.

The human fossil and archaeological record is discussed readably but sometimes incautiously in Pfeiffer's *The Emergence of Man* (1969). Somewhat more authoritative works, mostly emphasizing archaeology, include those of Clark (1967, 1969), Braidwood (1967), Bordes (1968), and Brace (1967). Materials concerning language may be found in such standard textbooks as Gaeng· (1971), Hocket (1962), and Gleason (1961) or in less technical treatments such as Sapir (1921), Hall (1961), or Greenberg (1968). Also of interest is Gudschinsky's *How To Learn an Unwritten Language* (1967).

Problems and questions

1. John Smith is said to be exactly like his maternal grandfather. What percentage of his genes actually came from his grandfather?
2. Carefully examine a male and female of any species and their children. Are there any phenotypic characteristics, such as ear form, stature, or hair color, in which the children closely resemble one parent and not the other. Do you find it hard or easy to identify the genotype by examining the phenotype?
3. Using published census materials and/or observations of the people around you, consider the kinds of factors that influence reproductive fitness (the number of children an individual is likely to produce). Would you attribute any observed differences between groups to "natural" selection, to "social" selection, or to both?
4. Observe the behavior of household pets of the same species in at least two different households and/or interview household members concerning the behavior of their pets. Do pets raised in different households behave in the same way or are there differences which you might attribute to training or experience?

2

What cultural anthropologists do

The field of anthropology includes four major subdisciplines: cultural anthropology, physical anthropology, archaeology, and linguistics. Physical anthropology approaches the study of the human species from a biological viewpoint. It is concerned with human biological evolution, comparisons between human beings and other animals, and the nature of human biological variation. Archaeology and linguistics are, in a sense, highly specialized subdivisions of cultural anthropology, archaeology being concerned with the reconstruction of past cultures through the study of their material remains and linguistics being concerned with the development and nature of language. Cultural anthropology, because it is broadly concerned with the nature of culture, provides general understandings that are utilized by the other subdisciplines. More specifically, cultural anthropology is concerned with the description and comparison of cultures for which historical records are available or which exist in the present and may be studied by direct observation and through the use of

31

interviews. This chapter is intended to provide insights into the problems and nature of cultural anthropology through a discussion of the kinds of problems encountered in the study and description of other cultures.

Fieldwork: how do you begin?

Imagine yourself suddenly set down surrounded by all your gear, alone on a tropical beach close to a native village, while the launch or dinghy which has brought you sails away out of sight. Since you take up your abode in the compound of some neighboring white man, trader or missionary, you have nothing to do, but to start at once on your ethnographic work. Imagine further that you are a beginner, without previous experience, with nothing to guide you and no one to help you. For the white man is temporarily absent, or else unable or unwilling to waste any of his time on you. This exactly describes my first initiation into fieldwork on the south coast of New Guinea. I well remember the long visits paid to the villages during the first weeks; the feeling of hopelessness and despair after my obstinate but futile attempts had entirely failed to bring me into real touch with the natives, or supply me with any material. I had periods of despondency, when I buried myself in the reading of novels, as a man might take to drink in a fit of tropical depression and boredom (Malinowski 1961:4)

Because human behavior is so deeply conditioned by the influence of verbal and nonverbal cultural messages, the scientific study of human beings requires that the observer or *ethnographer* place himself in a position to receive and learn the cultural messages transmitted among the members of a group. Unlike any other kind of scientist, the cultural anthropologist must become a part of the object of study, gaining acceptance by the group (establishing rapport) and learning to display at least some of the behaviors appropriate to group membership.

The quotation from Malinowski represents the extreme case in which the ethnographer, without the help of prior knowledge, must single-handedly establish contact with persons whose way of life is radically different from his own. Because the ethnographer's training differs radically from that of the people he studies, the cultural message is thrown into sharp relief. Where the ethnographer works with his own group or with a closely related group, the content of the cultural message is not easily perceived. People tend to view the characteristic behaviors of their own groups as natural and proper. Because they have learned their own traditions without conscious effort and often without conscious awareness of having learned, they are incapable of recognizing what they have been taught. Without a basis for comparison, such customs as eating with a fork or having only one wife may appear to be expressions of universal human tendencies. Although many anthropologists study their own culture or closely related cultures, they do so with knowledge of other cultures. The recognition of culture and the existence of cultural anthropology as a discipline depend upon the cross-cultural method, the conscious or unconscious comparison of the group being studied with other different groups. Our knowledge of the range of human behavior and the varieties of human culture depends, in turn, upon the ability of individual ethnographers to encounter strangers and to secure their help and acceptance. Like a good salesman, a good ethnographer has the courage to raise his arm and press his finger upon a strange doorbell. What happens next?

When the door opens, what then?

Napoleon Chagnon began his fieldwork among the Yanomamo with the aid of a missionary who was familiar with them. He describes his introduction as follows:

> My heart began to pound as we approached the village and heard the buzz of activity within the circular compound. Mr. Barker commented that he was anxious to see if any changes had taken place while he was away and wondered how many of them had died during his absence. I felt into my back pocket to make sure that my notebook was still there and felt personally more secure when I touched it. Otherwise, I would not have known what to do with my hands.
>
> I looked up and gasped when I saw a dozen burly, naked, filthy, hideous

men staring at us down the shafts of their drawn arrows! Immense wads of green tobacco were stuck between their lower teeth and lips making them look even more hideous, and strands of dark-green slime dripped or hung from their noses. We arrived at the village while the men were blowing a hallucinogenic drug up their noses. One of the side effects of the drug is a runny nose. The mucus is always saturated with the green powder and the Indians usually let it run freely from their nostrils. My next discovery was that there were a dozen or so vicious, underfed dogs snapping at my legs, circling me as if I were going to be their next meal. I just stood there holding my notebook, helpless and pathetic. Then the stench of the decaying vegetation and filth struck me and I almost got sick. I was horrified (1968:5).

When Christoph von Fürer-Haimendorf began his study of the Apa Tanis of Assam, he insisted upon entering their country without the military escort eagerly proffered by government officials. The members of this "hostile, treacherous and unpredictable" tribe were so astonished at the sight of a peaceful visitor that they welcomed him with open arms. A mob of over two thousand armed tribesmen surrounded his party examining his equipment and body and so trampling the ground that he could scarcely find a place to set up his tent (Fürer-Haimendorf 1956:17–18). In other places enthusiasm may be tempered with understanding:

We arrived at Tonghia in the middle of a bright, clear November morning. The long rainy season was recently over, the marshes below the village were green, and the men and women were in the fields gathering the last of the crops. We sat on a low wooden platform in front of the chief's house and waited for him to return from his labors. Children peeked from behind fences, an audience assembled in the courtyard, the tall and ancient chief arrived, and my assistant introduced me. He said that I was a student who had come to learn the language and observe the customs of the Badyaranké, and that I was hoping to become a teacher—as part of my education, I had come to Africa to learn how they live and work, and to write about them for others in America to read. The chief accepted this introduction, praised the motives, and gave us a tidy thatch-roofed house in his compound. He ridiculed the bag of rice which I had brought, for rice was then abundant in his village. Tonghia proved to be a happy choice, and I passed the ensuing year in the chief's family, i.e., with the persons living in his compound, and shared the food from his granaries (Simmons 1971:5–6).

In his encounters with strangers, the ethnographer copes with reactions ranging from deadly hostility to smothering friendliness. The fact that different peoples have different ways of dealing with strangers and different levels of understanding of the ethnographer's task represents one of the central problems of cross-cultural study: How can you make general statements about encounters with groups of people who are so different in their behaviors and in their way of thinking? We can deduce certain rules of thumb, but always with the certainty that an exception will be found somewhere.

First, friendliness and openness are critical to gaining acceptance. Feelings of contempt or dislike are, in the long run, difficult to conceal and are likely to be heartily reciprocated. Elaborate cover stories or phony justifications of the ethnographer's activities usually represent an unfounded contempt for the intellectual powers of those being studied. Where people sense a lack of genuineness, they are not likely to be cooperative or truthful. Most people are flattered when they encounter a stranger who is friendly and interested in their way of life and will go out of their way to make sure he has the correct information. Although Simmons's explanation of himself approaches the ideal, not all peoples understand such concepts as research or teaching. Here, the ethnographer must limit his explanations to easily understood propositions such as, "I am interested in learning your language" or "I am studying your folklore or your local history." It is unethical and an invasion of privacy to study people without their knowledge or without explaining the possible consequences of the study.

Second, and particularly as the ethnographer's stay lengthens, he must in some way contribute to the life of the group. This derives from a moral obligation not to exploit people who are very often defenseless, as well as from the fact that exchange is fundamental to social life. Although direct payment is possible and necessary in many situations, it may create and maintain the social distance characteristic of master-servant relationships. Often, the ethnographer pays his way by being interesting or by giving people the opportunity to display a powerful and exotic stranger. Depending on circumstances he may provide aspirin, trade goods, advice on educational matters, or free photographs. Keiser's presence among the Vice Lords of Chicago was made legitimate by the fact that he was writing a book (Keiser 1969:228), but the Rohners achieved general acceptance from the Kwakiutl only when they helped to recover the community motion picture projector from the Indian Agent (Rohner and Rohner 1970:12). There are limits to the magic of friendliness and generosity. Chagnon discovered that he could work with the Yanomamo only when he became "sly, aggressive, and intimidating" (Chagnon 1968:9).

Third, as illustrated by the plight of Malinowski (page 32), who received little help, fieldwork is always made easier when there is a Mister Barker or a "field assistant" who can mediate initial communications between the fieldworker and the people he studies. Sentences like "So and so said you could help me" will open many doors. With the exception of a few isolated groups like the Polar Eskimo, human groups have relationships with other human groups. These relationships are mediated by various contact-persons. "Contact-persons" tend to have a cosmopolitan outlook and may serve to introduce the ethnographer to the most hostile of groups.

Finally, because the accuracy of an ethnographic report depends upon the establishment of trust and fluent communication, a period of six months to two years of residence and participation in the activities of a group is often required:

Indeed, in my first piece of ethnographic research on the South coast, it was not until I was alone in the district that I began to make some headway; and, at any rate, I found out where lay the secret of effective field-work. What is then this ethnographer's magic, by which he is able to evoke the real spirit of the natives, the true picture of tribal life? As usual, success can only be obtained by a patient and systematic application of a number of rules of common sense and well-known scientific principles, and not by the discovery of any marvellous short-cut leading to the desired results without effort or trouble. The principles of method can be grouped under three main headings; first of all, naturally, the student must possess real scientific aims, and know the values and criteria of modern ethnography. Secondly, he ought to put himself in good conditions of work, that is, in the main, to live without other white men, right among the natives. Finally, he has to apply a number of special methods of collecting, manipulating and fixing his evidence (Malinowski 1922:5–6).

The following section deals with the problems of bias and prejudice as they affect our ability to describe other cultures as they really are.

What does it all mean?

Despite his possession of "real scientific aims," the ethnographer, like Malinowski or Chagnon, may yet encounter difficulties in coming to terms with the "real spirit of the natives." Every human being is the slave of his own cultural tradition. Everyone is influenced by the biases and preconceptions that he bears as a representative of a particular group of people at a particular time and place. The encounter with persons whose basic conceptions of morality and proper behavior are radically different from one's own and whose conceptions of the very structure of the universe and of the way things are to be named and classified are completely unfamiliar, can be a shattering experience perhaps best described by the term *culture shock*. As he enters an alien world, the ethnographer encounters problems of communication and translation. How do you explain what people think when the very terms of their thought are radically different from your own? Consider the Polar Eskimo:

In search of the Northwest passage, while following the shores of a cold and barren land, John Ross and the members of his party heard voices hallooing across the ice. As they sailed toward the distant sound, figures on the ice resolved themselves into Eskimoes driving their dog sleds back and forth. When the ships tacked to avoid drifting ice, the Eskimoes fled. John Ross and his men placed a pole upon the ice with a flag bearing a representation of the sun and the moon painted over a hand holding a sprig of heath (the only notable vegetation on that stony shore). To the pole was attached a bag containing presents and a picture of a hand pointing toward a ship. When the

Eskimoes failed to approach the pole, Sacheuse, an Eskimo who had volunteered to sail with the expedition, walked across the ice shouting "Kahkeite" ("Come on."). To this the strange Eskimo replied, "No, no, go away" (Adapted from Ross 1819:80–81).

After some four hundred years of isolation, the Polar Eskimo, confronted with the opportunity of rejoining the human species, could only say, "No, no, go away." Only the presence of Sacheuse, and his knowledge of the Eskimo language, prevented the failure of the encounter. John Ross and his men did all that they could, hoisting a flag bearing "universal" symbols and relying upon the "universal" value of gifts. Universal though the message might have been, it could not be translated by the men John Ross encountered.

Men do not communicate by means of universal symbols. They communicate by means of symbols that are given an arbitrary meaning within a system of language and social interaction. Men differ in the way they arbitrarily subdivide and measure the universe around them. They differ in the things they recognize and in the labels they apply to things (see Chapters 5 and 6). For the ethnographer the existence of the "translation" problem means that he cannot study a cultural system until he is able to cope with the system of meanings and perceptions characteristic of that system. Having learned the system of meanings, the ethnographer still faces the task of expressing an alien way of thought within the confines of his own language and culture. Although the problem of translation has been partially solved, it remains one of the most difficult and controversial obstacles to the scientific description of other cultures.

Ethnographers, like all other men, tend to perceive reality in the light of their own culture-bound experience. A chemist comes to the study of salt filled with the attitudes and beliefs about salt he acquired at his mother's knee. As a rule, people do not *feel* very strongly about salt, and the chemist does not feel a need to praise or condemn the substance that he studies. It is different with people:

> Their physical type is everywhere the same—wild blue eyes, reddish hair and huge frames that excel only in violent effort. They have no corresponding power to endure hard work and exertion, and they have little capacity to bear thirst and heat. When not engaged in warfare, they spend some little time in hunting, but more in idling, abandoned to sleep and gluttony. They show no self-control in drinking. You have only to indulge their intemperance by supplying all that they crave, and you will gain as easy a victory through their vices as through your own arms (Tacitus 1960:4, 113, 120).

Here, writing about the tribes of Northern Europe, the Roman historian cannot conceal his disgust at their barbarian ways. Later historians might wonder whether the Romans ran out of alcohol or the Germans became temperate. Writing of South India, the French cleric, Dubois, states: "It has struck me that a faithful picture of the wickedness and incongruities of polytheism and idolatry would by its very ugliness help greatly to set off the beauties and perfections of Christianity" (1947:9). The Abbé also notes: "Being fully persuaded of the superlative merits of their own manners and customs, they thnik those of other people barbarous and detestable, and quite incompatible with real civilization" (1947:303).

Ethnocentrism is the feeling that one's own culture is somehow more important or more central than any other culture. It usually takes the form of negative value judgments (idolatry is ugly) or of selective reporting which emphasizes the "bad" features of another culture. What Malinowski called "real scientific aims" include the attempt to describe other cultures objectively, without bias or prejudice. For some anthropologists, the desire to avoid ethnocentric reporting gives rise to the doctrine of *cultural relativity*; namely, that all cultures are equally good and/or equally bad. Although some consider this doctrine parallel to, "Each to his own taste as the lady said when she kissed the pig," the habit of passing judgment upon other peoples appears to be immature and pretentious. If there are divinely inspired individuals who are competent to pass judgment upon other cultures, then the best means of helping them in their judgments is an accurate and objective description of what others do. The "ethnographer's magic," then, has to do with his ability to overcome his ethnocentric feelings, and this ability, in turn, rests upon his ability to place himself in "good conditions of work."

What is the secret of fieldwork?

If, as Malinowski suggested, we imagine ourselves to be stranded on the beach, not far from a collection of houses occupied by the members of an unfamiliar culture, we will be confronted with problems affecting our ability to survive as well as our ability to collect useful information. When, like Chagnon or Simmons, we enter the settlement, we are at once confronted with concrete evidence concerning the manner in which strangers are received. As we attempt to obtain food, to form sentences, or to make friends and acquaintances, we are again confronted with evidence of the responses to the stimuli we provide.

Because our initial attempts to behave properly in a strange setting are bumbling, incompetent, and confused, our first reaction parallels the culture shock described by Chagnon:

> As we walked down the path to the boat, I pondered the wisdom of having decided to spend a year and a half with this tribe before I had even seen what they were like. I am not ashamed to admit, either, that had there been a diplomatic way out, I would have ended my fieldwork then and there. I did not look forward to the next day when I would be left alone with the Indians: I did not speak a word of their language, and they were decidedly different from what I had imagined them to be. The whole situation was depressing, and I wondered why I ever decided to switch from civil engineering to anthropology in the first place. I had not eaten all day, I was soaking wet from perspiration, the gnats were biting me, and I was covered with red pigment, the result of a dozen or so complete examinations I had been given by as many burly Indians (Chagnon 1968:5–6).

In walking the few steps from the beach to the settlement, we have lost control of ourselves and our lives. Where we were once competent and self-confident adults, we are now a curious hybrid, part clown, part lunatic, and part child. The secret of anthropological fieldwork lies in the ability of the ethnographer to become as a little child, to learn as a child learns, but at the same time to record what he learns. Anthropological fieldwork is the science that every child knows but that most adults have forgotten.

The child commences the process of learning to speak by babbling incessantly. When people respond to some of his noises and not to others, he begins to make certain noises more frequently. As he proceeds, the child forms hypotheses and performs experiments to test their validity. Hearing, "Yesterday, I walked in the park," the child attempts, "Yesterday, I runned in the park." Laughter, rejection, the pain of failure or immediate punishment inform the child that his experiment has failed. He now modifies his hypothesis and attempts further experiments until his ability to predict the results of his linguistic behavior approaches 100 percent. He confidently asserts, "Yesterday, I ran in the park."

Every human being is an ethnographer. Through careful, prolonged, and often painful research he has developed a theory concerning the nature of the culture in which he was raised. For the majority of human beings, this internalized theory of culture is sufficient to permit the generation of appropriate behavior and successful participation in the activities of his group. Because the ordinary human being does not perform his experiments consciously nor consciously formulate his theory of culture, he cannot tell you what he knows. The goal of the ethnographer is to keep a written record of his experiments and of the theory of culture he develops. The contrast between the conscious experimentation of the ethnographer and the partly unconscious experimentation of the child emerges most clearly from an examination of the methodology of linguistics.

Ethnography: can you say it right?

As Bloomfield says, "The ancient Greeks studied no language but their own; they took it for granted that the structure of their language embodied universal forms of human thought or, perhaps, of the cosmic order" (1933:5). Unlike the child or the ancient Greek, the anthropologist is aware of the artificial nature of human languages and he has some idea about what he might expect to find when studying a language different from his own. He knows that all known languages consist of a small number of basic sounds or *phonemes*. He is able to begin his work, then, with a series of systematic experiments, designed to identify the phonemes of the language (see Chapter 1, pp. 9 and 10). The anthropologist points to a dog and a native speaker who is assisting him utters a series of sounds which may or may not be relevant to the anthropologist's actions. The anthropologist attempts to write down or "transcribe" the sounds uttered by the native speaker. The native speaker bursts into laughter and repeats what he said before. In extremity, the field-worker may seize a dental mirror and thrust it into the mouth of the native speaker to discover how the sounds are produced. Eventually, the ethnographer learns to make the correct sounds, but he still doesn't know which sounds are important or significant in determining correct pronunciation.

The speaker of a language makes all kinds of noises when he says "dog," but only some of the noises he makes are essential to meaning. In the initial stages of his experimentation, the ethnographer attempts to write down the sounds in such a way that when he reads them out loud he can pronounce them correctly (that is, so that the native speaker finds them informative and not laughable). Gradually, the ethnographer assembles a box of file cards with a different "word" written on each card. Searching through his cards he attempts to find words that are different only in minor details. For example, having started with "dog," he might eventually encounter the word "bog." When he points to a dog and says "bog," his helpers burst into laughter. Plainly, the difference between dog and bog is significant or meaningful. He forms the hypothesis that "d" and "b" are both phonemes; that is to say that the difference between them makes a difference in the meaning of utterances.

Shuffling through his slips of paper, the fieldworker encounters "bug" and "dug." Again, he discovers that the difference between "b" and "d" is meaningful. After a few weeks of hard work, he has a list of the thirty to fifty basic types of sounds out of which the entire language is constructed. With more effort, he discovers how these thirty to fifty sounds may be combined to form words or parts of words (morphemes and bound morphemes). Using similar techniques, he discovers how words are to be combined to form phrases and sentences. The grammar of one language might consider "Dog digs" to be a correct sentence, while the grammar of another language might favor "Digs dog." Word order is arbitrary, not part of the cosmic order.

A grammar of a language is a set of rules which enables the fieldworker, or for that matter anybody else, to generate sentences in the language which are formally correct. Because there might be several different ways of formulating a grammar and because the same effect might be produced by a different sort of grammar, the grammar developed by a fieldworker is not necessarily identical to that used by native speakers. All that can be asserted about it is that it is a part of a theory of culture that meets the test of predicting the behavior of native speakers.

There is much more to the study of a language than the formation of correct sentences. It helps to know what the words mean and when particular grammatical sentences are appropriate. The meaning of a word is determined by when and where it is used (its distribution and context) and by its effect on human behavior. The sentence, "Bring me a turnip," is appropriate only in certain contexts. Used in such an appropriate context, the fieldworker learns what a turnip is. The word "turnip" is an arbitrary label assigned in a particular culture to a particular object. There is no guarantee that a different language would contain a word for turnip or that if it had a word for turnip that it would be used in the same way or in the same contexts. When we point to a turnip and say, "What is this called?" the word we elicit may or may not mean the same thing as the word "turnip" in English. It is no simple problem to determine the meaning of a word, and even when the meaning is established it may not be possible to translate it into another language.

The grammar or rules of language enable the individual to generate correct sentences. Other kinds of rules permit him to make such sentences at appropriate times and in appropriate places. By extension we can think of a cultural tradition as consisting of a series of grammars which enable the individual to generate not just correct speech but correct behavior upon any occasion.

When people actually talk, they may speak in ungrammatical or improper ways, and when they carry out other forms of behavior they may also deviate from correctness or propriety. Thus, an ethnographic account of a group of people consists of replies to the following two types of question:

1. What is the proper way of doing X?
2. How do people actually do X?

The symbol "X" may represent any kind of process or activity: going through a doorway, sitting in a class, giving a lecture, making a date, planting potatoes, tuning a violin, getting dressed, eating breakfast, going for a walk, or training a dog. Because all of these processes are carried out within particular settings and in terms of particular social roles and kinds of equipment, an ethnography also contains statements of the general form: "What are the circumstances surrounding X"? Such circumstances include the environment within which the activity takes place, the kinds of people involved in the carrying out of the activity, and the kinds of clothing, tools, buildings, or other items of material culture involved in the activity. A complete ethnography also indicates the manner in which each of the activities described is related to other activities.

An ethnography represents the fieldworker's best guess concerning the nature of life in a particular group. It is, then, a theory concerning a particular cultural system and the various statements in it represent hypotheses concerning the nature of the culture. How does the ethnographer go about assembling the data required for the testing of these hypotheses?

What do you observe?

07.30 Circum utters a contact grunt and goes *northward* along the riverbed. Again the entire party follows for some 20 yards and then stops.

07.31 Circum again rises; he briefly looks back at Pater and then goes another 30 yards *northward*. No one follows. He stops, comes back until he is only 20 yards away from his closest female and sits down. All the while Pater has been watching him.

07.32 Circum rises and begins to move *west*, straight across the riverbed. Only his youngest female follows him. After a few seconds both come halfway back and sit down.

07.33 Circum sets out again, this time in a *southwest* direction. Now, Pater rises, and the whole party follows Circum in the same marching order as above (Kummer 1971:64).

The above represents an observation of the behavior of a troop of baboons. Ethologists, who are zoologists concerned with animal behavior, base their findings primarily upon written observations of the above kind. Human behavior may be studied in the same way:

Maud, with Otto following, circled back to the children's room and stopped just inside the doorway.
   She started away, as though to lead Otto again.
   Otto asked in a serious tone, "Can I be the horse?"
   Maud immediately agreed in an equally serious tone, "O.K."

In a loud, commanding voice Maud yelled, "See, you run away and I catch you." This was a new angle to the game.

Otto matter-of-factly gave Maud the rope and immediately darted through the hall and into the living room (Barker and Wright 1955:364–365).

Both of these observations place a primary emphasis on social interaction, decision making, and leadership. Both emphasize movement from place to place. Both describe vocalizations, but neither one gives much detail concerning hand, face, or eye movements. The difference between the two observations lies primarily in the fact that human beings talk about what they are doing. The baboons, in fact, spent nearly half a day deciding to go southwest, where Pater wanted to go. Of course, Kummer was not able to ask the baboons what they were doing, nor was he able to ask them about the meaning of the grunts and gestures they exchanged. The presence of verbal communication among human beings complicates the task of making observations (you have to learn the language) but it also provides additional evidence concerning what people are doing and why.

Each of the fieldworker's observations contains a heading giving the date, the place, and the observer's name. Depending upon circumstances an observation may contain a description of the setting and the persons involved and references to the time of day at which each separate notation was made. Each observation is copied and at least one copy is stored in a safe place. Ethnographic observations must often be written in code or stored under lock and key to protect the privacy of the individuals involved. After making an observation, the fieldworker reads it over, making comments in the margin concerning things to look for next time or questions to ask about what he saw and heard. When a series of observations have accumulated, the ethnographer arranges them in terms of a system of classification and compares those that are similar in kind. A single observation of children playing horse is an inadequate basis for making any very firm statements.

In many situations, the fieldworker is unable to follow people around making notes, and his observations, written after the fact, look something like this:

FUNERAL   A.R.B. *July 15, 1967* Santana

Not far from the village, near the approach road, is an adobe wall surrounding a large open space. At one side of the construction facing the road is an arched doorway upon which is written in fading letters, the Spanish words, "Ashes to ashes, dust to dust." [Spanish translation needed here, also more detailed description of the graveyard.] Inside the doorway are the mounds of earth, the crosses and the monuments constituting the graveyard in which the fathers and grandfathers and perhaps most often the young children of Santana have been buried for more than [how many?] years. [Note: what is the Zapotec vocabulary relevant to this setting; what is the evidence that death is a significant cultural theme?]

Standing in front of this monument to the futility of life . . . [Strike this out, meaningless editorializing and artsy craftsy.]

Sometimes, a passerby standing in front of the cemetery can look down the road just at dusk and see moving toward him myriad points of light. To his right, he can see the evening star and on the clouds the last remnants of daylight. The strong winds of the afternoon have died with the evening band. [Find out if there are two bands or not and if one plays only American Indian music; also what about recruitment to the band?] [Does the above belong here?]

Soon the procession is visible. At the front, walking almost in darkness comes the band. A relative [what relative?] of the deceased [why not say dead man?] is circulating among the players offering them an occasional sip of mescal. There are about fifteen men in the band carrying drums, trumpets, flutes, clarinets [get a better list and put it in a table or appendix]. Marching with the band is a small boy carrying a bottle of orange pop in his hip pocket. From time to time he hands it to his trumpet-playing father who takes a swig. [Is this an idiosyncrasy or does orange pop really help?]

Following the band is a figure of Christ on the cross. The figure hangs in a contorted position and in a better light it would be possible to see the agonized expression, the blood dripping from the wounds, and the phrase [what is it?] inscribed upon the cross. Behind the cross comes a plain black coffin of the standard octagonal [?] shape. It is carried by four pall bearers [Was it four, how were they selected, paid? Connie says, they were almost too drunk to stand]. Following the coffin is a group of women carrying candles. Every so often a candle blows out and the carrier holds it in the flame of another candle, lights it and continues to move solemnly in tune to the music. Behind the women come a group of men [check this]. Both men and women have been drinking heavily [were all of the women drinking?], but most can navigate reasonably well.

The procession is the concluding portion of the funeral of Luis Martinez, an old man who died, evidently of heart failure on the previous day [Connie says he was 85 and died during the night]. (From field notes taken by Alan R. Beals)

Such an observation, perhaps written in more detail, might serve as a basis for further investigation of the nature of the funeral process in the community of Santana in Mexico. Because Santana is a fairly small community, it might not be possible for the ethnographer to observe any other funerals. In such a case, the ethnographer has to collect information about other funerals by asking residents of the community what they remember about them. In presenting his material on funerals, the ethnographer may simply describe the funeral he observed and discuss the extent to which he felt it was typical. Alternatively, he might describe what he felt to be a typical funeral. Ideally, the ethnographer would present a set of rules, a gammar if you like, which could serve as a means of explaining and predicting any kind of funeral likely to be held in the community.

At the funeral, one man turned to the ethnographer and said, "Look at this man, he is dead. Soon I too will be dead. You too will die. We must all die." Statements like this might lead an ethnographer to wonder about the meaning of death and funerals to the people of the community, with the hypothesis that the attitude toward death plays some kind of important role in regulating a wide variety of different kinds of behavior. From an analysis of a wide variety of observations and interviews, the ethnographer might identify a general organizing principle of the following kind. "Because we are all going to die, we must preserve proper behavior at all times, acting without regard to physical danger or self-interest."

In this way, each observation made by the anthropologist leads to further questions about what is going on. As these further questions arise, the ethnographer applies a variety of additional research techniques in an attempt to find definitive answers. Having derived a variety of questions about the meaning of death from his observations of funerals, the ethnographer might formulate a series of specific questions and administer them to a randomly selected sample of individuals. Such a systematic questionnaire would provide data that could easily be manipulated by means of standard statistical techniques. A problem arises in that the questions are those of the ethnographer. There is always the danger that the questions reflect his view of life rather than that of the persons being interviewed. Other data concerning death and its significance might be obtained from casual conversations, from nondirective questions or statements (What did you think about last night's funeral?), or from an examination of gossip or folktales.

In both observations and interviews, the ethnographer is likely to select materials of special interest to himself or reflecting the biases of his own culture. One way of correcting for this sort of bias is to train members of the group studied to make observations or carry out interviews. In general, interview situations are more susceptible to bias because every gesture and statement made by the ethnographer may be used by the informant as a source of information concerning the answers sought by the ethnographer. When a person who has never thought about funerals at all is asked, "What did you think about that funeral?" he has little choice, particularly if he is being paid or otherwise rewarded for his cooperation, than to formulate a convincing answer.

In attempting to describe how other people live, the ethnographer inevitably introduces some degree of distortion and error. The best ways of reducing the extent of such errors are to spend a considerable period of time in the field, to learn the language, to allow the people being studied to speak for themselves as much as possible, and to apply a variety of formal and systematic methods, particularly in those areas where the fiindings are most likely to be subject to question. The observation that people live in thatched or tile roofed houses with walls of adobe brick is unlikely to be questioned, while a statement that they are incapable of forming strong emotional attachments to others requires extensive documentation. The ideal test of an ethnographic description would lie in the ability of another person to behave properly within the culture described on the basis of the ethnographic description. Where a given group or community cannot be restudied by an independent observer, the value of an ethnographer's account must be tested indirectly in terms of comparison with other studies of similar communities. Let us consider this matter further.

How Do We Know It's So?
In his history of Arctic explorations, John Barrow has the following to say about John Ross's observations of the Eskimo:

> Ross, indeed, suspects that this account "may appear in some points to be defective;" he may safely satisfy himself that it will not only *appear,* in some points, to be *defective,* but will be so pronounced by all: in point of fact, he never set his foot on shore, and could not, by any possibility, have known anything of the stuff he has set down, which is of that kind of manufacture not worth the paper on which it is printed (1846:33).

Years later, Knud Rasmussen's Eskimo informants corroborated John Ross's description. From the time of Marco Polo, also branded a liar, accounts of strange peoples and unusual customs have been greeted with incredulity.

A laboratory scientist who discovers an unusual effect can usually find another scientist willing to repeat his experiment and test his findings. The field scientist tends to work alone or in small groups and has no organized way of replicating his findings. Robert Redfield, who conducted an early study of a village in Mexico (Redfield 1930), was much concerned about replication and encouraged Oscar Lewis (1951) to conduct a restudy of the village of Tepoztlán. Where Redfield had found a peaceful and harmonious community, Lewis found a community filled with conflict and disagreement. Although Redfield and Lewis agreed concerning most of the features of Tepoztlán, they disagreed concerning the basis of social interaction in the community. Because Redfield was interested in quite small communities, he may have focused his interest and attention on outlying hamlets, while Lewis emphasized the more urban-influenced central community of Tepoztlán. Because some years had passed between the study and restudy, it is possible that the community had undergone rapid change. Perhaps the differences in the two accounts are nothing more than an expression of differences in the personalities or theoretical viewpoints of the two men. In this case, Lewis's replication of Redfield's study failed to lead to any very general confirmation or disconfirmation of Redfield's findings. In the end, verification of the Lewis and Redfield studies has had to rest upon the gradual accumulation of evidence concerning the nature of communities in Mexico. The general feeling arising from this sort of comparison is that, while Lewis's work contains certain characteristic biases, it represents a more detailed and better documented description of the community than does Redfield's work. In view of the fact that Lewis had the advantage of Redfield's experience, this is hardly surprising. In the end, the credibility of an ethnographic account rests upon documentation.

What Are Your Impressions?

Faced with the probability that for years to come he will be the only reliable source of information about Tepoztlán or some other community or group, the ethnographer feels a need to provide as much information as possible. Every minute or hour the ethnographer spends documenting one kind of fact is a minute or hour not spent documenting some other kind of fact. In preparing his final account of what a particular group of people is like, the ethnographer finds that the bulk of his information consists of little more than his own educated impressions of what the people are like. Because the impressions of a knowledgeable person are more useful than no information at all, some of the information contained in an ethnography represents little more than a series of assertions supported only by the fact that the ethnographer was there. Such statements take the following form:

> An individual normally worships the deity of his father, and some also worship their mother's deity as well. Many deities are identified with a particular clan in which case all members, male and female, are worshippers by virtue of birth into it. After marriage women return home for the annual festival of their own deity, but they assist in the performance of the annual festival of their husband's deity. If a woman is childless, despite prayers and sacrifices to her husband's and her own deity, she may seek the help of another deity (Bascom 1969:77).

Such a means of presenting data is particularly acceptable if: (1) the materials covered are so obvious as to make error unlikely, or (2) similar accounts exist elsewhere in the literature. Because such descriptions rest upon the ethnographer's impressions, they are generally described as *impressionistic.*

A slightly more convincing method of presenting data is the *anecdotal* method, where the ethnographer's impressions are supported by direct reference to observations or by direct quotations from informants. For example, Bascom supports his comments about institutionalized friendship with a quotation from a legend:

> Once there were two men who were best friends. One of them had a fight with another man and killed him. Escaping, he ran to the house of his friend and told him what had happened. He said that the king would arrest and punish him. His friend advised him to act like a crazy man, to dress in rags, and, when questioned, to speak nothing but nonsense (1969:47).

Where available and relevant, photographs (Collier 1967), motion pictures, tape recordings, or various kinds of documents may be used to support ethnographic statements.

Over the years, ethnographers have developed impressionistic and anecdotal accounts of a wide variety of peoples. The existence of these "natural history" accounts have tended to release ethnographers from the burden of providing "complete" descriptions of the peoples they study. It

is now becoming increasingly acceptable to produce ethnographies that
focus upon particular topics and apply relatively sophisticated methodologies to more limited areas of culture. Fifty years ago an ethnographer
having the opportunity to study a tribe of Indians living in the jungles of
the Amazon would have been ridiculed if he had studied nothing more
than their hunting techniques, their language, or their methods of raising
children. Today, when a number of general accounts of these tribes already
exist, the ethnographer is expected to carry out more detailed investigations
of some particular aspect of life. Such detailed investigation permits the
application of formal methodologies.

*Formal Approaches: How
Do You Know?*

In carrying out their study of the Menomini Indians of Wisconsin, George
and Louise Spindler confronted a situation in which there already existed
a considerable body of published material concerning the tribe. Most of
this material attempted to deal with the way the tribe was organized before
it had experienced changes resulting from the modernization and urbanization of the part of Wisconsin in which they lived. For the Spindlers, the
problem was not, "What are the Menomini like?" but "How have the
Menomini adapted to the changing world in which they live?" To answer
this question it was necessary to find some way of measuring the degree
to which individual Menomini or groups of Menomini had adapted to modern circumstances and to find some way of describing the different kinds
of adaptation characteristic of different groups of Menomini.

One of several ways in which the Spindlers attacked this problem was to use the Rorschach projective technique on individuals from each of several different groups of Menomini. This technique consists of presenting a series of cards depicting inkblots to the individual and asking the individual what he sees. The advantage of the technique is that it provides the informant with relatively few cues concerning what he is "supposed" to see. Particular characteristics of the responses such as references to color or to movement can be analyzed in numerical terms and a measure of the similarities and differences of individuals and groups to each other can be constructed. "Acculturated" Menomini gave responses similar to those given by white Americans, while "native-oriented" Menomini gave quite different responses (George and Louise Spindler 1971:28–29). Through the use of this and other systematic measures, it was possible to develop a consistent and well-documented description of the kinds of differences existing between different groups of Menomini. The resulting positive evidence concerning the least acculturated or native-oriented Menomini lends special conviction to the Spindlers' consequent description of the way of life of the native-oriented group.

The methods used by the Spindlers developed logically out of the kind of research question they were asking. The study of acculturation is improved by methods that measure its extent. A great many ethnographic questions are fundamental to a wide range of human groups and the methods for finding answers to such questions have become relatively standardized. A case in point is the method for studying language described previously (pp. 40–41). A similar case, reflecting a different sort of method, arises in the need to identify the individual members of a cultural system.

What Is Your Name?
Fairly early in the conduct of his research, the ethnographer wishes to assemble basic information such as the names, ages, and sexes of the people he studies. The most common means of assembling such information is through a household census. Typically, the ethnographer goes from door to door getting a list of the names of each person in the household along with qualifying information such as sex, age, relationship to household head, birthplace, years of schooling, occupation, income, and, if relevant, the previous relationship of husband and wife. From this data, the ethnographer can construct a population pyramid showing the distribution of individuals in terms of age and sex, and he can compute estimates of fertility, divorce, or migration. He can also determine whether or not the households represent nuclear families (father, mother, son, daughter), or some other kind of arrangement. If informants report that married couples always live in the household of the groom's parents, he can check their report against the facts revealed in the census.

Depending upon his interests, the ethnographer may also collect censuses dealing with house styles, household equipment, expenditures, political opinions, or religious beliefs. In a small community of less than one hundred households, the census is the only accurate way of collecting detailed information concerning the group as a whole. Where households are numerous, the same sorts of questions might be answered more economically by numbering the households and using a table of random numbers to select between twenty and one hundred households for systematic study. The sample survey has the drawback of providing information about what the group is like on the average, but not providing information about exceptional households or individuals. It would be easy, for example, to conduct a sample survey which would omit the households of particularly wealthy or influential individuals. In a small community people may become indignant if they are omitted from a sample survey.

Generally, a census or a sample survey fails to provide information concerning the kinds of relationships that may exist between households. Kin relationships between households are generally obtained by collecting genealogies that include all of the households in the community. The most common tactic, here, is to interview an older person concerning the identity of his ancestors and descendants. To begin with, the ethnographer might ask his informant if he remembers the name of his father's father or of his father's father's father. He then asks if the father's father had any older brothers or sisters or any younger brothers or sisters and writes down their names. He obtains the name, birthdate, deathdate, and other information about each individual mentioned, then he inquires about their wives, children, children's children, and so on. If he is interested in kinship terminologies, he asks how the informant would address and refer to each of these individuals and how each of these individuals would address and refer to the informant. One way of organizing materials in a genealogy is to assign the letter "A" to the oldest person in the genealogy. His oldest son would then be AA and his oldest son's oldest son would be AAA. His younger brother would be B and his younger brother's oldest son would be BA. Female relatives are indicated by a lower case letter. Thus A's oldest daughter would be Ab. Such a technique produces a list of all of the relatives in a particular male line, and it is possible that each of the women married into the male line would generate an additional patrilineal genealogy.

When enough genealogies have been collected, it is possible to determine how every household in the community is related to every other household. Marriages to cousins or other close relatives can be traced, or the genealogies may provide information essential to an understanding of the inheritance of property. Genealogies provide evidence of membership in lineages or clans and this may be useful in understanding how people choose sides in disputes or why a particular individual is influential.

Rorschach projective techniques, censuses, and genealogies represent only examples of the many kinds of formal methods now used in the collection of ethnographic information. Other examples will be mentioned in future chapters. Essentially a formal method involves the collection of information in terms of a standardized set of procedures often leading to mathematical or statistical analysis and verification. The standardization of procedures limits the ethnographer's ability to bias his data through unconscious selection. It permits others to verify his results by applying the same methodology and seeing if it leads to the same results. Because the formalization or standardization of methodology has a way of introducing its own kinds of biases, it is unwise to depend upon a single method such as sample surveys or life history interviews to the exclusion of other methods. A systematic description of a particular group of people constitutes an ethnography. What might such a description contain?

What is included?

Ideally, an ethnography is a grammar or rulebook from which a reader could reproduce any and all behaviors appropriate to membership in a particular group as well as an account of the range of behaviors actually encountered. In fact, individual ethnographers tend to select aspects of cultural systems that seem particularly important to the people being studied or are particularly relevant to the ethnographer's interests. Heider's description of the Dugum Dani of New Guinea has the following chapter headings: subsistence; social organization; conflict; man and the supernatural; language and categories; art and play; the natural environment; the body; and artifacts of culture (1970: xi). Elwin's *Bondo Highlander* (1950), a study of a tribe in India, has the following chapter headings: setting; social organization; economics; marriage; religion; ceremony; maladjustment; and Bondo character.

In general, the table of contents of an ethnography represents the ethnographer's interpretation of the kinds of parts into which a cultural system can be divided with special reference to the cultural system at hand. Because each ethnographer forms his own ideas concerning what is important about the people he studies, it follows that attempts to compare different cultural systems are often frustrating. Information concerning funerals is present in most ethnographies, but many fail to mention equally widespread and universal processes such as child training or cultural change.

Variations in the training and theoretical interests of different ethnographers combined with variations in the nature of individual ways of life make it difficult or impossible to formulate a universal framework for the description of culture. The organization of the chapters in this book reflects an attempt to arrange the materials of cultural anthropology in such a way as to provide a kind of framework particularly useful to the understanding of the relationships among different kinds of human activities.

Thus, the following chapter has to do with the nature of human groups and with concepts such as *culture, system,* and *process,* which are of value in defining such groups and explaining the kinds of things that go on within them. Chapter 4 deals with the nature of the human environment and the kinds of processes involved in the maintenance of relationships between cultural systems and their environments. Chapters 5 and 6 deal with those basic interpretations of reality that constitute the core of any cultural tradition. Together, Chapters 4, 5, and 6 constitute a description of the playing field or setting within which human groups operate and the set of rules or cultural tradition which governs the activities of their memberships. The remaining chapters of this book deal with the fundamental processes or activities that occur in all human groups—in effect, how the game is played.

Summary

Scientific explanation of the similarities and differences among cultural systems is dependent upon the ethnographer's ability to arrive at detailed and objective descriptions. Objective descriptions depend upon the ability of the ethnographer to establish rapport; that is, to establish relationships with the people he studies that will permit him to collect information from them. This usually involves openness, a willingness to contribute to the life of the group, use of intermediaries or contact-persons, and prolonged participation.

Once rapport has been established the ethnographer still faces the translation problem and the problem of his own ethnocentrism. The strangeness of a new situation and the ethnographer's incompetence in coping with it may lead to culture shock. As this is overcome, the ethnographer, like the child, begins to learn a new culture. The ethnographer learns faster and more effectively than the child because he maintains a record of his experiences and because he has special methods of "fixing his evidence." This process is illustrated by the methods used by linguists in studying unknown languages.

The evidence collected by the ethnographer involves the answers to such questions as what is the proper way of doing X, and how is X related to other activities or processes. Much of the ethnographer's information derives from his formal and informal observations of behavior and from interviews of various kinds. Such data, written in the form of field notes, provide the basis for further questions or observations.

As data accumulate the ethnographer must consider the kind and variety of documentation required for a convincing description of those aspects of the cultural system he chooses to emphasize. Some description is presented in impressionistic or anecdotal form, but other description requires the use of formal methods. Such formal methods, illustrated by Rorschach projective techniques, censuses, and genealogies, involve the collection of information in terms of a standarized set of procedures. Where possible, evidence concerning matters that are controversial or uncertain is collected through the use of a variety of formal methods. Because an ethnography or description of a way of life tends to represent those aspects of culture considered vital to its operation, an ethnography is likely to be a theory of how some particular human group operates. The ideal test of such a theory is for a third person to read the ethnography and on that basis to generate behaviors acceptable to members of the group described.

Further readings

General problems of research in anthropology are considered in Pelto (1970). Considerations relevant to professional careers in anthropology are given in Frantz' *The Student Anthropologist's Handbook* (1972) and in Fried's *The Study of Anthropology* (1972). The carrying out of fieldwork is discussed, often from a highly personal point of view, in Spindler's *Being an Anthropologist* (1970), Golde's *Women in the Field* (1970), and Freilich's *Marginal Natives* (1970). There are numerous accounts of ethnographic experiences such as *A Diary in the Strict Sense of the Term* (Malinowski 1967), *In the Company of Man* (Casagrande, 1960), *Return to Laughter* (Bowen 1954), *Travels in Arabia Deserta* (Doughty 1888), *The Oregon Trail* (Parkman 1849), and *Incidents of Travel in Yucatan* (Stephens 1871). Anthropological fieldwork for beginners is discussed and illustrated by student papers in *The Cultural Experience* (Spradley and McCurdy 1972). An introduction to more specific fieldwork techniques is provided by Maranda's *Introduction to Anthropology* (1972) and by the variety of specialized publications in the "Studies in Anthropological Method" series by Holt, Rinehart and Winston. Several of the case studies, such as Newman's on the Gururumba (1965), and Turner's on the Highland Chontal (1972) provide good discussions of the problems of the anthropologist in the field.

An idea of the nature and content of ethnography can be obtained by examining any of the Holt, Rinehart and Winston "Case Studies in Cultural Anthropology" or any of the ethnographies referred to in the bibliography, especially those by Arensberg and Kimball, Colson, Elwin, Evans-Pritchard, Firth, Kaberry, Lowie, Malinowski, Nadel, Sahlins, Rasmussen, Lewis, Whyte, West, Wilson and Warner.

Problems and questions

Warning: Before undertaking any projects involving observations of interviews of human beings, the student should consult with his instructor and carefully review the discussion of student fieldwork in the Preface.

1. To test your ability as a scientific observer, take notes concerning a

portion of a television program or of some public performance or activity and ask your instructor for criticism. Do the same thing with an interview.

2. Through interviews and observations of a patterned activity—such as playing a game, attending a lecture, or getting up in the morning—formulate a set of rules which would enable someone else to carry out the activity in an acceptable manner. Find a way to test your rules.

3. Conduct a census of five to ten households. The households could be neighboring households on a city street or they could be the parental households of a group of students. Does the population seem to be increasing or decreasing? What is the membership of the average household? Can you think of any explanations for the differences among households?

4. Collect one or several genealogies. What are the kinship terms used in referring to the various people on each genealogy? Do the genealogies reveal any differences in family size, patterns of migration, or causes of death between the generations?

5. After observing the people in it and asking questions about its different parts, draw a map of some particular social setting and discuss the significance of the different items in it.

6. When is it proper to raise your right hand above your head and waggle it repeatedly at the wrist? What happens if you do this at the wrong time and place?

7. Read any two chapters in *Being an Anthropologist* (Spindler 1970) in connection with the two corresponding case studies. What kinds of problems and/or successes were experienced by the anthropologists in gaining acceptance? Would you attribute these problems and successes to characteristics of the ethnographer or to characteristics of the cultural system being studied?

3

Culture, system, and process

In preparing an ethnography, the cultural anthropologist assembles information about some particular people. He discovers the cultural messages transmitted within the group and relates these to the various activities carried out by members of the group. Because there are many different kinds of human groups and because they overlap with each other or are related to each other in a variety of ways, an important theoretical question has to do with the definition of such things as groups, societies, and cultures. Equally important questions have to do with ways of conceptualizing the different parts or aspects of whatever it is the ethnographer is studying. Questions about the object of study and the parts into which it may be divided form the subject matter of this chapter.

What is the object of study?

Every human being and group of human beings takes form under the influence of cultural as well as biological and experiential messages. Although other animals engage in social interaction and therefore form groups, the influence of culture creates special characteristics of human groups. Therefore, there are special problems in the definition, description, and analysis of human groups. One way of arriving at an understanding of these special problems is to consider the implications of the kinds of things involved in a description of human behavior:

> In South India, an old man sits on a shady platform under a nim tree. With his hand he strokes a bundle of fibers against his naked thigh and twists it into a rope. Below, at ground level, Ganga and Bhima are sitting on a rock. Bhima, a three-year-old girl, is holding an empty tin can and a stick. She puts the stick into the tin can and causes the can to roll back and forth. A five-year-old girl comes out of a nearby windowless stone house. As she sits beside the old man on the platform, Bhima goes to her and says, "I will bring you two mango seeds and two for Ganga and two for me and we will play 'seed.' " The five-year-old answers, "Bring." Bhima disappears and returns with six mango seeds. Together the players arrange the seeds in a circle. The five-year-old takes a stone and throws it at the seeds so that they all bounce out of the circle. The five-year-old picks up all of the seeds. Bhima says, "Give me two seeds." The five-year-old turns and runs away. Bhima says, "I won't play with you again."
>
> A two-year-old boy is sitting nearby on a rock. Bhima goes to him and pushes him off the rock, taking his place. The small boy sits on a different rock. Bhima pours sand on the boy. The boy rises and follows his sister into the house. In a minute the boy emerges from his house with a rock in his hand. He throws it in the direction of Bhima and then goes back inside the house. Bhima wanders off and the old man is left sitting under the tree, surrounded by gray, featureless houses, a stretch of sandy street, and a fractious goat. (Adapted from field notes taken by Constance M. Beals)

In this incident, a group of human beings came together, established a cooperative enterprise, and abandoned it leaving nothing but a circle in the sand. Many sorts of categories can be used in thinking about or analyzing this episode, but the following seem to be most important.

The observed activities are carried out within a *setting or environment*. The setting is composed of sun and shade and other "natural" things. It is also composed of such things as tin cans, domesticated plants, and houses. All of these things bear the impress of human activity and might be lumped together under the term *artificial environment*. The term *material culture* refers to parts of the *artificial environment* that are shaped deliberately in response to plans and recipes contained within a cultural tradition. By their existence, these things represent an aspect of the cultural message and exert an influence upon human behavior. Such terms as *tools, equipment,* or *artifacts* are used to represent special aspects of material culture. A house is an artifact or constructed thing, but it is hardly a tool. The old man with his rope is evidently not a member of the children's play group being described, nor does it seem appropriate to describe him as an artifact. Human beings and human groups outside of the group being studied can be defined as representing the *social environment*.

The division of a setting or environment into parts labeled natural, artificial, and social is useful in describing how the environment came into being. For the purpose of understanding why the members of a group behave as they do, it is more useful to think of the environment as a series of influences or pressures upon the group. Together these influences may be described as the *external conditions* that provide opportunities for and limitations upon various kinds of activities. When external conditions change, problems are created which must be coped with if the group is to continue to operate. Such new influences or problems might be called *stresses*.

The human beings interacting within the described setting are defined as a group, in this case a children's play group. Their activity is partly *symbolic interaction*. Language and gestures, such as the throwing of a rock, involve the use of symbols that derive their meaning from arbitrary agreement within the group. Although it is often possible to define a human group solely in terms of frequency of interaction, the distinction between the members of the play group and members of the social environment is partly based upon behaviors and attributes that *symbolize* group member-ship. To make the distinction between member and nonmember often requires knowledge of the arbitrary meanings that define membership. The artificial environment, the forest of symbols within which the children operate, and such things as procedures for playing the game of "seed" represent aspects of the *cultural tradition* of the group.

To say that a human group involves a setting, warm bodies, symbolic interaction, and a cultural tradition is like saying that a clock consists of springs, wheels, and hands. The important thing about a group of human beings, or a clock, is the manner in which the parts are interrelated when it is functioning. When a group is functioning, each of the abstractions that might be regarded as parts or aspects of the group exerts its influence only in terms of its relationships to the other parts. A thing composed of func-tioning and interrelated parts is called a *system*. Because the cultural tra-dition represents the unique component of any functionng human group, the terms *cultural system* and *sociocultural* system are useful in describing the object of study of cultural anthropology. *A cultural system is the organi-zation created by the interaction of human beings and cultural traditions within a particular setting.* A *society* is that special kind of cultural system within which such vital processes as birth, marriage, and death are carried out. The operation of a cultural system leads to particular outcomes in terms of human behavior. What causes a group of people to behave in certain ways or to achieve particular outcomes?

System: what determines the outcome?

The B-29 is an obsolete airplane which was designed to carry a crew of eleven men who, in the words of an Air Force general, were "to drop the bomb on the target." If we were to follow a flight of such a plane, we would probably start with a briefing session in which the crew would be given precise instructions concerning when the plane should leave the ground, in what direction it should fly, what speed it should go, what altitude it should maintain, where it should go, what it should do when it got there, and so on. These instructions, together with other training and experience the crew has received or undergone, contribute to the cultural tradition of the crew. The members of the crew form a group or society, and the airplane constitutes a sort of combined environment and set of tools. The flight from briefing room to destination and return constitutes a significant part of the operation of the crew.

What determines the outcome of a particular flight? From the viewpoint of the "groundpounders" who decide where and when the plane is supposed to fly and who announce their instructions at the briefing session, the flight should proceed according to plan. A groundpounder, particularly if he has been told little white lies about what actually happened, might hypothesize that what actually happened was determined by the rules and orders making up the cultural tradition of the aircrew.

The captain of an aircrew, faced with the problem of explaining why the airplane failed to reach its destination, might point to the poor condition of the airplane or the presence of unseasonal and unpredicted tropical storms. The captain hypothesizes, then, that what actually happens is determined by the environmental forces or stresses acting upon the aircrew. Groundpounders, hearing such a report, might hypothesize that the aircrew, being poorly trained or incompetent, had failed to follow instructions.

The manual of instructions given to all members of the crew states that if there is an oil leak, the aircraft commander (pilot) must be notified immediately. Because B-29 engines leak oil in various quantities almost continuously, it is practically impossible to determine whether the engine has sprung a fresh leak or is merely dripping oil in the usual manner. When a crew member looks and sees oil, his reporting will depend upon his experience, the mood of the aircraft commander as revealed throughout the flight, and, perhaps more than anything else, upon the characteristic crew attitude toward such things as built up through weeks of training. At night, or under conditions of poor visibility, the probability that an oil leak will be reported is reduced.

We cannot, simply by writing a manual (cultural tradition) about oil leaks in B-29 engines, specify the circumstances under which any particular oil leak might come to be reported to the aircraft commander. The best that can be done is to suggest the probable outcomes of a wide range of different conditions. Prediction of oil leak reporting involves the simultaneous control of a widge range of information having to do with the environment (the nature of the airplanes, the weather, the rest of the Air Force), the membership (who belongs to the crew and what are their attributes and relationships), the cultural tradition (what it says in the manual, what was done last time), and, finally, the way these various parts of the system actually work together when the crew is in operation. The groundpounder's hypothesis: "All you have to do is know the rules and follow them"; The mechanic's hypothesis: "All you have to do is understand the airplane"; and the crew member's hypothesis: "The weather was bad and the plane poorly maintained"; are insufficient to an understanding of what goes on. In the same way, knowledge of aspects of cultural systems such as material culture, society, cultural tradition, religion, personality, or economy is useful only when the aspects are considered in relationship to other parts or aspects of the ongoing system.

Which Explanation Is Best?

The extent to which it is necessary to conceive of human behavior as a product of the operation of a system of interrelated parts depends very much upon the kind of behavior that is being observed and the kind of question that is being asked of that behavior. Human reproduction, human metabolism, and such things as heart beat, respiration, or resistance to disease can often be discussed quite fruitfully as purely biological processes. Here, the biological or genetic message is of such overwhelming importance that powerful predictions can be made without giving much attention to such things as cultural tradition, interaction between human beings, or the impact of the setting or environment. Such predictions would be more accurate with knowledge of customary dietary practices, sleeping habits, exercise, outside temperature, or the frequency of stressful social interaction, but for the purposes of medical treatment, a prediction based solely on the study of biological processes may be of sufficient practical value to make consideration of other factors unnecessary.

Because all the members of a group speak more or less the same language according to the same set of rules, a linguist can find out a great deal about a language by studying the linguistic behavior of a single person. A language, or for that matter any other set of symbols used in communication, cannot be effective unless there is very substantial agreement concerning meanings and the proper ways of expressing them. For the study of such things as meaning or the nature of grammatical rules, the groundpounder's hypothesis is perfectly adequate for there is very nearly a one-to-one or mechanical correspondence between linguistic behavior and the set of instructions that underlies it. If we wish to predict which sentences will be regarded as grammatical by the members of a group, we can make almost perfect predictions on the basis of a knowledge of the grammar of the language. In this sense, linguistics is an exact science. Because members of a group must be in substantial agreement concerning what is proper in terms of their cultural tradition, exact predictions can be made concerning the meanings that will be attributed to particular actions and concerning actions that will be considered proper behavior. From this viewpoint it could be argued that linguistics, formal logic, and some branches of mathematics constitute the only really exact sciences.

The prediction that people will agree about something about which they have already agreed could be viewed as trivial. When it comes to predicting what people will actually say or what results they will actually obtain when they apply a mathematical theorem, linguistics and mathematics become inexact. With a little talent and luck, we can arrive at an exact prediction concerning what will be regarded as the correct rules for playing "seed," but this, after all, tells us very little about what will happen when the game is played.

Sometimes human behavior follows the patterns specified as proper behavior in the cultural tradition quite closely. A stage play performed in accordance with a detailed script will resemble the script so closely that our predictions concerning the behavior of the players will be enhanced very little by knowledge of the personalities of the players or the nature of the setting. A religious ritual may also be so tightly scripted as to provide little room for variation. In these cases, human behavior is so responsive to arbitrary rules and definitions as to make the hypothesis that human behavior is determined by cultural traditions quite useful.

By contrast, knowledge of the rules of a game predict the behavior of the players in the vaguest sort of way. For basketball, the rules tell us how many players there will be, what the environment should look like, and so on, but the actual playing of the game depends upon strategies formulated by the players in response to their interaction among themselves and with members of the opposing team. Here, the hypothesis that human behavior is generated in response to social interaction becomes quite useful although it would be difficult to explain basketball without a knowledge of the rules or cultural tradition underlying the game.

In considering the outcome of the flight of a bomber crew, a pregnancy, a basketball game, or any other activity that takes place within the confines of a cultural system, it is sometimes possible to attribute the observed outcome to simple causes. In most cases, outcomes have to be explained in terms of the complex interrelationships between causes or factors that occur within the functioning cultural system. Very often the outcomes of human behavior represent the kind of reciprocal causation discussed in connection with human evolution. Although we may *say* that the home team lost the basketball game because of poor officiating or because the basketball didn't go through the basket with sufficient frequency, a real explanation of the loss has to be made in terms of the general properties of the cultural system represented by the basketball team functioning within its setting.

In explaining such natural events as the behavior of the members of a group, the scientist inevitably explores simple explanations first before

proceeding to more complicated explanations. Because the scientist generally wishes to explain some particular thing, rather than everything, a simple explanation or theory of causation may be chosen because it explains and predicts those things the scientist is interested in. The explanation of human behavior in terms of simple or partial causes is usually called *determinism*. Biological determinism is the doctrine that human behavior can be explained by a knowledge of human heredity. Economic determinism is the doctrine that it can be explained in terms of the material rewards that people seek. Technoenvironmental determinism, a phrase coined by Marvin Harris, seeks to explain human behavior in terms of the interaction between environmental factors and human techniques for dealing with them. Historical determinism suggests an explanation of behavior in terms of past behavior. Cultural determinism is the explanation of behavior in terms of the information contained in the cultural tradition. Political determinism may mean the explanation of behavior in terms of a struggle for power or influence. Psychological determinism may seek to explain group behavior in terms of individual behavior or individual behavior in terms of childhood experience.

It is efficient to seek a deterministic explanation of human behavior, particularly if it works. Although any sort of deterministic explanation may work somewhere under some conditions, the fact that deterministic explanations work sometimes should not be taken to mean that some particular determinism is superior to all others or applies in every case. Deterministic explanations, like the groundpounder's hypothesis or the mechanic's hypothesis, reflect an attempt to simplify a complex situation. Single factors or clusters of factors such as human biology, the weather, or the cultural tradition can be expected to explain restricted aspects of human behavior. More general explanations require an understanding of the complex interaction among the many variables involved in the formation and operation of a cultural system. Human behavior is determined, not by A or B or N, but by the interrelationships of A and B and N within a complex system.

The search for explanations of human behavior is not confined to cultural anthropology. All of the social sciences, including psychology, sociology, political science, and economics, such humanistic disciplines as art, literature, music, and history, and such practical disciplines as medicine, law, and business administration are equally concerned with human behavior. The special features of cultural anthropology have to do with: (1) the study of cultural systems as complex wholes, (2) the explanation of the role of cultural traditions in influencing human behavior, and (3) the cross-cultural comparison of cultural systems. Because the understanding of cultural systems requires an understanding of environment, human biology, human behavior, and cultural traditions, anthropology tends to form a connecting link among the arts, humanities, and sciences concerned with the nature of man. Although it is possible to say "psychology studies the individual," or "sociology studies society," the different disciplines concerned with humanity overlap and duplicate each other at many points. The defining method of anthropology and its basic research question has to do with the explanation of the similarities and differences among cultural systems.

How may cultural systems be defined?

The explanation of the similarities and differences among cultural systems begins with an understanding of the ways in which such systems may be defined and classified. This is made difficult by the fact that cultural systems are constantly forming, dissolving, dividing, merging, reproducing, growing, and shrinking. Often, like an aircrew or a children's playgroup, cultural systems are included within other cultural systems. Often cultural systems share similar cultural traditions or are connected to each other through the exchange or transmission of a variety of personnel, goods, or messages. Because cultural systems always operate within settings, one way of defining them is in terms of their territorial boundaries.

Where Is the Edge?
A village in India is identified as follows:

> The irregular high, rain-furrowed mud walls which faced us might have been mistaken for a deserted fortress. No dooryards, no windows were there to give glimpses of family life. Nothing but blank walls and more walls, so joined that it was often difficult to tell where one man's house ended and his neighbor's began (Wiser and Wiser 1963:1).

A tribe in Africa has formally established geographical limits:

Pondoland is a rugged strip of coastland separated from Natal by the umThamvuna River, from other Cape Native reserves by the umThatha River (Hunter 1936:6).

Eskimo communities:

The permanent camps reach from Cape Seddon in Melville Bay right up to Humboldt's Glacier. . . . This little handful of hunters is distributed over a stretch of 800 kilometers. The Polar Eskimos themselves classify their places of habitation according to the wind in the following districts:

> Nigerdlit: Those who live nearest to the southwest wind.
> Ankunarmiut: Those who live between the winds.
> Orgordlit: Those who live in the lee of the southwest wind.
> Avangnardlit: Those who live in the north wind (Rasmussen 1921:20).

A factory finds its existence in two different places:

Five miles from the main plant, in the neighboring town of Herford, the company has a branch which manufactures some of the same products and employs between 60 and 70 people. This was originally a competitor, but it was absorbed into the New Freedom Products Company early in the present century and now is so closely integrated with the rest of the company that it might almost as well be another department in Teasville (Ellsworth 1952:21).

In the case of Pondoland or the Eskimo districts, territorial boundaries or locations are specified formally. Group members may also define boundaries informally and inexactly or it may be possible to identify such boundaries only by observing the places where the group actually operates. Boundaries in space can be defined in precise and formal terms as concrete as a fence, or in imprecise and informal terms as tenuous as a dirty look. Spatial boundaries may change rapidly. Territory may be used in alternation with other groups, as in a lunchroom patronized by the Rotary Club; or a group, such as an aircrew or a street-corner gang, may occupy a series of territories at different times. It is important to know when a cultural system is operating and how long it is likely to operate. How, then, may the temporal boundaries of cultural systems be expressed?

How Long Is It?

Among the Blackfoot of the North American plains, men of stature and ability maintained their position in society by organizing war parties. In *My Life as an Indian*, J. W. Schultz describes his experience:

The young and middle-aged men of the tribes were constantly setting out for, or returning from war, in parties of from a dozen to fifty or more. That was their recreation, to raid the surrounding tribes who preyed upon their vast hunting ground, drive off their horses, and take scalps if they could. A few miles back from camp the returning warriors would don their picturesque war clothes, paint their faces, decorate their horses with eagle plumes and paint, and then ride quietly to the brow of the hill overlooking the village. There they would begin the war song, whip their horses into a mad run, and, firing guns and driving before them the animals they had taken, charge swiftly down the hill into the bottom. Long before they arrived the camp would be an uproar of excitement, and the women, dropping whatever work they had in hand, would rush to meet them, followed more slowly and sedately by the men. How the women would embrace and hang on to their loved ones safely returned; and presently they could be heard chanting the praises of husband, or son, or brother.

No sooner did one of these parties return than others, incited by their success and anxious to emulate it, would form a party and start out against the Crows, or the Assiniboins, or perhaps the Crees, or some of the tribes on the far side of the Backbone-of-the-world, as the Rockies were called. Therefore I was not surprised one morning to be told that they were about to start on a raid against the Assiniboins. "And you can go with us if you wish to," Talks-with-the-Buffalo concluded. "You helped your friend to steal a girl, and you might as well try your hand at stealing horses" (1956:20).

In some cases, should the leader of such a war party have a bad dream, the war party might dissolve before it got started. Not all military organizations are so short-lived.

This regiment had a long association with India. As the 32nd Foot, it had held the residency at Lucknow through the famous seige of 1857, during the Mutiny. When the walls crumbled, the mess silver, crated, was used to plug the gaps. At dinner we now ate off some of that silver; the rest, the pieces that had been twisted by enemy fire, hung in glass cases on the wall. Among them was a soup tureen with a hole in it where a musket ball had entered— and dents where the ball had ricocheted around and round—and the leaden musket ball itself. A little farther along hung a long row of bronze medals, each with a short piece of crimson ribbon. These were the Victoria Crosses won by men of the 32nd at Lucknow. So, in the glow of the Lucknow silver and the self-effacing sheen of the Lucknow Crosses, we laughed and talked and quarreled and felt ourselves lapped in the warm continuity of tradition— a tradition that reached years farther back than 1857. On parade every man of the regiment wore a single red feather in the front of his pith helmet. The light company of the other battalion of the regiment had taken part in a successful night attack on the Americans at Paoli on September 20, 1777. The Americans had vowed vengeance, and, in order that they should know who had done the deed, the light company stained red the white feathers they used to wear in their hats—and ever since then the Duke of Cornwall's Light Infantry had worn a red feather or a red patch behind the cap badge (Masters 1958:16).

The Plains Indian war party and the British regiment are from some points of view quite similar, yet they differ sharply along the dimension of time. In South India groups of young men of different castes or *jatis* are organized to produce traditional village dramas. A drama company tends to be inactive during the seasons of heavy agricultural work and vigorously operative during the long, sweaty nights of the hot season. A chart of the temporal existence of such a cultural system would rise and fall seasonally over a ten- or twelve-year period before disinterest or conflict would bring about its "death." For other examples of the importance of duration to a definition of cultural systems consider the Democratic Party, Citizens for the Recall of John Smith, the Class of 1966, and the Senior Citizen's Club.

Spatial and temporal boundaries together provide a definition of the setting within which a cultural system operates. An alternative means of defining a cultural system is in terms of its membership.

Who Are the Others That Belong?

In one of the Sherlock Holmes stories Mr. Jabeez Wilson is invited to join the "Red-Headed League." The league was said to have been founded by a wealthy American eccentric named Ezekiah Hopkins who, perhaps because his own hair was red, was partial to redheads. The purpose of the league was to provide soft jobs, "easy berths," for men whose hair was the correct shade of red. The American tendency to define groups on the basis of superficial criteria was rediscovered some time later by the Swedish sociologist Gunnar Myrdal who wrote:

> The "Negro race" is defined in America by the white people. It is defined in terms of parentage. Everybody having a known trace of Negro blood in his veins—no matter how far back it was acquired—is classified as a Negro. No amount of white ancestry, except one hundred per cent, will permit entrance to the white race. As miscegenation has largely been an affair between white men and Negro women, it is a fair approximation to characterize the Negro race in America as the descendants of Negro women and Negro or white men through the generations—minus the persons having "passed" from the Negro into the white group and their offspring (1944:113).

In some groups, membership is based upon age:

> Nyakyusa villages (*ifipanga*) are formed by groups of boys or men, all roughly of the same age, together with the wives and young children of those who are married. Women belong to the villages of their husbands, young children to those of their fathers. Girls live at home until they are betrothed, after which they visit their future husbands periodically, and soon after puberty each joins her husband in his village. Boys, who marry later in life, leave home at about the age of ten or eleven and set up villages of their own (Wilson 1963:19).

A similar practice occurs in California where housing developments

may be advertised as "For young couples on the way up," or as "A place in the sun for senior citizens."

The Bambara of Africa regard life as a progression from an animal-like state through a series of initiations and graduations to a state of union with the divine. A process of learning, doing, and suffering leads the individual through six major societies of initiation, each divided into subsocieties having their own initiations. The first initiation society, the children's society, has six gradations more or less like a primary school:

At a sign from the chief of the society and after payment of twenty cowry shells per candidate, each neophyte lies down with his face on the ground on top of the mound which he constructed previously. Each has, in a hand held on his back, the bone saved from the preceding banquet, and he covers his eyes with the free hand.

A "lion," initiated the previous year, then arrives and circles three times around the initiates, each time scratching their backs with the claw of a monkey. He goes and hides this, then he approaches the infants again and asks them if they can say what it was. They reply negatively and, then, lifting their hands from their eyes, they search without being able to find anything. Their seniors, already initiated, mock and tease them. The infants lie down again and cover their eyes and the "lion" returns with the monkey's claw. He goes again around the infants and, this time, he takes the bone which they have hidden behind their backs. He scratches them, hides the claw and returns asking the same question: "Do you know what that was?" All the infants reply, "No," and vainly set about searching for the bones. Then they return once more to their previous position and the "lion" repeats his performance with the wooden board which he causes to vibrate and then hides in the dust. The same question is put to the neophytes; the same fruitless search follows. Then the "lion" goes himself to get the paw of the monkey, a bone and the board. He shows them to the children explaining the functioning of the instrument-emblem. Finally, they take an oath, holding the board and repeating the following formula: "When thous hast heard the roaring of the lion of the Society of the Uncircumcised, know that it consists of cutting a piece of wood, making a hole in it, putting a string through it and swinging it around. It is that, the voice of the lion. Those who reveal this will have the heart and liver torn out, their loins removed, they will be dead even for the other world" (Zahan 1960:118).

After man's search for truth has been acted out, as above, and the initiates admitted to the secret of the voice of the lion, they become "lions" and are entitled to all the privileges of lions, consisting primarily of running errands for higher ranking initiates. Membership among the Bambara is a complicated process having to do with sequential admission to subcultural systems within a larger, ladderlike arrangement of cultural systems, all within the total cultural system of the Bambara. For the Bambara, all members are engaged in self-perfection and self-realization through an endless struggle onwards and upwards—a struggle which usually ends only with admission to the other world and a final separation from society.

In North America, life also involves a ladderlike progression of initiations:

The first experience of shock and insecurity seems to come to the child when he must "break away" from the home, if only for a half-day, to attend kindergarten. "I hated school that year," wrote one girl in her autobiography, "I would cry and make up excuses and not want to go." A boy remarked, "At first I was scared stiff. During that day almost everyone cried because it was the first time away from home." Similarly, a girl said, "I sure was scared. My mother took me the first day. When I saw all the different faces I started running home, but I didn't make it. She took me back." Another boy wrote, "I hated school and for the first few weeks I cried when my mother left me at the school" (Fichter 1964:33).

Membership in a human group is a matter as arbitrary as the meaning of a word. Although group membership may be informal to the point where

group members are unable to describe clearly what the criteria of membership are, it is often much more formally defined. An individual may be regarded as a member of a group because he has red hair or particular ancestors, or has endured an initiation ceremony, acquired wealth, or achieved a state of spiritual or educational development. Membership may also involve particular capacities or achievements ranging from being born in a particular place to being able to run a mile in approximately four minutes.

Membership, whether it is conferred formally or deduced by a sociologist from the examination of behavior, constitutes what is called a *status*. A *status is a position or location that an individual occupies in relationship to other persons*. An individual can have the status of member of a number of different cultural systems. Although a cultural system requires members in order to operate, the possession of any particular set of warm bodies is not essential. What is essential is that they be willing to play the *roles* required for the operation of the system. *A role is the set of duties or performances that are appropriate to a particular status* (see Chapter 6). When there is a meeting or gathering and the cultural system cannot operate because most of the members are absent, the situation is one in which there are an adequate number of persons having the status of member, but not enough persons prepared to play the role of member. When people play the role of member, they interact and communicate, exhibiting appropriate behavior toward the other members of the cultural system. An additional way of defining a cultural system, then, is in terms of the interactions and interrelationships among a set of members.

What Are the Names of Your Friends?

In South Indian villages there are small shops that sell cigarettes, sugar, salt, and other inexpensive and often used items. When a village is divided into hostile parties or factions, members of the different groups often patronize different shops. Even if there are no strong antipathies or feelings of separateness, groups may form around particular shops for the purpose of gossiping and drinking tea or coffee. The anthropologist who wants to know something about subgroups within the village can establish group boundaries by observing people entering and leaving particular shops or by asking people which shop they patronize. Among the Nyakusa of Africa:

> Between the ages of about six and eleven boys sleep at their father's houses and herd their fathers' cattle. This is a full-time, if not a very arduous, occupation. The cattle are driven out about an hour or two after sunrise and return to be milked about 1 P.M.; after an hour they are again driven out and do not come back until sunset. The cattle of a group of neighbours, usually five to ten, are herded together by their young sons; and so these boys spend all day together for several years of their lives. This group of boys is the germ of the future age-village; it is a community with a common activity in the herding of the cattle, with a leader and laws and customs of its own (Wilson 1963:19).

In *Street Corner Society*, Whyte discussed groups that formed primarily as a result of members' locations on the same street corner (see Figure 1):

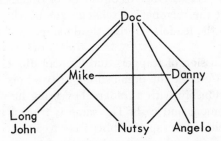

FIGURE 1   *Relationships among the leading Nortons* (after Whyte 1955:13).

Close friendship ties already existed between certain of the men, but the Nortons, as an organization did not begin to function until the early spring of 1937. It was at that time that Doc returned to the corner. Nutsy, Frank, Joe, Alec, Carl, and Tommy had a great respect for Doc and gathered around him. Angelo, Fred, and Lou followed Doc in making the corner their headquarters. Danny and Mike were drawn to Norton Street by their friendship for Doc and by the location of their crap game, right next to "the corner." Long John followed Danny and Mike.

The men became accustomed to acting together. They were also tied to one another by mutual obligations. In their experiences together there were innumerable occasions when one man would feel called upon to help another, and the man who was aided would want to return the favor. Strong group loyalties were supported by these reciprocal activities.

There were distinctions in rank among the Nortons. Doc, Danny, and Mike held the top positions. They were older than any others except Nutsy. They possessed a greater capacity for social movement. While the followers were restricted to the narrow sphere of one corner, Doc, Danny, and Mike had friends in many other groups and were well known and respected throughout a large part of Cornerville (1955:11–12).

Whyte's picture of the social relationships among the Nortons was derived from observation and participation in the affairs of the group. A similar picture can often be derived through an interview technique in which members of a set of individuals thought to form a group are asked to list their two best friends. "Leaders" might then be thought to be the persons named most frequently, and "followers" might be thought to be the persons named least frequently. It is a useful exercise to attempt to expose and diagram the relationships among the members of a small group.

The relationships among the members of a cultural system can be classified in a variety of different ways. Neighbors who meet over coffee may exchange gossip; stamp or bottle collectors may exchange goods. Questions can be asked about the kinds of things that are exchanged among the members of a group. Groups of friends, particularly if they view themselves as equals, may offer each other the same things that they receive. Such an exchange is *reciprocal* with tokens of esteem or friendship being passed back and forth among the members. Exchange among the Nortons tends to be *hierarchical* with the leaders offering "leadership," and the followers offering "followership."

In their discussion of trappers and tappers, Robert Murphy and Julian Steward (1956) describe the organization of two very similar groups. Trappers have a relationship with a trader; they bring him furs and he provides them with equipment and cash. The same is true of rubber tappers in the Amazon, they deliver the sap of rubber trees to an agent, and the agent provides them with cash and supplies. In both of these cases, the members of the cultural system are isolated from each other and linked together only by their common relationship with the trader or agent. Such patron-client systems exist, between doctor and patient, addict and supplier, or prostitute and customer. Here, what the patron offers the client is quite different from what the client offers the patron.

Because interaction takes many forms, usually involving a combination of reciprocal and nonreciprocal relationships, the drawing of group boundaries on the basis of interaction is difficult. In South India, many kinds of interaction, marriage, for example, may take place within groupings called castes or *jatis* and between villages. Is the cultural system the village or the set of people who intermarry or should we speak of two intersecting systems which together form a regional cultural system?

In one sense, the set of persons who interact is the entire human species. Depending upon the criteria used to describe interaction—frequency, type of interaction, or quality of interaction, the subdivision of the human species into cultural systems could take a variety of forms. The test of a definition of a cutural system has to do with the predictive value of the definition. There is little point in defining a set of Nortons or a set of Nyakyusa unless the definition contributes to our ability to predict some part of their behavior. A set of people occupying a territory must interact sufficiently to form and maintain a cultural tradition which, in turn, serves to guide their behavior as well as that of future members. Evidence for the existence of a cultural tradition and, therefore, of a cultural system is to be found in the existence of characteristic group behaviors or customs.

What Things Do You Do Together?

The quotation below is a translation of a statement made by a Navajo of the American Southwest. Presumably it reveals some aspects of characteristic Navajo behavior:

> One day, as we were herding at the edge of the woods, a man came riding out in the flat on the trail going to the northeast and southwest. When he'd almost passed by he looked up and saw us, so he turned his horse and started riding towards us. My father said, "Who's that fellow? Do you know him?" I said, "No, I don't know him." He rode up, and it was a fellow named No Neck. They called him No Neck because he had a big, round, short neck. He was an Along the Stream. His father's name was Little Wife Beater; he was a Reed People. My father recognized him and got up and shook hands with him, saying, "Where are you from? I haven't seen you for a long time, my cousin. I'm very glad to see you again." He said, "I'm from below Oraibi." "Where are you heading for?" my father asked him. "I'm going to my older brother's place. They say he lives around here somewhere, and I'd like to visit my relatives who live here. That's where I'm going." My father said, "When did you start?" "Yesterday morning I started from my place." Then my father said to him, "Tell me how the places are towards your home. Tell me how the weather is and what the land is like, the grazing, the water, the feed for the stock. Get down off your horse and tell me all about those things." As he got off his horse he said, "I've got nothing to tell." But when he sat down beside my father he said, "There's nothing from here on all the way down to Popping Rock Point. A little beyond there is good feed; that's where the feed begins. From there on this way there's nothing, but from there on over towards Cedar Standing, down in that flat, there's plenty of grazing and water" (Dyk 1967:133).

One of the cultural characteristics that might be suggested by the above is a characteristic Navajo method of presenting information. The statements below are responses made by Navajo and Hopi children who were shown a set of ambiguous pictures (Thematic Apperception Test) and asked to make up a story about each one. Does the quotation above suggest any Navajo characteristics which would help to identify the Navajo responses below?

1. He is mad. His mother must have scolded him because he refused to do it. He is going to do it.

2. I don't know what this boy is saying, maybe he is crying. When they get a scolding, they cry.

1. It is an Indian man. He was working in his field. He is tired. He will go back home.
2. He has a stick wth him. I don't know what he is doing.

1. He is crying. His parents spanked him because he did not want to do what he was told. He will do it now.
2. This boy is laying on a bundle and going to sleep (Henry 1947:7).

In each case the first reply was that of a Hopi boy and the second that of a Navajo boy. One rule which would have predicted which responses were Navajo is that the Navajo never speculate about motives or about past and future; like ideal scientists, they report exactly what they see and hear without interpretation or editorial comment. In these examples, the Hopi, who are close neighbors of the Navajo, always tell what they think might have happened in the past and what they expect will happen in the future. They always explain why people are doing what they are doing. This example demonstrates one way of identifying characteristic behavior; more data would be needed to reach any firm conclusions.

Widely separated groups of people constituting separate tribes or nations exhibit great differences in characteristic behavior. Language, tools, dress, marriage rules, statements of religious beliefs, and a thousand other behaviors can be used to express such differences. Where attention is focused upon different villages within a region or upon schools or teams within a larger cultural system, a great many characteristic behaviors are likely to be shared. To an outsider, one airplane crew is pretty much like any other. Nevertheless, within a short period following the formation of the the crew, special crew caps and other characteristic ways of dressing appear. The language of crew members is filled with special code words expressing crew unity or referring to unique incidents of which only this crew is aware. All aircraft crews possess the same statuses: aircraft commander, copilot, bombardier, navigator, and so on, but different individuals play their roles in different ways. Members of some crews may exchange their statuses frequently; members of other crews may "go by the book." Differences among closely related subtribes, villages, teams, schools, and airplane crews often turn out to be surprisingly large. Such groups may be described as possessing the "same" language or the "same" cutlure, but there are always differences.

But What Is the Essence of a Cultural System?

The boundaries of a cultural system may be expressed in terms of territory, duration, membership, interaction, characteristic behavior, or by several criteria together, depending upon convenience or the kinds of research questions being asked. The comparison of cultural systems depends in part upon our ability to establish types of cultural systems, such as nations, tribes, or work groups, which are defined in the same way. Because it is easy to set up classes of human beings, like men and women or carpenters, who do not form cultural systems, we cannot be sure that we have a cultural system unless we are aware of some minimal property which a set of individuals must possess before they can form a cultural system. One way of interpreting this minimum property or essence of cultural systems can be derived from the following quotations:

> There is no wonder in the fact that Chan Kom decided to become a pueblo. Sooner or later nearly every settlement containing a score or more of houses in this part of Yucatan became a pueblo, or tried to, under leadership provided from the city and under the stimulus of ambition and the desire for material advantage. What is notable is the unusual zeal with which the Chan Kom people, above all others in the neighborhood, worked to attain their objective and the outstanding success they achieved. Once they had made the decision, they set their feet firmly on the path to progress, and no exertion was too great, no discipline too firm, for the enterprise. Beginning as a cluster of thatched huts deep in the brush, no different from several others similarly situated, in the course of thirty years the village became the recognized and authoritative community of an area fifty miles across (Redfield 1962: 22–23).

> The mutineers now bade adieu to all the world, save the few individuals associated with them in exile. But where that exile should be passed, was yet undecided; the Marquesas Islands were first mentioned, but Christian, on reading Captain Carteret's account of Pitcairn Island, thought it better adapted to the purpose, and accordingly shaped a course thither. They

reached it not many days afterwards, and Christian, with one of the seamen, landed in a little nook, which we afterwards found very convenient for disembarkation. They soon traversed the island sufficiently to be satisfied that it was exactly suited to their wishes. It possessed water, wood, a good soil, and some fruits. The anchorage in the offing was very bad and landing for boats extremely hazardous. The mountains were so difficult of access, and the passes so narrow, that they might be maintained by a few persons against an army; and there were several caves to which, in case of necessity, they could retreat, and where, as long as their provisions lasted, they might bid defiance to their pursuers. With this intelligence they returned on board, and brought the ship to an anchor in a small bay on the northern side of the island, which I have in consequence named "Bounty Bay," where everything that could be of utility was landed, and where it was agreed to destroy the ship, either by running her on shore, or burning her. Christian, Adams, and the majority, were for the former expedient; but while they went to the forepart of the ship, to execute this businesss, Matthew Quintal set fire to the carpenter's store-room. The vessel burnt to the water's edge, and then drifted upon the rocks (Shapiro 1962:53).

In both of these cases, the members of a cultural system decided to change their cultural systems. The capacity of a set of people to make independent decisions gives rise to the development of a cultural tradition and those characteristic behaviors that lead to the formation of a cultural system. The minimum requirement for the existence of a cultural system is the capacity of a set of people to make independent decisions. Once that capacity is present, a village can decide to become a pueblo, and a ship's crew can decide to become a community.

Because the use of language and agreed upon symbols is basic to the formation of a cultural system, such systems cannot exist unless there is a set of people who are able to make independent decisions concerning membership, meanings attached to words and actions, and the activities of the membership. A cultural system must possess the capacity to build culture and that capacity can only exist in the presence of the ability, not necessarily conscious or deliberate, to make decisions as a group. *A cultural system comes into being when a set of human beings engage in decision-making activity.*

Process: what are you doing?

When people decide or in some way agree to form a cultural system, that is, when they decide to attach particular meanings to particular actions and to engage in particular behaviors, we must suppose that they do so with the stated or unstated purpose of obtaining particular outcomes such as getting food, finding new members, communicating, or protecting themselves. What they have in mind may not be consciously formulated, but, it is in some sense a plan. Observation of the happenings within a cultural system is observation of people executing plans designed to lead up to particular outcomes. Consider the following:

> Among the Cheyenne Indians of North America the body of a man is dressed in its finest clothing. It is wrapped in robes and transported outside the camp to be deposited in the crotch of a tree, on a scaffold, or on the ground under a pile of rocks. Favorite horses of the deceased are shot and left at the grave along with weapons or utensils which were used in life. Female relatives cut off their hair and gash their foreheads until the blood flows (Hoebel 1960:87).

> In Mexico, in the village of Tepoztlán, a person who is about to die is placed on a mat on the floor. After death, the corpse is dressed in clean clothing and there is a day of mourning. The corpse is then placed in a coffin and carried to a cemetery where it is buried. Nine days after the death, an offering of food is placed on the altar in the deceased's home in order to provide him with food during each of the months of the year. Wakes, in memory of the dead, are held on the night of the death, nine days later, and one year later. Mourning tends to be "restrained" (Adapted from Lewis 1960: 84–85).

On Palau, an island in the Pacific, Doab's funeral took place as follows:

> The corpse had been taken to the house of the head man of Doab's clan. It lay on a mat on the floor near one wall, dressed in its "best"—shirt, trousers, socks and shoes never worn in life and donated for the occasion by a relative. It had been washed with a heavily scented soap, in place of the old preparation of aromatic leaves, and its lips smeared with lipstick, a modern substitute for betel juice. A faded army cap lay on the pillow at one side of the head; on the other was a handbag containing the cherished possessions that were to accompany the corpse to the grave.
>
> As the mourning women arrived to take their places around the corpse, the younger ones handed Doab's clan "mother" a few yards of dress goods; the older ones gave her finely made mats. These goods were to be used to reward the rest of the women for the food they brought and for their preparation of it. The mourners arrived one by one over the period of an hour. Some of them wept and brought tears to the eyes of the rest as they approached the body. Between their arrivals there were muted conversations among those already present and among the detached cluster of men. Betel nut was sent for and distributed by the head of the house to all persons in the room. A coffin maker was at work in the yard in the midst of a crowd of squatting men who gave advice. At one point he passed a tape measure in the window, asking one of the women to measure the corpse. Later he returned to ask for some of the dress goods with which to line the coffin (Barnett 1960:63).

Doab's funeral represents an *ethnographic case*, a single observation of a group activity. The Cheyenne and Tepoztecan funerals represent *ethnographic hypotheses*. They are predictions about what would be considered by the members of the cultural systems involved to be appropriate or typical funerals. The funeral represents the carrying out of a plan or program for dealing with persons who have died. Carrying out such a funeral is one of the processes or activities characteristic of each of these cultural systems. When a cultural system is regarded as something that functions or operates, then the parts of the cultural system can be regarded as the series of *processes* that take place within it.

Processes, such as producing a crop, carrying out a funeral, getting up in the morning, or decorating the Christmas tree, share certain features in common. Like cultural systems they all involve settings, personnel, and traditional ways of doing things. Unlike cultural systems they all involve definite beginnings and endings and they may be repeated with different sets of personnel. A funeral process starts with the death or imminent death of an individual and continues until it comes to a specified end point such as disposal of the corpse, the sending away of the spirit of the deceased, or the last memorial feast. *A process is a series of interlinked events commencing under culturally defined conditions, following a culturally defined plan or pattern, and reaching a culturally defined endpoint.* "Culturally defined" means that the members agree as to the meaning, form, and content of the process.

Because all cultural systems, by definition, must contain sets of human beings engaged in decision-making processes, it is possible to list a series of processes essential to the survival of cultural systems and therefore present in all of them. First, any cultural system must have a means of *regulating membership*; that is, it must have a way of securing new members or getting rid of old members that will permit it to stabilize at an appropriate size. Second, any cultural system must have a way of *changing the status* of members so that appropriate duties and responsibilities may be assigned. Third, any cultural system must have a means for the *transmission of culture* because it is pointless to acquire members and assign them to statuses if they don't know how to play their roles properly. Fourth, because culture is not always transmitted accurately and because human beings often encounter problems not dealt with by the cultural tradition, any cultural system must contain *processes of social control*, means of influencing and controlling the behavior of its membership. Fifth, because cultural systems must adapt to changes in the setting within which they operate, any cultural system must contain mechanisms for *cultural change* involving the revising and updating of its cultural tradition. These five fundamental processes are discussed separately in Chapters 7 through 11.

Other kinds of processes are widespread among cultural systems because they are relevant to human biological requirements or to general features of all human environments. Although a bridge club or a class in mechanical engineering need not provide opportunities for eating, such subcultures or partcultures must be connected to cultural systems that provide their memberships with such opportunities. Every human being must be connected to a cultural system that provides for the various stages in the human life cycle and that copes with universal needs for food, sleep, sociability, and protection from the elements. Some writers reserve the term *society* for those cultural systems or collections of related cultural systems that provide for universal human needs from the cradle to the grave.

The fundamental processes required for the existence of cultural systems and the universal processes arising out of basic human characteristics are to be found every place that human beings are found. One approach to the explanation of the similarities and differences between cultural systems lies in the comparison of the manner in which the *same* process is defined and executed in different societies or cultural systems. In considering the funeral process, the facts that all people die, that corpses are often smelly and unsanitary, and that people are affected by the loss of a fellow member of their group lead us to believe that funerals or something like funerals are likely to be found everywhere. We can define the funeral process as the set of events centering about and triggered by the death or impending death of an individual. Because there are limited ways of disposing of a corpse or of its property and because we suspect that human reactions to death are likely to be limited by human psychology and biology, we expect that a *principle of the limitation of possibilities* will operate to produce similarities among funeral processes wherever they are found. Malinowski suggests that the following uniformities might be found to characterize the funeral process:

The mortuary proceedings show a striking similarity throughout the world.

As death approaches, the nearest relatives in any case, sometimes the whole community, foregather by the dying man, and dying, the most private act which a man can perform, is transformed into a public, tribal event. As a rule, a certain differentiation takes place at once, some of the relatives watching near the corpse, others making preparations for the pending end and its consequence, others again performing perhaps some religious acts at a sacred spot. Thus in certain parts of Melanesia the real kinsmen must keep at a distance and only relatives by marriage perform the mortuary service, while in some tribes of Australia the reverse order is observed.

As soon as death has occurred, the body is washed, anointed and adorned, sometimes the bodily apertures are filled, the arms and legs tied together. Then it is exposed to the view of all, and the most important phase, the immediate mourning begins. There is always a more or less conventionalized and dramatized outburst of grief and wailing in sorrow, which often passes . . . into bodily lacerations and the tearing of hair (Malinowski 1955:48–49).

Malinowski's theroy of mortuary proceedings is a *descriptive* theory. It lists the sorts of things that might or ought to be found in funeral processes, but does not attempt to explain why such things are present or why some things should be present in one cultural system and absent in another. For example, it might be suggested that bodily laceration and the tearing of hair tend to occur where individuals are trained to feel responsible for the death of others or to fear that they will be accused of such responsibility. In terms of such an explanation, demonstration of extreme grief could be considered a means of demonstrating innocence. Some other possible explanations would be that such demonstrations are the result of strong psychological attachment or frequent situations in which the cause of death is difficult to determine.

A method for developing such explanations was suggested by Franz Boas in 1896:

We have another method, which in many respects is much safer. A detailed study of customs in their relation to the total culture of the tribe practicing them, in connection with an investigation of their geographical distribution among neighboring tribes, affords us almost always a means of determining with considerable accuracy the historical causes that lead to the formation of the customs in question and to the psychological processes that were at work in their development. The results of inquiries conducted by this method may be three-fold. They may reveal the environmental conditions which have created or modified cultural elements; they may clear up psychological factors which are at work in shaping the culture; or they may bring before our eyes the effects that historical connections have had upon the growth of culture (Boas 1948:276).

In other words, the study of variation within a single process in a particular region provides a kind of experimental control that permits an explanation of the process in terms of the relative importance of universal psychological characteristics, environmental factors, and shared cultural traditions. If the members of Tribe A engage in bodily laceration while the members of Tribe B do not, the explanation for bodily laceration is to be sought in other differences in the environment or the cultural traditions of the two tribes. If the same sorts of factors account for the presence and absence of bodily laceration in other regions, it is evidence of a universal pattern that might be attributed to biological uniformities of the human species, to universal characteristics of cultural systems, or to an invention made so long ago as to be the property of all cultural systems.

A process acquires its particular form as a result of the interaction of universal human properties, particular environments or ecological niches, and particular cultural traditions. The general research strategy used in searching for explanations of the similarities and differences among cultural systems is to identify the role of each of these factors or clusters of factors in affecting the form of particular cultural systems and processes. Although the work of the cultural anthropologist begins with the study of some particular cultural system, the relative importance of different factors in influencing the development of the cultural system or the processes carried out within it can only be established by methods of cross-cultural comparison which study similar cultural systems in different environments, or the worldwide or regionwide distribution of particular characteristics and processes. In the following chapter, the relationships of cultural systems to their settings or environments are considered.

Summary

Human beings carry out their activities within an environment or setting formed by the interaction of people, other natural things, and cultural messages. For some purposes, the setting can be divided into natural, artificial, and social environments; for other purposes the setting can be regarded as a series of external conditions exerting particular influences upon the group. Important new influences arising in the environment are called stresses. Human beings interacting symbolically within a setting in terms of a cultural tradition form cultural systems.

Outcomes of the operation of cultural systems can often be explained in terms of relatively simple determinants as implied by such terms as biological determinism, economic determinism, historical determinism, cultural determinism, or psychological determinism. All such determinisms represent simplifications of the complex variables that interact to determine the outcomes or results of the operation of cultural systems. Consequently, general explanations of human behavior and cultural systems require an understanding of the manner in which different variables affect them. Cultural anthropology is most closely related to sociology and psychology, but it is also connected to all the disciplines that deal with man ranging from history to medicine. Among the disciplines concerned with the study of man, cultural anthropology has the special responsibilities of explaining the influences of cultural traditions and the operation of cultural systems viewed as organized wholes. The basic research question in cultural anthropology centers about the explanation of the similarities and differences among cultural systems.

The complex nature of cultural systems makes it possible to define and classify them in a variety of ways. The basic criteria for the definition of cultural systems include territory, duration, membership, interaction, and characteristic behaviors. However defined and classified, cultural systems cannot exist unless decision-making processes are carried out within them. The operation of cultural systems involves the carrying out of culturally defined processes ranging from getting up in the morning to disposing of a corpse. The fundamental processes required for the operation of a cultural system include regulating membership, changing status, cultural transmission, control of behavior, and cultural change. Widespread or universal kinds of processes take place within the limitations imposed by the nature of cultural systems and human beings. This limitation of possibilities makes possible the comparison of similar processes taking place within different cultural systems.

Isolation of the variables that account for the content of a particular process or explain the similarities and differences between cultural systems or similar processes in different cultural systems may be accomplished by the study of variation among a set of neighboring cultural systems, the selection of cultural systems that have something in common, such as similar environments or similar group organizations, or the study of the worldwide or regionwide distribution of similar processes. Particular beliefs or other characteristics of cultural systems may be examined in the same way.

Further readings

Almost all basic and theoretical works in the social sciences involve themselves in the definition of such basic terms as personality, cultural tradition, process, cultural system, environment, and structure. Introductory texts dealing with these problems and others include those of Beals and Hoijer (1971), Hoebel (1972), Keesing (1971), CRM Books (1971), and Harris (1971). The authoritative compilation of definitions of culture is Kroeber and Kluckhohn (1963). A readable appraisal of the effects of culture on human beings is Bates' *Gluttons and Libertines* (1958). The ethnographic literature cited at the end of the previous chapter contains a variety of perspectives on the nature of culture. Readable accounts of anthropologists and their theoretical contributions are *From Ape to Angel* (Hays 1964) and *They Studied Man* (Kardiner and Preble 1961).

Various problems concerning the definition of cultural systems are dealt with in the Case Studies, especially Downs' *The Navajo* (1972), the Spindlers' *Dreamers without Power* (1971), Keiser's *The Vice Lords: Warriors of the Streets* (1969), Boissevain's *Hal-Farrug* (1969), Quintana and Floyd's *Que Gitano!* (1972), and Uchendu's *The Igbo* (1966).

Problems and questions

1. Interview someone concerning the various kinds of groups and organizations to which he belongs or has belonged. What would be some ways of classifying these different cultural systems?
2. Using the "Case Studies in Cultural Anthropology" or other ethnographic sources, compare similar processes (such as producing food, training children, or holding a funeral) among several different peoples. Suggest some explanations of the observed similarities and differences in terms of environment, a common humanity, or historical experience.
3. Observe a small group or organization. How may the boundaries of the observed cultural system be defined?
4. Observe a small group of people doing something together. Take notes on some particular type of activity, such as giving orders or asking questions, and prepare a diagram showing the frequency and type of interactions among the members. (See page 69.)
5. Through interviews and observations concerning dining rituals, recreational patterns, or other traits, try to establish some of the content of a family cultural tradition.

4

Environment and ecology

Cultural systems take form as groups of human beings begin to act in terms of the earnest policies contained in their cultural traditions. Both the earnest policies and the actions that derive from them depend for their perpetuation and/or further development upon the nature of the developing relationships between the cultural system and the setting within which it operates. Selection is the final editor of the biological message and cultural message as well. It is to be expected, then, that the nature of cultural systems will have something to do with the nature of their environments. This chapter deals with the problems of describing the environments within which cultural systems operate and the nature of the relationships that obtain between the cultural system and its environment.

Where are they now?

From the Himalayas to the Arabian Sea, the valley of the Indus River is over one thousand miles long. Four or five thousand years ago, a civilization spread across the valley. Mohenjo Daro, one of the great cities of that civilization, was three miles in circumference and contained granaries, bathing pools, citadels, broad streets, a drainage system, great houses, and artistic works in clay and metal. Today, the city and civilization are in ruins, their once fertile lands covered with useless brush and scrub. Overgrazing, the silting up of irrigation works, accumulation of salt in the soil, destruction of forests to make bricks and smelt metals, flooding, an upthrust of coastal lands, overpopulation, internal dissension, and invasion by barbarians—some or all of these things led to the fall of the city and the destruction of the Indus civilization.

In every part of the world abandoned campsites, wrecked villages, or ruined cities bear testimony to the inability of the human species to come to terms with the environment. In the process of their dying, ancient cultural systems have contributed to new cultural systems so that over the years the sum of knowledge and experience accumulated in the cultural traditions of humanity has increased. The Indus civilization contributed to the rise of a new civilization in the Ganges Valley which through a process of constant change and adaptation has persisted to the present day.

The example of the Indus civilization is proof that human cultural systems are not excluded from the necessities of adaptation and survival. It is a proof that an adaptive capacity, such as the culture-building capacity, is useful only when it is used in an adaptive way. The building of cultures can take place only within limits and restrictions imposed by the environment. The research questions underlying this chapter and serving to define the subdiscipline of environmental or ecological anthropology have to do with the relationships between cultural systems and their environments. As indicated in Chapter 3, the environment consists of those natural, artificial, and social forces within which a given cultural system operates. The relationships between an environment and a cultural system constitute the *ecology* of that system. Ecological anthropology is concerned with the description of environments, the description of relationships between cultural system and environment (the ecological system), the explanation of the impacts of environments and cultural systems upon each other, and assessments of the adaptive value of particular cultural systems or processes. A first step in answering such questions is the discovery of suitable ways to describe human environments.

What is out there?

In the heart of the country they inhabited when first encountered by White men, the Menomini Indians . . . reside today on nearly 400 square miles of heavily timbered reservation on the Wolf River in northeast central Wisconsin. The natural environment—consisting of many waterfalls, streams filled with trout, and pine forest inhabited by bear, lynx, and wolves—remains the same.

The largest portion of the reservation is thickly forested and provides a sharp, oasis-like contrast to the flat, cleared farmlands of the White farmers to the north. This abrupt change in the terrain experienced as one enters the reserve from the north has an interesting psychological effect upon the tourist. Cars slow down as they approach the veritable wall of trees, and all of the superstitions and beliefs regarding the "scalp hunting Indians of the forest" are brought to the fore. Members of the Mitawin Dream Dance group living in this area relate with great amusement the fear-ridden condition of tourists who have been forced to come to their houses at night for various kinds of assistance (L. Spindler 1962:21).[1]

A few Menomini have experienced other things:

That's how my aunt died. They said after she died they watched her grave and found a bird and a couple of dogs they couldn't kill. My dad caught a dog one time. If any relatives were sick he watched with a gun, but the best way to catch one is to hide. My dad saw the light in the dog's eyes and just kept still. They put you to sleep if they catch you. Dad hollered at him and it was some old woman from Keshena. He hollered first before it saw him and it changed into a woman. When he surprised her she didn't have anything on but a necklace of tongues and hearts of people she had killed. She said not to do anything to her and she would quit witching (adapted from L. Spindler 1962:71).

Having defined a cultural system and specified the boundaries of the environment within which it operates, the ethnographer prepares a description of the environment. Such a description may involve elaborate maps and photographs or careful measurement of rainfall, wind velocity, temperature, and other variables, but its particular goal is to identify and classify those things that have or are likely to have an influence upon the cultural system and its members.

The description of the Menomini environment leads to a major problem: Is the environment to be regarded as consisting of those things that can be recognized by the anthropologist or is it to be regarded as consisting of those things that are recognized by the members of a cultural system? Assuming that Louise Spindler in her role of scientific observer might never encounter an old woman from Keshena attired in the tongues and hearts of her victims, there is a discrepancy between the real world of the scientific observer and the real world of the Menomini. By the same token, a scientific observer is likely to note many things in the environment that influence the Menomini but which the Menomini fail to recognize.

It is convenient to define the environment perceived by an outside observer as representing *scientific reality* and the environment perceived by the members of a cultural system as representing *cultural reality*. A more

---

[1] The Menomini Reservation became a county in the state of Wisconsin upon termination of federal support in June 1961, and the wolves have departed.

accurate, if less convenient, assumption would be that the observer perceives reality in terms of *his* culture, while the Menomini perceive reality in terms of a different culture. Whether we distinguish between scientific reality and cultural reality or see both as two kinds of cultural reality, there is a difference between them, and it is instructive to consider its implications. The remainder of this chapter deals with environment and ecology perceived in terms of scientific or observer reality, while the following chapter deals with environment perceived in terms of cultural reality. Whether people survive or not depends upon the extent to which they are adapted to the environment as it is, but what people do depends upon what they think the environment is like. Because survival depends upon adaptation to external conditions, it is fruitful to look upon cultural systems as devices for solving adaptive problems. Because any cultural system is by definition adapted, at least in the short run, there must be some sense in which it "fits" its environment. Consider the Tiwi from this perspective.

Do culture and environment dovetail?

The Tiwi live on Melville and Bathurst Islands off the coast of Northern Australia in an environment containing a relative abundance of edible wild plants and a fair amount of game. Extremes of temperature and climate appear not to have presented problems, nor is there much disease or ill health. Tiwi women and children spend most days gathering vegetable foods in the region surrounding their campsites. Young men often spend their time hunting, but are probably none too successful. Tools used by men consist of spears and throwing sticks, while the women use baskets and various digging implements. Women spend many years learning when and where to find food. Men become skilled hunters after years of effort. That survival requires the maintenance of extensive and complicated skills was demonstrated by the famine which took place between 1942 and 1946 when warfare cut off the supply of imported foodstuffs upon which the Tiwi had become dependent. They had lost their traditional skills and could no longer survive without outside help.

In the Tiwi household, the old men collect as many wives as possible, and the younger men—unable to marry—are treated as hangers-on, marginal members of the family. The wives, under the leadership of a skilled older woman, handle the collection of vegetable foods. Young men hunt for animal food and, because they are marginal, are free to move to other households when the supply of wild animals shifts. The old men, freed from the labor of the food quest by their multiple wives, are able to devote themselves to artistic, ceremonial, and political affairs.

The Tiwi cultural system appears to dovetail at every point with the requirements of the environment. Tiwi young men are freed for hunting; Tiwi women are organized into efficient work groups; and Tiwi old men

are given freedom to manage political relationships among the different groups of Tiwi. The Tiwi seem to exist in almost perfect equilibrium with their environment. They appear to eat well and to have peaceful relationships with other Tiwi (Hart and Pilling 1960). Granted the limitations of Tiwi knowledge and technology, the Tiwi cultural system appears almost to have been dictated by its external conditions. Can we, then, explain the similarities and differences among the external conditions that affect them? Does the goodness of fit between cultural system and environment justify an environmental determinism of the kind discussed earlier?

Must We Conform to the Environment?

In South India there are two major kinds of agriculture. Where water is abundant, irrigated rice is grown; where water is scarce, various millets and legumes sown together form the major crop. The environment offers a vast range of possibilities—hunting, collecting vegetable products, spice raising, coconut growing, wheat farming, sweet potato raising, tea planting, and so on. Although there are a few communities devoted almost exclusively to each of these types of subsistence activities, most communities specialize in the raising of rice or millet or a combination of both. Are all of these adaptations equally suitable and can the existing diversity be accounted for by the external conditions affecting each community? Consider some of the characteristics of rice and millet farming as practiced in South India.

To grow irrigated rice using the usual South Indian methods it is necessary to redesign the environment, leveling the ground and forming a kind of artificial swamp. Once the swamp is formed, constant attention is required to keep the water where it belongs and prevent it from washing away the crop. There are many weeds where there is much water, and where the yield is great the application of fertilizer must be great. In some places there are two or three crops per year, and the life of the rice farmer is one of steady labor. Because the crop requires extra attention during certain periods, a supply of temporary agricultural laborers is required. Rice land, when it has to be leveled and irrigated, is expensive. Men who are rich enough to buy such land are usually too rich to have to work for a living. Rice farming, then, tends to involve classes of investors or capitalists, farmers and laborers. Millet farming requires little preparation of the land. There is usually only one crop per year. The farmer owns his own land and hires relatively little labor. Millet farming communities support relatively few investors or laborers.

In both of these cases, the choice of an agricultural technique has sweeping implications. Rice agriculture, of the kind described above, does not encourage social equality:

. . . their masters may beat them at pleasure, the poor wretches having no right either to complain or to obtain redress for that or any other ill-treatment their masters may impose on them. In fact, these Pariahs are the born slaves of India, and had I to choose between the two sad fates of being a slave in one of our colonies or a Pariah here, I should unhesitatingly prefer the former.

This class is the most numerous of all, and in conjunction with that of the *Chucklers,* or cobblers, represents at least a quarter of the population. It is painful to think that its members, though so degraded, are yet the most useful of all. On them the whole agricultural work of the country devolves, and they have also other tasks to perform which are still harder and more indispensable. . . .

They live in hopeless poverty, and the greater number lack sufficient means to procure even the coarsest clothing. They go about almost naked, or at best clothed in the most hideous rags.

They live from hand to mouth the whole year round, and rarely know one day how they will procure food for the next. When they happen to have any money, they invariably spend it at once, and make a point of doing no work as long as they have anything left to live on (Dubois 1947:49–50).

South Indian rice agriculture requires a large class of laborers who work but do not own or control the land on which they work. Millet agriculture, particularly where the soil is poor and the yield small, cannot support a large laboring class. In the "poor" sections of South India, where little rice is grown, most people are artisans or small farmers. The class of agricultural laborers is small and relatively prosperous. In rice areas, village councils tend to be made up exclusively of members of the landowning castes, whereas in millet areas village councils tend to be made up of one man from each caste, lineage, or household.

The traditional situation in South Indian millet-raising areas is comparable to that of the United States of more than a century ago:

In America there are, properly speaking, no farming tenants; every man owns the ground he tills. It must be admitted that democratic laws tend greatly to increase the number of landowners and to diminish that of farming tenants. Yet what takes place in the United States is much less attributable to the institutions of the country than to the country itself. In America land is cheap and anyone may easily become a landowner; its returns are small and its produce cannot well be divided between a landowner and a farmer. America therefore stands alone in this respect, as well as in many others, and it would be a mistake to take it as an example (Tocqueville 1960, II:96).

Today, in many parts of the United States, yields have become large, agriculture has become industrialized, population has increased, and "democratic institutions" have changed their form. In India, "democratic institutions," developing perhaps as a result of industrialization, have begun to have an impact upon those places where rice agriculture is practiced. In earlier times, the spread of rice agriculture and irrigation works may have pressed upon the democratic institutions of millet-raising villages, just as urban industrial democratic institutions now press upon rice-growing villages.

But Which Choice Is Adaptive?

In South India rice agriculture ordinarily produces more pounds of food than does millet agriculture, but in many places the silting up of dams and irrigation works limits to a few hundred years the time period during which effective rice agriculture can be practiced. Rice agriculture under these conditions fails to lead to equilibrium between external conditions and the cultural system. It is not clear, then, that rice agriculture in South India is necessarily a more adaptive choice than millet agriculture. Rice agriculture also requires more water than other equally productive crops. Why, then, rice instead of coconuts, black pepper, or sweet potatoes? In broader terms, what accounts for a variety of adaptations and cultural systems coexisting within the same environment or occupying similar environments?

One possible explanation is that cultural systems form a part of the environment of other cultural systems. Therefore the growing of a given crop in a given village community depends in part upon the demand for that crop in village communities that do not produce it. The presence of a variety of cultural systems within a given environment may, then, increase the adaptability of each one of them. If millet was the most adaptive crop and everyone therefore raised it, the overall adaptive advantage might be much less than that provided by a situation in which many different crops were grown.

Another not necessarily alternative explanation has to do with commitment or entailment. When the members of a cultural system decide to raise rice, their commitment to rice agriculture entails modification of the environment and cultural system. Once the commitment has been made, the cost in effort and adaptive loss involved in deciding to do something else is increased. In the case of rice agriculture, where the environment may have been irreversibly changed, some alternative ways of adapting may have been placed out of reach forever.

Acting within the limits of the information contained in their cultural tradition or in the cultural traditions of neighboring peoples, human beings select particular technologies or means of coping with the environment. If they always chose the most adaptive technology, the correlation or goodness or fit between environment and cultural systems would tend to be quite high. In real life, human technologies usually do not permit the discovery of the one and only one best solution to human problems. People make mistakes and then adapt to their mistakes by making additional decisions about what to do.

Because each decision involves a cost, it becomes increasingly difficult to go back to the beginning and start all over again with a different crop or a different technology. As in the case of the Indus civilization, a long series of maladaptive choices may lead to ruin. In the case of two neighboring cultural systems where one is somewhat better adapted than the other, there is always the possibility that one will replace the other; that is, unless both cultural systems taken together are more adaptive than either one taken separately.

Two cultural systems operating in virtually identical desert environments in Africa and North America are not likely to be identical in character because: (1) they are likely to base their decisions upon different sources of traditional information; (2) they are likely to make different sorts of mistakes in the search for the one and only one best solution to their adaptive problems; and (3) they are likely to have different social environments. If, besides controlling the environments so that they are identical, we control the level of technology so that both groups consist of deer hunters or potato farmers, other similarities between the two cultural systems will increase.

As an explanation of the similarities and differences between cultural systems, then, the environment can be seen as setting limits upon what can be done with the technology at hand. The environment alone, or even the technology and the environment alone, cannot determine exactly the nature of particular cultural systems. Although a severe environment, one in which there are only a few possible ways to survive, has a greater effect than a more permissive environment, human beings and their cultural systems survive, not because they have achieved the one and only correct solution to each of the problems posed by the environment, but because they have solved their problems well enough to get by.

So far, adaptation to the environment has been considered primarily as adaptation to the *natural* environment. With reference to nature, we can classify cultural systems in terms of such processes as hunting, fishing, collecting, growing crops, practicing plow agriculture, herding, or using machinery. These processes differ in the extent to which they consume resources available in the natural environment and capture energy or materials which can be used to increase the population size or complexity of the cultural systems. Although the natural environment is critical in the sense that it is the ultimate source of the energy and materials required for the support of cultural systems, the impact of *artificial* and *social* components of the environment upon particular cultural systems may be of equal importance and may even dictate the choice of technologies used in coping with the natural environment.

Why not change the environment?

The crew of a B-29 consisted of eleven men (see Chapter 2). In order to "drop the bomb on the target," the crew carried on its operations within a complex machine. That machine, the B-29, was, at once, the major portion of the crew's environment and an instrument for dealing with the natural environment. External conditions, instead of being primarily a series of natural things, consisted of the machine itself and the crew's status as a part of a military hierarchy composed of other human beings.

The machine itself was built by civilian designers and builders whose main concern was to find a means of carrying heavy loads long distances at rapid speeds and great altitudes. The plane also had to be a superfortress, relatively immune to attack. In effect, then, the environment within which the aircrew was to operate was designed and built without too much regard for the cultural system of the aircrew or for the role of the aircrew in the larger military cultural system within which it also operated.

The aircrew came from the Army Air Corps, later the Air Force. These men had originally been civilians, but had been trained to interact in terms of a military organization which had developed in response to the problems encountered in land warfare by an infantry platoon. Because the activities of the infantry platoon were relatively simple and the men in it relatively untrained, members of such a platoon operated under control of a platoon leader whose orders were to be followed with "unthinking obedience." For the purposes of land warfare, an authoritarian organization in which a well-trained leader directed the activities of untrained followers was probably efficient.

In adapting this organization to the B-29, it was decided that there should be a commanding officer, very much like the platoon leader or the captain of a ship. He would possess absolute authority while the plane was in flight. Under the captain there would be a staff of officers consisting of a bombardier, a radarman, and a copilot. Other crew members, the flight engineer, radioman, and gunners were usually noncommissioned officers. Of the four gunners, several were likely to be privates. According to organizational charts, even the gunners were ranked—central gunner, right gunner, left gunner, and tail gunner.

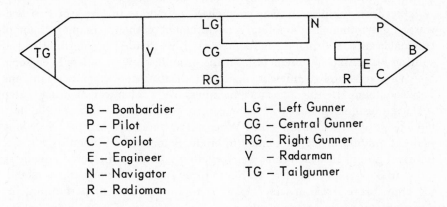

B — Bombardier
P — Pilot
C — Copilot
E — Engineer
N — Navigator
R — Radioman

LG — Left Gunner
CG — Central Gunner
RG — Right Gunner
V — Radarman
TG — Tailgunner

Although all the members of an aircrew were more highly trained, better paid, and higher ranking than most members of an infantry platoon, the operation of the crew was considered parallel to the operation of an infantry platoon: The aircraft commander gave orders, the crew members followed them. In practice, things were different. Few of the officers were in a position to observe, let alone supervise, the activities of the enlisted men. The tail gunner was completely isolated from the rest of the crew and beyond supervision. In flight, perhaps because of close confinement and boredom in the small tail compartment, he often fell asleep leaving the rest of the crew to wonder if he had set himself on fire or jumped out of the airplane. The aircraft commander, being trained almost exclusively in the complex art of piloting the airplane, had little or no idea what the other members of the crew were supposed to be doing. Each man on the crew was a trained specialist whose activities were often mysterious and incomprehensible to the others. Theoretically, the bombardier was an armaments officer, who supervised the activities of the relatively untrained gunners. Because the bombardier was situated in the nose of the plane and had other duties as well, he was in no position to oversee the gunners. In practice, because the central gunner was located in a bubble in the center top of the plane and had access to the gun controlling machinery and a good view of the action, the gun crew, including the bombardier, was directed by the central gunner.

In flight, the flight engineer, who alone possessed the equipment and skills required to calculate most efficient speeds and altitudes, instructed the aircraft commander concerning the speed and altitude at which he was to fly. The navigator, radarman, and radioman told the aircraft commander where he was and what he should do to get back on course. When the plane reached the target area, the aircraft commander was required by regulations to obey the orders of the bombardier. In the event of attack by enemy airplanes, it was the task of the gunners to instruct the aircraft commander concerning the maneuvers required to evade attack and to bring maximum firepower to bear upon an enemy he often could not see.

In effect, the aircrew was compelled to operate in terms of two contrasting environments: A military environment with its complex chain of command and an airplane environment with its divided responsibilities and shifting leadership requirements. On the ground, crew members lived separately, ate separately, and wore badges indicating the differences in rank between them. In the air, crew members wore identical clothing, often replacing insignia of rank with crew caps bearing letters indicating the individual's position within the crew. When crews remained together over long periods, military discipline tended to erode. Some crews formed tightly knit informal groups in which rank was forgotten and all participated equally in crew drinking parties and recreations. In aircrew mythology the outstanding crews were those in which every man was capable of performing the duties of every other crew member.

From the standpoint of the traditional military organization, the environment provided by the B-29 was clearly wrong. By 1952 Air Force generals were publicly advocating the development of new aircraft which would require small crews of very highly trained men; ultimately, there were to be no enlisted men or noncommissioned officers aboard. An all-officer crew could fraternize and be "democratic" without violating military tradition.

The case of the B-29 illustrates, among other things, that the requirements of a cultural system may generate powerful pressures toward the finding of problem solutions consistent with existing patterns and procedures. It is for this reason that people "pre-adapted" to the practice of rice agriculture and its various social and economic consequences are likely to attempt rice agriculture even in a situation where it represents a less efficient problem solution than might a new technique. Intensive rice agriculture, the construction of a city like Mohenjo Daro, or replacement of one airplane by another represent a great deal more than simple adaptation to the natural environment. They represent planned and systematic destruction of an existing environment and its replacement with one thought to be more suitable.

What is a good adaptation?

Rice agriculture can be regarded as an adaptation to the natural environment, while the building of a new airplane to replace the B-29 can be regarded as an instance of adaptation to the social environment. The trouble with thinking in such terms is that it obscures the fact that an adaptation can be successful only if it works simultaneously within the natural, artificial, and social environments. Rice agriculture can be successful only in appropriate artificial and social environments; a new airplane representing a successful adaptation to the social environment is useful only if it also flies.

In these terms, we can think of every process carried out within a cultural system as contributing to the solution of a problem existing simultaneously in the natural, artificial, and social environments. As a problem solution, a process must be reasonably compatible with other processes and consistent with the varieties of knowledge and experience contained within the cultural tradition. Writing about religion, Emile Durkheim, a father of sociology and mother's brother[2] of anthropology, said:

> There are basically no false religions. All are true in their fashion. All stem from the conditions of human existence (1912:3).

Durkheim argued that anything that was false and therefore inefficient or maladaptive would sooner or later meet an obstacle it could not overcome. In other words, every process carried out in every cultural system must be adaptive because anything that is maladaptive will be edited by processes of selection. Because the editing might often take place later, rather than sooner, it cannot be concluded that "all that is" is adaptive.

In sum, the survival of a cultural system involves much more than the solution of problems posed by the natural environment. It involves coming to terms with changes in the environment resulting from the operation of the cultural system. It involves coming to terms with characteristics of the cultural system itself because anything that people do must be in some degree consistent with all the other things that they do. And finally it involves meeting possible competition from other cultural systems. The com-

[2] In many cultures, the mother's brother, rather than the father, passes on his property to his nephews and instructs and disciplines them.

plexity of the survival problems handled by each of the processes carried out during the normal operation of a cultural system makes it difficult to estimate the extent to which a given process is adaptive or even what it is an adaptation to. More than a thousand years passed before the Indus civilization encountered an obstacle it could not overcome; before that it would have been hard to say just how the civilizaton was maladapted. A cultural system could not long survive if all its processes were maladaptive, but it can long survive when only some of its processes are. To the optimist most human cultural systems appear to be ingeniously adapted in almost everything they do. To the pessimist almost nothing seems adapted. Consider, in the following section, the difficulties involved in judging the adaptive value of the Karimojong way of life.

Are the Karimojong Adapted?

The Karimojong live in the southern part of Karimoja District in Uganda and depend for their subsistence upon cattle raising, hunting, collecting, and agriculture. The Karimojong maintain large herds of cattle which tend to overgraze the regions surrounding the campsite and force migrations to other regions. Cattle are regularly milked and all cattle, except pregnant or lactating cows and bulls reserved for breeding, are bled to provide blood for human consumption. Despite the large herds, the Karimojong eat relatively little meat. Oxen and sometimes a barren cow may be slaughtered to provide food at religious ceremonies or when other food is not available, but there is no attempt to slaughter surplus male cattle or cows that produce little milk or few offspring.

As individuals Karimojong dedicate themselves to the acquisition of as many cattle as possible and treat them with great affection. As a boy, a Karimojong is given a specially named male calf. He decorates the calf elaborately, sings songs about it at dances and beer parties, and makes

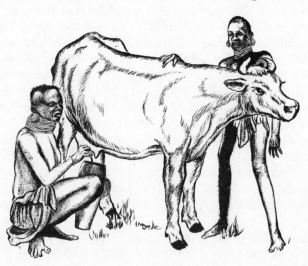

references to it in naming himself. It is hard to imagine how overgrazing or the maintenance of inefficient milk cattle can be adaptive, particularly if adaptation is considered in terms of maximizing the production of milk, meat, and blood. Is there any way in which Karimojong cattle raising makes sense?

One of the most significant factors in the Karimojong environment are enemy tribes who themselves seek greener pastures. If the Karimojong reduce their herds to maintain lush and abundant grasslands, the neighboring tribes may redouble their efforts to take them away. The need for unity in preventing cattle and land theft requires each cattle herder to have the support of friends and neighbors. In Karimojong society, this support is gained through gifts of cattle to relatives and in-laws. The man who owns a large herd has many friends and much protection. The rainfall in Karimojong country is uncertain and crops often fail. Here, again, a large herd of cattle provides insurance against famine. Cattle represent a means of storing wealth and rendering it portable where there are no banks, insurance companies, or elaborate food storage facilities.

> Even in modern times, the market for Karimojong beef is none too good. Four hundred pounds of dressed meat will buy less than three hundred pounds of cornmeal. (Dyson-Hudson 1969:76–89).

After reviewing only a few of the complexities of Karimojong life, it is difficult to reach enthusiastic judgments concerning the extent to which it might be considered adaptive or maladaptive. The Karimojong world is hardly the best of all possible worlds, but what other world is better? With these same questions about adaptation in mind, consider the equally complicated world of the Tsembaga.

Are Tsembaga Pigs Necessary?

The Tsembaga of New Guinea hold a periodic ritual called the *Kaiko*. At a Kaiko observed by Rappaport (1967), some 105 pigs were slaughtered yielding between 7000 and 8000 pounds of meat. Of this meat, between 4500 and 6000 pounds were distributed to 2000 or 3000 guests from 17 neighboring groups.

Pigs are useful in keeping residential areas free of garbage and feces. In gardens, they root up weeds and soften the ground. They also eat tubers and other materials that human beings would normally throw away. When there are too many pigs, it becomes expensive to feed them and they are inclined to invade gardens and to compete with human beings for the available food. One function of the Kaiko ritual, and of other similar rituals, would appear to be to reduce the pig population to manageable size, but this could also be accomplished by simply killing and eating pigs.

On the other hand, groups in New Guinea tend to be rather small and, at least in former times, often engaged in warfare. Frequent and uncontrolled warfare might have unfortunate consequences for the human population; carefully regulated warfare might help to control human populations or might contribute to the smoothing out of man/land ratios by forcing smaller groups to relinquish lands to larger groups. Traditionally, the waging of war and the making of peace was closely tied to ritual activities. The Kaiko ritual apparently served to promote contact and trade between otherwise isolated groups and it also led to marital and military alliances. To fight a war, it was necessary to have a lot of pigs which could be used to hold rituals and gain allies. Rituals held at the termination of a war created alliances which could only be changed after the enemies had again accumulated pigs and formed appropriate alliances.

Rappaport argues that this constitutes a "ritually regulated ecosystem," adaptive because it establishes an equilibrium among pigs, people, and the environment. Although it might turn out that ritually regulated ecological relationships are more or less adaptive than other kinds (if there are other kinds), it appears likely that change in any important part of the Tsembaga system of relationships would create severe adaptive problems. Without completely redesigning the cultural system, it would be difficult to improve upon the traditional adaptation. The Tsembaga, like the Karimojong, pass the major tests of adaptation. They have managed to survive over substantial periods of time, and, in terms of their tightly knit traditional cultural systems, it is hard to find much that has a demonstrably negative effect upon their chances of survival.

Who Needs a Superpotato?

The potato was developed in ancient Peru at least two thousand years ago. In Peru, there are many varieties of potatoes and traditional farming practices until recently ensured that the potatoes in any one field were of many different kinds. Instead of carefully selecting the best potatoes and using them for seed, the Peruvians traditionally used whatever was handy. Around 1588, potatoes were introduced into Ireland. Due to problems of shipping and the need to transport only the best potatoes, it is probable that these potatoes were superpotatoes, perhaps representing only one variety. After several centuries of selection by Irish farmers, who tended to plant only the biggest and best of potatoes, the Irish potato crop was totally destroyed in 1845 and 1846 by the previously unknown fungus *Phytophtora infestans*. Within a few decades, the population of Ireland had fallen from nine million to four million people. In the process of selecting potatoes for cultivation, the Irish farmer had apparently eliminated those varieties of potatoes that were resistant to *Phytophtora infestans* (from Salaman 1952).

The question of the superpotato raises some interesting problems concerning the ability of modern civilizations to disseminate new technological adaptations rapidly across wide areas. Might not atomic power, insecticides, new crops, or supersonic airplanes, like the superpotato, carry hidden within them the seeds of destruction? Might not the spread of a single set of closely related cultural systems over the entire planet create a kind of superculture every bit as vulnerable as the superpotato? Were all men and all cultures essentially the same and adapted to their environments in essentially the same way, would the human species have the same protection against rapid environmental change that it now possesses through the existence of a variety of cultures and kinds of man? The poet has many kinds of grass, dandelions, and daisies in his lawn; the efficiency expert has a lawn consisting entirely of the "best" variety of bluegrass. Who has the lawn most fitted to survive? For that matter, is the poet or the efficiency expert fitted to survive? The next section considers the possibility that the culture-building capacity itself is maladaptive.

Why Are Clams Happy?
Over the millennia, the so-called "higher" animals embarked upon a course of evolution emphasizing the importance of cooperation within the species and of learning through experience. Using hindsight, it appears almost inevitable that this should lead in time to the emergence of a culture-building species such as *Homo sapiens*. Ultimately, should the culture-building capacity prove adaptive (that is, if we survive as a species), it seems inevitable that this capacity will overwhelm the biological message so that human biological evolution becomes a reflex of the cultural message. This next great evolutionary step is implicit in our developing capacity to understand and hence to modify the genetic code.

The evolutionary "success" of the so-called higher animals might be thought of as a consequence of their adaptive failures. The higher animals, most particularly *Homo sapiens*, have rarely achieved a state of equilibrium with the environment. Like the flying Dutchman, the ancestors of *Homo sapiens* and *Homo sapiens* himself fled through the corridors of time seeking, first through biological and then increasingly through cultural evolution, new solutions to the problems of survival. Through these same millennia and more, the happy clam has merrily reproduced himself, maintaining, with few apparent changes, the genetic message with which he started his career.

With the emergence of the culture-building capacity, human survival appears to have depended upon the increasingly rapid development of new means of adaptation. Following the first inventions, leading to the use of tools and the hunting of large animals, human cultures changed but slowly. Then, with the invention of agriculture less than ten thousand years ago human beings began to alter and sometimes to destroy their environments with increasing rapidity. Human beings are not the only life forms that destroy their environments. It has been pointed out that if the first plants had preserved the "balance of nature," the earth would perhaps still have an atmosphere of methane and ammonia.

Whether we speak of the use of bows and arrows, fire, plows, bulldozers, or repeating rifles, the impact of human inventions upon the environment has been to simplify it and to dramatically reduce the number of plant and animal species. Humanity has solved its problems with a meat-axe, cutting out those species which were useless or threatening and replacing them or allowing them to be replaced with species which were more useful or better adapted to the presence of humanity. More and more, human beings have adapted the environment to themselves rather than adapting themselves to the environment. Without exception, certainly from the time of the Indus civilization, such drastic revisions of the environment have failed to promote the kind of equilibrium that might be described as adaptation. With the creation of superpotatoes, pesticides, and atomic bombs, it would appear that the survival of the species has come more and more to depend upon the solution of problems that the species itself has created. As *Homo sapiens artificialis* or synthetic humanity emerges from the drawing boards of the biologist, is there any guarantee that he will be better adapted than the superpotato?

Unlike the clam, the human species has never reached the safe harbor of relative equilibrium. In every environment and cultural system there have always been problems that were not solved and human beings who were considerably less happy than clams. What is the impact of such problems upon the development of cultural systems? Consider the case of the Nyoro, a tribe of Africa.

Why this, why now, why to me?

Yowana bought a piece of timber to make a door with, but it was stolen before he could use it. After searching the village he found it in the house of a neighbor, Isoke. He accused Isoke of stealing it, but since Isoke denied the theft and there were no witnesses, the charge failed. A few days later Yowana's house was burned down and he lost all his property. He did not know who had done this (though he suspected Isoke), so, informants afterwards said, he obtained from a vendor of powerful medicines a substance which if smeared on those of the posts of the burned house which remained standing would cause the incendiarist to suffer from dysentery and burning pains in his chest. Yowana is said to have applied the medicine as directed, and four days later Isoke became ill. His brothers consulted the local diviners, who said that Yowana's medicine was the cause of the illness. Isoke then summoned Yowana, confessed to him that he had burned his house and also that he had stolen the timber, and promised to make restitution. Isoke's brothers begged Yowana to get an antidote from the vendor of the original medicine so that Isoke might be cured. Yowana promised to do so, but unfortunately Isoke died. In this case complaints were made to the Protectorate police and Yowana was arrested for suspected murder, but an autopsy on Isoke's body showed no signs of poisoning, and Yowana was released. Nonetheless, nobody doubted that Yowana had killed Isoke by sorcery, least of all Yowana, who was heard to boast at beer parties of his prowess (Beattie 1960:74).

Throughout the world men like Isoke, strong enough to carry away another man's timber and mean enough to become involved in neighborhood quarrels, have a tendency to fall ill, sometimes to die. It appears likely, although Isoke's confession was obtained under duress, that he had committed the crimes of which he was accused. In other cases, perfectly innocent men may die as a result of sorcery or perfectly healthy men may die quickly and unpleasantly of unknown and unusual diseases. The germ theory of disease, however useful it may be for some purposes, fails to explain why Isoke got sick and not Yowana.

The Nyoro explain the matter as follows:

A sorcerer is a person who wants to kill people. He may do it by blowing medicine toward them, or by putting it in the victim's food or water, or by hiding it in the path where he must pass. People practice sorcery against those whom they hate. They practice it against those who steal from them, and also against people who are richer than they are. Sorcery is brought about by envy, hatred, and quarreling (Beattie 1960:73).

In some ultimate sense, perfect adaptation would involve perfectly stable and predictible relationships with the environment. Because the rains do not always come on time or are too heavy when they do come and because men die inexplicably or encounter misfortune, human beings inevitably face the problem of explaining that which cannot be explained. Such explanations, often partaking of the qualities of religion, may have adaptive consequences. For the Nyoro, sorcery and illness may be avoided by avoiding envy, hatred, and quarreling. Thus, the unsolved problem of illness appears to be used to promote qualities of behavior that enhance the adaptive virtues of unity and cooperation.

North Americans explain colds and other illness by saying, "I guess I've been staying up too late," "not eating properly," "too much boozing around," or " I should have worn my sweater." The fact that others who got drunk or forgot their sweaters did not get sick is ignored. Here, illness is not the result of sorcery, but the result of one's own misbehaviors. Small wonder that a sick person is confined in a small room, dressed in special clothing, deprived of the companionship of friends and family, forced to consume poorly cooked food served on a tray, allowed to do things only at rigidly specified times, and forced to undergo pain and humiliation. Criminals are punished in much the same way.

The North Americans also believe in sorcery:

There are many roads to insanity and our culture has probably trod them all. It is difficult to find in any other society a form of madness, or a pathway to it, that cannot be duplicated by us. The opposite is not true: that all cultures have developed as many forms of psychosis or found as many ways to attain it as we. In this we are secure in our riches. We are as highly developed in psychopathology as in technology.

Psychosis is the final outcome of all that is wrong with a culture. Coming to intense focus in the parents, the cultural ills are transmitted to their children, laying the foundation for insanity. The parents, blinded by their own disorientation, confusion, and misery, sometimes half mad themselves, make fearful mistakes; but only an observer who sees these with his own eyes can really know exactly how the tragedy was prepared (Henry 1963: 322–323).

Science tells us that human beings sometimes cause their own illnesses and that their illnesses are sometimes caused by others. There is a tendency, as among the Nyoro and the North Americans, to convert these sometime explanations into general explanations. The resulting processes of diagnosis and treatment are directed not so much at coping with the environment as at coping with the anxiety and hostility that arise because it is impossible to explain why one man became ill and not another.

In thinking about the problem of the relationships between cultural systems and their environments, it is useful to think of the various processes carried out within the cultural system as involving solutions or attempted solutions to problems posed by the environment. Because not all problems can be solved, because the correct solution is not always found, and because some problems are solved by radically changing the environment, it is not easy to draw direct connections between what the problem is and what people do in response to it. Because designing a process to solve a problem involves some sort of recognition of the nature of the problem, one of the problems of studying the environment is that of recognizing the problem and discovering the connection between problem and process.

But was that the problem the solution solved?

Raymond picked himself up and started pulling the wagon westward, along the side of the Vocational Training building. As he walked along, he muttered to himself, "I'll go get my crate." He ran around the back of the building and headed for the pit, where he had been playing with the crate in the afternoon. When he reached the pit, he crawled down into it and went straight to the crate. He began tugging and pulling at the crate, trying hard to raise it up to the level of the vacant lot. He worked hard (Barker and Wright 1955:242).

Had Raymond not announced the nature of his problem, the outside observer would have had difficulty understanding what Raymond was up to. It is not obvious that he was getting the crate, for he might have been cleaning out the pit.

In South India, an outside observer might see something like the following: In the rice fields ten women are standing in line. At one end stands an elderly woman who is peering along the line. She begins to sing a

strongly rhythmic and repetitive song. As she sings, the women step backward one step, bend over, and thrust rice seedlings into the ground. Looking at this behavior, the outside observer is likely to conclude that the
environmental problem here is that of planting rice seedlings in straight
rows, and that this is solved by the process observed. Even here, where
the problem seems easily identified and where the women would almost
certainly say that they were planting rice if they were asked, other problems
are mixed in. The songs the old woman is singing involve a kind of instruction and, in this sense, the observed process is educational. Similarly, the
arrangement of the women under the leadership of the old woman could
be interpreted as a process of assigning status or social position.

As Raymond or the women of South India carry out particular activities
and processes, they exert impact upon the environment. The sum of the
human activity carried out within a cultural system determines the nature
of the ecological relationships between the cultural system and its environment. In many cases, the carrying out of a particular activity represents
a conscious plan, such as "getting the crate," formulated with a view toward
establishing some particular relationship to the environment. Of course,
there is a distinction between planning to get the crate and actually getting
the crate and there is a difference between planting a crop of rice and
harvesting a crop of rice. In many cases, as noted in the Bible, people quite
literally "know not what they do," and processes carried out with one purpose in mind may lead to undreamed of consequences. Human beings may
solve their adaptive problems without planning to do so, or in planning to
solve some particular problem, they may create new ones. A part of the
problem of understanding cultural systems and their relationships to the
environment is that of understanding why a given process is carried out
and what its specific impacts are, not only on the environment, but upon

other aspects of the cultural system. In thinking about ways of planting rice, women in South India cannot think solely of the one and only one best way of planting rice, for they must also consider a variety of social and educational impacts that any method of planting rice must have. In selecting ways of doing such things as planting rice, human beings are guided by their general understanding of the nature of the environment and of the place which they occupy within it. This understanding, loosely classified under the heading of "world view," is part of the subject of the next chapter.

Summary

The disappearance of the Indus Valley civilization demonstrates that the survival of cultural systems and, therefore, much of their content is dependent upon their ability to adapt to environmental circumstances. Ecological anthropology is concerned with the description of human environments and the study of the relationships between environments and human beings. One of the problems involved in the understanding of human environments is that scientific and cultural realities may be quite different. Although, ideally at least, scientific reality is what really happens, cultural reality is what people see and react to.

Because cultural systems, like biological systems, are edited by selection in terms of their capacity to persist within the environment, there has to be a significant correlation or fit between the environment and the cultural system. The case of the Tiwi illustrates that such a fit is likely to occur and leads to questions concerning the extent to which cultural systems are to be regarded as products of their environments.

Patterns of agriculture in South India suggest that environmental circumstances may often provide the possibility of a wide range of choices all of which are adaptive, perhaps because a variety of adaptations are more adaptive than just one or because human beings find some way to avoid the consequences of a bad choice. Although, as may have been the case with the Indus civilization, a long series of bad or maladaptive choices may lead to ruin, disaster can often be postponed for centuries.

In the meantime, the members of any particular cultural system bring their own theories of survival and patterns of life into their dealings with the environment. These unique perspectives, combined with the various mistakes that are made in the process of working out adaptations to the environment, assure that environment alone or even environment and technology together will never be adequate to explain the similarities and differences between cultural systems. The tendency of the members of cultural systems to seek adaptations consistent with preexisting patterns of behavior is exemplified by the history and ultimate replacement of the B-29. In other cases as well, adaptation consists of the planned and systematic destruction of the environment.

Because relationships between cultural systems and their environments are moderated by complex ecological systems often involving reciprocal causation, it is difficult to estimate the adaptedness of a particular cultural system or of some particular part of it. Even where adaptation can be measured, adaptations to the natural environment may not be consistent with adaptations to artificial or social environments. A new airplane, conceived as an adaptation to the social environment, is successful only if it flies. Each part of a cultural system must be adapted to the other parts of the cultural system that constitute *its* environment, as well as to the environment itself. Although, as illustrated by the cases of the Karimojong and the Tsembaga, there may be no false religions, it is doubtful that there are any completely true religions. Cultural systems are just sufficiently adapted to get by.

The case of the superpotato illustrates the point that not all new ideas are good and suggests some of the dangers implicit in the modern habit of rapidly changing and simplifying environments. The experience of the superpotato argues in favor of diversity and in opposition to the belief that there is one and only one right way to do everything. When compared to the slow-changing clam, *Homo sapiens* seems to have fled through the corridors of time desperately papering over the evolutionary mistakes of his ancestors.

Two final problems of human adaptation are that human beings seem unable to solve all problems or to admit that some problems are unsolvable. Elaborate and apparently unrealistic beliefs concerning the causes of such things as misfortune and illness may themselves be adaptive because they provide psychological satisfaction or encourage cooperation. Much of human behavior is consciously or unconsciously dedicated to the solving of problems posed by the environment. Here, too, the complexities of ecological and cultural systems make it difficult to understand the nature of the problem or the purpose of the solution.

Further readings

An overview of anthropological studies of environment and ecology is provided by *Environment and Cultural Behavior* (Vayda 1969). "Worlds of Man," a series of volumes published by Aldine and edited by Walter Goldschmidt, includes such titles as *Northern Plainsmen: Adaptive Strategy and Agrarian Life* (Bennett 1969), *Amazonia: Man and Culture in a Counterfeit Paradise* (Meggers 1971), and *Rice and Man: Agricultural Ecology in Southeast Asia* (Hanks 1972).

General discussions are to be found in *The Forest and the Sea* (Bates 1960), *Human Ecology* (Bressler 1966), and *Theory of Cultural Change* (Steward 1955: 30–42). Ecologically oriented ethnographies include *Moala, Culture and Nature on a Fijian Island* (Sahlins 1962), *The Nuer* (Evans-

Pritchard 1940), *Pigs for the Ancestors* (Rappaport 1967), and *Hill Farmers of Nigeria* (Netting 1968).

Case Studies dealing with environmental problems and adaptations include the Spindlers' *Dreamers without Power* (1971), Hart and Pilling's *The Tiwi* (1960), Hudson's *Padju Epat* (1972), Hitchcock's *The Magars of Banyan Hill* (1965), Beals' *Gopalpur* (1962), Rivière's *The Forgotten Frontier* (1972), Diamond's *K'un Shen* (1969), Klima's *The Barabaig* (1970), and Ekvall's *Fields on the Hoof* (1968).

Problems and questions

1. On the basis of what you read in three or four case studies or other ethnographies, select cultural systems sharing similar environments such as the Hopi and Tewa (Dozier 1967) and the Navajo (Downs 1972). To what extent do environmental similarities contribute to similarities between the cultures?

2. Collect information concerning utilization of an important resource such as coal, copper, or water in modern US or European society. Does the data you have collected indicate that the society has reached an equilibrium with its environment? If not, what sorts of changes in technology or in other aspects of culture seem to be required in order to reach equilibrium?

3. Consider the natural, artificial, and social environments within which some particular family, club, or other small group operates. What sorts of environmental problems does the group face and how might its adaptations be improved?

4. Interview several individuals to find out how they explain and prevent misfortune and illness. How closely do these beliefs and actions conform with what you take to be realistic or "scientific" approaches to the problem?

5. Examine an ethnography, perhaps one of those listed under "Further Readings," and consider how well the various processes described (such as getting food, preventing and curing disease, or carrying out rituals) seem to fit in with the overall requirements for adaptation to the environment.

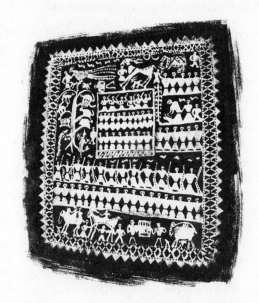

5

The nature
of tradition

*Chapter 4 dealt with the kinds of
relationships that obtain between cultural
systems and their surroundings. From
this perspective, many of the activities
characteristic of the members of cultural
systems can be seen as responses to
environmentally inspired requirements and
limitations. At the same time that human
beings respond to the environment, they
must also respond to the heritage of
messages and ideas handed down in the
form of a cultural tradition. Human behavior
can be interpreted as a complex outcome of
an interplay between environment and
tradition. This chapter, then, is concerned
with the nature of cultural traditions and
especially the manner in which cultural
traditions lead to ideas about the nature
of things and to the labeling and
classification of things.*

Was it right, what you did?

A cultural tradition is a set of ideas,
a message if you like, which is trans-

105

mitted with varying degrees of accuracy and completeness to each of the members of a cultural system. Like any message a cultural tradition may contain illogical, inconsistent, or false information. It need not solve all problems or provide the answers to every question. It must, if the cultural system is to survive, meet two criteria: (1) it must succeed in convincing most of the membership most of the time that their best interests are served by conformity to the cultural tradition; and (2) it must provide the information and technology required for adaptation to the environment.

If there were one and only one correct solution to every problem and if the cultural tradition contained such solutions, human behavior might well involve blind obedience to the dictates of tradition. Because some problems are never solved, because cultural traditions are silent or vague concerning other problems, and because some human beings fail to get the message, the membership of a cultural system cannot operate in perfect conformity to the cultural tradition. When we ask if man is the slave of culture or culture the servant of man, the answer must be equivocal. Under some circumstances individuals conform to that which is considered right and proper in terms of their cultural traditions. Under other circumstances, the individual has freedom to do whatever he thinks is best.

Two kinds of questions can be asked about cultural traditions: "What does the traditional message say?" and "What is the influence of the message upon behavior?" Such questions as, "Is that sentence grammatical?" or "Is that the right thing to do?" set up a situation in which there is one and only one right answer. Because languages and cultural traditions are arbitrary or conventional, because they are codes of behavior, the study of correct behavior can follow the model of exact or mechanical science.

It is wrong to eat peas with a knife; it is wrong to drive on the left hand side of the street; it is wrong to say, "School to go I." To the extent that anthropology explores the laws of human beings and not the laws of nature, anthropology is the only exact science. To the extent that human beings obey the law, speaking in grammatical sentences, driving on the right hand side of the street, and eating peas with their forks, a knowledge of traditional rules permits the prediction of behavior. Where human beings fail to do the right thing, the cultural tradition becomes one of several factors influencing their behavior. When human beings decide what to do, they take into account what they are *supposed* to do, and sometimes for various reasons they do something else. Anthropology now becomes an inexact or probabilistic science which makes statements about the likelihood that individuals will drive on the right hand side of the road or eat peas with forks. "What did you do?" is a different question from, "Did you do the right thing?"

Although a cultural tradition may be viewed as a set of instructions (what to do upon any occasion), it can hold the allegiance of the membership of a cultural system only if it contains convincing explanations of the correctness of the instructions. People must know not only what is right, but why it is right to do the right thing. A cultural tradition must explain the nature of things in a satisfying way before it gets down to specifics about what should be done. Such a general explanation of the nature of things is called *world view*. Because it is a statement about why things are the way they are as well as a statement about the way things are, a world view always goes beyond the limits of exact or practical knowledge about the world. Because it deals with unanswerable questions about the purpose of human life and the nature of birth and death, it partakes of the quality of religion.

The following, taken from Verrier Elwin's discussion of Saora religion, provides an example of what is meant by world view. One of the questions that might be asked about Saora world view, as about any other, has to do with its function: In what way does allegiance to this particular set of ideas contribute to the maintenance of the Saora cultural system?

World view: why are the dead so lonely?

The Saora are a tribe of some 100,000 people living in a mountainous district in India. For centuries they have preserved their way of life despite continuous pressure from the great civilizations of the Indian plains regions. Much of the time they have been subjugated:

> The Saora's threshing floor in Ganjam is indeed one of the saddest places in India. This symbol of a lifetime's toil, this shrine into which Mother Earth pours her choicest gifts, is the scene of persistent and wholesale economic trickery and exploitation (Elwin 1955:60).

Despite the necessity for paying tribute to powerful neighboring peoples, the Saora way of life and the Saora themselves continue to survive. The Saora are efficient collectors and producers of food. Each day, the men obtain quantities of the nutritious and mildly intoxicating sap of the palm trees surrounding their villages. Between meals there are snacks of land crab, chili, and mush. Protein rich foods are easily obtained and include buffalo, land crab, fish, field rats, and red ants with mushrooms. The Saora suffer heavily from malaria and other endemic diseases, and there are always problems in dealing with avaricious members of powerful neighboring groups. The Saora explain their situation in the world, more or less as follows:

There are two separate worlds, this world and an underworld. When a man dies, his spirit descends briefly to the underworld. Later, the spirit finds his way out of the underworld and wanders about the earth pestering everyone. When the spirit's friends and relatives sacrifice a buffalo and give an expensive feast to their kinsmen and neighbors, the spirit returns to the underworld and temporarily refrains from bothering the living.

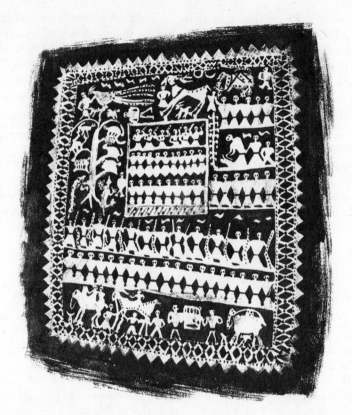

Although most Saora are contented with their roles as farmers and members of an unimportant tribe, a few Saora seek a life of greater usefulness and importance. Such individuals are likely to become shamans. That is, they are likely to be visited by the spirits of wealthy and important Hindus who threaten them and quite literally drive them out of their minds until they agree to marriage. Once married to such a Hindu tutelary spirit, the living Saora undertakes a variety of special obligations including communication with the underworld and the healing of the sick. In carrying out these obligations, the shaman may visit the underworld and be possessed by individual spirits and speak with their voices. This direct experience gives the Saora detailed knowledge of the nature of spirits and the underworld:

> The underworld is like this world; there are hills, rivers, rocks, and trees, but it is always moonlight there. There is no brighter light than that, there is no sun and the clouds are very low. You cannot recognize people at a distance, the light is so dim. The tutelaries (spirits of Hindus) are the officials and the ancestors are the peasants of the land. Since there is so little light, the ancestors cannot get about very much. But when they do find a path, they come to this world and cause a lot of trouble.
>
> It is hard to get sufficient food, though the ordinary dead plough their

fields. But the rulers, the tutelaries, who dress and behave like Hindus, are rich and prosperous; they sleep on beds; sahibs and forest officers come to their marriages; they keep many servants and soldiers; they ride on elephants and horses and have lizards, snakes and tigers as pets. As men keep dogs, they keep tigers in their houses. But the ancestors who are the peasants of that country, look just as they did at the time of death, thin, weary, deformed and sad. They cannot get proper clothes to wear and it is always cold under the infernal moon. The wind too blows so hard that it carries their thin bodies up into the air. When they can find the way, they come to their old homes on earth and give their relatives fever and ague; that is why we shiver when we get fever, because the dead who give it are themselves shivering with cold; they do not let us be until we give them clothes (Elwin 1955:69–70).

Pathetic creatures, neglected by their living relatives, the spirits desperately attempt to attract the attention of the living. Acting through grief, loneliness, and dire need, deceased parents attempt to carry off sons or grandchildren so that they will have someone to care for them in the underworld. Through the shamans, the living hear the pleas and demands of the dead and conduct appropriate ceremonies to cure the living and provide for the economic needs of the spirits.

There are also a variety of deities. These deities, as well as the spirits, are continually journeying from place to place. Although they are invisible to man, they may be encountered anywhere:

You who live in clearings now overgrown with trees, you who live in pits, you who live above, you who live in water, you who live in water where there are fishes, you who live in the fish, you who live in bones, you who live in the bones of men, you who live in the stone walls between fields, you who live in the trees of the forest, you made us and gave us birth; come all of you to take your offerings (Elwin 1955:328).

Walking along a trail, a Saora may inadvertently interfere with the activities of spirits or deities invisibly picnicking there. Should he accidently kick over their bowl of rice, they will be enraged and he will fall ill. Illness, then, is the consequence of failing to provide proper offerings to the ancestors or of accidentally or deliberately failing to treat deities with proper respect. Illness is cured through the holding of a ceremony in which the spirit or deity possesses the shaman, explains the cause of his anger, and is propitiated by means of gifts of food and drink. Any serious illness requires the sacrifice of a buffalo. The buffalo is obtained by borrowing money from neighboring groups so that most Saora are in debt to the moneylender. Although this sort of indebtedness is an aspect of the economic exploitation of the Saora by neighboring groups, it is worth noting that the moneylender now has a vested interest in the economic success of his client. Indebtedness, by providing the Saora with the protection of powerful moneylenders, may be one of the means by which the Saora have maintained themselves as a group despite pressures to adopt the customs and religion of their more powerful neighbors. Another characteristic of illness among the Saora is that wealthy men fall ill with greater frequency than do poor men. The man of wealth apparently establishes his social status and his importance through a form of hypochondria in which he provides gifts of food and drink not only to the spirits, but to the living as well.

The Saora world view presents an organized picture of the Saora world and provides explanations for the great questions of life: "Why do some men fall ill and not others?" "Why do men die?" "Why is the world the way it is?" The concept of an underworld occupied by spirits that cause disease leads to the performance of shamanistic healing rituals. These rituals have the purpose of curing disease, but in practice they appear to be multipurpose instruments that contribute to the solution of a variety of Saora problems. The role of shaman provides an outlet for those who might otherwise fail to find satisfaction in the Saora way of life. The feasting and buffalo sacrifice provides an opportunity for joyous unification of the community and for the display and circulation of wealth by the rich. Because male buffaloes are economically useless, except for eating, the buffalo sacrifice helps to control their numbers. Finally, because buffalo sacrifice leads to indebtedness to members of neighboring groups, it provides an avenue of social and economic interaction between the Saora and their neighbors. The Saora world view seems useful, but is it really?

Does It Work?
The Saora world view helps to maintain the Saora cultural system by providing an explanation of why things are the way they are and why people should do the things they do. The role played by a part of a cultural system in maintaining that system is called its *function*. In broadest terms, the function of world view is to explain the world in such a way as to convince the membership that the things they are called upon to do as members of a cultural system are right and proper. In the same way, although the purpose of the Saora curing ritual is to cure people, its functions have a great deal to do with maintaining social relationships within the group and between the group and neighboring groups. There is a difference between purpose and function.

Because any cultural system that survives can be said to be adapted to its environment, it is possible to argue that whatever the members of a cultural system are saying or doing must in some way contribute to adaptation. It might be argued that because the Saora believe in spirits and because they perform curing rituals, these beliefs and activities *must* be adaptive. Looking at our own or other cultural systems, there is a danger of concluding that "everything is for the best in this best of all possible worlds," or that "whatever is is good." If there are wars, it must be because wars are functional. If people believe things that are not so, it must be because those false beliefs are more adaptive than true beliefs.

If adaptation depended upon always doing the right thing and always perceiving the environment as it really is, human beings would have become extinct long ago. In fact, survival happens, not because every act and every belief contributes to survival, but because acts and beliefs contributing to survival outweigh those which make no contribution or a negative one. Most of the things that people say and do must be functional in the sense that they contribute to the maintenance of the cultural system or to the survival of its membership, but that does not mean that everything they say and do must be functional. Quite possibly, Saora buffalo sacrifice is dysfunctional and Saora indebtedness to neighboring peoples works against the long-term survival of the Saora. Saora survival may, in fact, come about through other means.

The only way to settle such questions definitively would be to try to discover what would happen to the Saora if they did not practice buffalo sacrifice. This calls for a fiendish experiment in which the Saora are forbidden to sacrifice buffaloes in the expectation that: (1) the Saora will become extinct, (2) nothing will happen, or (3) they will be better off than ever before. Less fiendish would be a search for situations in which people have abandoned or taken up animal sacrifice as part of the natural development of their cultural systems. Comparisons of peoples practicing animal sacrifice with peoples who do not might be instructive. Almost certainly investigations would show that animal sacrifice does not have the same functions among all peoples and that its positive or negative role in contributing to survival is different in different places. Still, this would put us in a good position to advise the Saora, if they should ask, about possible alternatives to buffalo sacrifice.

In thinking about the things the Saora do to cure malaria, a practitioner of modern medical and public health techniques might well propose a variety of strategies that would lead to more effective control or treatment of the disease. In this context, the Saora's lack of exposure to modern medical knowledge seems positively immoral. But what if the eradication of malaria led to a runaway increase in Saora population? What if the possession of modern medical knowledge led to abandonment of traditional Saora beliefs concerning the cause of illness?

The best guess about a particular world view or about any other aspect of a cultural system is that it contributes in some way to survival, that it is functional. Some things, runaway population growth or wholesale destruction of the environment, are more obviously dysfunctional than other things, but on the whole, there is no royal road to the determination of what is functional and what is not. Because all systems of world view explain things that are not known or not knowable, it follows that all systems of world view contain explanations which may later turn out to be false. There is no correct world view, but might not some world views be more correct than others? Might not another world view be more correct or functional than the Saora world view? Consider the Eskimo.

Is Eskimo Belief More True?
The Iglulik Eskimo have reason to believe that danger and hardship are everywhere, and they consider themselves to be hard-boiled and practical. Their world is governed and dominated by the "rules of life." All living things contain "souls" and "names" which render them sensitive to these rules. If the rules are violated by sinful and unclean human beings, the souls of animals killed in the hunt become evil spirits causing harm and death:

> It is strictly forbidden to sleep out on the ice-edge while hunting. Every evening the hunter must return either to land, or to the old, firm ice which lies some distance back from the open sea. The sea spirit does not like her creatures to smell human beings when they are not actually hunting (Rasmussen 1929:76).

Because there are a great many such rules, it is practically impossible for an ordinary person to avoid violating them from time to time. For the Eskimo, as for the Saora, supernatural beings are everywhere and constantly on watch for violations. The Saora is carefree, well aware that he is doing the right thing, and free of any strong fears of punishment. The Eskimo must constantly consider the rules of life, for he knows that the slightest mistake, the slightest error in handling his weapons or in dealing with other people, will result in cruel and inevitable punishment. The man who falls asleep on the ice-edge while hunting is likely to be caught there by the sister of the moon spirit who creeps up and cuts out his entrails with her semicircular knife. Children who play noisily while left alone by their parents are certain to attract the attention of the spanking monster and suffer painful punishment.

Rasmussen tried to find out why the Eskimo had so many rules:

> It had been an unusually rough day, and as we had plenty of meat after the successful hunting of the past few days, I had asked my host to stay at home so that we could get some work done together. The brief daylight had given place to the half-light of the afternoon, but as the moon was up, one could still see some distance. Ragged white clouds raced across the sky, and when a gust of wind came tearing over the ground, our eyes and mouths were filled with snow. Aua looked me full in the face and pointing out over the ice, where the snow was being lashed about in waves by the wind, he said:
> "In order to hunt well and live happily, man must have calm weather. Why this constant succession of blizzards and all this needless hardship for men seeking food for themselves and those they care for? Why? Why?"
> We had come out just at the time when the men were returning from their

watching at the blowholes on the ice; they came in little groups bowed
forward, toiling along against the wind, which actually forced them now and
again to stop, so fierce were the gusts. Not one of them had a seal in tow;
their whole day of painful effort and endurance had been in vain.

I could give no answer to Aua's "Why?" but shook my head in silence.
He then led me into Kublo's house, which was close beside our own. The
small blubber lamp burned with but the faintest flame giving out no heat
whatever; a couple of children crouched shivering under a skin rug on the
bench.

Aua looked at me again and said: "Why should it be cold and comfortless
in here: Kublo has been out hunting all day and if he had got a seal as he
deserved his wife would now be sitting laughing beside her lamp, letting
it burn full without fear of having no blubber left for tomorrow. The place
would be warm and bright and cheerful. The children would come out from
under their rugs and enjoy life. Why should it not be so? Why?"

I made no answer and he led me out of the house into a little snow hut
where his sister Natseq lived all by herself because she was ill. She looked
thin and worn, and was not even interested in our coming. For several days
she had suffered from a malignant cough that seemed to come from far down
in the lungs, and it looked as if she had not long to live.

Aua looked at me again, and said. "Why must people be ill and suffer pain?
We are all afraid of illness. Here is this old sister of mine; as far as anyone
can see, she has done no evil; she has lived through a long life and given
birth to healthy children, and now she must suffer before her days end. Why?
Why?"

This ended his demonstration, and we returned to our house to resume with the others the interrupted discussion.

"You see," said Aua, "you are equally unable to give any reason when we ask you why life is as it is. And so it must be. All our customs come from life and turn towards life; we explain nothing, we believe nothing, but in what I have just shown you lies our answer to all you ask.

"We fear the weather spirit of earth that we must fight against to wrest our food from land and sea. We fear Sila.

"Our customs all come from life and are directed toward life; we cannot explain, we do not believe in this or that, but the answer lies in what I have just told you.

"We fear.

"We fear the elements with which we have to fight in their fury to wrest our food from land and sea.

"We fear cold and famine in our snow huts.

"We fear the sickness that is daily to be seen among us. Not death, but the suffering.

"We fear the souls of the dead, of human and animal alike.

"We fear the spirits of earth and air.

"And therefore our fathers, taught by their fathers before them, guarded themselves about with all these old rules and customs, which are built upon the experience and knowledge of generations. We do not know how or why, but we obey them that we may be suffered to live in peace. And for all our angakoks (men who deal with the spirit world) and their knowledge of hidden things, we yet know so little that we fear everything else" (Rasmussen 1929:55–56).

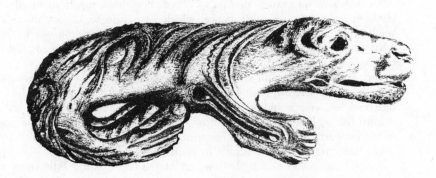

When things go wrong, when even the most careful attempts to follow the rules and customs fail to insure good weather or good hunting, the Eskimo gather together, and, under the leadership of an *angakok*, confess to all of the violations they have committed. When the spirits and the souls of the dead are satisfied that all sins have been confessed and forgiven, the sky clears and the animals emerge once more where they can be hunted.

Because the Eskimo live in one of the harshest and most demanding environments known to man, their world view must be regarded as helpful to them or at least noninjurious. The habit of conforming to a wide variety of rules and the mechanism of group confession in a sort of sensitivity session appear to contribute to the smooth functioning of the tiny and isolated communities in which the Eskimo live. The conformity of every person to the rules of life seems to be an asset in maintaining stable relationships with the environment. Would it not be better, then, if the Saora believed as the Eskimo do?

The Eskimo system works for small communities in a harsh environment, while the Saora system works for larger communities where the physical environment is rich and complicated and where the main problems of life have to do with disease and neighboring peoples. The Saora world view works for the Saora and the Eskimo world view works for the Eskimo. These different forms of world view do not arise directly from the environment, rather they develop slowly as a result of a continuing process of interaction between the cultural system and the environment. Different cultural systems with different world views might well be adapted to the same environment. One system might support more people, survive for a longer time, or be more or less subject to change than another system. Where there are two cultural systems and two world views, it is not always easy to decide that one is more functional, more adaptive, or better than another.

We might argue that world view based upon truths established through science would be superior to any other world view. We might even argue that such a world view exists and that we possess it or are so close to possessing it that it makes no difference. But does man live by truth alone?

The overestimation of the reliability of scientific results is not restricted to the philosopher; it has become a general feature of modern times, that is, of the period dating from the time of Galileo to our day, in which period falls the creation of modern science. The belief that science has the answer to all questions—that if somebody is in need of technical information, or is ill, or is troubled by some psychological problem, he merely has to ask the scientist in order to obtain an answer—is so widespread that science has taken over a social function which originally was satisfied by religion: the function of offering ultimate security. The belief in science has replaced, in large measure, the belief in God. Even where religion was regarded as compatible with science, it was modified by the mentality of the believer in scientific truth. The period of Enlightenment, into which Kant's lifework falls, did not abandon religion; but transformed religion into a creed of reason, it made God a mathematical scientist who knew everytihng because he had a perfect insight into the laws of reason. No wonder the mathematical scientist appeared as a sort of little god, whose teaching had to be accepted as exempt from doubt. All the dangers of theology, its dogmatism and its control of thought through the guarantee of certainty, reappear in a philosophy that regards science as infallible (Reichenbach 1959:43–44).

Only if science were infallible and contained the answers to every important question, would it be possible to construct a world view based upon a perfect understanding of the nature of things. World view must go beyond the ordinary to provide answers to questions that have no answer. It must do this because it must succeed in convincing the membership of the cultural system that what they are called upon to do is worth doing. Where a cultural system exists, it exists, in part, because the membership retains its allegiance to a particular world view consisting of explanations and understandings which reach beyond science and above truth.

The members of any cultural system regard their own particular view of the world as more accurate, useful, beautiful, or in some way better, or better for them, than any other world view. If they did not, they would change their views. Our own particular view of the world leads to questions about the effectiveness of other views. Is the Eskimo world view more or less consistent, more or less realistic, or more or less effective in its functioning than the Saora world view? Is it better to view the things in nature as something to be used up and consumed or as something to be cared for and preserved? Is it more useful to think of human beings as high class apes or as supernatural beings? Would it be better for the species as a whole if all the human beings in all the cultural systems shared the same world view or would it be better if they all had different world views?

It is easy to grade world views, cultural traditions, or cultural systems along various dimensions, but it is difficult to establish the value of any particular system of grading. Even if the rating of world views did not involve important moral and philosophical questions, most cultural anthropologists would feel that two other sorts of questions would have to be answered first: "How may we investigate and describe world view?" and "How may we explain the similarities and differences among different world views?"

Because it is impossible to answer any questions about world view without achieving descriptions of world view that are accurate and comparable, a major thrust of current anthropological research deals with the problem of description.

Description: where is the pattern?

In the beginning God created the heaven and the earth. And the earth was without form, and void; and darkness *was* upon the face of the deep. And

the Spirit of God moved upon the face of the waters. And God said, Let there be light: and there was light. And God saw the light, and it *was* good: and God divided the light from the darkness. And God called the light Day, and the darkness he called Night. And the evening and the morning were the first day.

And God said, Let there be a firmament in the midst of the waters, and let it divide the waters from the waters. And God made the firmament, and divided the waters which *were* under the firmament from the waters which *were* above the firmament: and it was so. And God called the firmament Heaven. And the evening and the morning were the second day.

And God said, Let the waters under the heaven be gathered together unto one place, and let the dry *land* appear: and it was so. And God said, Let the earth bring forth grass, the herb yielding seed, *and* the fruit tree yielding fruit after his kind, whose seed *is* in itself, upon the earth: and it was so. And the earth brought forth grass, *and* herb yielding seed after his kind, and the tree yielding fruit, whose seed *was* in itself, after his kind: and God saw that *it was* good.

The above statement is a myth, an authoritative or trusted explanation of things. It is accepted by a variety of cultural systems sharing access to the *Old Testament*. If we could simplify some aspect of this statement and reduce it to order or identify some part of the pattern in it, it would provide a starting point for an understanding of the world view of these cultural systems.

One way of beginning an analysis is to regard the statement as a kind of classification or taxonomy. The statement is among other things a list of certain things that exist in the world. Within the list things are arranged in a particular order. Some things precede other things in a temporal way and some things are on top of or within other things. An analysis of the statement might then lead to a diagram of the following sort:

WATERS				
WATERS ABOVE	FIRMAMENT (HEAVEN)	WATERS BELOW		
		SEA	LAND	
			GRASS	HERB	FRUIT TREE

To persons steeped in the particular world view of which this genesis story forms a part, most of the distinctions made seem perfectly logical and natural. Surely it is only human nature to distinguish heaven from earth, land from water, fruit from seed, and so on. But consider an aspect of Tikopian classification and Tikopian human nature.

Can You See Things as They Are?

It is hard for anyone who has not actually lived on the island to realize its isolation from the rest of the world. It is so small that one is rarely out of sight or sound of the sea. The native concept of space bears a distinct relation to this. They find it almost impossible to conceive of any really large land mass. I was once asked seriously by a group of them, "Friend, is there any land where the sound of the sea is not heard?" Their confinement has another less obvious result. For all kinds of spatial references they use the expressions *inland* and to *seawards*. Thus an axe lying on the floor of a house is localized in this way, and I have even heard a man direct the attention of another in saying: "There is a spot of mud on your seaward cheek" (Firth 1963:19).

On Tikopia, an island in the Pacific, the world view contains, as we might assume that all world views must, a way of expressing the spatial relationship among things, but the Tikopians approach the problem of defining location in a fairly unique way. It may be natural and human to have a system of coordinates for locating things in space, but there is evidently nothing in nature that says that all human beings must use the same set of coordinates. World views often differ in terms of the most basic and fundamental ways of classifying things:

To dispose things spatially there must be a possibility of placing them differently, of putting some at the right, others at the left, these above, those below, at the north of or at the south of, east or west of, etc., etc., just as to dispose states of consciousness temporally there must be a possibility of localizing them at determined dates. That is to say that space could not be what it is if it were not, like time, divided and differentiated. But whence come these divisions which are so essential. By themselves, there are neither right nor left, up nor down, north nor south, etc. All these distinctions evidently come from the fact that different sympathetic values have been attributed to various regions. Since all the men of a single civilization represent space in the same way, it is clearly necessary that these sympathetic values, and the distinctions which depend upon them should be equally universal, and that almost necessarily implies that they be of social origin (Durkheim 1961:23–24).

Durkheim's argument is that the basis of human thought and perception derives from the arbitrary or "made-up" nature of the principles, coordinates, or relations that are used to divide up the space-time continuum. If, as Durkheim suggests, fundamental categories are simply invented by the members of cultural systems and passed along as a part of the cultural tradition, it becomes impossible to perceive reality except as one's perceptions of reality are conditioned by culture. Because the scientific method itself depends fundamentally upon the idea of intersubjectivity; namely, that different observers will perceive the same experience in the same way, Durkheim's suggestion places an obstacle in the way of all general scientific theories about the nature of things. Modern physical theories, involving such violations of common sense as *N-dimensional space* or *relativity*, illustrate both the strength of such obstacles and the possibility of overcoming them.

Although it is easy to understand that concepts like "landward" and "seaward" are arbitrary categories made up by members of a group, many anthropologists suspect that there might be fundamental categories that arise from common human experience or the biological similarity of human beings. Psychoanalytic theories sometimes argue that the early experiences and the development of the human infant lead to the development of universal symbols and ways of perceiving. It might be argued, for example, that because the human infant's first experiences have to do with ingestion, defecation, and urination, all later experiences are likely to be classified in oral, anal, and genital terms (Erikson 1950). Biologically oriented theorists might argue that such things as the structure of the human eye place fundamental limitations upon the human capacity to divide up the space-time continuum. Because none of these possibilities have gained general acceptance, the safest guess would seem to be that there are universal categories of thought but that we cannot speak of them with precision because they lie hidden in a thicket of arbitrary or culturally derived categories of thought.

In linguistics, the relatively small number of distinctive speech sounds made by people speaking different languages suggests that biological factors having to do with the nature of the speech organs place powerful limitations upon the kinds of noises that can be made.

That some peoples produce highly distinctive speech sounds and that every language has its own particular set of speech sounds suggests the power of arbitrary or cultural categorizations in overriding or distorting biological limitations. An examination of the numeral systems of various peoples appears to indicate that counting is almost universally associated with the number of fingers and toes that people possess. The decimal system is based upon a unit of ten fingers, other systems are based upon five fingers or the sum of the fingers and toes. There are peoples who count the spaces between the fingers and toes instead of counting the fingers and toes, and they end up with systems that run: 1, 2, 3, one hand, one hand plus 1, one hand plus 2, one hand plus 3, two hands, two hands plus one, and so on. The early experience of having ten fingers and ten toes creates a predisposition to divide up the world not in some particular way, but in a limited variety of particular ways. There appear to be no methods of counting based upon 3, 6, 7, or 9, and the binary system (one, one hand, one hand plus one, one hand plus one hand) appears to be a recent invention. The creation of a numeral system to the base three poses no problem

(1, 2, trio, 1 trio 1, 1 trio 2, 2 trio, 2 trio 1, 2 trio 2, and so on), and is, therefore, natural enough even though uncommon in nature.

To the extent that human beings see things as they are taught to see them, speak as they are taught to speak, and count as they are taught to count, human beings are dreamers living in dreamworlds of their own, or rather of their ancestors' construction. Is it possible for a man immersed in the dreamworld of his culture to enter the dreamworld of another culture? If so, we must assume some common basis underlying all human world views. The most common assumption is that all world views represent a division of the space-time continuum into subjects or items and relationships between them. In other words, there must be things related to each other in terms of specific principles of classification such as sex, number, location, developmental state, origin, or temporal order. How may we discover what the principles of classification are?

What are your principles?

The following table by Hjelmslev, quoted by Sidney Lamb (1964:68), represents a way of classifying animals. The manner in which the items in the table are related serves to indicate their meaning.

ANIMAL	ADULT		INFANT
	Male	*Female*	
sheep	ram	ewe	lamb
horse	stallion	mare	colt
chicken	rooster	hen	chick

The fact that sheep, horses, and chickens may all be placed in the same table suggests that they are in some way things of a kind. Thus, within something which might be called the domain of animals, there is a type of animal whose subdomain is divided in terms of the principles given in the table. What are the principles of classification? There is a distinction between infant and adult animals and between male and female adults. These distinctions could be labeled principles of sex and maturation. In the culture represented by the table, one way of dividing the space-time continuum is in terms of principles of maturation and sex. Further study would be needed to determine how widely these principles are applied. Is everything in the world classified in terms of sex and maturity; if not, what kinds of things are so classified? Because all animals of the sheep, horse, and chicken kind are classified in terms of maturity, but only mature animals in terms of sex, it might be guessed that in this culture developmental state is more important than sex.

Here is another list (Lamb 1964:68):

SIZE	BIG	LITTLE
length	long	short
width	wide	narrow
depth	deep	shallow

In this table, the space-time continuum is divided into things that have size, and presumably things that do not, and the domain of size is divided into big and little things. The implications for the perception of things and behavior toward things are striking. If this were the only way of dealing with the domain of size, it would be impossible to describe a box of average size. The anthropologist brought up as a speaker of English and having a tendency to think of the animal domain or the size domain in these particular ways would have difficulty navigating in a cultural world that used different principles of classification or even the same principles in different ways or with different emphases. One of the goals of modern anthropology has been to find ways of eliciting or discovering principles of classification different from those of English.

What Is It That There Is?

Q: In the world, what what is there?
A: Houses, trees, water, huge factories, ordinary factories, bus stops, railroad stops, airplane companies, and hills, working people, cattle, birds, and snakes.
Q: In houses, what what is there?
A: Roof tiles, beams, men, radios, pictures, cooking utensils, cows, and rats.
Q: In roof tiles, what what is there?
A: Flat tiles from Bangalore, flat tiles from Chikkbalapur, ordinary tiles, and VJI tiles.
Q: In beams, what what is there?
A: Main beams, supporting beams, and rafters.
Q: In men, what what is there?
A: (Gives names of household heads in his family)
Q: In radios, what what is there?
A: Radio, pocket radio, and hand radio.

The interview method used here involves the use of a linguistic frame. A single question, "In the _____, what what is there?" is asked repeatedly making use of words supplied by the informant. The object of linguistic frame interviewing is to obtain as much information as possible from the person being interviewed while minimizing the bias that might be introduced by a series of perhaps unrelated questions asked by the interviewer. After the first question, in effect, the person interviewed supplies all future questions.

The example given above leads to a taxonomy, to a classification of the things that exist in the world:

WORLD																	
HOUSES													TREES	BEAMS	HUGE FACTORIES	ORDINARY FACTORIES	ETC.
ROOF TILES				BEAMS			MEN	RADIOS			PICTURES	ETC. COOKING UTENSILS, COWS, RATS					
BANGALORE TILES	CHIKKABALLAPUR TILES	ORDINARY TILES	VJI TILES	MAIN BEAMS	SUPPORTING BEAMS	RAFTERS	HOUSEHOLD HEADS FROM 1 TO n	ORDINARY RADIO	POCKET RADIO	HAND RADIO							

What kinds of questions can we ask about such a taxonomy? Presumably, it tells us something about the processes of human memory. How many items can there be in a list? How finely detailed can a classification be? It also tells us something about the person being interviewed. What are his interests? What are his areas of knowledge? How typical are his responses compared to those of other members of his group? Finally, such a classification, when compared with classifications given by other members of the group tells us something about the culture. What aspects of the environment are considered important? What principles are used in classifying? Is there any pattern in their scheme of classification? How closely does their scheme of classification resemble a similar set of responses, perhaps given by a college student in another culture? Finally, how do people generate such lists and classifications? Is there method in their madness?

In the example, everything listed exists in nature. From the scientific standpoint, the view of the environment is perfectly accurate, but it is difficult to imagine anyone but an urban-influenced South Indian interpreting a house as containing roof tiles, beams, radios, pictures, cooking utensils, cows, and rats. That persons in different cultural systems propose different world views does not mean that they are out of step with reality, it may only mean that they classify and interpret the world around them in different but equally valid ways.

In anthropology, the term *ethnoscience* has come to refer to highly systematic and formal studies of the systems of labeling and classification which the members of different cultural systems apply to the things they believe to exist. A history of the development of the ethnoscience approach is given in Sturtevant (1964) and formal methodologies are discussed by Frake (1964) and by Metzger and Williams (1963). Although ethnoscience has sometimes been treated as if it were a "new ethnography" with the implication that older forms of ethnography are therefore obsolete, it is in fact a useful and efficient way of gaining access to at least some of the content of the cultural message. Several writers, perhaps infatuated with the success of new methodologies in understanding cultural messages, have given the impression that an adequate cultural anthropology would dedicate itself solely to the study of cultural traditions. The position taken in this book is that full understanding of the similarities and differences among cultural systems is to be attained only through an understanding of the complex and systematic relationships among cultural traditions, environment, and actual behavior.

Ethnoscience is, in fact, a part of a new ethnography which has arisen as cultural anthropologists of all persuasions have brought increasingly systematic methodologies into the study of all aspects of cultural systems. The wholesale borrowing of methodological approaches from psychology, linguistics, statistics, mathematics, and computer science has not so much rendered the "old ethnography" obsolete as it has enhanced it by providing access to more accurate and systematic information about cultural systems. The new methods, perhaps most particularly the use of linguistic frames, lead specifically to questions about human behavior. One of the most important of these questions, considered in the following sections, has to do with the relationship between individual behavior and the cultural message. Specifically, how do individual members of a cultural system generate behaviors their fellows consider to be appropriate?

Where Do You Get Your Ideas?

In his responses to the linguistic frame, "In the _____, what what is there?" the young South Indian generates a classification which reflects the cultural tradition of his particular village. Within the framework provided by his culture, his responses are unique. No other human individual would provide precisely the same responses to that particular linguistic frame. A key question in anthropology is, "How is it possible to be a unique and creative individual and at the same time to exhibit the behavior characteristic of a particular cultural system?" One possible answer to this question, proposed in connection with language by Noam Chomsky (1966), is that cultural tradition exists in the form of rules, analogous to the rules of grammar, that permit the generation of uniquely individual behavior which nevertheless is accepted as culturally appropriate.

In South Indian culture, for example, two of the rules used in generating classifications seem to be: (1) that the environment is divided into a series of places; and (2) that each place contains characteristic things, plants, animals, people, and supernatural figures. Although not every place contains things in all of these categories, it seems likely that people respond to a question like, "In houses, what what is there?" by listing some of the things—plants, animals, and so on—that they remember as being characteristic of houses. The order of listing and the number of things in each category reflect the individual's personal interests and experience, but the particular things that can be in a house and the general method of classification reflect the cultural tradition.

What Kinds of Nails Are There?

Table 1 offers a taxonomy or classification of the kinds of nails that exist. The obvious function of such a classification is that of permitting communication among the members of a cultural system. To order a nail of a particular kind over the telephone, it would be necessary to have a grasp of this classification. In order to communicate, the individual must be capable of exhibiting behaviors other people can interpret accurately. To start a fight with another person, it is necessary to exhibit an angry frown, a threatening gesture, or some other indication of opposition. Human beings live in a forest of symbols and classifications, and, if they are to do the right thing at the right time, they must know how to generate correct behaviors and interpret the behaviors generated by others.

Lacking access to the system of classification and meaning, the member of a cultural system finds himself unable to function or compelled to seek the assistance of someone who does understand the system. Most people cannot order nails over the telephone, they must take the nail to a hardware store and ask a specialist to classify it for them. If so simple a thing as a classification of nails is too difficult for an ordinary person to learn, we are left with the puzzling question: "How do people manage to exhibit meaningful behavior most of the time?" In other words, how can the human individual have filed away in his head and instantly accessible all of the things he needs to know in order to function as a member of his cultural system? When the anthropologist asks, "How many kinds of trees are there?" how is it possible for the individual, acting virtually without hesitation, to generate an appropriate list of trees? How is it possible for a student during an examination to respond to a question with an answer that is interpreted by the instructor as correct, but is at the same time so unique and individualistic that the instructor is convinced that the student obtained the answer from his own head?

The conclusion is almost inescapable that when a human being performs such routines as classifying trees, buying nails, starting a fight, plowing a field, making a date, or passing through a doorway, his behavior depends in part upon habit or memorized sequences of behavior, but it depends perhaps even more upon the presence somewhere inside his body of a mechanism which permits him to generate behavior that is at once uniquely individual and culturally appropriate. For example, people do not remember all of the numbers in their numeral systems, rather the numbers

TABLE 1   *Nails advertised by Smith Nails and Fasteners*
(what dimensions are involved in the classfication?)

	COMMON NAILS		BOX NAILS	FINISHING NAIL BRAD HEAD	
	Length (in inches)	Gauge	Gauge (length is same)	Gauge	
60d	6	2	(not listed)	00	(not listed)
50d	5.5	3	(not listed)	00	(not listed)
40d	5	4	8 ("nonstock")	00	(not listed)
30d	4.5	5	9 ("nonstock")	00	(not listed)
20d	4	6	9	10	("nonstock")
16d	3.5	8	10	11	("nonstock")
12d	3.25	9	10.5 ("nonstock")	11.5	("nonstock")
10d	3.00	9	10.5	11.5	
9d	2.75	10.25	11.5 ("nonstock")	12.5	("nonstock")
8d	2.50	10.25	11.5	12.5	
7d	2.25	11.5	12.5	13	("nonstock")
6d	2.00	11.5	12.5	13	
5d	1.75	12.5	14.00	15	("nonstock")
4d	1.5	12.5	14.00	15	
3d	1.25	14	14.5	15.5	
2d	1.00	15	15.5 ("nonstock")	16.5	("nonstock")

Casing nails, countersunk head, are the "same length and guage specification as Box Nail."

Additional Information

1. "All types of nails available with ring or screw shank for greatly increased holding power."
2. "Galvanized finish provides mamixum rust resistance and may be specified in any Keystone nails."
3. "Cement coated—an adhesive resin coating that increases holding power may be specified on any type of nail."
4. "Other popular Keystone nails" include:
   a. concrete—"oil quench hardened, plain or screw shank"
   b. flooring—"nonslit blunt point."
   c. lath—"sterilized blued."
   d. plasterboard—"blued, flat head."
   e. pole barn—"stiff stock ringshank."
   f. roofing—"large head polished or galvanized."
   g. scaffold—"double head."
   h. spikes—"up to 12″ in length."

are supplied by applying a succession of rules to a small number of basic terms. Presumably these rules themselves are not independent of other rules and might themselves be generated by some set of even more basic rules. These considerations lead to two kinds of questions: first, what is the nature of the rules or, if you like, the grammar underlying a particular classification or a particular type of behavior, and second, what are the basic and general rules underlying a particular cultural tradition? Consider how the first of these questions applies to the making of beer.

What Makes Good Beer?
One of the important items in the culture of the Subanun of the Philippines is beer. The making of beer requires yeast cakes, and yeast cakes require the mixing of spices, rice, water, and old yeast. The quality of Subanun beer is believed (by the Subanun) to depend upon the particular spices that are added to the yeast cakes. Using linguistic frames to determine what sorts of things could be added to spices, Charles Frake (1964:139–140) received the answers "young leaves," "underground parts," "fruits," and "stems." Such expressions as "young leaves" do not mean the same in English that they do in Subanun, but with practice and further interviewing and observation, the ethnographer can learn, or come to think that he has learned, to make the same distinctions that the Subanun make.

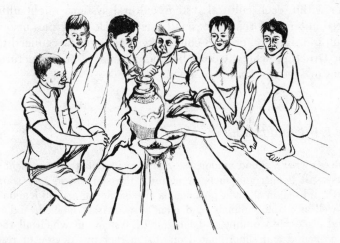

Continuing with the use of linguistic frame questions, Frake arrived at the following rules governing the making of spices: Select plant parts which include: (1) the "fruits" of "chili"; (2) the "stem" pieces of "sugar cane"; (3) "young leaves of selected trees"; and (4) the "underground parts" of selected "herbs" including "ginger" and "rice" if available. These reflect only a small proportion of the rules that must be followed if good beer is to be made, but they are sufficient to indicate the general properties of the grammatical rules that impose cultural limitations upon behavior. The first two rules give little scope for individual behavior; the second two rules provide a wide range of options. All Subanun beer spice is the same in that it is likely to contain chili and sugar cane, yet each individual recipe is different in that it is likely to contain different young leaves and underground parts. In the same way, a correct response to an examination question must involve both the correct information and an individual or personal style. There are many ways of making good beer, but you can't make good beer in just any way.

When the ethnographer, using systematic interview techniques or carrying out careful observations, arrives at a list of items and a set of rules he believes can be used to generate correct behavior with reference to the items, he may test his selection of items and set of rules by attempting to generate correct behavior. The test of a set of rules for beer making would lie in the ability to make good beer by using those rules. Having formulated a set of rules that work, it is tempting to assume that those are the rules that people actually use, but that too is a question for investigation.

There is nothing earthshaking about knowing how to classify nails or make good Subanun beer. The importance of the study of such trivial matters is that the reduction of a complicated variety of behavior to a set of comparatively simple items and rules increases the possibility of making comparisons both within and between cultures. Because it must be assumed that there are certain fundamental rules governing the generation of proper behavior within each cultural system, cultural systems might ultimately be compared in terms of relatively small lists of basic principles or orientations. Each cultural tradition or each cultural system might be reduced to a simple form or structure which would be comparable to the structure of other traditions or systems. Can it be done?

Where is the magic key?

> Indeed, what we find among the Zuñi is a veritable arrangement of the universe. All beings and facts in nature, "the sun, moon and stars, the sky, earth and sea, in all their phenomena and elements; and all inanimate objects, as well as plants, animals, and men," are classed, labeled, and assigned to fixed places in a unique and integrated "system" in which all the parts are co-ordinated and subordinated one to another by "degree of resemblance."
>
> In the form in which we now find it, the principle of this system is a division of space into seven regions: north, south, west, east, zenith, nadir, and the centre. Everything in the universe is assigned to one or another of these seven regions (Durkheim and Mauss 1963:43).

In writing about systems of classification in 1903, Durkheim and Mauss sought to reduce systems of world view to a simple scheme in which all aspects of culture could be shown to be simple reflexes of a single over all classificatory scheme. They sought a kind of magic key which would not only unlock the secrets of Zuni culture but permit the systematic comparison of Zuni culture with that of the Australian aborigines, other American Indian cultures, and ultimately the cultures of China and Europe.

Writing somewhat later, Ruth Benedict attempted to approach the question of fundamental cultural structure in more psychoanalytic terms. Benedict saw the great range of possible personality types as being in some way fundamentally divided between Dionysian and Apollonian emphases. The Dionysian pursues the values of existence through escape into extraordinary and even frenzied experience, while the Apollonian avoids excess and seeks moderation and temperance. The materials of culture were then seen as deriving from differing emphases upon different personality types.

Psychoanalytic theorists like Benedict, Kardiner, and Erikson have sought to explain culture as a kind of secondary expression of individual personalities. By contrast, Durkheim and Mauss, and the more recently celebrated Lévi-Strauss, have sought to explain culture in terms of systems of classification which they tend to see as originating or finding their basic expression in terms of the categories of kinship. These different searchers for the magic key have attempted to grasp the fundamental structure of culture by means of dramatic intuitive leaps. They have tried to grasp the essence of culture, not by the slow accumulation of data, but by means of a sudden and, very generally inexplicable, understanding of the whole. Both sets of theorists place the handles of their magic keys in very nearly the same place. The psychoanalytic theorists tend to emphasize early childhood experience, while the classification-oriented theorists tend to place their emphasis upon classifications of kinsmen, which must surely be among the first classifications learned by the growing child. If there is a magic key to culture, it is certainly to be found among the cultural materials made available to the new member of the cultural system.

In a different frame of mind, Bronislaw Malinowski (1961) sought to arrive at a "clear outline of the framework of the natives' culture in the widest sense of the word" by the method of "statistic documentation by concrete evidence" (p. 17). Ultimately the bits of concrete evidence were to be gathered and arranged in a basic master chart expressing the fundamental structure of the culture. Because the Trobriand culture studied by Malinowski, like all cultures, is exceedingly complicated, Malinowski never arrived at a clear outline of a cultural framework. Franz Boas, the "father of American anthropology," believed that any search for a magic key or basic framework was premature. Thus most American and British anthropologists, following Malinowski and Boas, have either postponed the search for fundamental unities of culture or attempted to develop a groundwork for such a search through the refinement of methodological approaches. In recent years, the search for a magic key has been guided by the thought that once sufficiently rigorous and formal descriptions of culture are available, the search for uniformities among the rules and classifications characteristic of particular cultures might take advantage of the modern computer's prodigious capacity for the storage and manipulation of data. For the present, the possibility of simplifying and reducing to order the vast and complex content of cultural traditions is supported only by the fact that it is hard to see how cultural traditions could exist in any other form.

Summary

A cultural tradition must be sufficiently convincing so that people believe it and follow it, and it must be sufficiently effective, in a practical sense, to permit survival. Because cultural messages are complicated and sometimes inconsistent or contradictory, human behavior involves conformity to cultural traditions in some areas of life and almost unlimited freedom in other areas of life. Because a particular bit of information is either part of the cultural message or not and because a given behavior is either proper or not in terms of tradition, the study of cultural traditions may have the characteristics of an idealized exact science. When individuals fail to exhibit correct behavior or disagree concerning the content of cultural messages, anthropology ceases to be an exact science and becomes as inexact and probabilistic as any other.

World view is a general explanation of the nature of things which answers unanswerable questions and explains why it is right to do the right thing. For example, the Saora world view contains answers to many of the great questions of life. In explaining why it is right to carry out particular activities, the Saora world view serves the *function* of encouraging the membership to perpetuate behaviors that appear to contribute to Saora adaptation. Although to an outside observer the Saora world view might appear to convey false information or to encourage maladaptive behaviors, it is impossible to discount the possibility that such things as animal sacrifice or a belief in ancestral spirits are in fact vital to Saora survival in a confusing and multifaceted environment.

By contrast, the Eskimo world view appears in many ways to be more realistic and practical than that of the Saora. In fact, these two world views have different functions to perform and different environments within which to perform them. Differences in the psychological attractiveness of different kinds of world view, differences between environments, and differences in patterns of ecological relationships between cultural systems and environment make it virtually impossible to reach firm conclusions concerning the "truth" or adaptive value of different kinds of world view. Although it sometimes appears that scientific investigations might provide a means for the evaluation of systems of world view, the most vital portions of any system of world view have to do with fundamental philosophical and theological questions which cannot be resolved by the methods of science. Science cannot tell us the meaning of life; we must figure it out for ourselves.

Anthropological descriptions of world view may be stated in general terms along the lines of the description of Saora and Eskimo world view, but they may also, following the various approaches used by students of ethnoscience, center upon the problem of exposing the principles of classification used to organize the various things in the world. Such principles of classification may, like the Tikopian concepts of landward and seaward, represent artificial or arbitrary conventions, or they may in some sense derive from psychological or biological characteristics of the human species. Limitations upon the kind and number of speech sounds characteristic of human languages and the limited number of possible numeral systems actually encountered in real life suggest the powerful influence of universal human characteristics upon human behavior, but they also indicate how easily such universals may be overridden and how difficult it is to be sure what they are.

One common interpretation of all systems of world view is that they may be analyzed in terms of items and relationships. The differences among sheep, horses, and chickens illustrate how the various items within the domain of animals may be classified in terms of maturation and sex. Similarly the domain of size can be divided in terms of bigness and littleness. The domain of cultural anthropology that deals with these problems is called ethnoscience, and an illustration from South India shows how linguistic frames can be used in the discovery of taxonomies.

Although the individual members of a cultural system share the same cultural message and classify the things around them more or less in the same way, individuals tend to behave in markedly different ways. Variation in the behavior of individuals sharing the same cultural tradition seems to be accounted for by the existence of grammars or sets of rules which permit them to generate behavior that is at once uniquely individual and culturally appropriate. The example of Subanun beer making illustrates some of the ways in which a person who follows the rules of beer making may nevertheless make a uniquely individual beer. One of the tests of our understanding of Subanun beer making or of any other aspect of a cultural tradition is to see if we can develop a grammar or a set of rules which will permit us to make beer or do something else in a manner that is both creative and acceptable.

The possibility of discovering basic mechanisms which permit the generation of culturally appropriate behavior within limited spheres leads to the even more fascinating possibility of discovering magic keys or basic structures representing underlying uniformities in cultural systems. Whereas Durkheim and Mauss and Lévi-Strauss sought such uniformities in terms of classifications of kinsmen, psychoanalytic theorists sought them in early childhood experiences. Both kinds of theorists attempted to grasp such fundamental unities by means of dramatic intuitive leaps. Malinowski and Boas, in contrast, appear to have believed that such fundamental unities, if they existed, could be reached only through the careful assembling of detailed evidence. Today, the rigorous methodologies characteristic of the new ethnography combined with the use of computers offer new approaches to the discoverey of such "magic keys."

Further readings

Materials relevant to world view and to basic perceptions of nature are often classified under the headings of "religion" or "science." Lessa and

Vogt's *Reader in Comparative Religion* (1965) offers important articles dealing with belief systems and religious practices. Special publications of the *American Anthropologist*, such as *Transcultural Studies in Cognition* (Romney and D'andrade, eds. 1964), *The Ethnography of Communication* (Gumperz and Hymes 1964) and *Formal Semantic Analysis* (Hammel, ed. 1965), contain discussions of ethnoscience and of other new approaches to the understanding of cultural traditions. Recent and important is *Cognitive Anthropology* (Tyler 1969).

Case Studies emphasizing various aspects of world view include Kearney's *The Winds of Ixtepeji* (1972), Dentan's *The Semai* (1968), Beals' *Gopalpur* (1962), and the Spindlers' *Dreamers without Power* (1971).

Problems and questions

1. Examine an ethnographic account of another culture. List some important aspects of that culture's world view and consider some possible ways in which the world view might contribute to success in coping with the particular problems faced by people in that culture.
2. After observing some simple process, such as exchanging greetings, passing through doorways, buying beer, or eating breakfast, list some of the rules that seem to govern "proper" behavior.
3. Through interviews or by examining some novels or television plays, derive some suggestions concerning an aspect of world view in the United States. For example, what are believed to be the major differences between men and women?
4. Using linguistic frames such as "What kinds of plants are there?" or "What kinds of students are there?" construct a diagram that would explain some of the principles involved in the classification.
5. After observing and interviewing a group of people to determine what they do and what they say they do in some particular situation, discuss the influence of their traditions upon their behavior.

6

The human domain

As members participate in the operation of a cultural system, they communicate to each other a body of knowledge and experience which becomes a cultural tradition. The cultural tradition offers a world view: a set of understandings about what the world is like and of the purpose of human life. In the form of language, the cultural tradition provides communication through which the members of a cultural system acquire "knowledge" of the kinds of things, events, and situations that exist in the world. From the cultural tradition, the members receive the message: "These are the things and situations you are likely to encounter, and these are the things you should do about them."

The preceding chapter stressed the importance of the cultural tradition as a means of organizing and directing the operation of a cultural system within its environment. In order to carry out those processes, such as hunting, planting crops, taking shelter, or preventing disease, which facilitate adaptation to the environment, the members of the cultural system must be identified and each member must contribute in an appropriate manner. Besides giving information about "what is out there," the cultural tradition must provide information concerning who the members are and what they are supposed to be doing. The cultural tradition, then, provides a taxonomy or classification of the membership and a set of instructions concerning the duties and behaviors appropriate to each member. This chapter deals with the problems of naming, classifying, and explaining people.

What kinds of people are there?

A woman of the Makah Tribe (Indians of the northwest coast of the United States) describes a portion of her social world as follows:

> They just had to get married to the same kind of class they belonged. For one reason, them chiefs wanted to marry the same class of people as they were themselves. So when they got children, they didn't want their children —well, like if I got mad at you and said, "You're low class, part slave!" you'd be hurt. So they wanted to get married same class generation after generation so all the children were the same class. So if I married a low-class person, then well my niece could call my son a low-class boy. That's what my father used to tell me. That's how I found out. That's why they used to marry the upper class, so all the time they would stay the upper class; the middle class, the middle class; the slaves, the slaves. Only crazy ones didn't obey orders. Even to my day they used to say that, "Slaves!" Now (turning to her niece), I know that your family was chiefs, and I tell you this. They didn't want no slaves for their children! They didn't want anybody to be able to say that to them (Colson 1953:206).

When Elizabeth Colson tried to find out if the Makah continued to maintain class distinctions, she discovered that "the line-up of important men of earlier days changed, a man would shift from slave to commoner to chief with the particular informant questioned" (p. 207).

In this example, the cultural tradition suggests that there are three major kinds of Makah and it gives some indication of the kinds of relationships supposed to exist among them. The relationship of marriage was supposed to occur only within each type and the types were related to each other hierarchically with the chiefs being high and the slaves low. Evidently, orders and instructions flowed down this hierarchy from chiefs to middle class to slaves, while obedience was extended upwards.

We could regard the Makah situation as a case of *cultural lag* in which, possibly under the liberating influence of democracy, every man has become a chief while the cultural tradition continues to refer to a previous situation in which some men were commoners or slaves. We could also argue that the cultural tradition in this case represents *ideal culture*, rather than *real culture.* Perhaps the three-class system represents an ideal pattern, a plan or program, which no one ever paid any attention to. It might well be that no Makah ever willingly admitted to being a slave or a commoner.

Why, then, should there be a discrepancy between the ideal described in the cultural tradition and the behavior actually exhibited by the members? One way of answering this question is to consider the effect of the classification upon the behavior of the members—everybody tries to exhibit chiefly behavior and to avoid slavelike behavior. The function of the official class system might be to promote a struggle for status in which each person attempts to acquire the attributes and behaviors of a chief. Among the Makah this struggle was often acted out in elaborate ceremonies or *pot-latches* in which men advanced their claims to chiefly status by providing lavish gifts and entertainments to their competitors. When Indian agents, horrified by these acts of conspicuous consumption, forbade such costly displays, the Makah reverted to elaborate birthday and Christmas parties. It is not, after all, conspicuous consumption itself that is bad, but the other fellow's conspicuous consumption.

Although members of cultural systems, as in driving on the right-hand side of the street, often obey the dictates of their cultural traditions with diligence or even slavishness, the case of the Makah illustrates that it is unwise to assume the literal existence of all of the kinds of people ("abominable snowmen?") described in the tradition or to believe that all of the rules and regulations ("Thou shalt not kill.") are literally and slavishly followed. A cultural tradition is a long and complicated message. Some parts of the message are poorly and vaguely worded; some parts, like "Catch 22," are well-guarded secrets; some parts have nothing to do with past or present reality; and some parts mean things quite different from what they seem to mean. Thus, the "real" meaning of "Thou shalt not kill," is "Thou shalt not kill without legal sanction."

That part of the cultural message that deals with the kinds of people in the world and what to do about them provides information about a *social structure*. A social structure consists of a set of defined positions or *statuses*, each occupied by an individual or a group (*subcultural system*). The cultural tradition provides *labels* or names for some, but not necessarily all, of these statuses such as "chief" or "slave." It indicates the arrangement of these statuses or the *relations* between them (chief is higher than slave or above slave), and it defines the *roles* each is to perform (chief supervises, slave does manual labor). Bearing in mind the differences among labels, statuses, and roles, consider the following set of puzzling events reported by the Tikopians of the South Pacific:

> . . . a lad went down to surf at Namo, leaving his *maro*, his waistcloth, near a canoe house. When he returned from the beach it had disappeared. Peering around he located it in the possession of a woman at the back of the shed. He called out to her:
> "Bring me, mother, my *maro*."

"Come and take it away," she replied.
"Bring me, grandmother, my *maro*."
"Come and take it away."
"Bring me, aunt (unmarried mother), my *maro*."
"Come and take it away."
"Bring me, sister, my *maro*."
"Come and take it away."
"Bring me, friend, my *maro*."
"Now that's it then!" (Firth 1963: 182)

Here, the young man, whom we shall call Ego, has been placed in an awkward predicament by a young woman whose status is unknown to Ego. Because the young woman has already adopted the role of a person qualified to view Ego's nude body, Ego attempts to resolve his predicament by assigning an appropriate status to the young woman. He begins by reciting a series of labels, "mother," "sister," and so on, which apparently apply to close relatives who can look upon Ego's naked body without sexual risk. When the young woman refuses to accept the status assignments implied by the labels, Ego has no recourse but to label her "friend." Although we may assume that a Tikopian person having the label "girl friend" may sometimes look upon the naked body of her "boy friend," our own cultural experience may lead us to believe that there is something not quite legitimate about the equation of the status, "friend," and the role of *maro* bringer. Ego resolves this last problem by seizing his "friend" firmly by the wrist and taking her to his house where they are married. She now has the label and status of "wife" and may legitimately play the *maro* fetching role for many happy years to come.

Kinship: what do you call your mother's child?

The anthropologist, seeking to understand the system of names and labels that the members of a cultural system apply to each other, often begins with questions of the following kind:

Q: What do you call the woman who gave birth to you?
A: Janet.
Q: I see. That's her name. Isn't there some more general way of referring to her?
A: Do you mean, "mother"?
Q: Would "mother" refer to any woman who gave birth to children?
A: Yes.
Q: What does Janet call you?
A: She calls me "son."
Q: Is there anyone else you call "mother?"
A: Yes. My wife's mother.
Q: What's a "wife"?

In this series of questions, a rather naive anthropologist is trying to discover the different terms that Ego, his informant, uses for his kinsmen. The anthropologist's goal is to obtain a list of *primary* kinterms including "mother," "father," "son," "daughter," "brother," "sister," "husband," and "wife." Once he has such a list of primary kinterms, he can begin to develop a genealogy by combining the primary terms:

Q: What is the name of your father's father's father?
A: I don't know.
Q: What about the name of your father's father?
A: Horace.
Q: What was his wife's name?
A: Charity.
Q: Did he have any brothers or sisters?
A: Yes, I think he had an older brother.

Once Ego's genealogy has been collected, it can be arranged in the form of a genealogical diagram (Figure 1). In the diagram, circles represent females and triangles represent males. Marriages are indicated by an "equals" sign and descent is indicated by the vertical and horizontal lines. Essentially, the genealogical diagram illustrates the network of persons who are connected to Ego through the relationships of marriage and descent. Relative age of a set of siblings (brothers and sisters) can also be indicated by placing the oldest sibling at the right. Other material such as age, date of birth, or birthplace can be written directly under the circle or triangle representing each individual. The death of an individual can be indicated by drawing a slanting line through his circle or triangle or by writing in his date of death.

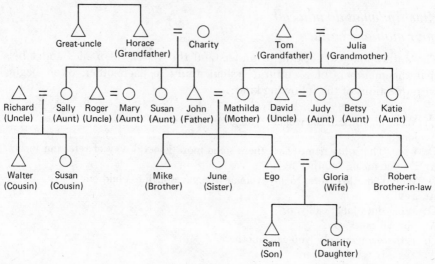

FIGURE 1

Now, with the genealogy in hand, the anthropologist can ask Ego how he refers to each of his relatives. He writes a *kinterm* ("uncle," "cousin," "sister") under each of the individuals in the diagram. Looking at the diagram among the set of persons one generation older than Ego, we find that both of John's sisters are called "aunt." Because both Sally and Susan are Ego's father's sisters, they can be regarded as occupying the same position on the diagram; that is, as representing the same *kintype*. A kintype is any type of relative that can be referred to by the same combination of primary terms (father's sister, mother's brother's daughter, or father's brother's wife's brother's daughter).

The appropriate kinterm for the kintype, father's sister, is "aunt." Is "aunt" a descriptive kinterm like "father" which applies to one and only one kintype or is it a classificatory term which applies to several kintypes? Looking at the diagram again, we find that "aunt" is also applied to mother's sister, father's brother's wife, and mother's brother's wife. The term, "aunt," covers four different kinds of relatives. Why should this be so? For one thing, it is very inconvenient to have a different term for all of the different kintypes that a given Ego might have. Just as it would be awkward to have a different term for each of the trees in a forest or each of the numbers up to one hundred, so it would be ridiculous to go around saying things like "father's father's brother's wife's daughter" every time you wanted to call attention to the fact that somone was related to you.

What Are Your Principles of Classification?

In classifying trees, people choose certain features, perhaps leaf shapes or kinds of flowers, in order to apply such terms as "oak," "ash,", or "poplar."

We might ask, then, what features all the people called "aunt" have in common? In other words, what kind of logic is involved in placing father's sister, mother's sister, father's brother's wife, and mother's brother's wife all together under the term, "aunt"? Related questions are: How might we as anthropologists find rules which would help us to apply the term, "aunt," to the appropriate kintypes or what might possibly be going on in Ego's head when he uses the term, "aunt"?

A shrewd guess is that because we are dealing with genealogical relationships, the answers to these questions are likely to be found in the genealogical properties of the various individuals labeled "aunt." We might say that an "aunt" is the sister of a parent or the wife of a parent's brother. Or, thinking about the qualities of "auntness," we might observe that an "aunt" is a female one generation higher than Ego. Because "aunts" are found on either side of the direct line of descent leading to Ego, we might use the term *collateral* (on the side) to express the distinction between "aunt" and "mother." Thus, a "mother" is a female *lineal* relative one generation higher than Ego, while an "aunt" is a female *collateral* relative one generation higher than Ego or the wife of a male collateral relative one generation higher than Ego.

In thinking about the English kinship system as a whole, it would appear that all of the kinterms except "cousin" involve more or less the same distinctions that can be observed for "aunt." In effect, relatives are differentiated in terms of sex, generation, and closeness to Ego (for example, lineal-collateral-distant). For a great many Egos, "cousin" seems to be used to refer to any distant relative, while the term "in-law" tends to be used for relatives by marriage. For Ego, who has made use of the English kinship terminology throughout his lifetime and has no knowledge of any other method of classifying relatives, the English terminology seems right and proper even though he can't explain exactly how the classification works.

Consider, now, the Kannada (South Indian) kinterms given in the genealogy in Figure 2. Here, at least in the simplified version given in the diagram, it turns out that there are only four terms used to describe all persons one generation older than Ego. As in English, a distinction is made on the basis of generation and sex, but there is no apparent distinction between lineal relatives and affinal relatives and there is no apparent distinction among close, collateral, and distant relatives. As anthropologists, what are we to say about the rule governing the use of such terms as "amma" and "atti"? If we asked which term is the Kannada term for "aunt," we would be asking a nonsensical question because both terms include kintypes covered by the term "aunt."

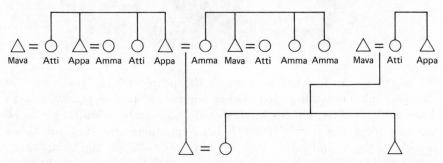

Mava   Atti   Appa Amma Atti   Appa   Amma Mava Atti   Amma Amma   Mava   Atti   Appa

FIGURE 2

The problem appears to be simple, for all we have to do is find a rule that would permit us to divide all the women in the generation above Ego into two classes. One interpretation of this situation would be to assume that all siblings of the same sex are considered similar and that they always marry spouses of the same kind. In terms of this rule, an "amma" is any female one generation older than Ego who is his mother, his mother's sister, the wife of an "appa," or the sister of an "amma." A "mava" is any male one generation older than Ego who is his mother's brother, the brother of an "amma," or the husband of an "atti." A wife's father is a "mava" because, if he were an "appa," Ego would be marrying his "sister." Because Kannada speakers regard all human beings as kinsmen, terms like "amma" and "mava" can be applied to any older man or woman whom Ego thinks of as being like a father's wife or a mother's brother. When Ego is asked what "mava" means he is likely to reply, "Bridegiver." Thus, "mava" is any man who might conceivably have a daughter that Ego might marry or any man to whom the respect due to a father-in-law is owed.

One interpretation of this situation is that "mava" is basically a kinship term referring to mother's brother, but that its meaning is extended to cover all persons whom Ego wishes to treat like a mother's brother. Another interpretation would be that there are two kinds of older men in the world, "appas," who are treated with a warm and personal respect, and "mavas," who are treated with a cold and distant respect, the differences being similar to that between neighbors and strangers. In the Kannada terminology, Ego's relationship to such men is not fictitious because Ego starts with the supposition that all men are related. Similar extensions of kinship terms in English are regarded as fictitious. The term "aunt" may be applied to a friendly neighbor woman who gives cookies to the children, or, in some Southern communities in the United States, to a Black woman who is old enough and close enough to merit some degree of respect, but not white enough to be addressed properly by name.

Kinship terminologies refer to people who are classified in terms of genealogical principles such as sex, age, generation, consanguinity (common "blood" or common descent), and affinity (marital status or marriage-ability). Cultural anthropologists regard such terminologies as important for a variety of reasons. The most fundamental is that kinship terminologies exist in one form or another in every known human society. Kinship terminologies seem to be basically human and tell us important things about the way human beings think about the world around them and about the origins of those fundamental social groupings associated with the early evolution of the human species. On a more frivolous level, kinship terminologies provide neat puzzles which, like other kinds of mathematical puzzles, can often be solved in elegant and exciting ways. Perhaps, in the end, it is the ability to make some kind of sense out of kinship terminologies that gives cultural anthropologists the hope that they may someday make sense out of the rest of culture.

Whatever it might be about kinship terminologies that fascinates anthropologists, the people who use them are concerned with identifying people towards whom they are to act in particular ways. How should relatives be treated?

What do you do to your "amma" and what does she do to you?

In 1907 I experienced a good sample of the relevant behavior. I was in the tent of David Stewart, my interpreter, and wished to draw out his mother-in-law concerning the games played in her youth. Though she was only a few feet away, Stewart did not ask her directly, but put each question to his wife, who repeated it to her mother and then repeated the answer to her husband. In 1910 James Carpenter did not speak to his wife's mother or grandmother and would not pronounce the Crow word for "to mark, to write" because his mother-in-law's name was Marks-plainly. In 1931 he still kept up these taboos. Even a man of preponderantly white blood may maintain the rule, presumably in deference to the old women's feelings (Lowie 1956:31).

The quotation above provides an example of what anthropologists describe as a *formal* role. When a person is termed, "mother-in-law," Ego behaves toward her in certain clearly specified ways. What is interesting about such formal role relationships as the avoidance relationship described above is why such formality should be necessary.

In the case of mothers-in-law, the fact that the wife's mother is so frequently the target of avoidance relationships, mother-in-law jokes, and even accusations of witchcraft leads us to suspect that the frequent formalization of relationships to mothers-in-law has to do with the possibility that Ego and his mother-in-law might get along too well or not well enough. Adams and Romney have argued that mother-in-law avoidance develops to prevent conflict between husband and mother over control of the daughter-in-law (1959). More broadly it can be argued that formal relationships are a means of preventing individual decision making in areas where conflict is likely to occur. Where Ego's obligation to his mother-in-law is simply the formal one of attending Sunday dinner, Thanksgiving, and Christmas, Ego's status as a good son-in-law is easy to evaluate and there need be no conflict over whether or not Ego is doing the right thing by his wife's mother.

What, then, happens to a formally defined relationship when powerful informal ties develop between the kinsmen concerned?

The taboos described are never conceived as the expansion of hostility but rather of the utmost respect. A substantial gift can, however, sometimes abrogate the taboo. If a man gives two or three horses to either parent-in-law, the ban may be lifted; according to one informant, a donation of a hundred dollars might suffice. Further, abolition of the customary rule occurs particularly after a wife's death; then her mother may absolve her son-in-law from all prohibitions by addressing him as "son," whereupon his relationship to her is assumed to have become filial and is not dissolved even if he should remarry. It is also possible for the son-in-law to take the initial step.

There was some variation in this procedure. Sometimes gifts were offered, yet the taboo persisted. Thus, Gray-bull once gave a horse to his father-in-law, and another to his mother-in-law, but spoke only to the former thereafter. The same informant gave his son-in-law Yellow-brow one or two horses, pronouncing the formula of adoption: "You, too, I shall make my child." Since then he would speak to Yellow-brow and smoke with him as if he were his son, but Gray-bull's wife was not affected by this arrangement (Lowie 1956:31–32).

It is easy to see how useful an avoidance relationship can be, particularly in connection with relatives that one would prefer to avoid. Other kinds of relationships are more difficult to explain:

There is a joking relationship between a boy and the husbands of his father's sisters. In fun these uncles are called "grandfathers" by the boy. There is no such relationship among the girls and women. A grandfather may come and sprinkle cold water on the boy early in the morning, or may carry him out and dip him in the spring, or may continually tease him by word and manner or play practical jokes on him.

The boy retaliates in kind. The boy may offer to carry a load which his "grandfather" has just gotten to the top of the mesa, but upon being trusted with it, he may proceed to take it back down the trail and deposit it at the foot of the cliff. Another trick is to dig a shallow pit in a trail frequented by a "grandfather" and to camouflage it so that he will step into it. Other tricks are improvised as the occasion warrants. A "grandfather" is the only adult who may be teased by the boy; least of all would he tease his true grandfathers (Dennis 1940:65–66).

Because boys may often have close relationships with their father's sisters, the father's sister sometimes undertaking responsibilities for the sexual education of the male child, the joking relationship may well serve to institutionalize and therefore control very real feelings of jealousy and hostility. Of course, relationships between relatives need not be sharply defined, and they may in fact be quite vague:

In America the family, in the Roman and aristocratic signification of the word, does not exist. All that remains of it are a few vestiges in the first years of childhood, when the father exercises, without opposition, that absolute domestic authority which the feebleness of his children renders necessary and which their interests, as well as his own incontestable superiority, warrants. But as soon as the young American approaches manhood, the ties of filial obedience are relaxed day by day; master of his thoughts, he is soon master of his conduct.

In a democratic family the father exercises no other power than that which is granted to the affection and the experience of age; his orders would perhaps be disobeyed, but his advice is for the most part authoritative. Though he is not hedged in with ceremonial respect, his sons at least accost him with confidence; they have no settled form of addressing him, but they speak to him constantly and are ready to consult him every day (Tocqueville 1960, II 203–206).

More recent students of the North American family than Alexis de Tocqueville, who wrote in the 1830s, have found that the father often does not know what to do. In the quotation below Crestwood Heights is a suburban community in Canada.

Both father and mother, within and without the home, perform their various roles largely, as we are now aware, "for the sake of the children." With only rare exceptions, Crestwood parents pretty well take for granted their responsibility for the physical care and social training of their children. But beyond their fundamental and obvious legal responsibility, Crestwood Heights parents often wonder "what to do next" with their children, since they are given no support by traditionally sanctioned methods of child-rearing. There is great variation in the patterns of child care and control, and considerable parental uncertainty.

Nor are the father and mother commonly agreed even in uncertainty as to how this function is to be discharged (Seeley, Sim, Loosley 1963:193).

In a relatively unchanging society, parents know what to do because they are permitted and encouraged to do substantially the same things their parents did. Neighbors and relatives also know the right thing to do. The North American father and mother, after debating with the Italian grandparent, the French grandparent, the Egyptian grandparent, and the Norwegian grandparent, finally turn toward books as a source of information concerning the definition of proper role relationships between parent and child. It is almost a case of the ethnography becoming the cultural tradition. Many doubts about the democratic and permissive nature of North American society that were current in de Tocqueville's time continue to be expressed today.

So far, anthropologists have had a tendency to discuss the roles played by kinsmen in terms of examples, "Gray-bull once gave a horse to his father-in-law," or in rather vague general terms, "the physical care and social training of their children." More recently, partly under the influence of the new ethnography, it has come to be felt that ideas concerning the proper relationships between kinsmen and the proper means of expressing such relationships can be subjected to the kind of systematic study that makes it possible to express a kinship terminology in terms of a few principles, a simple drawing, or a formula. A joking relationship can be maintained, for example, only if the participants exchange symbolic phrases or activities that indicate joking is involved. Because not all joking occurs in a context of kinship and because some jokes are "not funny," there must be clear limits to the kind and quality of jokes that may be inflicted upon kinsmen. Insofar as the jokes involved are "practical jokes" designed to humiliate or mildly injure the opponent, there must be formal mechanisms that prevent a joking relationship from escalating to full-scale combat. To function as a joking relative, a man must have a set of rules which enables him to create fresh and amusing situations that fall within "the limits of decency." Inasmuch as a child has no difficulty learning such rules and operating within them, anthropologists have often hoped that a scientifically trained adult may also not only learn such rules but develop a conscious understanding of their nature. So far, the magnitude of the descriptive task undertaken by the ethnographer has prevented the use of detailed methodology except within such limited spheres as that of kinship terminology. In the future, as ethnographic studies become more specialized, we can expect more systematic reporting and analysis.

Anthropologists, and human beings in general, tend to place great emphasis upon kinship and particularly upon the supposed biological ties between the persons who occupy the same kinship diagram. For the anthropologist and members of cultural systems, kinship is often a convenient fiction. Human beings do not love, honor, or obey their biological relatives unless they have an appropriate sociological relationship to them. For example, in the South Indian kinship terminology, an "appa" or "father" can be a very distant relative, by the standards of the English kinship terminology, not a relative at all. In some aboriginal Australian kinship systems, all human beings and many other living things are classified as kinsmen and ways of acting toward them are specified. The belief in a mystical tie among biological relatives is probably the force which leads people to attempt to extend their kin relationships as far as possible. The mystical brotherhood of church, lodge, labor union, or clan is in many ways superior to actual brotherhood, for mystical brothers can be endowed with virtues that real brothers may lack. If a stranger can be treated as "daddy" or "buddy," it is unnecessary to learn new ways of treating him.

Varieties of consanguinity and affinity appear to be recognized by all human beings. For most people, the earliest experiences of life are in a family-based household. Real and supposed kinship relationships and ways of treating kinsmen probably form the basis of the bulk of human social classifications and are of psychological importance even where kinship is not overtly present. At the same time, there is probably no society where biological kinship is the only basis of human relationships. The following sections deal with terminological classifications of human beings that are either distantly related or totally unrelated to kinship terminologies.

What other kinds of people are there?

You know, we have some Negroes in this country that are as white as you and I, and when I fill out marriage licenses for them I have sometimes put them down as white and they have told me they are Negroes. Of course, this is no insult to them. They know they look white, and being taken for white is no new experience for them. But the ones I have trouble with are these Croatans. We always record them as white in this office, and when I think someone is a Croatan I just mark the license white and say nothing about it. But the trouble is with the dark ones. Really, some of them do look for all the world like Negroes, or like mulattoes anyway. And you know I hate to come right out and ask them, because they don't like that (Berry 1969, p. 48).

In the United States, the people in the world are often thought of as divided into different *racial groups* such as "white," "black," "oriental," "Mexican-American," and "Indian." Very often these racial classifications are further subdivided into *ethnic groups* in terms of religion or tribal and national origin. Most people believe that membership in a racial category is easily determined on the basis of such superficial physical traits as skin color, eye color, hair color, hair form, or various facial characteristics. Very often it is believed that members of some or all ethnic groups can also be identified by such characteristics. Where the supposed racial characteristics fail to make positive identification possible, it is often assumed that habits of speech, occupations, gestures, or other behavioral characteristics are infallible indicators of group membership.

In the above example, the judge in charge of issuing marriage licenses encounters the fact that actual or real membership in racial or ethnic groups has to do not with the individual's physical characteristics but with such sociological factors as who his parents are, to which church he belongs, or which school he attends. The Croatans, who may or may not represent some complex mixture of ethnic groups, consider themselves to be quite distinct from "Negroes" and may violently resent being classified as such. Should the judge fail to apply an unworkable racial classification correctly, he may consider himself fortunate to escape with a punch on the nose. The point is: It is fairly easy for Ego to classify people in terms of kinship and it is fairly easy for the anthropologist to arrive at an understanding of what the classification is about; other kinds of classification are likely to be much more complicated and to involve criteria which are poorly understood both by Ego and the anthropologist.

Ethnic groups in the United States seem to be classified in terms of various combinations of biological attributes and behavioral characteristics. Terms like "Jewish mother," "Irish policeman," or "white Anglo-Saxon Protestant," bring to mind stereotyped images of individual physical characteristics and at the same time images of characteristic behaviors. Of course, many other statuses are defined within North American culture. Consider "fireman," "boss," "New Yorker," "Rotarian," "Episcopalian," "radical," "friend," "roommate," "suburbanite," "patient," and "neighbor." Some of these terms imply classification in terms of occupation or activity, some imply status hierarchies ("boss"), some imply equality, some make reference to birthplace or residence, others make reference to group membership. In all cultures each individual has many statuses and plays many roles. Ego's selection of, or assignment to, some particular status depends upon the nature of the process that is being carried out at any particular moment. A man who carries out the process of "visiting mother" is a son, but when he carries out the process of "putting out a fire," he may be a fireman. Even in less complicated societies, such as that of the Crow Indians of the North American Plains, part of the interest of the game of culture and part of the problem of predicting human behavior lies in Ego's multiplicity of statuses and roles. How should Ego really treat his barā'ace?

> A man is extremely circumspect in the presence of his brother-in-law, whom he addresses as bā'aci and refers to as barā'ace. These terms embrace the wife's mother's brother as well as the wife's brother and his sister's husband, since a maternal uncle always figures as an older brother. Two brothers-in-law are supposed to be extremely friendly and to exchange gifts. They are permitted to speak lightly on impersonal matters, but under no condition must they bandy personal remarks savoring of obscenity. There is apparently no objection to telling an obscene myth before a brother-in-law, but according to Leforge even this was deemed gravely indecorous. The bond and the taboos linked with it sometimes outlast the marriage on which the relationship rests. On the other hand, adoption into a society might transform a brother-in-law into a "son." A distinction is drawn between the wife's own brother and her remote kinsmen addressed by the same term. It is her closest "brothers" that enjoy the greatest respect, while some jesting is possible with the others, especially on military matters. Thus, White-man-runs-him married one of Old-dog's clan sisters, and the two men would jocularly say to each other, "You have never been on a war party." Similarly, Gray-bull was wont to chaff Scolds-the-bear, who was at a disadvantage, being afraid to respond because of Gray-bull's superior prestige as a warrior.
>
> Even in such distant relationships of the brother-in-law category personal allusions to sex are rigorously barred. I once pretended to be Arm-around-the-neck's brother-in-law, but mispronounced the proper term of address so that it was mistaken for a reference to my informant's genitalia. Playing the assumed part, he at once dealt me a light blow. Even outsiders respect this taboo. A man at once breaks off a ribald remark if he sees his victim's brother-in-law entering the scene (Lowie 1956:29–30).

Here, although sex is a taboo topic when Ego is in association with any "brother-in-law" no matter how remote, other aspects of Ego's role behavior toward his "brothers-in-law" are strongly conditioned by their other statuses such as close or distant relative, more or less prestigious warrior, or membership in one society or another.

Structure: what are you building here?

When the ancient Babylonians attempted to contrive a tower reaching up to Heaven, the deity destroyed the common enterprise by assigning a different language to each of the builders. Without a vehicle for the transmission of the cultural message and without the means of assigning appropriate roles and statuses, the cultural system of the builders of the tower of Babel promptly collapsed as did their building later. The curse that afflicted Babylon still afflicts the human species, and, when our cultural systems become so large as to threaten Heaven, difficulties of communication and understanding inevitably develop.

Among nonhuman primates, who lack language altogether, the largest possible group—the equivalent of a tribe or nation—is called a troop. A troop of primates is generally associated with a particular piece of land or territory and generally has little to do with other troops. Troops have been observed numbering anywhere from two to seven hundred individuals, but the most common range of variation for all primate species is between ten and eighty animals (Kummer 1971:31). Modern tribes of hunters and gatherers, whose means of coping with the environment resemble those of archaeologically known early human groups, consist, on the average, of about five hundred individuals. Joseph Birdsell suggests that one limiting factor affecting the size of such human groups is language (1968:229–240). In other words, as groups of human beings become increasingly large, the development of different dialects in different subgroupings makes communication increasingly difficult. Particularly in desert regions, hunter-collectors tend to form relatively tiny bands or subgroups which are isolated by geographical distance. Increasing distances and numbers make it difficult for the different bands to maintain close contact and the result is that their languages and cultural traditions tend to diverge.

How, then, can there be large tribes of hunter-collectors, agriculturalists, or industrialized peoples within which many thousands or millions of people share common languages? One answer is to use roads, horses, or airplanes as a means of transcending the limitations of geography. Another is to use writing, printing, telephones, or radios as a means of promoting communication among individuals separated by geographical distances. Another technique, perhaps more basic and fundamental, is exemplified by the case of Dimal, a two-year-old aborigine from the Kimberly Division in Western Australia:

> Dimal was generally referred to by her subsection name of Nambin, as was also her half-sister, Buma, aged about nine. The mother belonged therefore to the nadjili subsection and her father to the djangala. Dimal like all others had a djering, in this case, dilly-bag, and was found at Mindjari, a water-hole in her father's horde country of Bibiban, lying about 40 miles to the northwest of the camp in the Lunga territory. Her subsection totem was opossum, and from her father she had inherited his *guning*, dream totems, which were

tfimili (baobab tree) and *ngali* (paper-bark). Buma, since she had another father, possessed a different horde country and a different *guning*, but like Dimal had the right to live in her mother's horde country, her *kamera*.

Dimal's name was that of another woman of the same tribe and subsection whom she had never seen, but whom she would regard henceforth as her *naragu* or namesake (the same term being used also for the subsection totem). The elder woman on hearing that the small child had been named after her, had sent a frock and for the rest of their lives, the two would continue to exchange gifts and visit one another when possible.

Dimal then, from the moment of her birth was equipped with a *noera:da:m*, a *wanyegoara da:m*, four totems, a namesake, and a subsection; i.e., her relationships were already defined in regard to certain strips of territory, the totemic system, and to individuals, since the subsections stand in a kinship relation to one another (Kaberry 1950:49–50).

The trick involved in providing Dimal with all of these statuses and roles consists of dividing the membership of the tribe into a variety of groups and classes and providing the individual with different patterns of interaction or relationship which she may use in dealing with members of the different groups or classes. Dimal and the other members of her tribe escape the limitations of geography and biological kinship by creating systems of classification in which geographically or biologically distant persons are brought affectively or emotionally close by belonging to the same group or class as Ego or persons close to him.

One of the techniques used by Dimal's people to extend the membership of their groups and hence to extend the circle of individuals with whom close communication is possible is to deny the facts of paternity:

> Questioned on the function of sexual intercourse natives admitted that it prepared the way for the entry of the *djinganara:ny*. "Him make 'em road belonga picanniny: young girl no got 'em road." Most women believed that the semen remained in the vagina and had nothing to do with the child. "Him nothing," was the trenchant reply, when after circuitous inquiry I finally suggested the facts in the case (Kaberry 1950:40).

Due to the denial of paternity, Dimal, besides being able to inherit statuses from her actual mother and father, is in a position to acquire statuses and memberships by virtue of the fact that her "spirit" was found in a distant water hole and possessed particular properties associated with the "dilly-bag." Dimal has a lot of connections, and it is only natural that in the course of her life she will make practical use of them in communication and social interaction. Such interaction will involve linguistic communication with people who are geographically and biologically distant and will have the effect of counteracting in some degree the Babylonian curse.

What Can You Do for Me?

The easiest way to deal with strangers, as in traditional Tiwi culture, is to kill them. Such a response to those who cannot be named or classified as members has an inhibiting effect upon trade or other useful contacts with people outside of Ego's close group of kinsmen and neighbors. As in the case of Dimal, above, a system of categorizing people which provides statuses and roles for at least some strangers facilitates communication and makes these strangers psychologically, economically, or socially useful and acceptable. Once large groups of people have been divided into kinds or classes, it is useful to imagine that all of the members of any particular category fulfill some function that is of special importance to Ego or to the group as a whole. Consider the case of the Tewa, a group living in close association with the Hopi Indians of Arizona:

> I am of the Bear clan,. Our mothers' mothers' mothers and our mothers' mothers' mothers' brothers were Bear clan people. They came a long time ago from *Tsawadeh*, our home in the east. Our sisters' daughters' daughters' children, as long as women of my clan have children, will be of the Bear clan. These are our clan relatives, whom we trust, work with, and confide in. My mother's older sister guards the sacred fetish which is the power and guardian of our clan and which was brought in the migration from *Tsawadeh*. My mother's older sister feeds our fetish and sees that the feathers are always properly dressed. At important ceremonies, my mother's brother, erects his altar and sets our fetish in a prominent place within the altar. My mother's older sister and my mother's brother make all the important decisions for our clan, and such decisions are accepted with respect and obedience by all Bear clan members. My mother's older sister and her brother are called upon to advise, to reprimand, and to make decisions on land and ritual affairs for all of us who are of the Bear clan. My mother's older sister's house is where our fetish is kept, and therefore it is a sacred house to us and there we go for all important matters that concern our clan (Dozier 1966:42).

Other neighboring tribes and groups such as the Hopi and Navajo have clans which can be identified with Tewa clans when it is convenient to do so.

> When I asked if the Hano (Tewa) Corn clan was also similarly related (i.e., to Hopi clans), my informant, a Corn clan woman, replied that the Tewa were not Hopi and she could not believe that a Hopi clan, even though similar in name, could be related to a Tewa clan. With regard to the association of Fir and Bear clans with certain Hopi clans, she remarked that these people "were trying to deny their Tewa heritage and wanted to be like Hopi." Yet when this same woman was on a visit to Mishongnovi in the winter of 1951, she sought out Patki (a theoretically related clan) households. At that time she remarked: "These are our people; they treat us kindly when we visit them, and when they come in our village they stay in our houses" (Dozier 1966:45).

The above example shows how the concept of clan brotherhood and sisterhood can be used to convert perfect strangers into helpful relatives. Clan solidarity, as in the case of the Capulets and Montagues or Martins and Coys, may lead to situations in which rivalries or feuds poison the relationships between clans. In the Romeo and Juliet story or the story of the Martins and the Coys, the conflict between clans was resolved quite typically by the affection of a boy in one clan and a girl in another. That clans tend to be exogamous—that marriage must take place outside of the clan—contributes powerfully to the cementing of relationships among clans and to the fact that feuds between clans tend to be better regulated than wars between strangers. The mothers' brothers, the male members of a matrilineal clan, must always consider that the enemy includes some of their wives, wives' children, and sister's husbands.

How else may clans be made interdependent?

> The *Sumakolih* is a curing association whose members wear masks like Kachina impersonators. The *Sumakolih*, now controlled by the Cloud clan, was formerly owned and managed by the extinct Sun clan. The association cures "sore eyes"; but any Tewa or even a Hopi from First Mesa may request the association to dance, either to effect a personal cure or to secure well being for the community in general (Dozier 1966:78).

Most of the Tewa clans are charged with the management of particular associations charged with practical and religious duties vital to the carrying out of life. Individuals from a variety of different clans, sometimes voluntarily, sometimes at the request of their parents, and sometimes as a result of accidental involvement in the affairs of the association, are initiated into some particular association, and thus, in collaboration with members of other clans, carry out important duties. War between clans now threatens to become war between members of the same club and among its costs must be included the disruption of those vital practical and ceremonial activities which prevent illness, bring rain, or secure the general well being. The case of the Swazi illustrates some more complicated ways of joining clans together.

Why Do You Have So Many Wives?

The Swazi form a political state in South Africa consisting of thousands of people occupying a region the size of Hawaii. The Swazi are organized into large patrilineal clans, but also in terms of a complex and hierarchical political system dominated by a king and a queen mother:

> . . . clan exogamy is recognized as an effective way of extending and creating social ties, and the king is expected to unify and centralize his position by taking women from all sections of his people. When he marries a clan sister (a special privilege reserved for kings), her father is automatically removed from the royal Nkosi Dlamini clan, and becomes the founder of a separate subclan. This also limits the number of Dlamini; a nobility always tries to maintain itself as an exclusive minority (Kuper 1963:17).

The king puts himself and his clan above clan rivalries by making his own clan rather small and special, and he may eliminate rivals within his own clan by marrying their daughters. He ensures that important clans have access to the kingship by taking additional wives, one king had forty, from a variety of different clans. The king was also surrounded by "blood brothers" who performed important parts of the rituals of kingship and government and were also drawn from a variety of clans.

At lower levels there were regimental age classes:

> Age groups cut across the boundaries of local chiefs and across the bonds of kinship, incorporating individuals into the state, the widest political unit. Between members of the same regiment, and particularly those in permanent residence, there is a loyalty and camaraderie. They treat each other as equals, eat together, smoke hemp from the long hemp pipe that is part of their joint equipment, work together, and have a central meeting place or clubhouse in the barracks. They call each other "brother" or "my age mate," "my peer," and the ties between them are said to be stronger than those between kinsmen of different generations. Towards other age sets there is often openly expressed rivalry and occasional fights. . . . (Kuper 1963:53).

Because the individual Swazi recognizes and belongs to a variety of groups and classes and because the activities of all of the complex organizations are orchestrated by a powerful political hierarchy, many thousands of people can be brought into a cultural system which seems to operate as effectively as an Australian tribe containing five hundred individuals. The institutions of the Swazi—the kingship, the clans, the age classes, the households, and other territorial groupings—constitute a social structure which may be appreciated in architectural terms in the same way that we appreciate the structure of a crystal, a mollusk, or a symphony. Though we may appreciate their beauty, it is more difficult to evaluate the effectiveness of the structures built by the Australian aborigines, the Tewa, or the Swazi. Would some other system provide for better communication, more cooperation, or more efficient regulation of internal conflict? To compare such systems in terms of numbers is not unlike judging a symphony by the number of instruments involved or judging a house by the number of square feet it contains. Consider the sharp parallels and remarkable contrasts existing between India and Mexico.

Should You Marry Out and Trade In or Trade In and Marry Out?

Throughout most of India, the ideal pattern of social structure consists of a series of ranked castes or *jatis*. Birth into a high ranking jati is usually considered to be a reward for virtuous conduct in a previous life, while birth into a low jati is a punishment for previous sins. For the most part, jatis are divided into exogamous clans, and marriages take place between the clans but within the castes. The reward or punishment, the "fate," assigned to each caste consists of particular occupations, special ritual duties, special restrictions on the foods that may be eaten, and special dress or other characteristics. Each village or group of related villages consists of representatives from a variety of different jatis. In theory, and to a considerable extent in practice as well, the representatives of each of the jatis, in the process of working out their fate, have the right and obligation of performing particular religious or economic tasks vital to the welfare of the village. A member of the Barber jati has the unique privilege of cutting hair. The Farmer raises grain, the Carpenter makes plows, and the Potter makes pots. If the Barber wishes to arrange his daughter's marriage, members of other jatis in the village perform special services essential to the ceremony. Thus, the Priest conducts the ceremony, the Goldsmith manufactures the bridal jewelry, and the Astrologer determines the future prospects of the bride and groom.

Because one Barber can serve many persons, a village is unlikely to contain many practicing families of Barbers. Naturally, if the Barber is the victim of unfair competition or if he wishes to raise prices, he calls upon the members of his jati in other villages to support him. Here, the Barber jati operates like a trade union. When the Barber arranges his son's marriage, he must communicate with his kinsmen in other villages in order to find a bride. Because the Barber jati is a small one and there are only a few Barbers in each village, the son's bride may come from a considerable distance. Intermarriages within the Barber jati create a network of kinship involving many villages and covering many square miles of countryside. A small village containing perhaps twenty jatis, might find itself in the center of twenty kinship networks covering several hundred different villages.

Under these circumstances, in contrast to the more typical human situation where a man lives within a community composed largely of relatives, the local community may consist almost entirely of persons who are not considered relatives of Ego and with whom marriage is unthinkable. Because the village is the setting for Ego's daily life, almost every other kind of important social tie operates across jatis within the village. Ego's friends, the people he works with, his neighbors, the fellow members of a drama company, and his fellow worshippers at the village temple are very largely members of other jatis. Regardless of Ego's jati, he must maintain smooth relationships with the members of most other jatis or face a situation in which he cannot get a haircut, have his sheep butchered, hold a wedding, or even be buried. The basic pattern of the Indian village community enfolds millions of people and has persisted for several thousands of years.

The pattern of the Indian village is basically one of marrying outside the village and trading or economic exchange within the village. The result has been the creation of large areas or regions within which people speak the same languages, raise children in similar ways, accept the same religion, and so on. What would happen if the pattern were reversed so that marriages took place only within the village, but different villages tended to manufacture particular necessities of life? Something like such a mirror image of the Indian situation exists in parts of Mexico.

In the Valley of Oaxaca, marriages take place almost entirely within the village. Whereas individual families in Indian villages exhibit considerable differences in wealth, occupation, and social status, individual families in Oaxaca villages tend to be of roughly equal wealth and status and to follow the same occupations. Persons of relatively high wealth and status in Oaxaca villages are often chosen to direct and financially support elaborate religious ceremonies or fiestas. Thus, if a man does become wealthy, he may be compelled to donate a considerable portion of his wealth to the community.

Specialists who provide the goods and services required for the day-to-day carrying out of the life of the village are located in market towns or in other villages having unique economic specializations. One village weaves blankets, another produces grinding stones, another bakes bread, another makes pottery, and another sells milk products. Relationships between villages take place at weekly markets where large numbers of people congregate for purposes of conviviality and for the buying and selling of goods produced in different villages. In Oaxaca, attendance at weekly markets is practically compulsory, while in India, weekly markets tend to be small and to offer relatively few products for sale.

In both India and Oaxaca the basic pattern of organization involves the exchange of products between economically specialized endogamous groups. In India marriage takes place within castes and economic exchange takes place between castes within the village; in Oaxaca marriage takes place within the village and economic exchange takes place between villages. What are the consequences of these two different arrangements? In the Valley of Oaxaca, several different languages are spoken and differences in dialects often make communication, except in Spanish, difficult between persons from different villages where the same language is spoken. Even following the advent of modern roads and systems of communication, Mexican national culture retains great regional variation, while the cultural uniformities characteristic of India seem much greater. While this difference can be attributed in part to the mountainous nature of the Mexican terrain and the difficulties of communication between villages, the patterns of social structure governing the relationships among individuals and villages offer more important explanations. In particular, it would seem that market relationships are less effective than kin relationships in promoting similarities between villages.

In comparing the social structures of traditional India and Mexico it is possible to reach judgments concerning the effectiveness of the structures for particular purposes. Marrying out and trading in is plainly more effective in maintaining linguistic and cultural similarities over large regions than is marrying in and trading out. One of the costs of this kind of effectiveness is the disappearance of interesting people such as the Zinacantecos of Mexico (Vogt 1970), but perhaps their traditions are doomed in any case by the advent of roads and transistor radios.

Summary

The cultural tradition provides the members of a cultural system with sets of terms, statuses, and roles that constitute their social structure. Because a cultural tradition has the properties of a message or set of instructions, discrepancies among the terms, statuses, and roles defined in the cultural tradition are always possible. There may be terms for kinds of individuals that do not exist; there may be statuses for which there are no terms or for which appropriate roles are ill-defined. As in the plan of the Makah class system, there may be an ideal culture which is only loosely connected to the real culture represented by consistencies in the actual behavior of the members. Where discrepancies between terms, statuses, and roles become obtrusive, members often attempt to resolve the inconsistencies through direct action. Thus, the Tikopian youth married the woman who insisted on playing the role of wife.

One of the most pervasive and thoroughly studied aspects of social structure is the labeling or classifying of genealogically related persons. Here, combinations of primary kinterms define kintypes, which are classified in terms of such principles as sex and generation and are largely derived from genealogical relationships. Sets of kintypes are then lumped together under such kinterms as "aunt" or "amma." The contrast between the English and Kannada systems of kin terminology illustrates that, whereas the decision to lump particular kintypes under some particular kinterm is arbitrary, it tends to be consistent in terms of the methods of classification used by the members of a particular cultural system.

Because sets of kinship terms are defined by relatively simple gene-alogical principles, it is relatively easy for members and anthropologists to arrive at an understanding of the connection between an individual's status and the label that should be applied to him. There are many other ways of classifying the members of a cultural system, and the case of the Croatans illustrates that even the members of cultural systems may have great diffi-culties in deciding which label to apply to which person. The members of a cultural system may be classified by the roles they play, their occupations, their position in a ranked hierarchy of statuses, their group membership, physical appearance, and many other ways.

Very often, as in the case of a man who is both a "son" and a "fireman," Ego has the option of assigning a variety of terms and statuses to any par-ticular individual, and, depending upon the situation, any particular indi-vidual may assume one of the terms, statuses, or roles to which he is entitled rather than another. The Crow Indians are supposed to treat their "brothers-in-law" in particular ways, but in real life they modify their behaviors in order to take into account other statuses and roles occupied by particular brothers-in-law.

The use of language in the dissemination of cultural traditions makes it possible for human beings to develop groupings that are considerably larger than those found among other primates. Where human groups are small and geographically dispersed, the number of persons who can share a single mutually intelligible dialect tends to be quite small, perhaps less than one thousand. As illustrated by the case of Dimal, the requirement that human beings interact only with persons who are biologically and geographically close can be overcome through the use of social structures that mandate close interaction among persons who are normally biologically or geograph-ically distant.

The cases of the Tewa, the South Indians, and the Oaxacans illustrate how the assignment of individuals to a variety of statuses can be used to create a social structure which insures interaction and communication among thousands or even millions of individuals. The manner in which individuals are assigned membership in different groups or subcultural systems and the kinds of relationships that obtain between the different groups have much to do with the kinds of communication, cooperation, and conflict that take place within particular tribes, states, or nations. The pat-tern of social structure in South India, although it is virtually a mirror image of the social structure of Oaxaca, seems to ensure much wider communica-tion and interaction than does the social structure of Oaxaca. The social structure of Oaxaca apparently has the virtue of maintaining a variety of distinctive local cultures. In all of these cases it is difficult to decide whether the multiplication of groups and subgroups should be regarded as an art form or as a necessary response to the problem of ensuring communication and cooperation among the members of large cultural systems. Most social structures seem more complicated than they need to be, and because conflict *does* take place between clans, villages, age classes, and kings and commoners, the practical value of particular kinds of social structures may sometimes be called into question.

The following chapters deal with the processes by which members of cultural systems are recruited, assigned statuses, trained, and controlled. What are the problems involved in finding sufficient members to occupy the statuses defined within the social structure?

Further readings

General techniques for the analysis of kinship terminologies are discussed in Schusky's *Manual for Kinship Analysis.* Also worth consulting are *Kinship and Marriage* (Fox 1967) and *Kinship and Social Organization* (Buchler and Selby 1968). Other aspects of social classification are dealt with in *Politics, Law and Ritual in Tribal Society* (Gluckman 1965), *Social Anthropology* (Bohannon 1963), *Primitive Social Organization, Second Edition* (Service 1971), and *Comparative Political Systems* (Cohen and Middleton, eds. 1967).

In the Case Studies, kinship and social classification is emphasized in Dozier's *Hano* (1966), Beidelman's *The Kaguru* (1971), Basso's *The Cibecue Apache* (1970), Beattie's *Bunyoro* (1960), von Fürer-Haimendorf's *The Konyak Nagas* (1969) and Kuper's *The Swazi* (1963).

Problems and questions

1. Collect a genealogy writing down the kinship term used by Ego in addressing each of the persons in it. What are some principles of classification that would explain the application of the terms?
2. Asking questions such as "How should a person treat his mother-in-law, his father, his brother, etc.," try to determine whether there are any cultural rules governing the treatment of different types of kinsmen.
3. Study a particular family or other small group. What are the statuses of the different members and what are the roles that they play?
4. Conduct some interviews concerning policemen, carpenters, college professors, etc. What are some traditional beliefs about the statuses and roles implied by these terms?
5. Write the names of some social categories such as occupations, churches, clubs, or athletic teams on a set of three by five cards and ask your informants to arrange them in order putting the highest or best on the top and the lowest or worst on the bottom. Is there any consistency in the rankings you obtain?
6. From an ethnographic account of another culture prepare a list or chart showing the different kinds of groupings and social classifications that are recognized.

7

The regulation of membership

A cultural tradition provides the members of cultural systems with understandings of the kinds of things that there are in the world, the kinds of situations that exist, and the kinds of actions that are appropriate in each situation. Like the rules of a game, the script of a play, or a recipe in a cookbook, the cultural tradition has an effect upon the real world only when the structures it proposes and the actions it suggests are used and employed by living human beings. A cultural system becomes an operating entity only when human beings begin to carry out the processes essential to its functioning. This chapter concerns the processes by which a cultural system obtains the warm bodies required to fill the statuses defined within the cultural tradition and constituting its social structure.

Where will we get the members?

If a cultural system is viewed as a social structure, a set of statuses or positions to be filled by members, then processes for the regulation of membership are those by which the cultural system obtains the persons it needs and moves them from status to status within its structure. Given limits on the loaves of bread that can be won from the environment and on the capacity of the cultural system to provide jobs or statuses for human beings, processes for the regulation of membership must provide enough warm bodies to solve manpower needs, but not so many as to exhaust environmental resources or available positions. Because human beings grow old and die, because they lose interest or move away, the membership of every cultural system must be constantly renewed. Because too many human beings are little better than too few, so far as survival is concerned, processes designed for the renewal of membership must be balanced by processes designed for the limitation of membership and for the circulation of members from job to job or status to status.

The fundamental processes that regulate membership are, of course, those that concern the regulation of human biological reproduction. Processes that simply transfer members from one status to another within the social structure would soon lose their point unless the supply of human beings were constantly replenished through birth. In discussing processes for the regulation of membership, then, the distinction between a society, which includes all of the processes required for the reproduction and survival of human beings, and a part- or subcultural system is extremely important. Processes carried out within societies and having to do with marriage, fertility, birth, life support, and mortality encounter special problems posed by the biological characteristics of the human species. What are some of these problems?

How many people can there be?

In 1798, Thomas Malthus published an essay concerning the rapidity with which the human species might reproduce:

> . . . if the necessaries of life could be obtained without limit, and the number of people could be doubled every twenty-five years, the population which might have been produced from a single pair since the Christian era, would have been sufficient, not only to fill the earth quite full of people, so that four should stand in every square yard, but to fill all the planets of our solar system in the same way, and not only them but all the planets revolving around the stars which are visible to the naked eye, supposing each of them . . . to have as many planets belonging to it as our sun has (Malthus 1798; quoted in Heilbroner 1961:86).

For his computations, Malthus assumed only that the human population would double each twenty-five years. For this, all that is required is that each living female produce, on the average, two living female children each twenty-five years. A small number of male children would also be needed. Considering that human females have the capacity to produce children roughly every two years while they are in their teens and retain that capacity for more than twenty years, Malthus' predictions are modest.

Under the assumption that the necessities of life can be obtained without limit, the earth should have been filled with people many centuries ago. Lacking the benefit of any accurate knowledge of human behavior much beyond what he could see, Malthus believed that the failure of human populations to reproduce at the expected rate was the result of an absence of necessities. He arrived at the anthropological law that the members of any society would reproduce themselves until they attained a state of overpopulation that could be remedied only by famine, pestilence, or mass killing.

How Fast Is the Population Growing?

Although even today, we are only beginning to make accurate estimates of the size of the human population, there have been several attempts to estimate the rate of increase of the human species. Choosing, as did Malthus, the quite recent beginning of the Christian era for his estimate, Dorn (1962:285) arrives at the following figures:

YEAR (A.D.)	POPULATION IN BILLIONS	NUMBER OF YEARS TO DOUBLE
1	0.25 (?)	1650 (?)
1650	.50	200
1850	1.1	80
1930	2.0	45
1975	4.0	35
2010	8.0	?

These figures do not take into account the time, perhaps starting ten thousand years ago, when the development of agriculture triggered one great increase in the size of the human population; nor do they take into account earlier population explosions such as might have been triggered by the invention of language or even fishnets. The limited information available points to a rapid increase in the human population over the last few hundred years. Foerster, Mora, and Amiot (1960:1291) go so far as to predict that we will all be literally squeezed to death on November 13, 2026, when the human population approaches infinite size.

The recent vast increase in the human population is the result of the introduction of new crops and technologies which have *seemingly* led to the multiplication of the necessaries of life without limit. It may also have to do with rapid changes in the character of human cultural systems which have swept away traditional processes for the regulation of population. Because unlimited increase in the production of the necessaries of life leads to unlimited consumption of irreplaceable resources (including space), it seems to be only a matter of time before we run out of air, water, energy, space, or some other vital resource and become extinct.

Long before vital resources are completely used up, the planet will probably be swept by famine, pestilence, or mass killings which will substantially reduce world population. Such a solution to the population problem, usually called a *Malthusian solution,* has undesirable features. Human reproduction is a costly and time-consuming process, and so, even without considering moral issues, it seems stupid to raise people to maturity and then kill them off. A more practical solution would appear to be to discover, perhaps rediscover, methods of regulating population so that the number of individuals conceived and born is just large enough to maintain equilibrium with the environment—using resources, but not using them up.

The regulation of human populations involves, as does the regulation of any other species, the interruption of the normal biological life cycle in such a way as to produce a balance between the number of individuals who are born and the number of individuals who die. Such regulation can take the form of the prevention of mating, the prevention of conception, the prevention of live births, or the killing or weakening of infants, children, or adults. In one form or another, most of these techniques are used, not always deliberately, in all human cultures, but cultures differ greatly in the frequency and manner in which these techniques are applied. Consider some of the ways in which population is regulated on Tikopia, an island in the South Pacific.

Regulation: do they castrate their sons in Tikopia?

According to Dillon, the population of Tikopia in the early years of the nineteenth century was in an anomalous state. The number of females was "at least treble that of the males." This discrepancy he attributed to artificial means, alleging that all males except the first two were strangled at birth, the reason assigned by the natives being to prevent an undue increase in population. The Englishmen found on the island by Dumont D'Urville denied this. Gaimard speaks of the number of children in a family as varying from three to eight, while John Maresere, eighty years later, stated that the family was limited in size to four, any number beyond this being buried alive as a rule. Moreover in contradistinction to Dillon, he said that girls rather than boys were destroyed. Durrad, who lived for two months on the island and was a careful observer, stated that the people had large families and that there was an excess of males over females. . . .

The utter worthlessness of casual observation derived from the stay of a day or so which the *Southern Cross* and other vessels make was demonstrated by a statement which I received as a serious explanation from an engineer on the way down to the island. He said that he believed that large numbers of the boys were castrated soon after birth, and alleged that he had ripped off the waistcloth of three and found this to be the case. Hence he accounted for their great stature—almost a legend among white people—and their general mild nature. This, as I noted with some skepticism at the time, would account for restriction of the population, but not for a differential sex ratio. Moreover, the effects should be perceptible in families without children, if such lads afterwards married. The statement, as might be imagined, I found later to be entirely without foundation, but it is true that the Tikopia do endeavor to control their population in ways that are hardly less striking (Firth 1963:367–368).

Firth found the population of Tikopia to be distributed as follows:

	MALE		FEMALE	
	Married	*Unmarried*	*Married*	*Unmarried*
Children and adolescents (under 18)	00	338	00	249
Adult to middle-aged (18–40)	132	117	149	101
Above middle age (over 40)	85	15	76	19

Among the children there are substantially more males than females. Among the eighteen to forty group there is a balance of males and females, while the above forty group shows slightly more males than females. The large number of children under eighteen cannot be accounted for by lowered mortality such as might result from better diet or improved medical care because there is no particular increase in the number of females. Firth suggests that the discrepancy between the number of males under eighteen and the number over eighteen can be accounted for by the fact that sizable numbers of males are killed or disappear during long and dangerous sightseeing voyages. Female infanticide might explain the relatively small number of females under eighteen, but while Firth was in Tikopia slightly more females were born than males. A tendency to neglect female children would, however, have the same impact as deliberate infanticide. In former times, Tikopian population was controlled by the following methods: Younger brothers in a large family were expected to remain single, both unmarried and married people with "sufficient" children practiced *coitus interruptus*, abortion was practiced by unmarried girls, infanticide was practiced at the discretion of the family head, and young or unmarried men often set out on sea voyages from which they did not return. When the island became crowded, one section of the population was attacked and forced to emigrate. Such attacks sometimes involved conflict between districts and sometimes involved attacks on persons of low rank by persons of high rank. The principal means of controlling population on Tikopia was probably the prevention or delay of the marriage of large numbers of women.

In the Tikopian case, the introduction of laws forbidding abortion or infanticide would tend to increase the frequency of long and suicidal sea voyages and/or genocidal conflicts. The prevention of sea voyages and killing, measures often adopted by colonial powers in the South Pacific, leads to overpopulation resulting in famine, the importation of the necessities of life, and/or mass migration. The processes involved in the regulation of membership in the Tikopian cultural system can be evaluated in terms of cost and effectiveness. Assuming the unavailability of any modern technology for birth control, what might be an ideal means of controlling Tikopian population? Consider, now, processes for regulating population in Ireland.

Ireland: After the Famine, What?

Tom Casey, K————, is a very poor holder with thirty acres of mountain and a bog. Two sons and a daughter are still at home, and a bachelor brother works with him. Another daughter works for herself as a domestic servant in Ennis. One son Tom is apprenticed to a carpenter in Ennis. A daughter emigrated through the good graces of her aunt.

Michael Dunn of T———— has twenty acres, but has not prospered. His two sons left at eighteen and twenty respectively to drive hackney automobiles in Ennis, an uncle there giving them a start. Another son now thirty and a daughter are still at home working the farm.

In a mountain townland, Pat Looney's father prospered, won the good graces of the landlord's agent, amassed four farms, the largest fifty acres, the smallest eighteen. He married off two daughters with two hundred pound fortunes, settled three sons and a daughter with her husband in each of the farms. Pat himself, the eldest, now about eighty, got the largest farm but not the one he wanted. He has been warring with his brothers and his neighbors ever since. He held out against his father for five years, refusing to marry and take his farm. In Pat's youth, land agitation and reform had not yet prevented subdivision and acquiring of new farms by a successful tenant. Pat on his fifty-acre mountain farm has married off a daughter locally at three hundred pounds and sent two sons out to America. Another daughter works in England. Two sons, aged forty-three and thirty-six, are at home and Pat hasn't made up his mind yet which one shall get the land (Arensberg and Kimball 1948:147–148).

It will be recalled that the introduction of the superpotato to Ireland led to a dramatic increase in the Irish population and, ultimately, to a disastrous famine. Over one hundred years after the famine, Ireland still maintained one of the highest rates of fertility in the world, over 250 births per one thousand *married* women. The typical Irish wife was producing one child every four years. Presumably the cause of this high rate of fertility was that both the Irish government and the Catholic church strongly opposed birth control and encouraged large families.

Despite the high rate of fertility, Ireland's rate of population growth remained small. Her annual birthrate was 21 babies per thousand people. How was it possible for each thousand married women to produce 250 babies, but to have only 21 babies for each thousand people? Taking note of the above quotation concerning Tom Casey, imagine a small family farm just large enough to support a married couple and their children. Assuming that the family has at least two male and two female children and that the male children will farm the land while the female children marry men farming other small plots, it would be evident that the small farm could not produce sufficient resources to support both sons and their wives and children. One son (in Ireland this was generally the oldest) had to leave the farm and take his chances in the city, England, or the United States. If they remained on the farm, the daughters would have to wait until a farmer came along who had sufficient resources to support them. All other things being equal, the daughters might wait a very long time before such a prince appeared. Most probably, one daughter might never marry and bear children, and the other daughter might not begin to bear children until she was thirty. Even if the married daughter produced a child every two years until she was forty, she could only produce five children, while the unmarried daughter would produce none at all. Irish population, then, appears to have been controlled by a combination of emigration and spinsterhood.

We are often led to believe that the control of human populations depends entirely upon the development of safe, cheap, and effective devices which will prevent the conception of children. The Irish case is one in which population control was achieved, at least for a time, by creating circumstances that delayed or prevented the marriage of women. For such a method to be effective, cultural rules forbidding sexual relationships outside of marriage must be effectively enforced.

India: Can You Afford It?
In K. Sagar's *Modern Complete Letter Writer*, the following is given as a typical matrimonial advertisement:

> Match for M. A., 25 years, beautiful employed Arora virgin. Early decent marriage. Dowry seekers please excuse. Apply Box 2589 Hindustan Times, New Delhi 1. (Sagar N.D.:220).

To the reader, this advertisement conveys the information that this is a Brahmin lady, well past the normal age of marriage, who is unable to provide the dowry usually regarded as a requirement. Brahmins are one of the highest ranking of all the Hindu *jatis* (castes). This is partly because they are a pure, vegetarian, and priestly jati, but it also derives from their control of land, their access to higher education, and their great wealth. Over most of India, Brahmins are a numerically small jati with a birthrate that is lower than that of most other jatis. How is this small birthrate achieved?

The lady in the advertisement is twenty-five years old and has no dowry. Over much of India, a Brahmin woman can be married only if her father is comparatively wealthy. Even in villages, the minimum dowry required amounts to some three times the annual earnings of an ordinary laborer. In the city, the bride's father may well have to provide for the bridegroom's education, perhaps even for years of foreign study. Already ten to fifteen years past the normal age for an early decent marriage, the Arora virgin may hope to marry only some gentleman sufficiently modern or wealthy to disregard dowry or, if she herself is modern, a gentleman from some other jati. The *Modern Complete Letter Writer* offers a reply from a civil engineer of active habits and good disposition but who is a member of a non-Brahmin jati.

In a complex society, such as that of India or the United States, where people are divided into jatis or ethnic groups and where membership in a particular class, caste, or ethnic group has an impact upon the life chances of the individual, differential access to medical care or other resources may also have an impact upon population size. In the United States, poor people, American Indians, American Negroes, and Mexican-Americans may lack access to education, medical care, and jobs and consequently tend to have a lower life expectancy than do members of other groups. Often high mortality is balanced by a high birthrate to produce a net increase in population mostly consisting of children doomed to early death. Among poor people in the United States, especially those living in urban slums, the depressing prospects of future survival, combined with a virtual absence of effective or responsive law enforcement, sometimes leads to heavy use of dangerous drugs and high rates of crime, murder, suicide, and divorce. Where the mother must work to support her children, the absence of public child care facilities may lead to the neglect and death of younger children.

In most complex urban societies, casual or calculated inequalities in the distribution of goods and services lead to a kind of cryptogenocide in which some kinds of people have high rates of infant mortality and short life expectancies. In all societies, the distribution of opportunities and resources helps to determine who shall be married, who shall have children, how long the children will live, and whether or not those children shall, in turn, have the opportunity to bear children.

What Are All the Methods of Control?

In sum, human populations everywhere are regulated by a variety of mechanisms operating at every stage in the life cycle. Before marriage or mating takes place, the high cost of marriage, institutionalized forms of spinsterhood such as convents, malnutrition, poor medical care, or drug taking severely limit the prospect that some individuals will bear children. Once married the high cost of childbirth or the presence of numerous children may lead the husband and wife to abstain from sexual relationships, to practice interrupted sexual intercourse, or to use birth control devices. Once a child has been conceived, drugs or mechanical means may be used to secure abortions. Amateurish, illegal, or self-help abortions often limit population by destroying the mother as well as the fetus. Where abortion is legalized and performed effectively, it has roughly the same impact as birth control devices. As of 1969, for example, the populations of the United States and Japan were both growing at the rate of about 1 percent per year, presumably as the result of legalized contraception in the United States and legalized abortion in Japan. The widespread use of contraception in Japan and illegal abortions by perhaps one fourth of all mothers in the United States make this a less than perfect example.

As in the story of Moses, the abandonment of unwanted children has a long history in human society. In the United States unwanted children are beaten to death with surprising, but not accurately measured, frequency. In South Indian villages, first-born and second-born male children are generally taken to scientifically trained medical practitioners when they fall ill. Later-born male children and female children often receive no medical care at all. There is some evidence that a mere absence of affection may often lead to debilitation, illness, and even the death of human infants. Certainly the love and attention which greets the first-born child can hardly be expected for the fifth-born child. In most societies, although there are exceptions, the first-born child receives the education or expanded opportunity. Very often it is the first-born who makes the "proper" marriage and has the greatest chances of bearing children. The seventh son of a seventh son has dreary prospects indeed. Neglect in infancy is one of the major causes of human mortality.

For all human societies, extraordinary drought, newly introduced epidemic diseases, or other temporary restrictions upon resources or life chances may result in sharp increases in mortality. New technology or more successful adaptations may also lead to needs for rapid reproduction. When this happens, restrictions on population growth tend to be removed and sometimes forgotten. The resulting increase in population may produce a situation in which there are more people than required for efficient operation of the cultural system and more people than the environment can conveniently support. The consequences of such unlimited increase are mass migration, famine, pestilence, or killing.

All cultural systems deal with the problem of having just enough, not too many or too few, warm bodies. The problem is complicated because changing environmental factors and technologies cause constant fluctuations in the size of populations and the need for bodies. Because children are born ten to twenty years before the need for them can be determined and because the number of children born depends upon the number of women who become pregnant, regulation of population requires a degree of knowledge, accurate prediction, and detailed calculation which no cultural system has achieved. For the United States, we do not know how many women have illegal abortions or how many die as a consequence of one. We do not know how many children die of neglect or beatings. We do not know in any detail how many people we need to man our institutions or to maintain our equilibrium with the environment, especially twenty years from now. "Modern" methods for the regulation of population, virtually unaided by the trivial sums expended on population research, are markedly inferior to those employed by groups we sneeringly call "primitive."

The mere production of warm bodies can be achieved with little training and vast enjoyment by almost any human male and female. Almost certainly, it was the puritanical belief that pain must follow pleasure which led Malthus to conclude that human societies must commit the sin of over-population and suffer the punishments of famine, disease, and genocidal war. Comparative examination of a variety of human societies suggests that although these deadly processes occur almost everywhere, their impact is lessened by more benign processes which limit human marriage and fertility. Once processes for the regulation of population have provided a reasonable balance between numbers of people and resources available, other processes are required to ensure the movement of people among the various sub-cultural systems within the society and the occupation of the various statuses provided within the social structure of each of these systems. What are the processes involved in the movement of people within and between cultural systems?

What if you want a male child?

Each time a woman bears a child there is a 50 percent chance that it will be male. If a woman bears two children, there is a 25 percent chance (.5 times .5) that both will be male. In thinking about such things as kinship terminologies and family structures, anthropologists like to visualize nuclear families composed of father, mother, son, and daughter. In real life, a host of factors may create situations in which a nuclear family household lacks a mother or a father or possesses two sons and no daughters. If the adequate operation of the tiny cultural system represented by the nuclear family requires that it be staffed by some particular set of people, severe problems are created by their absence.

In South India, according to one version of the cultural tradition, "A woman should have nine children and treat her husband as the tenth." Most women do not have such proverbial ambitions, but nearly all wish to have four or five children, and, because male children inherit the family farm and may often support the parents in their old age, most women wish to have one or two sons. Because household tasks such as bringing water from the well, grinding grain, and preparing food require large amounts of time, it is very difficult for a single individual to live alone and still have time to earn his living. As a kind of minimum, a household should consist of a working husband, a housewife, and a male heir. Any other condition threatens survival. Consider the following table representing all the households in a single jati in a South Indian village:

HOUSEHOLD NUMBER	HOUSEHOLD COMPOSITION
1	husband, wife, 3 sons
2	husband, wife, 2 daughters
3	husband, wife, 2 sons, 2 daughters
4	husband, wife, 4 sons, 3 daughters
5	adult male
6	adult female
7	mother, 3 sons, 1 daughter
8	adult male, his mother, his sister, his sister's daughter, his sister's husband, his brother's wife
9	husband, wife, husband's father, husband's 3 sisters, husband's 2 sister's daughters

Out of nine families, only three possess husband, wife, and male heirs. In Household 8, the role of the missing wife is filled by a mother and a brother's wife. In Households 8 and 9, the absence of male heirs has been attacked by bringing in women likely to produce sons. There are other things that can be done. If a wife is childless or produces only daughters, she can be divorced or a second wife, often the wife's sister, can be obtained. Where there are daughters and no sons, or where a household owns more land than can be worked by the existing number of sons, it is possible to "adopt" the daughter's husband. In former times, more rarely today, a daughter could be married to one of the deities. Following the marriage, she could have intercourse with persons of any respectable jati who contributed money to the temple of the deity. Her male offspring could inherit her father's property. A husband who suspected that he was responsible for the childlessness of his wife, might prevail upon a friend to have secret intercourse with his wife with the hope of producing a male heir.

A woman, living alone with her children, might rent her fields on a sharecropping basis to a brother or close relative or might earn a living through prostitution, concubinage, or the sale of cooked food. A single adult male would generally remarry as quickly as possible. During the interim, he might obtain cooked food from a neighbor or obtain a concubine, often belonging to another jati. A childless husband and wife might borrow or purchase a son, usually from a close relative. The roles played by missing or sick household members can be filled by visiting relatives or by hiring replacements.

All of these arrangements for the exchange of persons between households have to do with the regulation of membership, and all of them depend upon the existence of a larger cultural system which permits cooperation and the exchange of personnel between households. Because chance factors deeply affect the membership of households, means for the permanent or temporary exchange of personnel between households seem essential. Households tend to be linked together to form bands, neighborhoods, or communities which carry out, among other things, processes regulating the membership of households.

Can You Use Another Hand?

The following excerpt from the life history of a Nunivak Eskimo indicates how such processes may affect the individual:

First thing I remember, I was riding in a sled, but I don't remember where I was going or whom I was with. Next thing I remember, I was living with an old couple. I thought they were my parents, but they were really my grandparents, I learned later. After a while, some children told me they were my grandparents. At first, I wouldn't believe them, but gradually I believed them.

Then my grandfather died. That was the first time I had seen a dead person. I went to live with my father's sister named AMa'Gakh. She was poor and I had a very bad time while I was with her.

I don't know how long I lived with my grandparents or with my aunt. Then Isaac Aiya-qsaq took me: he was my father's brother.

When I went to Isaac, I learned for the first time that I had a real mother and real brother somewhere.

I tried to help Isaac; I wanted to help him. But then Isaac died, the year the church was built. A year later, or a little more than a year later, I married Agnes, Lewis' daughter, Dick's sister, and I came to live with Lewis at Nash Harbor. Lewis' home was a good place. Lewis was like a father to me.

I have had four children. My little girl died of measles in 1942. I have three boys now (Lantis 1960:84–88).

The same sort of thing happens on Alor in Indonesia:

Once my mother wanted me to cut (clear) the fields, but I didn't want to, so she tied my hands together and left me in the house. I gnawed the rope through and ran away to Alurkoma (mother's mother's sister's husband, called grandfather). I lived with Alurkoma for about a year. But I thought about my mother's tying my hands, and so I got part of a knife blade and pounded it to make it hard and went to cut the field. When it was all cut and burned over, my father and mother came to plant it. Then I cared for the field myself and weeded it. When the food was ripening, my mother came to harvest it. I remembered her tying my hands, and I said she could not take the food. She remembered how I had gnawed through the cord and ran away, and she said the crop was hers. She told me I could not cut her gardens any more, and if I wanted to cut gardens I had better go to my father's. She herself got the corn.

All this time I was living with Alurkoma. Alurkoma's wife, Tilamau, said I had better go work at Ruataug, where my father's garden was. So I went there to cut the garden. The first year I got a hundred bundles of maize and sold them in Likuwatang and bought a knife. The next year I got only forty bundles, the year after only thirty, the year after only twenty. Then I stopped working there. (Question) Mother and father lived together all this time. (How many years did you live with your grandparents?) Four years. (Then?) Then I returned to live with my mother and father. At this time I had a friend called Fanmale. We used to shoot at a banana trunk target. When Fanmale hit the target many times, I would beat him over the head with a bow. When I hit the target many times, he would hit me over the head with a bow. We were always quarreling. Then we said we had better stop target shooting. We stopped being friends, and I made friends with Malemani. I threw out Fanmale. I was maybe twelve or thirteen at this time.

Malemani made a house in the fields. His mother was dead. Young men and women gathered. Girls and boys planned whom they would marry. They slept together in this house. The house was near the Limbur ravine. We played there for three years. I stayed there and didn't live with my mother and father. There were many gardens there and enough to eat.

After we had been there awhile I said, "We play only with women and do not think of anything else. Let us think of collecting a brideprice" (DuBois 1961:194–195).

During his childhood, Mangma, who gave the above account, lived with several other relatives including his father's first cousin:

I liked him because he took good care of me. Langmai had no wife. I followed him around, ran errands for him, getting areca, water, fire, tobacco, or whatever he sent me for. I was there alone with him. Langmai said, "My older brother has many children; you come and stay with me" (DuBois 1961:197).

A year later, Mangma went off to stay with another family. On Alor, in contrast to most human societies, the relationships between parents and children appear to be particularly fragile. This is reported to have an impact upon the kinds of people Alorese children turn out to be, and it may have great ecological importance in that it eliminates the role of chance factors in affecting household composition. An Alorese household can apparently contain whatever assortment of male and female children appears desirable at the moment.

All in the family?

Next to the human individual, the individual family household is the fundamental operating unit out of which most cultural systems are constructed. The chances of biology and the life chances of individuals war constantly upon the household, depriving it of needed members and interrupting its functioning. Processes of adoption, marriage, visiting, and employment mobilized within the larger cultural systems represented by bands, neighborhoods, and villages permit replacement of missing or ineffective household members and the continued effective functioning of the unit. Just as the human infant cannot survive without the support of human adults, so the human household cannot survive without the support of larger cultural systems. As households exchange their memberships in order to maintain themselves, a network of communication and interaction between households is established with the result that different households come to share virtually the same cultural tradition.

A community of interacting households may be quite small and it, too, is affected by the problem of getting the right person in the right place at the right time. Small and isolated communities tend to produce a large proportion of their memberships and to rely upon their internal processes for the staffing of the various statuses required for effective operation. More commonly neighborhoods and communities are engaged in wider processes for the permanent or temporary exchange of membership with other cultural systems. The following sections consider the special case of exchange between the city and the small community.

Where Have All the Young Men Gone?

The city of Bombay is located on a peninsula which forms one of the largest and most beautiful harbors in the world. To this harbor come ships laden with the oil, manufactured products, and foodstuffs of Europe and the Near East. Foreign and domestic industrial concerns build their factories and the stately mansions of their managers here. Because the peninsula is small and because factories and stately mansions require considerable space, Bombay, like Manhattan Island or San Francisco, is crowded.

Men who work as laborers in the city take up their residence in crowded slums with unpaved streets. The flushing toilet is unknown; there is no garbage disposal, running water, electricity, or municipal service of any kind. The climate of Bombay is warm and wet and people shelter themselves in impromptu shacks just large enough to contain a bed and a one-burner kerosene stove. To get to work in the morning, the factory worker puts on hip length rubber boots and wades, sometimes for miles, through the mixture of feces and garbage constituting his environment. People who are unable to obtain factory jobs which permit them to buy or rent shacks may find employment in stone quarries located outside the city. Here, there is slightly better housing, trees, and an occasional blade of grass. The barefoot, barehanded worker, his wife, and children gather rocks dynamited from a cliff-face and load them into trucks.

People come to Bombay from the village of Gopalpur, three hundred miles away, for a variety of reasons, but mostly because they are poor and even the stone quarries pay a wage four times larger than can be obtained in the village. Although the population of Gopalpur has grown very slowly and there have been few changes in the village or its region over the past years, people have had an increasingly difficult time maintaining their traditional forms of agriculture. Traditionally this depended upon the presence of a kind of landed aristocracy, which made agricultural loans available to the community and preserved wealth in the form of stored grain that could be released to clients in time of need. With modernization, the rural aristocracy began to move to urban areas and to use their resources for such personal benefits as the education of their children. Over the past two decades, those aristocrats who remained have begun to purchase tractors, jeeps, and other equipment with which to farm their own large acreages. Gopalpur lies, then, in the center of an increasing competition between industrialized farmers and peasant farmers. For the moment, the poor people of Gopalpur maintain their traditional form of agriculture and their competitive position by importing money from Bombay.

For many individuals the traditional form of peasant agriculture has become a kind of hobby supported by remittances from the city. Typically a man works in the city until he manages to save enough money to marry. Leaving his wife and children in the village or, in some cases taking them with him, he returns to the city until he earns enough money to buy land and cattle. His sons then plow the land until they, in turn, require money for their marriages and for expansion of the family agriculture. Permanent emigration to Bombay, while it takes place in some cases, is ruled out by the abysmal living conditions there. Many find it impossible to support their wives and children in the city, and, even if they take their wives, they often find it necessary to leave some or all of their children with grandparents or other relatives. There is a tendency for Gopalpur to become a village of children and old people with most of its young and middle-aged men living in the city.

For many families, the bright promise of a few years spent working in Bombay is marred by susceptibility to fatal and contagious diseases. In one family of Muslims, two brothers emigrated to Bombay and obtained prestigious jobs working in the railroad yards. A younger brother was left behind to care for the agricultural properties and the aged parents. In due time, one of the older brothers sent back his daughter who had contracted tuberculosis of the bone. Daily, the younger brother carried his niece to the dispensary two miles away, but one day, as we started out with our notebooks, we passed him in the Muslim cemetery. He had buried his niece quietly in the cold dawn and was weeping silently while he smoothed and decorated the mud over her grave. In another family, one of the young sons returned from Bombay with tuberculosis. The disease spread through his family, the search for wealth in Bombay ending in the death not only of the son but of most of the members of his household as well. For Gopalpur, the city of Bombay may well represent a kind of ecological trap into which she must pour her young men and thereby maintain a precarious existence between the tractor on the one hand and the cesspools of Bombay on the other.

Where Else Does This Happen?

The movement of rural populations to urban areas has an ancient history. An old Tamil (South Indian) poem translated by Dr. K. Gnanambal describes a city where the rain is falling and the entire population cowering indoors beside the glowing hearth. Everyone, that is, except the Greek mercenaries who are wandering about in the rain, singing and drinking wine. Perhaps, like the men of Gopalpur, they were thinking about wives and children left behind on rocky and unproductive farmsteads.

The following advertisements appeared in the *American Weekly Mercury* of February 18 and May 22, 1729:

> Lately arrived from London, a parcel of very likely English servants, men and women, several of the men Tradesmen; to be sold reasonable and Time allowed for payment.

> There is just arrived from Scotland, a parcel of choice, *Scotch Servants*; Taylors, Weavers, Shoemakers and ploughmen, some for five and others for seven years; . . . (Quoted in Parrington 1927, 1930:134).

With a few changes in working conditions and in the definition of terms, the North American territories have continued to require cheap labor:

The most dramatic occupational change and one which has become a major new source of income to the village is the *bracero* movement. In 1948, fewer than thirty Tepoztecans were *braceros*—that is, temporary agricultural workers in the United States; by 1957, over six hundred men had been *braceros* for periods that varied from forty-five days to over a year. This occupational change has made for other great changes in the village. In 1943, Tepoztlán suffered from an acute land shortage. Now, because in many cases the *braceros* return to the village only to rest a few months before setting out for another period in the United States, it suffers from a shortage of manpower, and many *milpas* go uncultivated (Lewis 1960:97–98).

In Ireland, parts of India, Scandinavia, Greece, Central Asia, all over the world, younger brothers hear of far-off places they will never visit, spinsters wait patiently beside hearths grown cold. A community of old people, women, and children wait for lovers who have gone to war, sons migrated to America, or older brothers working in the factories. In some cases, overcrowded communities become residual communities occupied by grandparents, mothers, and children while the able-bodied men serve in distant wars or factories returning in their old age to retire and raise their now departed children's children.

The above examples deal with the special case in which rural communities producing a surplus of population maintain an integration with urban communities by exchanging their young men for retired factory workers or soldiers. Such a condition is most likely to obtain when new territories, new occupations, or high urban death rates create a population shortage in urban centers. There are many other devices for the exchange of population between communities. One of them is marriage.

Marriage: who shall be chosen?

Marriage, and practices affecting the likelihood of marriage, may play an important role in determining who shall bear children. It is also an important means of regulating the exchange of persons between households and the creation of new households. At this level, incest taboos, forbidding sexual and/or marital relationships among members of the household, have the effect of compelling exchanges between households. Exogamous rules forbidding marriage with particular individuals or classes of individuals and endogamous rules requiring marriage within particular groups or classes, place further limitations upon marriage. Rules that the bride or groom must be beautiful or hardworking or a college graduate or older or younger also work to control the movement of individuals by marriage. Consider the situation in the French village of Peyrane:

By the time young people are ready to marry they are acquainted with other young people from the whole area of the Apt Basin and even from more

distant parts of the department. Family connections, visits, *promenades*, and, above all, the dances which they have attended have enlarged their circle of acquaintances beyond the limits of Peyrane.

Choosing a husband or wife from among these acquaintances is limited by both legal and popular restrictions. It is forbidden by law to marry a lineal relative, whether the relationship is legitimate or illegitimate, whether the relationship is by blood, marriage, or legal adoption. Marriage is also forbidden between brother and sister, uncle and niece, aunt and nephew, brother-in-law and sister-in-law (if divorced). . . . Popular and canonical restrictions go even one step further, to forbid marriage between first cousins. . . .

It may be that a common but less recognized prejudice still further limits the field of choice; young people apparently prefer to find a spouse living beyond the boundaries of the commune rather than to marry someone from the village whom they have always known. Unfortunately, the census records are incomplete on this point, so that we cannot know exactly to what extent people go outside of Peyrane to find a spouse. Of the eighty-two married couples for whom we have information, only seven were endogamous [both spouses from village] and seventy-five were exogamous [one spouse from outside the village] (Wylie 1964:124).

In addition the girl's father must give his consent to the marriage. He does this when the family feels that the young couple are truly in "love" and that both are *serieux*. Being *serieux* involves fidelity, hard work, frugality, and a host of other virtues. Because "a fool and his money are soon parted," the present financial status of the prospective bridegroom is not stressed. On the other hand, a father is unlikely to approve his daughter's marriage unless the prospective bridegroom has some means of support and the couple has a place to live. In order to get married, then, a young man has to establish himself economically. This process is usually delayed because the young man must complete his military service before his marriage. The period of military service begins at the age of twenty, and a considerable time elapses before a young man completes his military service, establishes himself in an occupation, and locates the right girl.

Although a young man may inherit a family farm and therefore bring his wife to his family homestead, such patrilocal residence is often impossible. Whether the new family lives patrilocally, matrilocally (with the wife's family), or neolocally (in a new place), depends upon the availability of occupations and houses. Thus, the concept of *serieux* requires the bride and groom to establish themselves in some location where they may be productively employed. The marriage pattern, then, creates a system for the exchange of brides and grooms between communities, and, by influencing the residence of the bride and groom, it adjusts the population of each community to the available resources. Complaining about the effect of military service upon marriage, Wylie states: "The State loses far more in economic productivity and a lower birth rate than it gains from their services [in the military] (p. 124)." On the other hand, France has been relatively free of overpopulation or high rates of unemployment.

In Peyrane, marriage and the selection of a place to live after a marriage depend primarily upon the earning capacity of the bridegroom. It is a fair guess that the goal of establishing a lasting relationship upon a sound economic foundation is fundamental to all systems of marriage. The individual who embarks upon the process of "getting married" or more likely upon the process of "arranging someone else's marriage" follows a complicated decision-making process which determines who shall be married and where the married couple will take up residence. Consider the preliminary steps involved in entering into the marital search procedure in South India (See Figure 1).

When Do We Search for the Bride?

The groom's father, uncle, or older brother must be prevailed upon to set in motion a process of bride-search which will ultimately lead to a costly marriage followed sooner or later by division of the family property. Faced with the prospect of considerable expense and the loss of a hardworking adult member of the household, prospective arrangers naturally prefer to delay a young man's wedding as long as possible, preferably until the bridegroom becomes increasingly rowdy and bumptious. His work suffers and he spends his nights womanizing, drinking, and/or gambling. Normally this sort of behavior indicates to the arranger that the groom is ready for marriage, and the arranger commences to search for a suitable bride. Where the

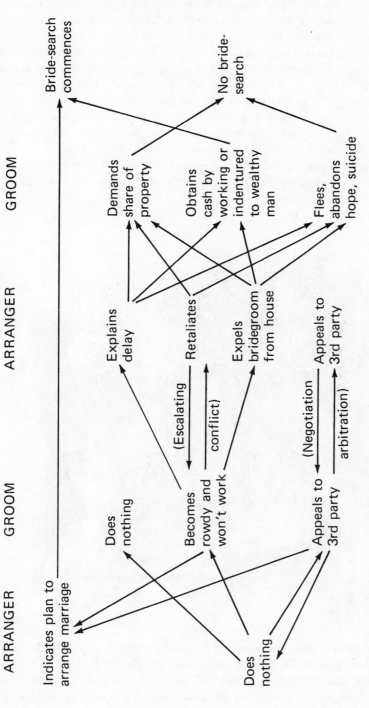

FIGURE 1   A fragment of a process: Initiating the search for a bride.

arranger has decided that there will be no marriage or that the marriage must be delayed, he may try to control the groom's behavior by force, by reason, or by getting rid of him altogether. Both the arranger and the groom may speak to friends and neighbors thereby setting in motion a process of negotiation and arbitration which may ultimately reconcile their differences. Where a lack of cash and other resources makes immediate marriage impracticable, the groom may go to the city or elsewhere to seek a job or he may indenture himself to a wealthy landlord in order to obtain the cash needed for his marriage. Sometimes, not shown in Figure 1, the interest and other charges due the landlord are so high that the groom or his family never receive any cash and the groom works the rest of his life to pay off his debts. In most cases the bride-search ultimately begins and the bridegroom ultimately obtains a bride.

The bride-search is influenced by the fact that the ideal bride, in addition to being beautiful, hardworking, and astrologically correct, should be related to the groom as a mother's brother's daughter, father's sister's daughter, or sister's daughter. Because landed property is handed down within a joint family consisting of the male descendants and younger brothers of the family head, residence after marriage is generally within the groom's joint family. Further, in any small caste or jati all of the households in the village are likely to belong to the same exogamous lineage. Very often all of the women in the village in the groom's jati are considered to be his "sisters." Except where two or more lineages within a village exchange daughters, marriages tend to involve bringing in a woman from another village.

Granted that the groom's mother would like to see her brother's daughter brought into the family, it stands to reason that she would argue in favor of mother's brother's daughter marriage. Now, and here we return to the subject of this chapter, if both the mother and the son's wife come from Village A to Village B, a one-way flow of women from A to B is established. Cash, the "brideprice," flows in the reverse direction form B to A. If we assume that the groom's father wishes to continue and maintain relationships with his sister, and brothers and sisters are considered very close, then the father's sister goes from A to B and the groom's wife goes from B to A. In other words, there is an exchange of women between the two villages, and also an exchange of cash. A similar condition of equal exchange exists when the groom marries his sister's daughter.

Let us go a little further and assume that Village B is a wealthy village where some families have more land than they know what to do with and that Village A is a poor village where some families have no land at all. Because a wife from a poor family will work harder and be less critical of her husband's house, the wealthy families from Village B will naturally wish to acquire women from Village A, while the poor families in Village A will shun women from Village B. Mother's brother's daughter marriage now becomes the favored form of marriage between the two villages. Being wealthy and faced with a shortage of labor, some of the fathers in Village B are likely to decide to obtain their sons-in-law as well as their daughters-in-law from Village A. Now, both mother's brother's daughters and mother's brother's sons are being brought into Village B and the population of Village A is declining. Ultimately, this movement of population would tend to wipe out the economic differential between the two villages and a pattern of sister's daughter or father's sister's daughter marriage might develop as a means of maintaining the restored economic and population equilibrium.

Although in real life, the patterns of marriage in South India are more complicated than the above description suggests, the system as a whole functions as a means of maintaining a good fit between the resources available to a village and the numbers of men and women living in it. In the United States, France, or South India, community size tends to be regulated by processes of job-hunting or bride-searching which cause individuals to move voluntarily from overcrowded communities to less crowded communities. What process might be anticipated where mechanisms for the exchange of population fail to produce an equilibrium? Consider the case of the Tsembaga, a tribal people in New Guinea.

What shall we do with the pigs?

The Tsembaga raise pigs, sweet potatoes, and manioc. Because both pigs and people eat sweet potatoes and manioc, the survival of pigs and people depends upon an adequate balance between them. (The general outlines of the Tsembaga situation were described on pp. 95–96.) When the pig population increases beyond reason, garden owners begin shooting other people's pigs, and pig owners begin shooting gardeners or their wives or pigs. When this happens, people move elsewhere if they can. Another possibility in traditional times was to hold a *Kaiko* or pig festival wherein groups from friendly tribes were entertained periodically over a period of about a year and everyone consumed as much pork as possible. The friendly visitors, most of them relatives from other groups, became military allies by virtue of their participation in the pig festival. When the pig festivals were completed, the community was prepared to attack an "enemy" group and lay waste their houses and gardens. The enemy abandoned its territory and took up residence among friendly groups. If the enemy did not lay claim to its territory within a reasonable time by performing a ceremony called "planting the *rumbin*," the territory could be clamied by the victors. Thus, a community which became overpopulated could regain its environmental equilibrium by expanding its territory.

Although environmental hazards, such as high rates of disease or competing groups, may cause a few human cultural and subcultural systems to suffer from a chronic shortage of members, the most common pattern is one in which tribes, villages, clubs, political parties, or other groups fluctuate in size more or less independently. In a well-run cultural system, mechanisms exist for transferring members from overcrowded groups to less crowded groups. Where groups become excessively large, and this is illustrated by the Tsembaga case, conflict may occur resulting in fission (division into two groups) or in the expulsion of some members. Another alternative, also illustrated by the Tsembaga, is to acquire the additional resources needed to provide for the increased membership. These processes can be observed in most human groups. For example, a physics department having too many students and faculty members may introduce tougher standards, firing some faculty and flunking some students. If resources are available, it may resort to fission, creating a new department of biophysics. It may also grow by taking over the resources of some other department which has been unsuccessful in recruiting students. The specific processes used in the regulation of the population of physics departments are different from those used in Peyrane, South India, or among the Tsembaga. One of the key questions for anthropology, then, is to consider the range of possible ways of regulating group size and the kinds of impact they have on the people who use them.

Summary

Every cultural system must cope with those features of its environment that influence the birth and death and the comings and goings of its members. One important aspect of the problem of population regulation is that human beings possess the capacity to multiply their populations with considerable rapidity. Over the last several centuries, the time required for the human population to double in size has been consistently shrinking. The potential for rapid population increase is present in all human societies, but in most it is controlled by mechanisms that limit this growth. These mechanisms operate by interrupting the human life cycle to prevent mating, conception, birth, or survival.

In any society, that of Tikopia, for example, a variety of processes work together to limit rates of population growth. Interference with or interruption of any of these processes leads to an increase in the number of individuals who survive to maturity. Unless the additional resources required to support the increased number of adults are made available or migration is feasible, the killing of adults through starvation, war, disease, or other means becomes inevitable. Because different processes for the regulation of population affect society in different ways, it is possible to evaluate them in terms of cost and effectiveness.

One of the most economical and effective ways of controlling population growth is through the prevention of mating. The cases of the Irish and the Brahmins illustrate techniques for delaying or preventing the marriage of women. Because men remain fertile virtually throughout their lifetimes and because one man can impregnate many women, systems for delaying the marriage of men are effective only if they also delay the marriage of women. In most complex societies, systems of social stratification and of the unequal distribution of goods and services tend to lower the life expectancies of deprived individuals and classes, thus limiting their rates of population growth. Although contraception, abortion, and infanticide occur in a wide variety of societies, the neglect and abuse of infants are probably the most common methods of regulating population.

Needs for rapid population increase may follow famines, epidemics, or periods of rapid expansion in technology and the availability of resources. Needs for the rapid expansion of population may result in the abandonment of traditional methods for the regulation of population and have led to a situation where the United States and other modern industrialized nations face major difficulties in the regulation of their populations. These difficulties are partly the result of a lack of scientific knowledge concerning systems of population regulation and partly the result of adaptation to rapid increases in resources.

Besides regulating the numbers of persons within any particular society, processes for the regulation of population must insure that the various groups and statuses within society are adequately staffed. The staffing of small subcultural systems such as the household is made difficult by unpredictable variation in the number of children who might be born or survive in any particular household. The presence of such unpredictable variation in household composition requires the exchange of populations between households. Examples of this are drawn from South India, the Eskimo, and the Alorese.

Communities formed by neighboring and interacting households also face problems in the regulation of their populations. Examples from Gopalpur and other ancient and modern rural communities illustrate the special case where rural communities regulate their populations through the temporary or permanent migration of their young men to urban communities. Examples from Peyrane and South India explore the manner in which complex systems of bride-search and marriage may act as a means of adjusting community populations to their resources.

Where the absence of an overarching political and social system places difficulties in the way of exchanges of population between communities, warfare between neighboring communities, illustrated by the case of the Tsembaga, may serve as a means of enlarging the territories of overpopulated communities. In sum, where mechanisms for the regulation of population fail to operate through the exchange of population between groups, groups that become excessively large may either undergo processes of fission or processes for enlarging the resources available to them. The following chapter considers processes involved in recognizing, asserting, and establishing the statuses of individuals or groups.

Further readings

The growth and decline of world population is a frequent topic of discussion in such journals as *Science* and the *Scientific American. Population, Resources, Environment* (Ehrlich and Ehrlich 1972) is a useful recent summary of the issues in this field. *Culture and Human Fertility* (Lorimer 1954) remains the principal source for anthropological discussions of population regulation. More recently, *Man, the Hunter* (Lee and DeVore 1969) provides discussion of population regulation among hunter-collectors.

Relevant Case Studies include Beals' *Gopalpur* (1962), von Fürer-Haimendorf's *The Konyak Nagas* (1969), Messenger's *Inis Beag: Isle of Ireland* (1969), Deng's *The Dinka* (1972), Horowitz's *Morne–Paysan,* and the Halperns' *A Serbian Village in Historical Perspective* (1972).

Problems and questions

1. Collect some evidence concerning premarital search procedures in your own tribe or group. What sort of impact do these search procedures have in determining who shall be married or in influencing the frequency of marriage?

2. Examine several ethnographic sources and compare the methods used to regulate household membership in each case. In each case, consider the extent to which the regulation of household membership involves the exchange of members among households, communities, or other groupings.

3. Conduct a census of a group of neighboring households or of the households to which the members of some particular group belong. Does your data suggest the operation of any mechanisms for regulating household size or composition?

4. Interview several students concerning the number of brothers and sisters they have and their plans concerning marriage and numbers of future offspring. Consider some possible explanations for differences among the students or between the students and their parents. Assuming that your data is typical, what might be concluded about future population growth or decline?

8

Symbolic messages and ritual processes

Processes for the regulation of membership provide the personnel required to carry out the various operations characteristic of any particular cultural system. A further set of processes, defined here as ritual processes, is required to inform the membership concerning what is going on and the nature of the activities expected of them. This chapter deals with the minor rituals that signal the status of the various participants in organized activities and the beginnings and endings of the various processes carried out in the normal operation of the cultural system. It also deals with the major rituals or ceremonies that signal important changes in the status of individuals or the patterns of group activity.

What good is the song of the meadowlark?

In the morning chickens feed in the village street, scratching in the dirt and clucking. At a hint of movement in the

184

sky above, the rooster puffs up to twice his normal size and dashes through the flock screaming "hawk, hawk." Silently the flock scuttles for safety. The social life of animals and people is marked by constant communication. Some of this communication, like the rooster's cry of "hawk," appears to involve messages that are direct and meaningful. Other forms of expression, like the song of the meadowlark, are not so easily understood. If the meadowlark merely wishes to announce his identity and location, his status if you like, why doesn't he cluck like a chicken? For that matter, does the chicken's cluck say, "I am here and all's well," or is it merely done to aid good digestion? Perhaps, if we could talk to chickens, they would have an answer. But if they are at all like human beings, they probably do not know why they do what they do. If they did, they might not tell all to an anthropologist.

In this book, much of what human beings do is discussed from a utilitarian perspective. Working through their cultural systems, human beings carry out a variety of useful activities or processes. "Hunting a wallaby," "planting corn," or even "arranging a marriage," can be conceived in utilitarian terms as means of obtaining food or regulating population. In the practical business of planting corn, we observe people interrupting their activity with horseplay, idle gossip, bursts of song, or even elaborate rituals and prayers claimed essential for the germination of the seeds or the bringing of rain. One of the most challenging problems in anthropology is the search for explanations of human activities that seem meaningless or impractical and that the ordinary person usually cannot explain. Why do you sing excerpts from "La Traviata" in the shower; why do you celebrate Christmas?

Although a great deal of human activity can be explained by the hypothesis that human beings, like chickens, are foolish creatures, most anthropologists cling to the idea that there must be method in such madness. Many human performances which seem necessary, yet seem to have little relevance to such practical matters as earning a living or reproducing the species, may have to do with the regulation of relationships within and between groups of people. If processes for the regulation of membership have the practical effect of ensuring the presence of the warm bodies needed for the various groups and task forces required for the operation of a cultural system, then another class of processes seems to be required to inform individuals concerning their membership status, the nature of the ongoing activity, and the presence and status of other members or groups. Some of these processes, like the prayer for rain which initiates the corn planting process, are parts of other processes, but others, like a high school graduation, seem almost entirely devoted to announcing and confirming status. The prayer for rain, while it could be regarded as a means of symbolizing the beginning of the corn planting process, might also be regarded as a morale boosting device that promises future status as successful corn planters to the supplicants.

Because singing in the shower or praying for rain has no easily identified practical purpose and because people are nevertheless inclined to feel that such activities are necessary, they come under the general heading of ritual. A *ritual* is an oft-repeated action lacking any obvious practical consequence yet stimulating discomfort or anxiety when it is not performed. A complicated and highly formalized ritual is often referred to as a *ceremony*, but anthropologists are not in general agreement concerning these definitions. A ritual, such as a prayer for rain, which takes cognizance of awesome or supernatural forces can be defined as a *religious* rather than a *secular* ritual. Here some anthropologists would define religion as having to do with a state of mind which regards some things as sacred or awesome, while others would rest their definition on a Western and presumably scientific distinction between the natural or "real" world and the supernatural world.

Rituals can be further defined in terms of the people they involve: personal, interpersonal, familial, community, tribal, intertribal, and so on; or they may be defined in terms of the kinds of events that cause them to take place. Thus, *rites of passage* mark stages in the life cycle of the individual such as birth, puberty, marriage, and death; *calendrical ceremonies* mark stages in the annual cycle of activities; and *crisis rituals* mark periods of illness, famine, or catastrophe. The simplest, most common, and least understood kinds of rituals are those interpersonal rituals that mark the day-to-day interaction of human individuals. What is the nature of such rituals? Can they be detected in an ordinary description of behavior such as the following?

Who's Who and What's Going On?

Suddenly Raymond ran *eagerly* to another tree.
He started climbing the tree with great energy.
He remarked *in an offhand way*, but with slight emphasis on the second word, "I hope I can climb this tree." *He seemed to say this to himself as a form of encouragement.*
In a high pitched, soft sing-song he said, "I hope, I hope, I hope."
Raymond continued climbing the tree, *cautiously* grasping one branch and then another, and fixing his feet firmly.
He called out to Stewart in a *playfully boastful manner*, "Stewart, this tree is harder to climb than the other one."
Stewart called back *very firmly and definitely*, "No, it isn't."
When Raymond was as high as it seemed safe to climb, he settled in a crotch of the tree with his hands gripped tightly around the branches.
Exuberantly he sang out, "Owww, owww, whee. Do you see me?" (Barker and Wright 1955:207).

In the above episode, the performances of Raymond and Stewart can easily be interpreted as representative of one of the processes characteristic of a particular cultural system. It can be given the label, "tree climbing process" and classified under the general heading of "children's play." In utilitarian or practical terms, the tree climbing process can be interpreted as a means of developing physical skills which will be useful in adult life. Although the observer has tended to ignore the problem of communication between Stewart and Raymond and, in particular, has only summarized their nonverbal communications, it is more difficult to understand and to "see" the interaction rituals that form a part of the tree climbing process. When Raymond runs "eagerly" to the tree and says, "I hope I can climb this tree," he seems to be performing a ritual which changes his status from that of a person watching Stewart climb a tree to that of a tree climbing person. When he says his tree is harder to climb, he seems to be establishing status as Stewart's competitor.

Raymond's assertions of his status with regard to Stewart are necessary if the tree climbing process is to be a social act. What is missing from this example, as it must be from most examples of human behavior, is the presence of the anxiety that would exist if the rituals were improperly performed. The more subtle rituals, especially those performed every day, tend to be invisible both to performers and observers simply because they are performed constantly. Is it really fair to classify Raymond's eagerness as a ritual and to give it the same significance as a prayer for rain? One approach to this problem is to consider what happens when two individuals meet and both perform inappropriate rituals.

Am I Not Sacred, Too?

Once last year as I was leaving my office in Jackson, Miss., with my Negro secretary, a White policeman yelled, "Hey, boy! Come here." Somewhat bothered, I retorted: "I'm no boy!" He then rushed at me, inflamed, and stood towering over me, snorting "What dija say, boy?" Quickly he frisked me and demanded, "What's your name, boy?" Frightened, I replied, "Dr. Pouissant. I'm a physician." He angrily chuckled and hissed, "What's your first name, boy?" When I hesitated he assumed a threatening stance and clenched his fists. As my heart palpitated, I muttered in profound humiliation "Alvin."

He continued his psychological brutality, bellowing, "Alvin, the next time I call you, you come right away, you hear? You hear?" I hesitated. "You hear me, boy?" My voice trembling with helplessness, but following my instincts of self-preservation, I murmured, "Yes sir." Now fully satisfied that I had performed and acquiesced to my "boy" status, he dismissed me with, "Now, boy, go on and get out of here or next time we'll take you for a little ride down to the station house!" (Kochman 1971: 67–68).

Here, the incident was almost certainly triggered by some improper aspect of Dr. Pouissant's demeanor. *Demeanor* is a term used by Erving Goffman (1967:56–84) to describe the manner in which one individual presents himself to another. Dr. Pouissant's demeanor involved his physical appearance as a "Negro" combined with costume and gestures which may have reflected his status as a physician or a middle-class person. Dr. Pouis-

sant's demeanor may have involved a breach of ritual etiquette which demanded that Negroes dress and act poor. Dr. Pouissant's demeanor, then, was a profanation or defilement of the policeman's sacred values comparable to that which might occur if a minister preached a sermon in his undershorts.

Goffman defines the proper exchange of rituals indicative of regard for the status of other individuals as *deference*. In this case, Dr. Pouissant further profaned the policeman's sacred values by claiming, first, an equal status as an adult, and, second, a superior status as a physician. This is what Goffman defines as *ceremonial profanation*. In response, the policeman brutally invaded Dr. Pouissant's personal space and destroyed his ritual status by touching (frisking) him. The normal and ceremonious conduct of everyday life depends upon deference, the tender and ritual regard which each person exhibits toward all other persons. Because interaction rituals are performed automatically without thought ("Good morning, how are you?" "I'm fine."), people are generally unaware of their ritual nature, the fact that they are performing them, or their precise meaning. In linguistic terms, "How are you?" seems to call for a medical report, but, in fact, its real meaning is closer to "I know and recognize you; do you know and recognize me?" Regardless of medical circumstances, the proper answer is "Fine." All rituals, including interaction rituals, involve the use of symbolic actions, gestures, objects, and words that seem to be meaningful but whose meaning is often unknown to the performer. How are such symbolic codes to be interpreted and understood?

What Does an Eyebrow Flash Mean?
The accompanying drawings illustrate a widely distributed human gesture known as an "eyebrow flash." According to Eibl-Eibesfeldt (1970:420), the

eyebrow flash occurs in a variety of widely distributed cultures as a part of the ritual of greeting expressing the fact that the greeter is in an especially good mood. How is the widespread distribution of the eyebrow flash to be explained? Eibl-Eibesfeldt feels that the eyebrow flash and various other gestures such as nodding, bowing, or smiling may derive in whole or part from a biologically rather than culturally inherited system of communication. Such gestures might be viewed as representing aspects of a prehuman or prelinguistic system of communication which, since it is biologically inherited, could be expected to be universally present among human beings. Because particular cultural systems might train their members to avoid smiles or eyebrow flashes or to use such gestures in highly restricted ways, Eibl-Eibesfeldt does not expect that the same gestures would have the same meanings in all human groups: "We know that innate behavior patterns can be suppressed by training" (1970:424). The facts of the case seem to be that interaction rituals tend to involve gestures and body movements many of which seem to have similar meanings in widely separated human cultures.

The same appears to be true of other kinds of rituals as well. Bruno Bettelheim (1954) notes that initiation rituals often involve surgical operations upon the male or female genitals. Why should this be so, and what does it mean? Bettelheim suggests that human beings might have a universal tendency to envy the sexual organs possessed by members of the opposite sex. The motive behind the cutting or manipulation of the male or female sexual organs might be to provide males with vaginas and females with penises. This is a dramatic and intriguing thought, but a great deal of evidence is required before it can be firmly rejected or accepted as correct. In this case, the argument for the existence of a universal system of meaning derives from the argument that human males and females tend to envy each other and to wish to be like one another. Although such envy might to some degree be of biological origin, it might also be attributed to universal aspects of cultural systems such as the division of labor between men and women in the human family. A recent and pioneering discussion of envy is that of Foster (1972).

The wide but by no means universal association between initiation rituals and operations performed upon sexual organs could be explained as an innate or biological characteristic which is suppressed in some cultures. Another possible explanation is that it is a very ancient idea which was once characteristic of all human societies, but which has been replaced by other ideas in some cultural systems. All human beings make use of fire, although one or two groups have been reported as being unable to make fire. Because human beings are the only animals that use fire, it could be argued that there is some connection between human biology and the use of fire, but it would also make sense to argue that fires are simply an ancient discovery that all men share. Fires often symbolize warmth and togetherness and play an important part in rituals of various kinds. The experience of heat from a fire can be thought of as a part of the biological basis for a universal symbolism of fire, but in any given culture fire symbolizes much more than warmth.

Is the symbol cultural or biological?

Because of their common biology and the universal possession of languages and cultural systems, human beings share a great many experiences so that there are widespread similarities in the meanings attached to different things and particularly to the symbols in rituals. It is hardly startling to discover that arrows are masculine or that pots are feminine. Feces, blood, and dead things often symbolize danger and pollution. If you ask someone to indicate the direction from which the sun rises, it is obvious that he is going to have to point with his finger, or his lips, or his chin or in one of the limited number of ways in which direction may be indicated. The shape of the human body and the distribution of human muscles place restraints on the manner in which pointing may be conveniently carried out and even if our man points awkwardly from our viewpoint with his shoulder or with his elbow, we are likely to get the message. Is the message, therefore, biological or is it cultural?

The United States Christmas ritual involves eggnog, Christmas trees, ornaments, Yule logs, the Virgin and Child, and the colors red and green. Do these things have a universal symbolic meaning? Could we say that eggnog symbolizes mother's milk, that the evergreen tree symbolizes life everlasting, that the ornaments symbolize fruitfulness, that the Yule log symbolizes the eternal flame of life, that the Virgin and Child symbolize fruitfulness, that red symbolizes menstrual blood, and that green symbolizes life and vegetation? If so, we could interpret the symbols of Christmas as having to do with fertility or with life and death in some way. The point is, we are just guessing. Perhaps the color red symbolizes death and red and green together symbolize death and rebirth.

How Do We Know What the Symbols Mean?
One of the best ways of finding out what things mean is to ask people. Imagine, then, walking up to a U.S. citizen and saying: "What is the mean-

ing of eggnog?" or "What does an eyebrow flash mean?" The hidden significance of eggnog, if it has a hidden significance, can only be understood in the context of the whole system of meanings that the members of a cultural system use in the communication of ideas and feelings. One way to begin to understand eggnog, for example, would be to examine the various ritual contexts within which the consumption of various drinks occurs. Or, since eggnog is more or less white, we might consider the various ritual contexts in which whiteness is important. Might we connect the fact that white symbolizes virginity in certain contexts with the fact that Christmas has to do with the Virgin Mary? Does the whiteness of the eggnog symbolize snow or does it symbolize nothing at all?

Does eggnog derive its meaning from some prelinguistic, biologically inherited system of communication or is its meaning culturally assigned? The answer to such questions depends upon what eggnog means or, more importantly, from whence its meaning comes. If the meaning of eggnog comes solely from the fact that it is a whitish fluid and if all whitish fluids signify mother's milk for all human beings, then we would have to say that at one level at least it can be interpreted as a universal and biologically based symbol. But a ritual drink like eggnog is freighted with all kinds of meanings and psychological associations. To the extent that these meanings are cultural; that is, to the extent that they are shared by a set of members of a cultural system, the meaning of eggnog is cultural. To say that something is cultural is to say that it arises in a complicated way out of interactions among human biological factors, environmental factors, and the various experiences that the successive sets of members of the cultural system have undergone.

Any kind of thing or action to which meaning can be assigned is likely to derive some part of its meaning from universal human characteristics. Such universal characteristics are likely to represent common human biology, common human experiences, or very ancient and widespread ideas. The proper question to ask about eyebrow flashes, eggnogs, and other such things is not whether they are of biological or cultural origin, but to what extent and in what way various different factors have affected their meaning.

An important point about rituals and ceremonies is that they involve things and actions that have meaning but whose meaning is not clear. The messages inherent in the casual rituals of daily interaction, as well as the messages inherent in more formal and complex rituals, are often unconsciously transmitted and received. We are cheered by cheery greetings, but, as informants, it is not clear to us precisely how the message was delivered or exactly how it triggered our own cheeriness.

How Close Are You?

For example, the psychological state of a given individual and his relationships to other individuals are deeply influenced by how close to other persons the individual is standing. But what does it mean when individuals stand close together or when they stand far apart? Is there a hidden message in the rituals of nearness and farness? For the United States, Hall (1959: 163–164) gives the following partial interpretation of the meaning of distance:

1. Very close (3-6")	Soft whisper; top secret
2. Close (8-12")	Audible whisper; very confidential
3. Near (12-20")	Indoors, soft voice; outdoors, full voice; confidential
4. Neutral (20-36")	Soft voice, low volume; personal subject matter
5. Neutral (4.5-5')	Full voice; information of non-personal nature
6. Public Distance (5.5-8')	Full voice with slight overloudness; public information for others to hear
7. Across the room (8-20')	Loud voice; talking to a group
8. Stretching the limits of distance (20-24' indoors; up to 100' outdoors)	Hailing distance, departures.

Granted a certain amount of local variation, it is plain that citizens of the United States could not manage themselves or their social lives unless they knew in some way how to maintain proper distance. Of course, they manipulate and influence each other through their management of distance. People use interaction rituals in subtle ways to influence each other and establish their status. Does this sort of thing also take place in those more formal and complicated rituals for which the term ceremony is appropriate? Do Hopi Indian ceremonies change individual behavior and, if so, how?

Ritual impact: how did you feel?

Among the Hopi Indians of the southwestern part of the United States, the infant in traditionally oriented groups is bound to a cradleboard soon after birth. He is taken off the cradleboard only for the changing of soiled diapers or for bathing. Eating, sleeping, and traveling all take place on the board. After he is three months old, the child is released for progressively longer periods. Children are usually nursed on demand or whenever they cry or whimper. As soon as the child begins to demand solid food, adults give him part of whatever they are eating. As the child approaches one year of age, he is encouraged to walk and to speak his first words. A child is weaned when the mother becomes pregnant with a second child, few babies nursing for more than two years. When the child can walk and understand, an effort is made to toilet-train him. The child comes home to eat when he pleases (but not when adults are eating), eats whatever he wants, and sleeps when he feels like it. Girls may spend the night in friends' houses while boys frequently sleep in a group at some distance from the family house. The child may touch everything he sees, but must stay away from the cliff, the stove, and the ladder leading down into the ceremonial house (*kiva*). He is told not to fight, tease, or injure anyone, but not really prevented from doing so. Until he is six, the male child has no duties. After six, he may be asked to accompany his father to the fields where he guards the cornfields against prairie dogs, runs errands, chops wood, picks fruit, and helps with the harvesting (Dennis 1940).

Hopi parents are not completely permissive:

> My child, tomorrow morning you will go for a bath. Just as the sun comes out you will pray (wish, will) that your life shall be good. Then the sun will come out and give you life. And you shall live happily. Here you happily will work for me and I'll eat those good things. With them I will grow strong. I shall continue to live well. I won't be sick. Going on (my road) I shall always be happy. And these people having something to live by will think (only) of continuing their good lives. And having made the good life for them, don't ever be mean (angry). Whoever is not mean will live long. Whoever is mean will surely die. Therefore anyone who is happy always sings. And so go take your bath. If you do that you will be strong, and your mothers and fathers (clouds, katcinas, the dead) will be happy when you work for them. They will be parents to your plants. One who lives thinking this way has a peaceful (Hopi) life and is always happy (Kennard 1937:491).

If children misbehave, a bugaboo katcina[1] may appear, masked and carrying a basket in which to stuff naughty children. Parents may have great difficulty in defending children from these monsters. Fathers tend to punish children only when they are annoyed, but the mother may ·call upon one of her brothers to punish all the children for the offense of any one. Good children, and of course there are no strong precedents for badness, receive gifts: "You have helped your father in the fields so the katcinas have brought you a nice bow and arrow" (Dennis 1940:47).

In the Hopi system of thought, thinking about good or appropriate things has a positive effect upon this world and the world of the katcinas. The good thoughts and actions of the katcinas affect this world. Katcinas bring gifts to children and rain. Trouble in the world comes from those who think "mean" thoughts, the "two-hearts." A great many Hopi, sometimes members of one's own family, are, often unknowingly, two-hearts who must bring illness and disaster upon their relatives or die a kind of supernatural starvation. Hopi rituals, which maintain a relationship between the Hopi and the katcinas, preserve what little good there is in the world.

All of this is soon recognized by the child. He knows that if he pretends to be sick, he may cause illness in others. He knows that a dream may spell danger to his friends and relatives. In a moment of rudeness a child may

[1] Katcinas or kachinas are supernatural figures sometimes impersonated by masked men. Their meaning and role in Hopi life are explained in the following examples.

offend someone who turns out to be a two-heart, and the child may sicken and die. For protection in this unsafe world, the child may rely upon the katcinas. No matter what happens, the katcinas will be there to enjoin correct behavior and prevent disaster.

Between the ages of six and ten, the child must prepare himself to undertake adult responsibilities. The child's passage from the permissive world of childhood to the harsher world of adult work and responsibility is marked by his initiation into either the Powamu or the Katcina society. Parents decide which of these societies is to be selected. The Powamu society has a relatively mild initiation rite which takes place on the fifth day of the Powamu ceremony. Initiation into the Katcina society is considered more difficult and takes place on the fifth day of the Powamu ceremony, or, if there is a Powamu initiation, on the day following. The initiates to both societies are present through ten days of intense ceremonial activity.

What Is the Ceremony Like?

At the climax of the sixth day of the Powamu ceremony the Katcina initiation takes place as follows: The chief priest of the Powamu society (dressed in white, holding in his left hand a gourd, four corn ears, and a knife-shaped wooden implement, and in his right a crook to which the corn ear and the cornmeal packets are fastened) takes a position to the right of the ladder leading down into the underground ceremonial room. He is Muyingwa, the god of fertility and growth. An old man asks: "Taa, hakah um pito?" (Well, where did you come from?) The katcina replies that he came from below. The old man says, "Tell us why you wander about?" The katcina explains how those below made a ladder with turquoise strands holding it together:

Eastward we came, traveling on a road marked with yellow corn seed (shelled corn). We beheld the house of the Akush Katcina chief. In a beautiful yellow mist was the house enveloped. So we went in. The Akush Katcina chief was there. He has beautiful yellow corn seed, beans, watermelons, muskmelons, and that way he lives. Here these Oraibi children, little girls, little boys, of different sizes, here at the *sipapu* shall they know our ceremonies; yes they shall know them. Beautiful ladder beam, beautiful ladder rungs, tied to the beam with turquoise strands. Thus, we came out.

Westward we came. On a road marked with beautiful blue corn seed we traveled. We beheld the house of the Nakachok Katcina chief. Beautiful white mist enveloped the house. Thus we went in. The Nakachok Katcina chief was there. Having beautiful blue corn seed, beans, watermelons, muskmelons, he dwells there. These Oraibi children here, little girls, little boys, of different sizes, here at the *sipapu* shall they know our ceremonies. Yes, they shall know them! Beautiful ladder beam, beautiful ladder rungs, with turquoise strands are they tied to the ladder. Thus we came out (Voth 1901:99).

And so it goes, westward again to the Hototo Katcina enveloped in red mist, southward to the Mastop Katcina enveloped in white mist, northward, westward, southward, eastward, southward, and northward. The deity continues:

And now you gather your people, your children, all of them, into your lap and hold them all very fast (protect them). But now this time open your hands to these people that this yucca may enlighten their hearts, and when their hearts have been enlightened here their heads will be bathed with roots of this yucca and then they will be done.

And thus then follow to the white rising and to the yellow rising this road marked with nice corn pollen and on which these four old age marks (crooks) are standing. On them you will support (or rest) yourselves, and over yonder, where the shortest one stands, may you fall asleep as old women and as old men. But I am not wandering alone. Here at the corner they have already arrived (referring to the four Koyemsi Katcinas behind the curtain in the corner of the kiva); come in, be welcome (Voth 1901:100–101)!

The deity sprinkles the candidates with water and leaves the kiva. The Koyemsi katcinas, who seem little more than boys, touch every candidate with a corn ear and a stone axe. They stand aside and there is silence. All know that soon other katcinas will come to flog the initiates. There is a

loud grunting noise; rattles and bells are heard. There are poundings on the
roof and the word *u'huhuhu* is howled repeatedly. The two Ho katcinas
enter the kiva and stand on either side of a large sand painting, grunting,
howling, rattling, trampling, and brandishing the yucca leaves to be used
as whips. The Hahai-i katcina stands at the southeast corner of the sand
painting holding a supply of whips.

> A sponsor seizes a nude candidate and drags him onto the sand mosaic
> holding both of his hands. The boy attempts to protect his sexual organs
> from the pointed tips of the yucca leaves as he is beaten on the legs and
> hips. Mothers and fathers shout encouragement at their children or accuse
> the katcinas of hitting too hard. Some children endure the flogging without
> flinching, others jump away and scream. Sometimes a frightened child mic-
> turates or defecates. When it is over the Hahai-i katcina is severely beaten
> by both Ho katcinas who then begin scourging each other while the initiates
> cheer. The katcinas leave and the initiates may now know ceremonial
> secrets. On following days the community is filled with katcinas and there are
> dances and ceremonies. On the tenth day, more recently on the ninth day,
> the katcinas appear in the village and order all people into their houses.
> Later, there is a procession in which the people accompany the katcinas. At
> the conclusion of the ceremonies, all parents are ordered to cover up or
> otherwise hide their children. As soon as this is done, the katcinas remove
> their masks. They are men, not gods (Voth 1901:100–125).

What Was the Effect?

Years later Don Talayesva described his experiences to the anthropologist, Simmons:

> I recognized nearly every one of them, and felt very unhappy, because I
> had been told all my life that the Kachinas were gods. I was especially
> shocked and angry when I saw all my uncles, fathers, and clan brothers
> dancing as Kachinas. I felt the worst when I saw my own father and when-
> ever he glanced at me I turned my face away.
>
> I kept thinking . . . about the Kachinas whom I had loved (Aberle 1950:
> 83–84).

The above description of the Powamu ceremony and the katcina society
initiation is fragmentary and incomplete. It is difficult for an outsider to
grasp all the complexities or to understand why the process of initiation
should take precisely the form that it takes among the Hopi. Anthropologists
disagree about the extent to which the dramatic discovery that the gods
are men is surprising or shocking to the children. The situation may be like
that in the United States where some children believe in Santa Claus and
others never take him seriously. Because most children only undergo the
relatively mild Powamu initiation, they are not whipped, but they do see
their friends whipped. The child learns that years ago, the katcinas did
actually visit the earth. Now, the two-hearts have frightened them away

and they appear as spirits inhabiting the masks worn by human beings. Such information must never be revealed to the uninitiated.

Anthropological understandings of such a complicated ceremony can be reached at many different levels. Historically, the Powamu ceremony can be compared with ceremonies held by neighboring groups and tribes and certain elements in the ceremony can be shown to have been borrowed and to have diffused or spread from group to group. Such a ceremony may also be understood as a complicated system of symbols, a kind of hidden message which is not fully understood even by the participants. Symbolic representations of fertility, for example, might be sought in the equipment, drawings, and decorations used. By comparing the Powamu ceremony with all other Hopi ceremonies or other processes that make up Hopi life, it might be possible to arrive at a picture of the basic organization of the cultural system.

Because the obvious intent of the Powamu ceremony is that of converting boys into men, we are inclined to wonder if it really does so and, if so, how it accomplishes its ends. Don Talayesva remembers:

> I thought of the flogging and the initiation as an important turning point in my life, and I felt ready at last to listen to my elders and to live right. Whenever my father talked to me I kept my ears open, looked straight into his eyes, and said, "Owi (Yes)" (Aberle 1950:84).

Why did the ceremony affect Don Talayesva in this way? One explanation is that the ceremony offers the initiate a clear choice. He may conclude that the katcinas are not real and accept the consequence that he can no longer be a Hopi, or he can accept the spiritual nature of the katcinas in which case all of the benefits of membership accrue. On its face, the whole ceremony involves trickery and meaningless cruelty ("when I saw my own father . . . I turned my face away")on the part of the very same people who have treated the child so indulgently in the past. Logically and emotionally, the child's only escape is the recognition that his parents and relatives behaved as they did as a means of countering the machinations of the two-hearts.

In general, where rituals are designed to produce striking changes in the daily behavior of individuals, a variety of psychological devices appear to be employed: drug taking, pain, fatigue, isolation, starvation, repetition, music, propaganda, dramatic performances, feasts, confessions, and processions. The combination of a number of such techniques to form an elaborate ceremonial process mobilizing all of the symbolic and behavior controlling apparatus of the cultural system almost certainly results in deep and irreversible changes in the personalities of many who are subjected to them. The cynical young child who does not believe in Santa Claus or who has never been deceived by the katcinas may not be so deeply affected by earnest endeavors to change his personality. Such individuals, and they exist in many if not in all parts of the world, may yet respond to ceremonies by dramatically changing their behavior. Whatever else it may do or signify, an elaborate initiation ceremony indicates that the adults mean business. The initiate must "grow up" or else. For further discussion of the influence of discontinuity on cultural transmission see Chapter 9.

Many rituals and ceremonies have importance, not so much for their role in changing individuals as for their role in changing relationships among individuals or in affirming the solidarity of particular groups. How is it possible for rituals to strengthen social bonds?

Have you come to eat the holigi?

One day during the slack period just after harvest, a group of well-dressed men and women arrive in Gopalpur in procession accompanied by musicians. These men and women are relatives of Siddanna who, along with several elders of their village, have come to discuss a possible marriage of one of their sons to Siddanna's daughter. After resting for a decent interval in the courtyard of the village temple, they march in procession to the open space in front of Siddanna's house. Men from Siddanna's house go through the village, stopping at every house and announcing, "*Biigaru* have come to our house, so come." Gradually, one or two persons from each house in the village, along with all of the children in the village, go to Siddanna's house and sit.

When all have gathered, someone says, "Is there anyone here from the Stoneworker's colony?" A man stands up and says, "Yes, we were invited." A messenger arrives from the Police Headman of the village, "I am not feeling well, but pretend I am there and talk." The Village Crier addresses the biigaru: "What is your village; why have you come?" The biigaru reply, "We have come because there is *holigi* in Siddanna's house. We have come to eat the holigi." The Crier turns to Siddanna: "Have you got holigi in your house? They have come to eat the holigi." Siddanna answers, "Yes there are holigi in my house. If they have come to eat the holigi, let them eat." The Crier asks the biigaru, "What is the *oli* on your side?" They reply, "It is 75 rupees; what is it on your side? How many saris do we have to give you?" Siddanna answers, "Here the oli is 110 rupees and two saris. One sari must cost 15 rupees, one must cost 20 rupees if the people are poor. The mother's sari and the full stomach sari are included in the oli. Are you ready to give this much oli or not?" The biigaru reply, "Yes." Siddanna's people say, "We must also be given an anklet weighing two seers, a leg chain weighing one half seer, a silver girdle weighing one seer, a bracelet of ten tolas, an upper arm bracelet of one seer, a gold earring weighing one tola, a nose star, a marriage necklace and one or two *masi*." (Usually the nose star and marriage necklace are not mentioned at this time.) The biigaru reply, "Yes."

The biigaru have brought a sari for the bride, flowers, and two blouses. The sari is placed on a plate and given to the bride along with the two blouses, rice, dried dates, betel leaf and nut, and a half coconut. A lamp is lit and placed before the bride. A diagram is drawn with rice. The bride and "the girl-who-sits-beside-her" sit on the diagram and put on the sari and the blouses. A blouse and one rupee are given to the girl-who-sits-beside-her. Turmeric powder is rubbed on the girls' foreheads and on everyone sitting nearby. Two half coconuts are filled with rice, areca nut, and other materials and poured into the bride's sari. This is called the *stomach filling*, and it gives the bride a somewhat pregnant look. Brown sugar is now given to the biigaru and other portions distributed to the Village Headman, the Police Headman, the Accountant, the Crier, the Blacksmith, the Priest, the Carpenter, "People from Other Villages," and to everyone present. All except the biigaru and the family leave. Siddanna's family prepares food and feeds the biigaru. Invited guests from the village then come and eat. All sleep. The next morning, the biigaru and other guests are given holigi and they return to their village.

People in South India do not rush hastily into marriage. The eating of the holigi is just one of a series of steps leading to a climactic marriage ceremony. Although either party can withdraw from the marriage at any point, the cost of the separate ceremonies along the way must have the effect of increasing commitment and reducing the chances of a withdrawal just before the final ceremony is to take place. Another easily seen characteristic of the ceremony is that it ensures the presence of a large number of witnesses to the unwritten marriage contract.

But why is it necessary that everyone in the village be invited, that anyone who can't come present his excuses, and that everyone receive and eat brown sugar? Villagewide participation in the ritual argues that: (1) no one in the village is sufficiently angry with Siddanna to refuse to attend; and (2) all know about and approve of the wedding. It is not so much a matter of the ceremony promoting or establishing social ties or social integration within Gopalpur as it is a demonstration of the preexistence of such ties. In fact, all public and community ceremonies in Gopalpur *must* be properly conducted, yet they cannot be conducted if there is open conflict in the village. Outstanding conflicts between the bride's village and the groom's village would also rule out the possibility of marriage. Because the enactment of a large ceremony, no less than the enactment of a minor interpersonal ritual, requires a process of cooperation and of recognition of status, it is possible to interpret rituals of all kinds as being enforcers and regulators of human relationships.

The Powamu ceremony and the various South Indian marriage ceremonies illustrate varieties of ritual which can, at least from some viewpoints, be interpreted in utilitarian or practical terms. Both varieties of ceremony appear to affect human behavior and to develop a broad acceptance of and commitment to specific changes in status and role behavior. The processes of becoming a man or a married couple seem to be directly facilitated by the ritual. In the same way, Rappaport's description of the Kaiko ritual in New Guinea (see pp. 94–95) attributes to it the practical effect or function of regulating populations of pigs and people. Although almost any ceremony can be explained in terms of the fact that it provides insurance by encouraging the accumulation of goods or that it gives everyone a good high protein meal or that it is good for business, many rituals and ceremonies are hard to explain in practical terms. What are the following rituals good for?

How did you overcome your problem?

I was born in Jaltal, an ailing child with a great head that caused my mother much pain. While I was still in the womb, my father mistook a snake for a bit of wood and struck it with his axe. This snake was really the God Ajorasum, and when I was born he made me very ill. But my father called a shaman, who sacrificed a fowl to the angry god and dedicated a pot with many promises and I recovered. Later, when I was old enough to play with other children and take the cattle out to graze, my father sacrificed a buffalo to Ajorasum on the bank of a stream (Elwin 1955:135).

Here, the purpose of these healing rituals is evidently that of restoring and maintaining health, but, it if works, it is not clear why it works. The following more complicated series of events is even harder to explain:

When I was about twelve years old, a tutelary girl called Jangmai came to me in a dream and said, "I am pleased with you; I love you; I love you so much that you must marry me." But I refused and for a whole year she used to come making love to me and trying to win me. But I always rejected her until at last she got angry and sent her dog (a tiger) to bite me. That frightened me and I agreed to marry her. But almost at once another tutelary came and begged me to marry her instead. When the first girl heard about it she said, "I was the first to love you, and I look on you as my husband. Now your heart is on another woman, but I'll not allow it." So I said "No" to the second girl. But the first in her rage and jealousy made me mad and drove me out into the jungle and robbed me of my memory. For a whole year she drove me.

Then my parents called a shaman from another village and in his trance my tutelary came upon him and spoke through his mouth. She said to my parents, "Don't be afraid, I am going to marry him. There is nothing in all this; don't worry, I will help the boy in all his troubles." My father was pleased and bought a she-goat, and two cloths, bangles, a ring and a comb and arranged the wedding. The shaman sat down in the house, put the gifts and a new pot in front of him, tethered the goat near by and, singing, singing, fell into a trance. My tutelary's mother, father and sisters brought her to me and I fell to the ground unconscious. Jangmai asked for her cloth and the shaman dressed me in it. Then she demanded the other things, gift by gift, and they put the ring on my finger and gave me the bangles and necklace, and did my hair with the comb (Elwin 1955:135–137).

A tutelary is a spirit from a high ranking jati who falls in love with and "marries" a male or female of the Saora tribe in India. After a "wedding" has taken place, the afflicted (or favored) individual becomes a shaman who can be possessed by spirits and so diagnose and cure illness. The position of shaman is one of great responsibility and importance. It is tempting, then, to think of Saora healing rituals as a means of providing a place for those Saora who seek some greater importance in life than the daily round of farming, eating, and sleeping which is the lot of the ordinary

person. In effect, ritual marriage to a tutelary spirit might be regarded as a means of preventing or treating mental illness. It is equally possible that Saora mythology concerning illness and tutelary spirits is itself responsible for the creation of the mental illness which it cures.

Why Healing Rituals?

The most obvious fact about magical or supernatural healing rituals in most cultures is that they operate in areas where practical cures are unavailable. In the United States, if there were a quick and easy cure for arthritis, people would hardly feel a need to cure it by wearing copper bracelets. Because the course of any illness is affected in some degree by the patient's state of mind, it can be argued that any authoritative treatment will be beneficial. Even where psychological assistance is of no conceivable value, the absence of any other effective treatment combined with the fact that psychological treatments often are effective would encourage people to attempt rituals that depend upon magic or supernatural agencies for their effectiveness.

Illness, especially severe illness, is a threat to the status of the individual as a member of his cultural system and also to the status of the family or work group of which the individual may be an important part. Healing rituals can be interpreted as a means of coping with the resulting anxiety. Because rituals in general tend to occur during those anxious moments when the individual or the group is undergoing a change in status, it is possible to argue that the fundamental source of human ritual activity is human anxiety and uncertainty.

In Saora healing rituals, the shaman identifies the precise cause of the illness and, while he is possessed by the spirit or deity responsible, reveals the exact steps required for treatment and cure. Fine if it works, but what if it doesn't work? How does that allay anxiety? The Saora tend to explain the failure of their healing rituals by appealing to the willful nature of supernaturals. Spirits and deities are easily offended and it is always easy to identify some failure or inadequacy in the performance of ritual which has offended the supernaturals. That rituals have to be performed in just the right way offers an escape clause which explains why some performances are ineffective. The same kind of error occurs in all processes carried out within cultural systems. Psychologically a ritual error may be no different from planting the seeds too deep or not planting them deep enough. It is a predictable sort of human error which does not challenge fundamental certainties.

One of the important characteristics of rituals, and of other cultural processes as well, is the element of repetition. Magical rituals in particular depend upon the correct performance of every detail of the ritual process. In everyday life, the omission of morning coffee or bedtime toothbrushing may create considerable anxiety. In most places, the use of inappropriate dress or of taboo or obscene language may provoke violent and even murderous reactions. The fact that rituals of all kinds may be spoiled by profane or sacrilegious acts has often led to the conclusion that there is one and only one right or normative way of carrying out the characteristic behaviors appropriate to any particular cultural system. Especially in the performance of magical or religious ceremonies there is an inclination to conceive of the individual member as a slave to his cultural tradition. The difficulties inherent in observing and describing large numbers of different activities lead anthropologists to speak of typical or normative ways of doing things rather than to attempt any systematic exploration of the range of variation which may actually occur. What, then, are the kinds of variation that can properly occur in the conduct of a ceremony?

Variation: how many chambelanes?

In an attempt to understand some aspects of variation in the conduct of wedding ceremonies in Tenejapa in Mexico, Duane Metzger and Gerald Williams (1963:1076–1101) began by collecting a series of phrases and sentences that people actually used in discussing wedding ceremonies. One such phrase was "Vamos a nombrar nueve chambelanes" (Let us appoint nine male attendants). One of the things you can do in planning a wedding, then, is to appoint different numbers of attendants. One way of interviewing people about the number of male attendants there might legitimately be would be to strike out the word "nine" in order to create the *substitution frame*: "Let us appoint _____ male attendants." Metzger and Williams discovered that any number of male attendants between zero and nine was acceptable. Another substitution frame, "Let us appoint _____ _____," led to the discovery that you could appoint *chambelanes, damas, padrinos, madrinas, madrinas de arras*, and *pajes*. There are, then, several types of attendants that can be appointed and different numbers of each type (see Table 1).

TABLE 1   *Variables in choice of participants in Tenejapa wedding ceremony*

NO.	CHAMBELAN	DAMA	PADRINO	MADRINA	MADRINA DE ARRAS	PAJES
0	X	X			X	X
1	X	X	X	X		
2	X	X	X	X	X	X
3	X	X	X	X		
4	X	X				
5	X	X				
6	X	X				
7	X	X				
8	X	X				
9	X	X				

Some additional rules apply, however. We must name the same numbers of *chambelanes* and *damas,* of *padrinos* and *madrinas,* and of *madrinas de arras* and *pajes.* If we name large numbers of *chambelanes* we must name the largest possible number of *padrinos* and *madrinas de arras.* If we name zero or a small number of *chambelanes,* then we can name zero *padrinos* and only one *madrina de arras.*

Decisions about the number of attendants to be appointed at a wedding are obviously based upon a weighing of expenses against the desirability of an elegant ceremony. Certain minimum performances are required if the ceremony is to be regarded as a wedding ceremony, but beyond that the holding of the ceremony offers a rich texture of alternatives that allow for the expression of individual style or the wealth and social position of the families concerned. Although "Hiya, buddy" and "How are you, sir?" represent the same ritual of greeting, their messages concerning status are expressive of very different personalities or situations.

Summary

Rituals and ceremonies are processes or parts of processes that are often repeated, lack obvious practical consequences, and create anxiety or discomfort when they are not performed. Distinctions can be made between ordinary rituals and ceremonies and between secular and religious rituals. Rituals can also be defined in terms of the people or groups involved or in terms of the events that lead to their performance. Although many different ends, including a variety of practical ends, may be accomplished through ritual, the principal function of ritual appears to center upon the announcement, confirmation, or reinforcement of the status of groups and individuals.

As illustrated by the tree climbing episode, it is difficult for observers and participants to maintain an awareness of the frequency or importance of ritual in everyday life. Interpersonal rituals in particular seem to become visible and significant only, as illustrated by the case of Dr. Pouissant, when they are not practiced. Because rituals tend to be made up of words or gestures or objects whose meanings cannot always be explained by informants, one of the problems in the study of rituals has to do with the meanings of ritual things or gestures. The example of the "eyebrow flash" opens up the possibility that the meaning of some ritual gestures might be rooted in human biological characteristics. The example of genital operations suggests a further explanation in terms of basic human psychological experiences. The example of eggnog and the United States Christmas ceremony confronts us with the complexities of ritual symbolism and the difficulties inherent in finding simple or general explanations of the meaning of ritual acts and objects. The pervasiveness and hidden nature of ritual meanings is further explored in terms of the meaning of distance in the United States.

Using the complex and veiled symbolism of distance and the other little rituals of daily life, individuals exert powerful influences upon the behavior of others. Formal and complicated ceremonial events such as the crowning of the king or the initiation of a child into manhood have the obvious effect of assigning new statuses and roles to individuals. As suggested by the example of the Hopi initiation ceremony, such complicated rituals may also mobilize a variety of psychological devices—drugs, pain, fatigue, isolation, starvation, repetition, music, propaganda, dramatic performances, feasts, confessions, and processions—to create deep and irreversible changes in the personality of individuals. Although it is difficult to estimate the impact of any single part of a ceremony upon any particular individual, one message that probably comes through in most initiation ceremonies is that the adults mean business. The child must become an adult or else.

The fact that a ceremony can be held at all may be testimony to the strength of preexisting relationships among groups and individuals. Thus the South Indian marriage ceremony, by involving many individuals and by steadily increasing the commitment of all parties involved, seems to strengthen and reinforce the social bonds of which the marriage itself is merely an expression. Rituals can be seen as devices for enforcing and regulating a wide variety of human relationships. Although this viewpoint stresses the direct practical value of rituals in building and maintaining social bonds, it should not be forgotten that rituals are routines which create breaks in the routine of daily life. They are among the things that make life worth living and they are a lot of fun besides.

Very often rituals are dedicated to the solution of practical problems arising out of illness or other individual or collective misfortunes. Saora rituals appear to be directed specifically at the healing of physical and mental illness. Here, where ordinary ways of coping with problems are ineffective or lacking in drama, the ceremony offers collective assistance and provides all concerned with "something-to-do." It can be argued that the fundamental source of human ritual activity is anxiety or uncertainty. Even if the ritual activity proves ineffective, anxiety is allayed by the fact that everything possible has been done to preserve and enhance the status of the sufferer.

The importance of conducting a ritual in the proper way and in a repetitive manner sometimes obscures the fact that rituals, like other processes, involve individual variations upon a common theme. The case of wedding ceremonies in Tenejapa is an example of the manner in which the cultural message, including those governing the conduct of ceremonies, offers a rich texture of alternatives that allow for the expression of individual style and status.

Further readings

Most of the works of Erving Goffman, especially *Interaction Ritual* (1967), deal with the rituals of everyday life. Lessa and Vogt's *Reader in Com-*

parative Religion (1965) provides a good summary of various approaches to rituals, ceremonies, and "religious" acts. Young's *Initiation Ceremonies* (1965) and Van Gennep's *The Rites of Passage* (1961, first published in French in 1908) discuss one variety of ritual.

Case Studies emphasizing ritual include Hoebel's *The Cheyennes* (1960), Vogt's *The Zinacantecos of Mexico* (1970), Deng's *The Dinka* (1972), Leis' *Enculturation and Socialization in an Ijaw Society* (1972), Buechler and Buechler's *The Bolivian Aymara* (1971), and Pospisil's *The Kapauku Papuans* (1963).

Problems and questions

1. Observe some rituals of greeting. Are there any differences in terms of situation or social status that would explain why different greetings are exchanged at different times or between different kinds of people?
2. Using ethnographic sources, compare marriage or other ceremonies from several different societies. What are the differences and similarities? Why?
3. Study an initiation ceremony in the modern United States. Does it seem to make any difference in the behavior of the initiate or of the people around him?
4. Discuss some possible functions of a particular ritual or ceremony. What sorts of data would you need to demonstrate that the ritual actually fulfilled the possible functions you suggest?
5. Describe some of the important symbols or symbolic acts involved in a particular ceremony and consider possible ways of interpreting or explaining their meaning.

9

The transmission of culture

This chapter is about how neonates become talking, thinking, feeling, moral, believing, valuing human beings—members of groups, participants in cultural systems. It is not, as a chapter on child psychology might be, about the growth and development of individuals. It is about how young humans come to want to act as they must act if the cultural system is to be maintained. It is also about special and virtually unmanageable burdens placed upon teachers and schools when the cultural system is caught up in transformative change and why minority populations in complex societies are disadvantaged by their schooling. A wide variety of cultures are examined to illustrate both the diversity and unity of ways in which children are educated. The educational functions that are carried out by initiation rites in many cultures are emphasized, and the concepts of cultural compression, continuity, and discontinuity are stressed in this context. Various other techniques of education are demonstrated with selected cases, including reward, modeling and imitation, play, dramatization,

verbal admonition, reinforcement, and storytelling. Recruitment and cultural
maintenance are analyzed as basic educative functions. The chapter is not about
the whole process of education but about certain parts of that process seen
in a number of different situations.

What are some of the ways that culture is transmitted?

Psychologists and pediatricians do not agree upon the proper and most
effective ways to raise children. Neither do the Dusun of Borneo, the Tewa
or Hopi of the Southwest, the Japanese, the Ulithians or the Palauans of
Micronesia, the Turkish villagers, the Tiwi of North Australia, the people of
Gopalpur, or those of Guadalcanal. Each way of life is distinctive in its outlook, content, the kind of adult personalities favored, and the way children
are raised. There are also many respects in which human communities are
similar that override cultural differences. All major human cultural systems
include magic, religion, moral values, recreation, regulation of mating,
education, and so forth. But the *content* of these different categories, and
the ways the content and the categories are put together, differ enor-
mously. These differences are reflected in the ways people raise their children. If the object of cultural transmission is to teach young people how to
think, act, and feel appropriately this must be the case. To understand this
process we must get a sense of this variety.

This Is How It Is in Palau

Five-year-old Azu trails after his mother as she walks along the village path,
whimpering and tugging at her skirt. He wants to be carried, and he tells
her so, loudly and demandingly, "Stop! Stop! Hold me!" His mother shows
no sign of attention. She continues her steady barefooted stride, her arms
swinging freely at her sides, her heavy hips rolling to smooth the jog of her
walk and steady the basket of wet clothes she carries on her head. She has
been to the washing pool and her burden keeps her neck stiff, but this is not
why she looks impassively ahead and pretends not to notice her son. Often
before she has carried him on her back and an even heavier load on her head.
But today she has resolved not to submit to his plea, for it is time for him to
begin to grow up.

Azu is not aware that the decision has been made. Understandably, he
supposes that his mother is just cross, as she often has been in the past, and
that his cries will soon take effect. He persists in his demand, but falls behind
as his mother firmly marches on. He runs to catch up and angrily yanks at
her hand. She shakes him off without speaking to him or looking at him.
Enranged, he drops solidly on the ground and begins to scream. He gives a
startled look when this produces no response, then rolls over on his stomach
and begins to writhe, sob, and yell. He beats the earth with his fists and kicks
it with his toes. This hurts and makes him furious, the more so since it has
not caused his mother to notice him. He scrambles to his feet and scampers
after her, his nose running, tears coursing through the dirt on his cheeks.

When almost on her heel he yells and, getting no response, drops to the ground.

By this time his frustration is complete. In a rage he grovels in the red dirt, digging his toes into it, throwing it around him and on himself. He smears it on his face, grinding it in with his clenched fists. He squirms on his side, his feet turning his body through an arc on the pivot of one shoulder.

A man and his wife are approaching, the hubsand in the lead, he with a short-handled adz resting on his left shoulder, she with a basket of husked coconuts in her head. As they come abreast of Azu's mother the man greets her with "You have been to the washing pool?" It is the Palauan equivalent of the American "How are you?"—a question that is not an inquiry but a token of recognition. The two women scarcely glance up as they pass. They have recognized each other from a distance and it is not necessary to repeat the greeting. Even less notice is called for as the couple pass Azu sprawled on the path a few yards behind his mother. They have to step around his frenzied body, but no other recognition is taken of him, no word is spoken to him or to each other. There is no need to comment. His tantrum is not an unusual sight, especially among boys of his age or a little older. There is nothing to say to him or about him.

In the yard of a house just off the path, two girls, a little older than Azu, stop their play to investigate. Cautiously and silently they venture in Azu's direction. His mother is still in sight, but she disappears suddenly as she turns off the path into her yard without looking back. The girls stand some distance away, observing Azu's gyrations with solemn eyes. Then they turn and go back to their doorway, where they stand, still watching him but saying nothing. Azu is left alone, but it takes several minutes for him to realize that this is the way it is to be. Gradually his fit subsides and he lies sprawled and whimpering on the path.

Finally, he pushes himself to his feet and starts home, still sobbing and wiping his eyes with his fists. As he trudges into the yard he can hear his mother shouting at his sister, telling her not to step over the baby. Another sister is sweeping the earth beneath the floor of the house with a coconut-leaf broom. Glancing up, she calls shrilly to Azu, asking him where he has been. He does not reply, but climbs the two steps to the threshold of the doorway and makes his way to a mat in the corner of the house. There he lies quietly until he falls asleep.

This has been Azu's first painful lesson in growing up. There will be many more unless he soon understands and accepts the Palauan attitude that emotional attachments are cruel and treacherous entanglements, and that it is better not to cultivate them in the first place than to have them disrupted and disclaimed. Usually the lesson has to be repeated in many connections before its general truth sinks in. There will be refusals of pleas to be held, to be carried, to be fed, to be cuddled, and to be amused; and for a time at least there will follow the same violent struggle to maintain control that failed to help Azu. For whatever the means, and regardless of the lapses from the stern code, children must grow away from their parents, not cleave to them. Soon or late the child must learn not to expect the solicitude, the warm attachment of earlier years and must accept the fact that he is to live in an emotional vacuum, trading friendship for concrete rewards, neither accepting nor giving lasting affection (Barnett 1960:4–6).

Is culture being transmitted here? Azu is learning that people are not to be trusted, that any emotional commitment is shaky business. He is acquiring an emotional attitude. From Professor Barnett's further description of life in Palau (Barnett 1960) we know that this emotional attitude underlies economic, social, political, even religious behavior among adult Palauans. If this happened only to Azu we would probably regard it as a traumatic event. He might then grow up to be a singularly distrustful adult in a trusting world. He would be a deviant. But virtually all Palauan boys experience this sudden rejection (it happens more gradually for girls)—not always in just this particular way—but in somewhat the same way and at about the same time. This is a culturally patterned way of getting a lesson across to the child. This culturally patterned way of treating the child has a more or less consistent result—an emotional attitude—and this emotional attitude is in turn patterned, and fits into various parts of the Palauan cultural system. What is learned by Azu and transmitted by his mother is at once a pattern of child training (the mother had it and applied it), a dimension of Palauan *world view* (Palauans see the world as a place where people do not become emotionally involved with each other), a modal personality trait (most normal adult Palauans distrust others), and a pattern for behavior in the context of the many subsystems (economic, political, religious, and so forth) governing adult life.

Azu's mother did not simply tell him to stop depending upon her and to refrain from lasting emotional involvements with others. She demonstrated to him in a very dramatic way that this is the way it is in this life (in Palau at least). She probably didn't even completely rationalize what she did. She didn't say to herself, "Now it is time for Azu to acquire the characteristic Palauan attitude that emotional attachments are not lasting and the best way to teach him this is for me to refuse to carry him." Barnett says that she "resolved not to submit to his plea." We can't be sure that she even did this, for not even Homer Barnett, as well as he knows the Palauans, can get into Azu's mother's head. We know that she did not, in fact, submit to his plea. She may well have thought that it was about time for Azu to grow up. Growing up in Palau means in part to stop depending on people, even your very own loving mother. But maybe she was just plain tired, feeling a little extra crabby, so she acted in a characteristically Palauan way *without thinking about it* toward her five-year-old. People can transmit culture without knowing they do so. Probably more culture is transmitted this way than with conscious intent.

Discontinuity between early and later childhood is apparent in the Palauan case. Most cultures are patterned in such a way as to provide discontinuities of experience, but the points of time in the life cycle where these occur, and their intensity, differ widely. Azu experienced few restraints before this time. He did pretty much as he pleased, and lolled about on the laps of parents, kin, and friends. He was seldom if ever punished. There was always someone around to serve as protector, provider, and companion, and someone to carry him, usually mother, wherever he might go. Much of this changed for him after this day at the age of five. To be sure, he is not abandoned, and he is still shielded, guided, and provided for in every physical sense, but he finds himself being told more often than asked what he wants, and his confidence in himself and in his parents has been shaken. He no longer knows how to get what he wants. The discontinuity, the break with the ways things were in his fifth year of life, is in itself a technique of cultural transmission. We will observe discontinuities in the treatment of children and their effects in other cultures.

How Is It Done in Ulithi?

The Ulithians, like the Palauans, are Micronesians, but inhabit a much smaller island, in fact a tiny atoll in the vast Pacific, quite out of the way and fairly unchanged when first studied by William Lessa in the late forties (Lessa 1966). The Ulithians educate their children in many of the same ways the Palauans do, but differently enough to merit some special attention.

Like the Palauans, the Ulithians are solicitous and supportive of infants and young children.

The infant is given the breast whenever he cries to be fed or whenever it is considered time to feed him, but sometimes only as a pacifier. He suckles often, especially during the first three to six months of his life, when he may average around eighteen times during the day and night. The great stress placed by Ulithians on food is once more given eloquent expression in nursing practices. Thus, if both the mother and child should happen to be asleep at any time and it seems to someone who is awake that the baby should be fed, both are aroused in order to nurse the baby. . . .

The care of the baby is marked by much solicitude on the part of everyone. One of the ways in which this is manifested is through great attention to cleanliness. The infant is bathed three times a day, and after each bath the baby is rubbed all over with coconut oil and powdered with turmeric. Ordinarily, bathing is done by the mother, who, as she holds the child, rocks him from side to side in the water and sings:

> Float on the water
> In my arms, my arms
> On the little sea,
> The big sea,
> The rough sea,
> The calm sea,
> On this sea.

[three sentences omitted]

An infant is never left alone. He seems constantly in someone's arms, being passed from person to person in order to allow everyone a chance to fondle him. There is not much danger that if neglected for a momnet he will harm himself (Lessa 1966:94–96).

Unlike the Palauans, the Ulithians do not create any special discontinuities for the young child. Even weaning is handled with as little disturbance as possible.

> Weaning begins at varying ages. It is never attempted before the child is a year old, and usually he is much older than that. Some children are suckled until they are five, or even as much as seven or eight. Weaning takes about four days, one technique being to put the juice of hot pepper around the mother's nipples. Physical punishment is never employed, though scolding may be deemed necessary. Ridicule, a common recourse in training Ulithian children, is also resorted to. The child's reaction to being deprived of the breast often manifests itself in temper tantrums. The mother tries to mollify the child in a comforting embrace and tries to console him by playing with him and offering him such distraction as a tiny coconut or a flower (Lessa 1966:95).

Apparently this technique, and the emotional atmosphere that surrounds it, is not threatening to Ulithian children. We see nothing of the feelings of deprivation and rejection suffered by Azu.

> The reactions to weaning are not extreme; children weather the crisis well. In fact, a playful element may be observed. A child may quickly push his face into his mother's breast and then run away to play. When the mother's attention is elsewhere, the child may make a sudden impish lunge at the breast and try to suckle from it. After the mother has scolded the weanling, he may coyly take the breast and fondle it, toy with the nipple, and rub the breast over his face. A man told me that when he was being weaned at the age of about seven, he would alternate sleeping with his father and mother, who occupied separate beds. On those occasions when he would sleep with his father, the latter would tell him to say goodnight to his mother. The boy would go over to where she was lying and playfully run his nose over her breasts. She would take this gesture good-naturedly and encourage him by telling him he was virtuous, strong, and like other boys. Then he would go back to his father, satisfied with his goodness (Lessa 1966:95).

We also see in the above account of Ulithian behavior that transmission of sexual attitudes and the permissiveness concerning eroticization are markedly different than in our own society. This difference, of course, is not confined to relations between young boys and their mothers, but extends through all heterosexual relationships, and throughout the patterning of adult life.

Given the relaxed and supportive character of child rearing in Ulithi, it is small wonder that children behave in a relaxed, playful manner, and apparently grow into adults that value relaxation. This is in sharp contrast with the Palauans, whom Barnett describes as characterized by a residue of latent hostility in social situations, and as subject to chronic anxiety (Barnett 1960:11–15).

Indeed, play is so haphazard and relaxed that it quickly melts from one thing to another, and from one place to another, with little inhibition. There is much laughter and chatter, and often some vigorous singing. One gains the impression that relaxation, for which the natives have a word they use almost constantly, is one of the major values of Ulithian culture (Lessa 1966:101).

Particularly striking in the transmission of Ulithian culture is the disapproval of unusually independent behavior.

The attitude of society towards unwarranted independence is generally one of disapproval. Normal independence is admired because it leads to later self-reliance in the growing individual, dependence being scorned if it is so strong that it will unfit him for future responsibilities. Ulithians talk a lot about homesickness and do not view this as improper, unless the longing is really for a spouse or sweetheart, the suspicion here being that it is really sexual outlet that a person wants. Longing of this sort is said to make a person inefficient and perhaps even ill. Homesickness is expected of all children and not deprecated. I was greatly touched once when I asked a friend to tell me what a man was muttering about during a visit to my house. He said he felt sad that I was away from my home and friends and wondered how I could endure it. Ulithians do not like people to feel lonely; sociability is a great virtue for them (Lessa 1966:101).

The degree and kinds of dependence and independence that are inculcated in children are significant variables in any transcultural comparison of cultural transmission. Palauan children are taught not to trust others and grow to adulthood in a society where social relationships tend to be exploitive and, behind a facade of pleasantness, hostile. Palauans are not, however, independent, and tend to be quite dependent for direction upon external authority (Barnett 1960:13, 15–16). The picture is confused in Palau by the greater degree of acculturation (than at Ulithi) and the threatening situations that the Palauans have experienced under first German, then Japanese, and now American domination. In American society, middle-class culture calls for independence, particularly in males, and independence training is stressed from virtually the beginning of childhood. But adolescent and adult Americans are among the most sociable, "joiningest" people in the world. Ulithian children are not taught to be independent, and the individual who is too independent is the object of criticism. Palauan children are taught a kind of independence—to be independent of dependency upon other people's affection—by a sudden withdrawal of support at about five years of age. But which is really the more "independent" adult? Palauans are independent of each other in the sense that they can be cruel and callous to each other and exploitive in social relationships, but they are fearful of independent action and responsibility, are never originators or innovators, and are dependent upon authority for direction. Ulithians are dependent upon each other for social and emotional support, but do not exhibit the fearful dependency upon authority that Palauans do.

This does not mean that there is no predictable relationship between the training of children in dependency or independence and the consequences in adulthood. It does mean that the relationship is not simple and must be culturally contextualized if it is to make sense.

Every society creates some discontinuities in the experience of the individual as he or she grows up. It seems impossible to move from the roles appropriate to childhood to the roles appropriate for adulthood without some discontinuity. Societies differ greatly in the timing of discontinuity, and its abruptness. The first major break for Azu, the Palauan boy, was at five years of age. In Ulithi the major break occurs at the beginning of young adulthood.

> The mild concerns of ordinary life begin to catch up with the individual in the early years of adulthood and he can never again revert to the joyful indifference of his childhood.
>
> Attaining adulthood is marked by a ritual for boys and another for girls, neither of which is featured by genital operations. The same term, *kufar*, is used for each of the initiations. . . .
>
> The boy's *kufar* is much the less elaborate and important. It comes about when he begins to show secondary sex characteristics and is marked by three elements: a change to adult clothing, the performance of magic, and the giving of a feast. All this occurs on the same day. . . .
>
> The outstanding consequence of the boy's ritual is that he must now sleep in the men's house and scrupulously avoid his postpubertal sisters. Not only must he not sleep in the same house with them, but he and they may not walk together, share the same food, touch one another's personal baskets, wear one another's leis or other ornaments, make or listen to ribald jokes in one another's presence, watch one another doing a solo dance, or listen to one another sing a love song (Lessa 1966:101–102).

Brother-sister avoidances of this kind are very common in human societies. There is a whole body of literature about them and their implications and consequences. The most important thing for us to note is that this is one of the most obvious ways in which restrictions appropriate to the young adult role in Ulithian society are placed on the individual immediately after the kufar. Transitional rites, or "rites of passage," as they are frequently termed, usually involve new restrictions of this sort. So, for that matter, do the events marking important transitions occurring at other times in the life experience. Azu lost the privilege of being carried and treated like an infant, and immediately became subject to being told what to do more often than demanding and getting what he wanted. One way of looking at Azu's experience and the Ulithian kufar is to regard them as periods of sharp discontinuity in the management of cultural transmission. Expressed most simply—what cultural transmitters do to and for an individual after the event is quite different in some ways from what they did before. Another way of looking at these events is to regard them as the beginning of periods of cultural compression. Expressed most simply—cultural compression occurs when the individual's behavior is restricted by the application of new cultural norms. After the kufar, the Ulithian boy and girl cannot interact with their mature opposite-sex siblings except under very special rules. Azu cannot demand to be carried and is told to do many other things he did not have to do before.

In Ulithi the girl's kufar is much more elaborate. When she notices the first flow of blood she knows she must go immediately to the women's house. As she goes, and upon her arrival, there is a great hullabaloo in the village, with the women shouting again and again, "The menstruating one, Ho-o-o!" After her arrival she takes a bath, changes her skirt, has magic spells recited over her to help her find a mate and enjoy a happy married life, and is instructed about the many *etap* (taboos) she must observe—some for days, others for weeks, and yet others for years. Soon she goes to live in a private hut of her own, built near her parent's house, but she still must go to the menstrual house whenever her discharge begins (Lessa 1966:102–104).

The discontinuity and compression that Ulithian young people experience after the kufar are not limited to a few taboos.

Adolescence and adulthood obviously come rushing together at young Ulithians, and the attitude of the community towards them undergoes a rapid change. The boy and the girl are admitted to a higher status, to be sure, and they are given certain rights and listened to with more respect when they speak. But a good deal is expected of them in return. Young men bear the brunt of the heaviest tasks assigned by the men's council. For their own parents they must help build and repair houses, carry burdens, climb trees for coconuts, fish, make rope, and perform all the other tasks commonly expected of an able-bodied man. Young women are similarly called upon to do much of the harder work of the village and the household. Older people tend to treat these very young adults with a sudden sternness and formality lacking when they were in their childhood. The missteps of young people are carefully watched and readily criticized, so that new adults are constantly aware of the critical gaze of their elders. They may not voice strong objections or opinions, and have no political rights whatsoever, accepting the decisions of the men's and women's councils without murmur. Altogether, they are suddenly cut off from childhood and must undergo a severe transition in their comportment towards others about them. Only in the amatory sphere can they find release from the petty tyranny of their elders (Lessa 1966:104).

What Is It Like To Be Initiated in Hano?

Like the Hopi, with whom they are very close neighbors on the same mesa in Arizona, the Hano Tewa hold an initiation ceremony into the Kachina[1] cult at about nine years of age. In fact the Hano and Hopi share

[1] This word is sometimes spelled Katcina, sometimes Kachina. Voth, used as the source in Chapter 8 for the description of the Hopi ceremony, spells it Katcina. Dozier, used as the source for the Hano Tewa, spells it Kachina. Either is correct.

the same ceremony. Further examination of this occasion will be instructive. Up until that time Hano children are treated about the way the Hopi children are (See Chapter 8). They are kept on a cradleboard at first, weaned late, by middle-class American standards, and on the whole treated very permissively and supportively by mothers, mother's sisters, grandparents, fathers, older siblings, and other people in and about the extended family household, admonished and corrected by the mother's brother, and half scared to death from time to time when they are bad by the Kachinas, or the threat of Kachinas. Of course nowadays the continuity of this early period is somewhat upset because children must start in the government day school at Polacca when they are about seven, and the teachers' ideas of proper behavior are frequently at variance with those maintained by Hano parents. Excepting for school, though, Hano children can be said to experience a consistent, continuous educational environment through the early years.

Things change when the initiation takes place at about age nine. A ceremonial father is selected for the boy, and a ceremonial mother for the girl. These ceremonial parents, as well as the real parents and for that matter everyone in the pueblo, build up the coming event for the child so that he or she is in a tremendous state of excitement. Then the day comes. Edward Dozier reports the initiation experience of one of his informants.

We were told that the Kachina were beings from another world. There were some boys who said that they were not, but we could never be sure, and most of us believed what we were told. Our own parents and elders tried to make us believe that the Kachina were powerful beings, some good and some bad, and that they knew our innermost thoughts and actions. If they did not know about us through their own great power, then probably our own relatives told the Kachina about us. At any rate every time they visited us they seemed to know what we had thought and how we had acted.

As the time for our initiation came closer we became more and more frightened. The ogre Kachina, the Soyoku, came every year and threatened to carry us away; now we were told that we were going to face these awful creatures and many others. Though we were told not to be afraid, we could not help ourselves. If the Kachina are really supernaturals and powerful beings, we might have offended them by some thought or act and they might punish us. They might even take us with them as the Soyoku threatened to do every year.

Four days before Powamu our ceremonial fathers and our ceremonial mothers took us to Court Kiva. The girls were accompanied by their ceremonial mothers, and we boys by our ceremonial fathers. We stood outside the kiva, and then two whipper Kachina, looking very mean, came out of the kiva. Only a blanket covered the nakedness of the boys; as the Kachina drew near our ceremonial fathers removed the blankets. The girls were permitted to keep on their dresses, however. Our ceremonial parents urged us to offer sacred corn meal to the Kachina; as soon as we did they whipped us with their yucca whips. I was hit so hard that I defecated and urinated and I could feel the welts forming on my back and I knew that I was bleeding too. He whipped me four times, but the last time he hit me on the leg instead, and as the whipper started to strike again, my ceremonial father pulled me back and he took the blow himself. "This is a good boy, my old man," he said to the Kachina. "You have hit him enough."

For many days my back hurt and I had to sleep on my side until the wounds healed.

After the whipping a small sacred feather was tied to our hair and we were told not to eat meat or salt. Four days later we went to see the Powamu ceremony in the kiva. As babies, our mother had taken us to see this event; but as soon as we began to talk, they stopped taking us. I could not remember what had happened on Powamu night and I was afraid that another frightening ordeal awaited us. Those of us who were whipped went with our ceremonial parents. In this dance we saw that the Kachina were really our own fathers, uncles, and brothers. This made me feel strange. I felt somehow that all my relatives were responsible for the whipping we had received. My ceremonial father was kind and gentle during this time and I felt very warm toward him, but I also wondered if he was to blame for our treatment. I felt deceived and ill-treated (Dozier 1966:59–60).

Like Don Talayesva, the Hopi who was quoted in Chapter 8, the Hano Tewa children are shocked, angry, chagrined when they find that the supernatural Kachinas they have been scared and disciplined by all their lives up until then, and who during the initiation have whipped them hard, are really men they have known very well in their own community, their clans, their families. To be treated supportively and permissively all of one's life, and then to be whipped publicly (or see others get whipped) would seem quite upsetting by itself. To find out that the awesome Kachinas are men impersonating gods would seem almost too much. But somehow the experience seems to help make good adult Hopis and good Hano Tewa out of little ones.

If the initiate does not accept the spiritual reality of the Kachina, and will not accept his relatives' "cruel" behavior as necessary and good for him (or her), he can stop being a Hopi or a Tewa. But is this a real choice? Not for anyone who is human enough to need friends and family who speak the same language, both literally and figuratively, and whose identity as a Hopi or Tewa Indian stretches back through all of time. Having then (usually without debate) made the choice of being a Hopi or a Tewa, one is a *good* Hopi or Tewa. No doubts can be allowed.

There is another factor operating as well. Children who pass through the initiation are no longer outside looking in, they are inside looking out. They are not grown up, and neither they nor anyone else think they are, but they are a lot more grown up than they were before the initiation. Girls take on a more active part in household duties and boys acquire more responsibilities in farming and ranching activities. And it will not be long before the males can take on the role of impersonating the Kachinas and initiating children as they were initiated. The ceremonial whipping, in the context of all the dramatic ceremonies, dancing, and general community uproar, is the symbol of a dramatic shift in status-role. The shift starts with just being "in the know" about what really goes on in the kiva and who the Kachinas are, and continues toward more and more full participation in the secular and sacred life of the community.

Dorothy Eggan sums it up well when she writes:

> Another reorganizing factor . . . was feeling "big." They had shared pain with adults, had learned secrets which forever separated them from the world of children, and now they were included in situations from which they had previously been excluded, as their elders continued to teach intensely what they believed intensely: that for them there was only one alternative—Hopi as against Kahopi.
>
> Consistent repetition is a powerful conditioning agent and, as the youngsters watched each initiation, they relived their own, and by again sharing the experience gradually worked out much of the bitter residue from their own memories of it, while also rationalizing and weaving group emotions ever stronger into their own emotional core—"It takes a while to see how wise the old people really are." An initiated boy, in participating in the kachina dances, learned to identify again with the kachinas whom he now impersonated. To put on a mask is to "become a kachina," and to cooperate actively in bringing about the major goals of Hopi life. And a girl came to know more fully the importance of her clan in its supportive role. These experiences were even more sharply conditioned and directed toward adult life in the adult initiation ceremonies, of which we have as yet only fragmentary knowledge. Of this one man said to me: "I will not discuss this

thing with you only to say that no one can forget it. It is the most wonderful thing any man can have to remember. You know then that you are Hopi. It is the one thing Whites cannot have, cannot take away from us. It is our way of life given to us when the world began" (Eggan 1956:364–365).

In many ways the preadolescent and adolescent period that we have been discussing, using the Ulithian kufar and the Hano Tewa and Hopi initiation ceremonies as representative cases, is the most important of all in cultural transmission. There is a considerable literature on this period, including most notably the classic treatment given by van Gennep (1960) that was first published in 1909, and the recent studies by Frank Young (1965), Yehudi Cohen (1964), Gary Schwartz and Don Merten (1968), and Whiting, Kluckhohn, and Albert (1958). Judith Brown provides a cross-cultural study of initiation rights for females (Brown 1963). But these studies do not emphasize the educational aspects of the initiation rites or rites of passage that they analyze.

One of the few that does so is the remarkable essay by C. W. M. Hart, based upon a single case, the Tiwi of North Australia (1955), but with implications for many other cases. Hart contrasts the attitude of cultural transmitters toward young children among the Tiwi to the rigorous demands of the initiation period.

> The arrival of the strangers to drag the yelling boy out of his mother's arms is just the spectacular beginning of a long period during which the separation of the boy from everything that has gone before is emphasized in every possible way at every minute of the day and night. So far his life has been easy; now it is hard. Up to now he has never necessarily experienced any great pain, but in the initiation period in many tribes pain, sometimes horrible, intense pain, is an obligatory feature. The boy of twelve or thirteen, used to noisy, boisterous, irresponsible play, is expected and required to sit still for hours and days at a time saying nothing whatever but concentrating upon and endeavoring to understand long intricate instructions and "lectures" given him by his hostile and forbidding preceptors. [sentence omitted] Life has suddenly become real and earnest and the initiate is required literally to "put away the things of a child" even the demeanor. The number of tabus and unnatural behaviors enjoined upon the initiate is endless. He mustn't speak unless he is spoken to; he must eat only certain foods, and often only in certain ways, at fixed times, and in certain fixed positions. All contact with females, even speech with them is rigidly forbidden, and this includes mother and sisters (1963:415).

Hart goes on to state that the novices are taught origin myths, the meaning of the sacred ceremonials, in short, theology, ". . . which in primitive society is inextricably mixed up with astronomy, geology, geography, biology (the mysteries of birth and death), philosophy, art, and music—in short the whole cultural heritage of the tribe." And that the purpose of this teaching is not to make better economic men of the novices, but rather ". . .

better citizens, better carriers of the culture through the generations. . . ."
(Hart 1963:415). In this view Hart agrees (as he points out himself) with
George Pettit, who did a thorough study of educational practices among
North American Indians, and who writes that the initiation proceedings
were ". . . a constant challenge to the elders to review, analyze, dramatize,
and defend their cultural heritage" (Pettit 1946:182).

Pettit's words also bring into focus another feature of the initiation rituals that is implicit in the description of these events for the Ulithians, Hano
Tewa, and the Tiwi, and that seems very significant. In all of these cases
dramatization is used as an educational technique. In fact a ceremony of
any kind is a dramatization, sometimes indirect and metaphoric, sometimes
very direct, of the interplay of crucial forces and events in the life of the
community. In the initiation ceremonies dramatization forces the serious-
ness of growing up into the youngster's mind and mobilizes his emotions
around the lessons to be learned and the change in identity to be secured.
The role of dramatization in cultural transmission may be difficult for
American readers to appreciate, because the pragmatization of American
schools and American life in general has gone so far.

These points emphasize the view of initiation proceedings taken in this
chapter—that they are dramatic signals for new beginnings and, at various
times before and throughout adolescence in many societies, the inten-
sification of discontinuity and compression in cultural transmission. Discontinuity in the management of the youngsters' learning—from supportive
and easy to rigorous and harsh; compression in the closing in of culturally
patterned demand and restriction as the new status-roles attained by successfully passing through the initiation period are activated. Of course this
compression of cultural demand around the individual also opens new
channels of development and experience to him. As humans mature they
give up the freedom of childhood for the rewards to be gained by observing
the rules of the cultural game. The initiation ceremonies are dramatic signals to everyone that the game has begun in earnest.

Initiation ceremonies and other rites of passage will not be stressed in
the cases that follow, though we will come back to them briefly when we
get to Japan. These processes have already been discussed in Chapter 8 and
the cases discussed above have made the points most relevant to understanding cultural transmission. There are other things to be understood now.

What Happens in Gopalpur?
In the village of Gopalpur, in South India, described by Alan Beals, social,
not physical, mastery is stressed.

Long before it has begun to walk, the child in Gopalpur has begun to develop
a concern about relationships with others. The period of infantile dependency is extended. The child is not encouraged to develop muscular skills, but
is carried from place to place on the hip of mother or sister. The child is
rarely alone. It is constantly exposed to other people, and learning to talk,

to comunicate with others, is given priority over anything else that might be learned. When the child does learn to walk, adults begin to treat it differently. Shooed out of the house, its training is largely taken over by the play group. In the streets there are few toys, few things to be manipulated. The play of the child must be social play and the manipulation of others must be accomplished through language and through such nonphysical techniques as crying and withdrawal. In the play group, the child creates a family and the family engages in the production of imaginary food or in the exchange of real food carried in shirt pockets (1962:19).

Children in Gopalpur imitate adults, both in the activities of play and in the attempts to control each other.

Sidda, four years old, is playing in the front of his house with his cousin, Bugga, aged five. Sidda is sitting on the ground holding a stone and pounding. Bugga is piling the sand up like rice for the pounding. Bugga says, "Sidda, give me the stone, I want to pound." Sidda puts the stone on the ground, "Come and get it." Bugga says, "Don't come with me, I am going to the godhouse to play." Sidda offers, " I will give you the stone." He gives the stone to Bugga, who orders him, "Go into the house and bring some water." Sidda goes and brings water in a brass bowl. Bugga takes it and pours it on the heap of sand. He mixes the water with the sand, using both hands. Then, "Sidda, take the bowl inside." Sidda takes the bowl and returns with his mouth full of peanuts. He puts his hand into his shirt pocket, finds more peanuts and puts them in his mouth. Bugga sees the peanuts and asks, "Where did you get those?" "I got them inside the house." "Where are they?" "In the winnowing basket." Bugga gets up and goes inside the house returning with a bulging shirt pocket. Both sit down near the pile of sand. Bugga says to Sidda "Don't tell mother." "No, I won't." Sidda eats all of his peanuts and moves toward Bugga holding his hands out. Bugga wants to know, "Did you finish yours?" "I just brought a little, you brought a lot." Bugga refuses to give up any peanuts and Sidda begins to cry. Bugga pats him on the back saying, "I will give you peanuts later on." They get up and go into the house. Because they are considered to be brothers, Sidda and Bugga do not fight. When he is wronged, the older Bugga threatens to desert Sidda. When the situation is reversed, the younger Sidda breaks into tears (Beals 1962:16).

In their play, Bugga and Sidda are faithful to the patterns of adult control over children, as they have both observed them and experienced them. Beals describes children going to their houses when their shirt pockets are empty of the "currency of interaction" (grain, bits of bread, peanuts).

This is the moment of entrapment, the only time during the day when the mother is able to exercise control over her child. This is the time for bargaining, for threatening. The mother scowls at her child, "You must have worked hard to be so hungry." The mother serves food and says, "Eat this. After you have eaten it, you must sit here and rock your little sister." The child eats and says, "I am going outside to play, I will not rock my sister." The child finishes its food and runs out of the house. Later, the child's aunt sees it and asks it to run to the store and buy some cooking oil. When it returns, the aunt says, "If you continue to obey me like this, I will give you something good to eat." When the mother catches the child again, she asks, "Where have you been?" Learning what occurred, she says, "If you bought cooking oil, that is fine; now come play with your sister." The child says, "First give me something to eat, and I will play with my sister." The mother scolds, "You will die of eating, sometimes you are willing to work, sometimes you are not willing to work; may you eat dirt." She gives it food and the child plays with its sister (1962:19).

This is the way the child in Gopalpur learns to control the unreliable world of other people. Children soon learn that they are dependent upon others for the major securities and satisfactions of life. The one with a large number of friends and supporters is secure, and they can be won and controlled, the individual comes to feel, through the use of food, but also by crying, begging, and working.

And among the Eskimo?

Eskimo children are treated supportively and permissively. When a baby cries it is picked up, played with, or nursed. There are a variety of baby tenders about, and after the first two or three months of life older siblings and the mother's unmarried sisters and cousins take a hand in caring for it. There is no set sleeping or eating schedule and weaning is a gradual process that may not be completed until the third or fourth year.

How is it then that, as white visitors to Eskimo villages often remark, the Eskimo have managed to raise their children so well? Observers speak warmly of their good humor, liveliness, resourcefulness, and well-behaved manner. They appear to exemplify qualities that Western parents would like to see in their own children (Chance 1966:22). American folk belief would lead one to surmise that children who are treated so permissively would be "spoiled." Norman Chance describes the situation for the Alaskan Eskimo.

Certainly, the warmth and affection given infants by parents, siblings, and other relatives provide them with a deep feeling of well-being and security. Young children also feel important because they learn early that they are expected to be useful, working members of the family. This attitude is not instilled by imposing tedious chores, but rather by including children in the round of daily activities, which enhances the feeling of family participation and cohesion. To put it another way, parents rarely deny children their company or exclude them from the adult world.

This pattern reflects the parents' views of child rearing. Adults feel that they have more experience in living and it is their responsibility to share this experience with the children, "to tell them how to live." Children have to be told repeatedly because they tend to forget. Misbehavior is due to a child's forgetfulness, or to improper teaching in the first place. There is rarely any thought that the child is basically nasty, willful, or sinful. Where Anglo-Americans applaud a child for his good behavior, the Eskimo praise him for remembering. . . .

Regardless of the degree of Westernization, more emphasis is placed on equality than on superordination-subordination in parent-child relations. A five year old obeys, not because he fears punishment or loss of love, but because he identifies with his parents and respects their judgment. Thus he finds little to resist or rebel against in his dealings with adults. We will find rebellion more common in adolescents, but it is not necessarily a revolt against parental control.

By the time a child reaches the age of four or five, his parents' initial demonstrativeness has become tempered with an increased interest in his activities and accomplishments. They watch his play with obvious pleasure, and respond warmly to his conversation, make jokes with him and discipline him.

Though a child is given considerable autonomy and his whims and wishes treated with respect, he is nonetheless taught to obey all adults. To an outsider unfamiliar with parent-child relations, the tone of Eskimo commands and admonitions sometimes sounds harsh and angry, yet in few instances does a child respond as if he had been addressed hostilely. . . .

After the age of five a child is less restricted in his activities in and around the village, although theoretically he is not allowed on the beach or ice without an adult. During the dark winter season, he remains indoors or stays close to the house to prevent him from getting lost and to protect him from polar bears which might come into the village. In summer, though, children play at all hours of the day or "night" or as long as their parents are up. . . .

Although not burdened with responsibility, both boys and girls are expected to take an active role in family chores. In the early years responsibilities are shared, depending on who is available. Regardless of sex, it is important for a child to know how to perform a wide variety of tasks and give help when needed. Both sexes collect and chop wood, get water, help carry meat and other supplies, oversee younger siblings, run errands for adults, feed the dogs, and burn trash.

As a child becomes older, more specific responsibilities are allocated to him, according to his sex. Boys as young as seven may be given an opportunity to shoot a .22 rifle, and at least a few boys in every village have killed their first caribou by the time they are ten. A youngster learns techniques of butchering while on hunting trips with older siblings and adults, although he is seldom proficient until he is in his mid-teens. In the past girls learned butchering at an early age, since this knowledge was essential to attracting a good husband. Today, with the availability of large quantities of Western foods, this skill may not be acquired until a girl is married, and not always then.

Although there is a recognized division of labor by sex, it is far from rigid at any age level. Boys, and even men, occasionally sweep the house and cook. Girls and their mothers go on fishing or bird-hunting trips. Members of each sex can usually assume the responsibilities of the other when the need arises, albeit in an auxiliary capacity (1966:22–26).

Apparently the combination that works so well with Eskimo children is support—participation—admonition—support. These children learn to see adults as rewarding and nonthreatening. Children are also not excluded, as they so often are in America, from the affairs of adult life. They do not understand everything they see, but virtually nothing is hidden from them. They are encouraged to assume responsibility appropriate to their age quite early in life. Children are participants in the flow of life. They learn by observing, and doing. But Eskimo adults do not leave desired learning up to chance. They admonish, direct, remonstrate, but without hostility.

The Eskimo live with a desperately intemperate climate in what many white men have described as the part of the world that is the most inimicable to human life. Perhaps Eskimo children are raised the way they are because a secure, good-humored, resourceful person is the only kind that can survive for long in this environment.

In Sensuron?

The people of Sensuron live in a very different physical and cultural environment than do the Eskimo. The atmosphere of this Dusun village in Borneo (now the Malaysian state of Sabah) is communicated in these passages from Thomas Williams' case study.

> Sensuron is astir an hour before the dawn of most mornings. It is usually too damp and cold to sleep. Fires are built up and the morning meal cooked while members of the household cluster about the house fire-pit seeking warmth. After eating, containers and utensils are rinsed off with water to "keep the worms off" and replaced in racks on the side of the house porch. Older children are sent to the river to carry water home in bamboo containers, while their mother spends her time gathering together equipment for the day's work, including some cold rice wrapped in leaves for a midday snack. The men and adolescent males go into the yard to sit in the first warmth of the sun and talk with male neighbors. The early morning exchange of plans, news, and recounting of the events of yesterday is considered a "proper way" to begin the day. While the men cluster in the yard center, with old shirts or cloths draped about bare shoulders to ward off the chill, women gather in front of one house or another, also trading news, gossip, and work plans. Many women comb each other's hair, after carefully picking out the lice. It is not unusual to see four or more women sitting in a row down the steps of a house ladder talking, while combing and delousing hair. Babies are nursed while mothers talk and small children run about the clusters of adults, generally being ignored until screams of pain or anger cause a sharp retort of kAdA! (do not!) from a parent. Women drape spare skirts about their bare shoulders to ward off the morning chill. About two hours after dawn these groups break up as the members go off to the work of the day. The work tasks of each day are those to be done under the annual cycle of subsistence labor described in the previous chapter. . . .
>
> Vocal music is a common feature of village life; mothers and grandmothers sing a great variety of lullabies and "growth songs" to babies, children sing

a wide range of traditional and nonsense songs, while adults sing at work in the fields and gardens during leisure and social occasions and at times of ritual. Drinking songs and wedding songs take elaborate forms, often in the nature of song "debates" with sides chosen and a winner declared by a host or guest of honor on the basis of "beauty" of tone, humor, and general "one-upmanship" in invention of new verse forms. Most group singing is done in harmony. Adolescents, especially girls, spend much of their solitary leisure time singing traditional songs of love and loneliness. Traditional verse forms in ritual, and extensive everyday use of riddles, folktales, and proverbs comprise a substantial body of oral literature. Many persons know much ritual verse, and most can recite dozens of stylized folktales, riddles, and proverbs.

Village headmen, certain older males, and ritual specialists of both sexes are practiced speechmakers. A skill of "speaking beautifully" is much admired and imitated. The style used involves narration, with exhortation, and is emphasized through voice tone and many hand and body gestures and postures. Political debates, court hearings, and personal arguments often become episodes of dramatic representation for onlookers, with a speaker's phrase listened to for its emotional expressive content and undertones of ridicule, tragedy, comedy, and farce at the expense of others involved. The verse forms of major rituals take on dimensions of drama as the specialist delivers the lines with skillful impersonations of voices and mannerisms of disease givers, souls of the dead, and creator beings.

By late afternoon of a leisure day people in the houses begin to drift to the yards, where they again sit and talk. Fires are built to ward off the chill of winds rising off the mountains, and men and women circle the blaze, throwing bits of wood and bamboo into the fire as they talk. This time is termed mEg-Amut, after the designation for exchange of small talk between household members. As many as 20 fires can be seen burning in yards through Sensuron at evening on most leisure days and on many evenings after work periods. Men sit and talk until after dark, when they go into houses to take their evening meal. Women leave about an hour before dark to prepare the meal. Smaller children usually eat before the adults. After the evening meal, for an hour or more, the family clusters about the house fire-pit, talking, with adults often engaged in small tasks of tool repair or manufacture. By 8 or 9 P.M. most families are asleep; the time of retiring is earlier when the work days are longer, later on rest days (1965:78–79).

Children in Sensuron are, like Eskimo children, always present, always observers. How different this way of life is from that experienced by American children! Gossip, speech-making, folktale telling, grooming, working, and playing are all there, all a part of the stream of life flowing around one and with which each member of the community moves. Under these circumstances much of the culture is transmitted by a kind of osmosis. It would be difficult for a child *not to* learn his culture.

The children of Sensuron do not necessarily grow up into good-humored, secure, trusting, "happy" adults. There are several factors that apparently interact in their growing up to make this unlikely. In the most simple sense, these children do not grow up to be like Eskimo adults because their parents (and other cultural transmitters) are not Eskimo. Dusun cultural transmitters (anybody in the community that the child hears and sees) act like Dusun. But cultural transmitters display certain attitudes and do certain things to children as well as provide them with models. In Sensuron, children are judged to be nonpersons. They are not even provided with personal names until their fifth year. They are also considered to be ". . . naturally noisy, inclined to illness, capable of theft, incurable wanderers, violent, quarrelsome, temperamental, destructive of property, wasteful, easily offended, quick to forget" (Williams 1965:87). They are threatened by parents with being eaten alive, carried off, damaged by disease-givers. Here are two lullabies sung to babies in Sensuron (and heard constantly by older children):

> Sleep, Sleep, baby,
> There comes the *rAgEn* (soul of the dead)
> He carries a big stick,
> He carries a big knife,
> Sleep, Sleep, baby,
> He comes to beat you!

or, as in this verse,

> Bounce, Bounce, baby
> There is a hawk,
> Flying, looking for prey!
> There is the hawk, looking for his prey!
> He searches for something to snatch up in his claws,
> Come here, hawk, and snatch up this baby!
> (Williams 1965:88).

None of the things that the adults of Sensuron do to, with, or around their children is to be judged "bad." Their culture is different from Eskimo culture, and a different kind of individual functions effectively in it. We may for some reason need to make value judgments about a culture, the character of the people who live by it, or the way they raise children—but not for the purpose of understanding it better. It is particularly hard to refrain from making value judgments when the behavior in question occurs in an area of life in our own culture about which there are contradictory rules and considerable anxiety. Take, for instance, the transmission of sexual behavior in the village of Sensuron.

In Sensuron people usually deal with their sex drives through ideally denying their existence, while often behaving in ways designed to sidestep social and cultural barriers to personal satisfaction. At the ideal level of belief the view is expressed that "men are not like dogs, chasing any bitch in heat," or "sex relations are unclean." Some of the sexuality of Dusun life has been noted earlier. There is a high content of lewd and bawdy behavior in the play of children and adolescents, and in the behavior of adults. For example, the eight-year-old girl in the house across from ours was angrily ordered by her mother to come into the house to help in rice husking. The girl turned to her mother and gave her a slow, undulating thrust of her hips in a sexual sign. More than 12 salacious gestures are known and used regularly by children and adults of both sexes, and there are some 20 equivalents of "four-letter" English terms specifically denoting the sexual anatomy and its possible uses. Late one afternoon 4 girls between 8 and 15 years, and 2 young boys of 4 and 5 years were chasing about our house steps for a half hour, grabbing at each other's genitals, and screaming, *uarE tAle!* which roughly translated means, "there is your mother's vulva!" Adult onlookers were greatly amused at the group and became convulsed with laughter when the four-year-old boy improvised the answer, "my mother has no vulva!" Thus, sexual behavior is supposed to be unclean and disgusting, while in reality it is a source of amusement and constant attention. . . .

Children learn details of sexual behavior early, and sex play is a part of the behavior of four-to-six-year olds, usually in houses or rice stores while parents are away at work. Older children engage in sexual activities in groups and pairs, often at a location outside the village, often in an abandoned field storehouse, or in a temporary shelter in a remote garden (Williams 1965:82–83).

We can, however, make the tentative generalization that in cultures where there is a marked discrepancy between ideal and real, between the "theory" of culture and actual behavior, this conflict will be transmitted and that conflicts of this kind are probably not conducive to trust, confidence in self and in others, or even something we might call "happiness." We are like the people of Sensuron, though probably the conflicts between real and ideal run much deeper and are more damaging in our culture. In any event, the transmission of culture is complicated by discrepancies and conflicts, for both the pattern of idealizations and the patterns of actual behavior must be transmitted, as well as the ways for rationalizing the discrepancy between them.

How Goes It in Guadalcanal?

Many of the comments that have been made about child rearing and the transmission of culture in other communities can be applied to the situation in Guadalcanal, one of the Solomon Islands near New Guinea. Babies are held, fondled, fed, never isolated, and generally given very supportive treatment. Weaning and toilet training both take place without much fuss, and fairly late by American standards. Walking is regarded as a natural accomplishment that will be mastered in time, swimming seems to come as easily. Education is also different in some ways in Guadalcanal. There is no sharp discontinuity at the beginning of middle childhood as in Palau, nor is there any sharp break at puberty as in Ulithi, or at prepuberty as among the Hano Tewa or Hopi. The special character of cultural transmission in Guadalcanal is given by Ian Hogbin:

Two virtues, generosity and respect for property, are inculcated from the eighteenth month onward—that is to say, from the age when the child can walk about and eat bananas and other things regarded as delicacies. At this stage no explanations are given, and the parents merely insist that food must be shared with any playmate who happens to be present and that goods belonging to other villagers must be left undisturbed. A toddler presented with a piece of fruit is told to give half to "So-and-so," and should the order be resisted, the adult ignores all protests and breaks a piece off to hand to the child's companion. Similarly, although sometimes callers are cautioned to put their baskets on a shelf out of reach, any meddling brings forth the rebuke, "That belongs to your uncle. Put it down." Disobedience is followed by snatching away the item in question from the child and returning it to the owner.

In time, when the child has passed into its fourth or fifth year, it is acknowledged to have at last attained the understanding to be able to take in what the adults say. Therefore, adults now accompany demands with reasoned instruction. One day when I was paying a call on a neighbor, Mwane-Anuta, I heard him warn his second son Mbule, who probably had not reached the age of five, to stop being so greedy. "I saw your mother give you those nuts," Mwane-Anuta reiterated. "Don't pretend she didn't. Running behind the house so that Penggoa wouldn't know! That is bad, very bad. Now then, show me, how many? Five left. Very well, offer three to Penggoa immediately." He then went on to tell me how important it was for children to learn to think of others so that in later life they would win the respect of their fellows.

On another occasion during a meal I found Mwane-Anuta and his wife teaching their three sons how to eat properly. "Now Mbule," said his mother, "you face the rest of us so that we can all see you aren't taking too much. And you, Konana, run outside and ask Misika from next door to join you. His mother's not home yet, and I expect he's hungry. Your belly's not the only one, my boy." "Yes," Mwane-Anuta added. "Give a thought to those you run about with, and they'll give a thought to you." At that point the mother called over the eldest lad, Kure, and placed the basket of yams for me in his hands. "There, you carry that over to our guest and say that it is good to have him with us this evening," she whispered to him. The gesture was characteristic. I noted that always when meals were served to visitors the children acted as waiters. Why was this, I wanted to know. "Teaching, teaching," Mwane-Anuta replied. "This is how we train our young to behave" (1964:33).

It appears that in Guadalcanal direct verbal instruction is stressed as a technique of cultural transmission. Hogbin goes on to describe the constant stream of verbal admonition that is directed at the child by responsible adults in almost every situation. And again and again the prime values, generosity and respect for property, are reinforced by these admonitions.

The amount of direct verbal reinforcement of basic values, and even the amount of direct verbal instruction in less crucial matters, varies greatly from culture to culture. The people of Guadalcanal, like the Hopi, keep telling their children and young people how to behave and when they are behaving badly. In American middle-class culture there is also great emphasis on telling children what they should do, explaining how to do it, and the reasons for doing it, though we are probably less consistent in what we tell them than are the parents of Guadalcanal. Perhaps also in our culture we tend to substitute words for experience more than do the people of Guadalcanal, for the total range of experience relevant to growing up appropriately is more directly observable and available to their children than it is to ours.

> Girls go to the gardens regularly with their mother from about the age of eight. They cannot yet wield the heavy digging stick or bush knife, but they assist in collecting the rubbish before planting begins, in piling up the earth, and weeding. Boys start accompanying their father some two or three years later, when they help with the clearing, fetch lianas to tie up the saplings that form the fence, and cut up the seed yams. The men may also allocate plots to their sons and speak of the growing yams as their own harvest. The services of a youngster are of economic value from the time that he is pubescent, but he is not expected to take gardening really seriously until after he returns from the plantation and is thinking of marriage. By then he is conscious of his rights and privileges as a member of his clan and knows where the clan blocks of land are located. As a rule, he can also explain a little about the varieties of yams and taro and the types of soil best suited to earth.
>
> At about eight a boy begins to go along with his father or uncles when the men set out in the evening with their lines to catch fish from the shore or on the reef. They make a small rod for him, show him how to bait his hook, and tell him about the different species of fish—where they are to be found, which are good to eat, which are poisonous. At the age of ten the boy makes an occasional fishing excursion in a canoe. To start with, he sits in the center of the canoe and watches, perhaps baiting the hooks and removing the catch; but soon he takes part with the rest. In less than a year he is a useful crew member and expert in steering and generally handling the craft. At the same time, I have never seen youths under the age of sixteen out at sea by themselves. Often they are eager to go before this, but the elders are unwilling to give permission lest they endanger themselves or the canoe (Hogbin 1964:39).

The children of Guadalcanal learn by doing as well as learn by hearing. They also learn by imitating adult models, as children do in every human group around the world.

> Children also play at housekeeping. Sometimes they take along their juniors, who, however, do not remain interested for long. They put up a framework of saplings and tie on coconut-leaf mats, which they plait themselves in a rough-and-ready sort of way. Occasionally, they beg some raw food and prepare it; or they catch birds, bats, and rats with bows and arrows. Many times, too, I have seen them hold weddings, including all the formality of the handing-over of bride price. Various items serve instead of the valuables that the grownups use—tiny pebbles instead of dog's and porpoise teeth, the long flowers of a nut tree for strings of shell discs, and rats or lizards for

pigs. When first the youngsters pretend to keep house they make no sexual distinction in the allocation of the tasks. Boys and girls together erect the shelters, plait the mats, cook the food, and fetch the water. But within a year or so, although they continue to play in company, the members of each group restrict themselves to the work appropriate to their sex. The boys leave the cooking and water carrying to the girls, who, in turn, refuse to help with the building (Hogbin 1964:37–38).

Children seem to acquire the culture of their community best when there is consistent reinforcement of the same norms of action and thinking through many different channels of activity and interaction. If a child is told, sees demonstrated, casually observes, imitates, experiments and is corrected, acts appropriately and is rewarded, corrected, and (as in the Tewa-Hopi initiation) is given an extra boost in learning by dramatized announcements of status-role change, all within a consistent framework of belief and value, he or she cannot help but learn, and learn what adult cultural transmitters want him or her to learn.

How Do They Listen in Demirciler?
In Demirciler, an Anatolian village in the arid central plateau of Turkey, a young boy, Mahmud, learns by being allowed in the room when the adult men meet at the Muhtar's (the village headman) home evenings to discuss current affairs.

Each day, after having finished the evening meal, the old Muhtar's wife would put some small earthenware dishes or copper trays filled with nuts or chick-peas about the room, sometimes on small stands or sometimes on the floor, and the old man would build a warm fire in the fireplace. Soon after dark the men would begin to arrive by ones or twos and take their accustomed places in the men's room. This was the largest single room in the village and doubled as a guest house for visitors who came at nightfall and needed some place to sleep before going on their way the next day. It had been a long time since the room had been used for this purpose, however, because the nearby growing city had hotels, and most of the modern travelers stayed there. However, the room still served as a clearing house for all village business, as well as a place for the men to pass the cold winter evenings in warm comfort.

The room was perhaps 30 by 15 feet in size, and along one side a shelf nearly 15 inches above the floor extended about 2 feet from the wall and covered the full 30 feet of the room's length. The old Muhtar sat near the center of the shelf, waiting for his guests to arrive. As the men came in, the oldest in the village would seat themselves in order of age on this raised projection, while the younger ones would sit cross-legged on the floor. No women were ever allowed to come into this room when the men were there. The Muhtar's wife had prepared everything ahead of time, and when additional things were occasionally needed during the evening, one of the boys would be sent out to fetch it. Opposite the long bench was a fireplace, slightly larger than those in the kitchen of the other village homes, in which a fire burned brightly spreading heat throughout the room. The single electric bulb lighted the space dimly and so the shadows caused by the firelight were not prevented from dancing about the walls.

Mahmud would have been happier if the electric bulb had not been there at all, the way it used to be when he had been a very small boy. Electricity had been introduced to the village only a year ago, and he remembered the days when only the glow of the fire lighted these meetings.

As the gatherings grew in size, Mahmud heard many small groups of men talking idly about all sorts of personal problems, but when nearly all of the villagers had arrived, they began to quiet down.

The Hoca posed the first question, "Muhtar Bey, when will next year's money for the mosque be taken up?"

"Hocam, the amount has not been set yet," was the Muhtar's reply.

"All right, let's do it now," the Hoca persisted.

"Let's do it now," the Muhtar agreed.

And Mahmud listened as the Hoca told about the things the mosque would need during the coming year. Then several of the older men told how they had given so much the year before that it had been hard on their families, and finally, the Muhtar talked interminably about the duty of each Moslem to support the Faith and ended by asking the head of each family for just a little more than he knew they could pay.

Following this request there were a series of discussions between the Muhtar and each family head, haggling over what the members of his family could afford to give. Finally, however, agreement was reached with each man, and the Hoca knew how much he could count on for the coming year. The Muhtar would see that the money was collected and turned over to the Hoca.

The business of the evening being out of the way, Mahmud became more interested, as he knew that he liked most of what was to come now. He had learned that he was too young to speak at the meetings, because he had been taken out several times the year before by one of the older boys and told that he could not stay with the men unless he could be quiet, so he waited in silence for what would happen next. After a slight pause one of the braver of the teen-aged boys called to an old man.

"*Dedem*, tell us some stories about the olden times."

"Shall I tell about the wars?" the old man nearest the Muhtar asked.

"Yes, about the great war with the Russians," the youth answered.

"Well, I was but a boy then, but my father went with the army of the Sultan that summer, and he told me this story" (Pierce 1964:20–21).

Is there any situation in the culture of the United States where a similar situation exists? When America was more rural than it is now, and commercial entertainments were not readily available for most people, young people learned about adult roles and problems, learned to think like adults and anticipated their own adulthood in somewhat the same way that Mahmud did. Now it is an open question whether young people would want to listen to their elders even if there was nothing else to do. Possibly this is partly because much of what one's elders "know" in our society is not true. The verities change with each generation.

At the end of the "business" session at the Muhtar's home an old man tells a story. The story is offered as entertainment, even though it has been heard countless time before. Young listeners learn from stories as well as from the deliberations of the older men as they decide what to do about somebody's adolescent son who is eyeing the girls too much, or what to do about building a new road. Storytelling has been and still is a way of transmitting information to young people in many cultures without their knowing they are being taught. Any story has either a metaphoric application to real life, provides models for behavior, or has both features. The metaphor or the model may or may not be translated into a moral. The elders in Demirciler do not, it appears, make the moral of the story explicit. In contrast, the Menomini Indians of Wisconsin always required a youngster to extract the moral in a story for himself. "You should never ask for anything to happen unless you mean it." "He who brags bites his own tail." A grandparent would tell the same story every night until the children could state the moral to the elder's satisfaction (Spindler 1963b). People in different cultures vary greatly in how much they make of the moral, but stories and mythtellings are used in virtually all cultures to transmit information, values, and attitudes.

What happens when the culture is changing?

In most of the culture cases used in this chapter to illustrate different ways of transmitting and acquiring culture the assumption is implicit that the culture is stable. As a matter of fact, all of the cultures in this chapter are changing, but at different rates. Some of them are on the brink of cataclysmic change, and were caught by the ethnographer just before it happened. The consequences of rapid culture change and acculturation are discussed in Chapter 11. Here in this chapter we must pay some attention to the problems of transmitting culture when the very culture to be transmitted is transforming. Whose culture should be transmitted? That of the grandparents' generation—as is so often the case in small, traditional societies like the ones we have been talking about so far? That of the parents' generation? But today this culture may be twenty years out of date. Should youth invent their own culture and transmit it to each other? That is what the young people in the United States do to a surprising extent. That adolescent tastes in music, cars, dress, dances, speech, and many other things are highly patterned among youth and quite different from the tastes of their parents on these same matters, is news to no one. Of course there are regional differences, class differences, school by school differences, and differences between cliques in the same schools, but there are a number of commonalities as well that are a part of "youth culture" in the United States. Advertising agencies and merchants know this, and adolescents spend millions of dollars a year, mostly on things their parents would be quite willing to have them do without.

The United States is not the only place where change is pulling apart what was once together. Take the case of Japan.

What Changes and What Stays the Same?

Every place around the world where rapid change is taking place, and that is almost everywhere, there are some things that stay the same and others that do not. In Japan, as is made clear in Chapter 11, the adaptation to rapid urbanization and industrialization has been relatively smooth, despite the dislocation of traditional patterns of behavior by Western, and particularly American, ways of doing things. This general statement applies to the way children are raised.

There is no "typical" Japanese community. There are many different ways of life, many different kinds of people. Takashima, a *buraku* of Kojima, a loose collection of formerly independent farming, fishing, and industrial settlements in Okayama Prefecture, is as typical as any single small settlement can be of the semi-rural and more traditional part of today's Japan. Children there are raised with a mixture of tradition and modernity.

> There had been some troubling moments during the infancy of all the children, when Hanako had been reluctant to follow the old customs which grandmother made ready to carry out. She had been unwilling to give the newborn infants the traditional infusion of bitter herbs which grandmother had in readiness, but she had finally pretended to do so. Many other old customs had been circumvented in the same way without giving offense to grandmother. Some of the customs surrounding pregnancy and childbirth were, of course, very simple to follow as well as being absurd. Hanako did not find it difficult during pregnancy to observe such taboos as those against eating octopus, lest her child be born boneless, or eating misshapen vegetables, lest the child be similarly misshapen. Grandmother had seen to it that the placentas and the bath water used at childbirth had been properly buried in the ground beneath the floor of the room where birth took place. She had also carefully wrapped the umbilici of the infants in cloth and paper and tucked them away in a drawer for possible future use of which even she was ignorant. Out of deference to grandmother, Hanako had tried to avoid other people for thirty-three days after childbirth, but this had been a trying and impractical custom. She had also tried to remember to sprinkle herself and the house with purifying salt when the prescribed period had ended. Grandmother spoke of making a "new fire" at this time, as she also had at the end of the mourning period when the great grandparents had died. But a new fire was built as a matter of course every day, and this old custom that grandmother attempted to follow had no meaning for Hanako.
>
> The rearing of the children had thus followed practices that combined tradition and innovation. When the children were ready for weaning at about two years of age, Hanako had followed the practice common when she was a child. Rubbing the juice of freshly broken chili peppers on her nipples had brought dramatically quick results. In other matters of child rearing, Hanako had leaned self-consciously toward the new. Well aware of theories of nutrition from lectures she had heard by visiting specialists in public health, and from reading articles in women's magazines, she watched the children's diet with care. After the death of their third-born child, she had not hesitated to consult a physician when symptoms of illness were evident. After the national program of socialized medicine reached Takashima, there had been no economic reason for failing to seek trained medical counsel. The children were healthy and all were so large that she habitually

purchased for them clothing a full two year-sizes larger than their actual ages. None had ever had physical punishment, and, if sometimes troublesome in early childhood, at least the elder two were now obedient and well mannered (Norbeck 1965:28, 29).

It is apparent that even in this more traditional sector of Japanese culture the old customs of child rearing have become almost irrelevant to present-day parents. The second son of the Matsui family of Takashima, described above, achieved an advanced education, became a salaried man in a large business, and married a city girl. Soon they moved to an apartment in a *danchi* (concrete multistoried low-cost housing) and shortly thereafter had their first child.

Two months after they moved into the *danchi*, Aki gave birth to their daughter Emi. By this time she had made friends with several neighbors, pregnant like herself or the mothers of young children. The birth, in a hospital, had been untroubled, and Jiro had shown no disappointment that their child was a daughter. They both hoped to have one more child, preferably a son but a daughter would also be welcome. The child was normal and healthy, but it soon was clear that Aki could not provide all the nourishment that the infant required. At their doctor's recommendation, bottles, nipples, and a sterilizer were purchased, and Emi became one of several dozen infants in the *danchi* living on a supplementary diet.

Domestic finance was considerably aided by gifts for the baby from Aki's parents and other relatives. Jiro's parents sent a brilliantly colored infant's *kimono,* in country taste, which was placed in a drawer and never worn. Recreation for Jiro and Aki now consisted of television turned down to a whisper, books and magazines, occasional chats with neighbors, visits with the relatives, and enjoyment of the baby. Jiro sometimes helped with the housework and felt no loss of masculinity for doing so (Norbeck 1965:77).

Jiro and Aki had no need to give even lip service to the old customs

surrounding the birth of their child and its early years. But there may not be the complete break with the past that this observation implies. It is probably true that many specific customs in child rearing can be laid aside without decisively influencing the way children are raised. This surely seems contradictory. What is meant is that it may not be so much exactly what is done with a child that counts but the general way in which it is done. For example, whether a child is given a bottle or the breast may be less important than whether it is held while being given the bottle or left to be alone while it sucks. And even in the circumvention of customs surrounding pregnancy and childbirth dear to grandparents in the Takashima household, the parents communicated to their own children the value of not offending and of respecting older people—and filial piety and respect are cultural values of long standing in Japan. The same kind of situation occurs in school as small children work conscientiously at learning to paint the traditional Japanese characters (borrowed from China), however "democratic" or "progressive" the setting otherwise, they learn patience at painstaking replication, obedience, and even some of the quality of Japanese artistic expression. There are other ways as well in which continuity between past and present is retained.

The grandfather still tells stories to his grandchildren in the Matsui household.

> . . . recounting the tales he had heard from his grandfather, spine-chilling stories of ghosts and demons. From grandfather, Makoto has learned that Jimmu Tanno, the first emperor of Japan, once lived in Takashima and that his ghost may be seen on moonlit nights walking the sands of Uragahama beach. Grandfather, and sometimes grandmother and Hanako, tell Makoto other tales that are less frightening but no less interesting—of the peach boy who sprang from the seed of a peach; the boy who went on a turtle's back to a fairyland at the bottom of the sea; and of the *Kappa*, creatures both frog-like and boy-like that live in streams. *Kappa* can lure people and horses into the water, but once tilted so that the liquid in the concave depressions at the top of their heads is spilled, they are powerless (Norbeck 1965:38).

But even in Takashima television displaces many of the time-honored family diversions and directly influences the transmission of culture.

> Grandfather and all his male descendants including Makoto like *chambara,* stirring dramas of the bold adventures and honorable exploits of ancient feudal lords and their retainers. When these are broadcast, the women of the household usually find other things to do. Makoto favors animated cartoons. Among his favorites are "Atomu," which concerns the adventures of a miraculous boy of the atom age named Atom; "Tetsujin," featuring the robot of the space age; "Popeye," and a variety of other American cartoons. Yuriko and her mother and grandmother like modern and period plays with Japanese themes in which rivers of tears flow. These Akira and Hajime frequently watch but deny liking. Everybody except grandfather and Makoto like the rebroadcasts of "I Love Lucy," "Rawhide," and the ancient Our Gang come-

dies, which have Japanese dialogue dubbed in. Akira and Yuriko agree in liking old American movies. The channel that broadcasts educational programs sees little use. As a result of television, bedtime is often later than usual by an hour or two; Akira sometimes does not go to bed until nearly eleven o'clock (Norbeck 1965:41).

Here again the recurring theme of change and continuity in cultural transmission appears. The *chambara* television dramas transmit values as well as some information meaningful in the perspective of Japanese history. They also furnish Japanese viewers with a means of identifying with their own cultural past, and this is an important part of cultural transmission. Doubtless the modern and period plays with Japanese themes that the females in the household like so well also reinforce long-standing Japanese values and attitudes. Perhaps even the "Atomu" series exhibits some continuity with the superman implications of the Samurai tales that have been favorites among Japanese for generations. Possibly even "Popeye" is a Samurai in disguise, however farfetched this may seem to Americans. But what about "I Love Lucy," "Rawhide," "Our Gang" comedies, and the American movies that Japanese see? It seems unlikely that they reinforce any Japanese values, unless by accident. Television has brought into, in fact transmitted within the Matsui household, an alien culture. No matter how innocuous and socially meaningless an American play, movie, or cartoon may seem to us, it projects a cultural stream of influence that alters the process and content of cultural transmission in this and millions of other Japanese households.

Despite the apparent changes within the Matsui household, and the sharp break between that household and the urban family of Jiro and Aki, it is probably true that the most telling break in the continuity of cultural transmission in Japan occurs during adolescence.

A decline in faith coupled with loss of the necessary personnel have denied to Akira one of the privileges of young manhood. The ancient ceremony initiating youths into the Young Men's Association, which formed part of the Autumn Festival of the tutelary god, is no longer conducted. Held annually or biennially for young men turned sixteen, the rite celebrated their maturity with a feast in which they and all other unmarried young men of the community participated. It was a time when the young men buried their enmities with other youths, and when all were allowed and expected to get drunk. Its climax was a procession of the drunken youths, in costume, carrying a heavy litter on which one of their number sat behind curtains beating a drum and impersonating the tutelary god. Scarcity of young men, lack of interest, and disapproval of drinking among the young recently put an end to this once popular event (Norbeck 1965:47).

It surely is not important in itself that adolescent males no longer celebrate their maturity by getting drunk and carrying one of their number around in a heavy litter. It is important that the Young Men's Associations mean much less or have ceased to exist, that the worship of tutelary gods is disappearing, or is defunct in many sectors, and that the whole complex of cultural forms of which the initiation was a part has, in varying degrees in different places, disintegrated. It is even more important that the Japanese, like ourselves, have not invented any new dramatic way of carrying adolescent males over the gap between childhood and adulthood. There are, of course, many relatively undramatized signals in both cultures, such as going away to school, starting to work, getting the keys to the car (in the United States), but none of them has the unifying and dramatic effect of a real initiation ceremony. Perhaps this is because there is little agreement in Japan, or in the United States, about what it is one should be initiated into. There are so many different directions to go in adult life, so many more status-role changes ahead of one during adult life, that a dramatic announcement of this preliminary status-role change seems beside the point.

Nevertheless, the startling rise in juvenile crime, the futile destructiveness of adolescent gangs, the experimentation with drugs, and other behaviors symptomatic of hostility toward adult cultural norms characterizing significant segments of the adolescent population in both countries, suggests that no effective way has been discovered to incorporate new generations into the cultural system of either country.

There is probably more continuity with the past in Japan than in the United States. Nevertheless, we know that the balance between change and continuity is precarious in both countries. There are more nations and communities all around the world that are like Japan and the United States in this respect, than there are like the Hopi or the Hano Tewa as we have described them.

What does cultural transmission do for the system?

So far we have considered (except for Japan) cultural transmission in cases where no major interventions from the outside have occurred, or, if they have occurred, we have chosen to ignore them for purposes of description and analysis. There are, however, virtually no cultural systems left in the world that have not experienced massive input from the outside, particularly from the West. This is the age of transformation. Nearly all tribal societies and peasant villages are being affected profoundly by modernization. One of the most important aspects of modernization is the development of schools that will, hopefully, prepare young people to take their places in a very different kind of world than the one their parents grew up in. This implies a kind of discontinuity that is of a different order than the kind we have been discussing.

Discontinuity in cultural transmission among the Dusun, Hopi, Tewa, and Tiwi is a process that produces cultural continuity in the system as a whole. The abrupt and dramatized changes in roles during adolescence, the sudden compression of cultural requirements, and all the techniques used by perceptors, who are nearly always adults from within the cultural system, educate an individual to be committed to the system. The initiation itself encapsulates and dramatizes symbols and meanings that are at the core of the cultural system so that the important things the initiate has learned up to that point, by observation, participation, or instruction, are reinforced. The discontinuity is in the way the initiate is treated during the initiation and the different behaviors expected of him (or her) afterward. The culture is maintained, its credibility validated. As the Hopi man said to Dorothy Eggan, "I will not discuss this thing with you only to say that no one can forget it. It is the most wonderful thing any man can have to remember. You know then that you are Hopi (after the initiation).[2] It is the one thing Whites cannot have, cannot take from us. It is our way of life given to us when the world began." (See pp. 218–219.) This Hopi individual has been *recruited* as a Hopi.

In all established cultural systems where radical interventions from outside have not occurred, the major functions of education are *recruitment* and *maintenance*. The educational processes we have described for all of the cultures in this chapter have functioned in this manner. Recruitment occurs in two senses: recruitment to membership in the cultural system in general, so that one becomes a Hopi or a Tiwi; and recruitment to specific roles and statuses, to specific castes, or to certain classes. We may even,

[2] Parenthetical insert by George D. Spindler.

by stretching the point a little, say that young humans are recruited to male or female, on the terms with which a given society defines being male or female. This becomes clear in cultures such as our own, where sex roles are becoming blurred so much that many young people grow up without a clear orientation toward either role. The educational system, whether we are talking about societies where there are no schools in the formal sense but where a great deal of education takes place, or about societies where there are many specialized formal schools, is organized to effect recruitment. The educational system is also organized so that the structure of the cultural system will be maintained. This is done by inculcating the specific values, attitudes, and beliefs that make this structure credible and the skills and competencies that make it work. People must believe in their system. If there is a caste or class structure they must believe that such a structure is good, or if not good, at least inevitable. They must also have the skills— vocational and social—that make it possible for goods and services to be exchanged that are necessary for community life to go on. Recruitment and maintenance intergrade, as you can see from the above discussion. The former refers to the process of getting people into the system and specific roles; the latter refers to the process of keeping the system and roles functioning.

Modernizing cultures: what is the purpose of education?

In this transforming world, however, educational systems are often charged with responsibility for bringing about change in the culture. They become, or are intended to become, agents of modernization. They become intentional agents of cultural discontinuity, a kind of discontinuity that does not reinforce the traditional values or recruit youngsters into the existing system. The new schools, with their curricula and the concepts behind them, are future oriented. They recruit students into a system that does not yet exist, or is just emerging. They inevitably create conflicts between generations.

Among the Sisala of Northern Ghana, a modernizing African society, for example, there have been profound changes in the principles underlying the father-son relationship. As one man put it:

> This strict obedience, this is mostly on the part of illiterates. With educated people, if you tell your son something, he will have to speak his mind. If you find that the boy is right, you change your mind. With an illiterate, he just tells his son to do something. . . . In the old days, civilization was not so much. We obeyed our fathers whether right or wrong. If you didn't, they would beat you. We respected our fathers with fear. Now we have to talk with our sons when they challenge us (Grindal 1972:80).

Not all of the Sisala have as tolerant and favorable a view of the changes wrought by education, however:

When my children were young, I used to tell them stories about my village and about our family traditions. But in Tumu there are not so many people from my village and my children never went to visit the family. Now my children are educated and they have no time to sit with the family. A Sisala father usually farms with his son. But with educated people, they don't farm. They run around town with other boys. Soon we will forget our history. The educated man has a different character from his father. So fathers die and never tell their sons about the important traditions. My children don't sit and listen to me anymore. They don't want to know the real things my father told me. They have gone to school, and they are now book men. Boys who are educated run around with other boys rather than sitting and listening to their fathers (Grindal: 83).

That these conflicts should flare up into open expressions of hostility toward education, schools, and teachers is not surprising. A headmaster of a primary school among the Sisala related to Bruce Grindal what happened when a man made a trip to a village outside Tumu.

He parked his car on the road and was away for some time. When he returned, he saw that somebody had defaced his car, beaten it with sticks or something. Now I knew that my school children knew something about this. So I gathered them together and told them that if they were good citizens, they should report to me who did it and God would reward them. So I found out that this was done by some people in the village. When the village people found out their children told me such things, they were very angry. They said that the teachers were teaching their children to disrespect their elders. It is because of things like that that the fathers are taking their children out of school (Grindal: 97–98).

The above implies that the new schools, created for the purposes of aiding and abetting modernization, are quite effective. Without question they do create conflicts between generations and disrupt the transmission of the traditional culture. These effects in themselves are a prelude to change, perhaps a necessary condition. They are not, however, the result of the effectiveness of the schools as educational institutions. Because the curricular content is alien to the existing culture there is little or no reinforcement in the home and family, or in the community as a whole, for what happens in the school. The school is isolated from the cultural system it is intended to serve. As F. Landa Jocano relates concerning the primary school in Malitbog, a barrio in Panay, in the middle Philippines:

. . . most of what children learn in school is purely verbal imitation and academic memorization, which do not relate with the activities of the children at home. By the time a child reaches the fourth grade he is expected to be competent in reading, writing, arithmetic, and language study. Except for gardening, no other vocational training is taught. The plants that are required to be cultivated, however, are cabbages, lettuce, okra, and other vegetables which are not normally grown and eaten in the barrio. [sentence omitted]

Sanitation is taught in the school, but insofar as my observation went, this is not carried beyond the child's wearing clean clothes. Children may be required to buy toothbrushes, combs, handkerchiefs, and other personal items, and bring these to school for inspection. Because only a few can afford to buy these items, only a few come to school with them. Often these school requirements are the source of troubles at home, a night's crying among the children. . . . [sentence omitted] In the final analysis, such regular school injunctions as "brush your teeth every morning" or "drink milk and eat leafy vegetables" mean nothing to the children. First, none of the families brush their teeth. The toothbrushes the children bring to school are for inspection only. Their parents cannot afford to buy milk. They do not like goats' milk because it is *malangsa* (foul smelling) (Jocano 1969:53).

Nor is it solely a matter of the nonrelatedness of what is taught in the school to what is learned in the home and community. Because the curricular content is alien to the culture as a whole, what is taught tends to become formalized and unrealistic and is taught in a rigid ritualistic manner. Again, among the Sisala of Northern Ghana, Bruce Grindal describes the classroom environment.

The classroom environment into which the Sisala child enters is characterized by a mood of rigidity and an almost total absence of spontaneity. A typical school day begins with a fifteen-minute period during which the students talk and play, often running and screaming, while the teacher, who is usually outside talking with his fellow teachers, pays no attention. At 8:30 one of the students rings a bell, and the children immediately take their seats and remove from their desks the materials needed for the first lesson. When the teacher enters the room, everyone falls silent. If the first lesson is English, the teacher begins by reading a passage in the students' readers. He then asks the students to read the section aloud, and if a child makes a mistake, he is told to sit down, after being corrected. Variations of the English lesson consist of having the students write down dictated sentences or spell selected words from a passage on the blackboard. Each lesson lasts exactly forty minutes, at the end of which a bell rings and the students immediately prepare for the next lesson.

Little emphasis is placed upon the content of what is taught; rather, the book is strictly adhered to, and the students are drilled by being asked the questions which appear at the end of each assignment. The absence of discussion is due partially to the poor training of the teachers, yet even in the middle schools where the educational standards for teachers are better, an unwillingness exists to discuss or explain the content of the lessons. All subjects except mathematics are lessons in literacy which teach the student to spell, read, and write.

Interaction between the teacher and his students is characterized by an authoritarian rigidity. When the teacher enters the classroom, the students are expected to rise as a sign of respect. If the teacher needs anything done in the classroom, one of the students performs the task. During lessons the student is not expected to ask questions, but instead is supposed to give the "correct" answers to questions posed to him by the teacher. The students are less intent upon what the teacher is saying than they are upon the reading materials before them. When the teacher asks a question, most of the students hurriedly examine their books to find the correct answer and then raise their hands. The teacher calls on one of them, who rises, responds (with his eyes lowered), and then sits down. If the answer is wrong or does not make sense, the teacher corrects him and occasionally derides him for his stupidity. In the latter case the child remains standing with his eyes lowered until the teacher finishes and then sits down without making a response (Grindal 1972:85).

The nonrelatedness of the school to the community in both the content being transmitted and the methods used to transmit it is logically carried into the aspirations of students concerning their own futures. These aspirations are often quite unrealistic. As one of the Sisala school boys said:

I have in mind this day being a professor so that I will be able to help my country. . . . As a professor I will visit so many countries such as America, Britain, and Holland. In fact, it will be interesting for me and my wife. . . . When I return, my father will be proud seeing his child like this. Just imagine me having a wife and children in my car moving down the street of my village. And when the people are in need of anything, I will help them (Grindal: 89).

Or as another reported in an essay:

By the time I have attained my graduation certificate from the university, the government will be so happy that they may like to make me president of my beloved country. When I receive my salary, I will divide the money and give part to my father and my wife and my children. . . . People say the U.S.A. is a beautiful country. But when they see my village, they will say it is more beautiful. Through my hard studies, my name will rise forever for people to remember (Grindal: 89).

As we have said, the new schools, like the traditional tribal methods of education and schools everywhere, recruit new members of the community into a cultural system and into specific roles and statuses. And they attempt to maintain this system by transmitting the necessary competencies to individuals who are recruited into it via these roles and statuses. The problem with the new schools is that the cultural system they are recruiting for does not yet exist in its full form. The education the school boys and girls receive is regarded by many as more or less useless, though most people, like the Sisala, agree that at least literacy is necessary if one is to get along in the modern world. However, the experience of the school child goes far beyond training for literacy. The child is removed from the everyday routine of community life and from observation of the work rules of adults. He or she is placed in an artificial, isolated, unrealistic, ritualized environment. Unrealistic aspirations and self-images develop. Harsh reality intrudes abruptly upon graduation. The schoolboy discovers that, except for teaching in the primary schools, few opportunities are open to him. There are some clerical positions in government offices, but they are few. Many graduates migrate in search of jobs concomitant with their expectations, but they usually find that living conditions are more severe than those in the tribal area and end up accepting an occupation and life style similar to that of the illiterate tribesmen who have also migrated to the city. Those who become village teachers are not much better off. One Sisala teacher in his mid-twenties said:

> I am just a small man. I teach and I have a small farm. . . . Maybe someday if I am fortunate, I will buy a tractor and farm for money because there is no future in teaching. When I went to school, I was told that if I got good marks and studied hard, I would be somebody, somebody important. I even thought I would go to America or England. I would still like to go, but I don't think of these things very often because it hurts too much. You see me here drinking and perhaps you think I don't have any sense. I don't know. I don't know why I drink. But I know in two days' time, I must go back and teach school. In X (his home village where he teaches) I am alone; I am nobody (Grindal: 93).

The pessimist will conclude that the new schools, as agents of modernization, are a rank failure. This would be a false conclusion. They are neither failures nor successes. The new schools, like all institutions transforming cultural systems, are not articulated with the other parts of the changing system. The future is not known or knowable. Much of the content taught in the school, as well as the very concept of the school as a place with four walls within which teacher and students are confined for a number of hours each day and regulated by a rigid schedule of "learning" activities, is Western. In many ways the new schools among the Sisala, in Malitbog, and in many other changing cultures are inadequate copies of schools in Europe and the United States. There is no doubt, however, that formal schooling in all of the developing nations of the world, as disarticulated with the existing cultural context as it is, nevertheless is helping to bring into being a new population of literates, whose aspirations and world view are very different than that of their parents. And of course a whole class of educated elites has been created by colleges and universities in many of the countries. It seems inevitable that eventually the developing cultures will build their own models for schools and education. These new models will not be caricatures of Western schools, although in places, as in the case of the Sisala or the Kanuri of Nigeria described by Alan Peshkin (Peshkin 1972), where the Western influence has been strong for a long time, surely those models will show this influence.

Perhaps one significant part of the problem and the general shape of the solution is implied in the following exchange between two new young

teachers in charge of a village school among the Ngoni of Malawi and a
senior chief:

> The teachers bent one knee as they gave him the customary greeting, waiting
> in silence until he spoke.
> "How is your school?"
> "The classes are full and the children are learning well, Inkosi."
> "How do they behave?"
> "Like Ngoni children, Inkosi."
> "What do they learn?"
> "They learn reading, writing, arithmetic, scripture, geography and drill,
> Inkosi."
> "Is that education?"
> "It is education, Inkosi."
> "No! No! No! Education is *very* broad, *very* deep. It is not only in books,
> it is learning how to live. I am an old man now. When I was a boy I went
> with the Ngoni army against the Bemba. Then the mission came and I went
> to school. I became a teacher. Then I was chief. Then the government came.
> I have seen our country change, and now there are many schools and many
> young men go away to work to find money. I tell you that Ngoni children
> must learn how to live and how to build up our land, not only to work and
> earn money. Do you hear?"
> "Yebo, Inkosi" (Yes, O Chief) (Read 1968:2–3).

The model of education that will eventually emerge in the modernizing
nations will be one that puts the school, in its usual formal sense, in perspective, and emphasizes education in its broadest sense, as a part of life
and of the dynamic changing community. It must emerge if these cultures
are to avoid the tragic errors of miseducation, as the Western nations have
experienced them, particularly in the relationships between the schools and
minority groups.

Why have minority groups in North America been disadvantaged by their schools?

In Harlem School?

A description of a first-grade class in a black ghetto in New York City
follows. It is not a school in the poorest of the districts. It was considered
"typical" for the grade.

> The teacher trainee (student teacher) is attempting to teach "rhyming." It
> is early afternoon. Even before she can get the first "match" (for example,
> "book" and "look") a whole series of events is drawn out.
> One child plays with the head of a doll, which has broken off from the doll,
> alternately hitting it and kissing it.
> The student teacher tells a boy who has left his seat that he is staying-in

after school. He begins to cry. Another child teases that his mother will be worried about him if he stays in after school. The boy cries even harder and screams at the teacher: "You can't keep me in until 15 o'clock."

A girl tries to answer a question put to the class but raises her hand with her shoe in it. She is told to put her hand down and to put her shoe on.

Another child keeps switching his pencil from one nostril to another, trying to see if it will remain in his nose if he lets go of it; he is apparently wholly unconcerned with the session in progress.

One child is lying down across his desk, pretending to sleep while seeing if the teacher sees him. Just next to him another child leads an imaginary band. Still a different child, on his other side, stands quietly beside his seat, apparenty tired of sitting.

While this is all going on the regular teacher of the class is out of the room. When she does return, she makes no effort to assist, or criticize, the student teacher. The student teacher later informed me that the regular teacher was not "just being polite." She rarely directed the student teacher, but simply let her "take over" the class on occasion. The student teacher also remarked that things were no different in the class when the regular teacher held forth.

Fifteen minutes had gone by, but little "rhyming" had been accomplished. A boy begins to shadow box in the back; another talks to himself in acting out a scene he envisions.

Still another child shakes his fist at the student teacher, mimicking her words: "cat-fat, hop-stop."

Two children turn to each other and exchange "burns" on one another's forearms, while another child arranges and rearranges his desk materials and notebook, seemingly dissatisfied with each succeeding arrangement.

A girl in the back has an empty bag of potato chips but is trying to use her fingers as a "blotter" to get at the remnants. She pretends to be paying attention to the lesson.

Another child asks to go to the bathroom, but is denied.

After a half-hour I left (Rosenfeld 1971:105).

As Gerry Rosenfeld, who taught in Harlem School and did an anthropological field study there, pointed out, the schooling of these children is already patterned for them at the age of six or seven. "Not much is expected from them," they are from poor families, they are black, and they are "disadvantaged." By high school many of them will be dropouts, or "pushouts," as Rosenfeld terms them. As they get older they become less docile than the children described above, and some teachers in ghetto schools have reason to fear for their own safety. The teachers of this classroom did not have reason to fear their pupils, but they were ignorant about them. Their preparatory work in college or in teacher training had not prepared them for a classroom of children from a poor ghetto area in the city. The student teacher knew nothing about the neighborhood from which the children in her class came. She knew only that she "did not want to work with 'these' children when she became a regular teacher" (Rosenfeld: 105).

As a teacher and observer at Harlem School, Rosenfeld found the teachers held an array of myths about poor children that they used to account for their underachievement and miseducation. At the benign liberal level they are beliefs about the nature of poverty and cultural disadvantage. These conditions become accepted as irrevocable givens. The child comes from such a background, therefore, there is nothing I, as a teacher, can do but try to get minimal results from this misshapen material. Among teachers who are explicitly bigoted in their views of the poor and black, the explanations for failure may be less benign. According to Rosenfeld, and his observations are supported by others, an underlying ethos pervades the slum school which prescribes and accepts failure for the child.

> Assistant principals function not as experts on curriculum and instruction but as stock boys and disciplinarians. Boxes are constantly being unpacked and children are being reprimanded and punished. The principal seems more concerned with maintaining a stable staff, irrespective of its quality at times, than with effecting school-community ties and fashioning relevant learning programs. Education appears as a process where children are merely the by-products, not the core of concern. Guidance counselors and reading specialists are preoccupied with norms and averages, not with the enhancement of learning for all the children. Theirs is a remedial task, and where one would not exist, they create it. School directives and bulletins are concerned with bathroom regulations and procedures along stairways, the worth of the children being assessed in terms of their ability to conform to these peripheral demands (Rosenfeld: 110).

The new teacher, however idealistic he or she may be at first, will be affected by the environment. He or she becomes a part of the social structure of the school. A socialization process occurs so that personal commitment and philosophy become ordered around the system. The clique structure among staff personnel also forces the newcomer to choose models and cultivate relationships. Communication must occur. There must be others with whom one can commiserate.

Teachers who keep their idealism, tempered as it is after a time by reality, turn more and more inward toward their own classroom. There one sees the results of the years of educational disenchantment. In the middle grades and beyond the children are already two or more years behind standard achievement norms. The teacher realizes that for the children the school is an oppressive and meaningless place. He comes to understand also that children have developed counterstrategies for what they have perceived as their teachers' indifference, confusion, despair, and in some cases, outright aggression. But if the teacher persists in the effort to understand his or her pupils, eventually they become individuals. Most are alert and active. They are potentially high learners and achievers. Some are subdued and permanently detached. Some are irrevocably hostile towards schools, teachers, and white people. Others have surface hostilities but are willing to give trust and confidence when it is justified. Some are fast learners with strong curiosity and an eagerness to learn about the world. Others are apathetic or simply dull. Once the children become individuals, with sharp differences, they can no longer be treated as objects or as a collectivity.

The next step for the teacher who is going to become effective as a cultural transmitter and agent of socialization, as all teachers are, is to learn something of the neighborhood and of the homes from which the children come. But this is the step that is rarely taken. Rosenfeld describes the situation at Harlem School.

> Though Harlem School belonged to the neighborhood, it was not psychologically a part of it. On the contrary, teachers felt unwanted, estranged. Perhaps this was why few ventured off the "beaten paths" to the "hinterland" beyond the school, into the side streets and the homes where the children played out their lives. Some teachers at Harlem School had never been to a single child's household, despite the fact that they had been employed at the school for many years. Nothing was known of community self-descriptions, the activity and social calendar in the neighborhood, the focal points for assembly and dispersal, or the feelings of residents toward the "outside world." Teachers could not imagine that they could foster a genuine coming-together of neighborhood persons and themselves. They hid behind their "professionalism." They failed to realize that the apathy and disparagement they associated with parents were attributed by the latter to them. It is not to be underestimated how "foreign" teachers feel themselves to be at Harlem School, how disliked by the children. Why then do they remain on the job? Part of the answer is in the fact that the rewards of one's work are not always sought on the job itself, but in the private world. Teachers have little stake in the communities in which they work; that is why it may be necessary to link more closely teachers' jobs and children's achievement. It is my guess that all children (except those with proven defects) would achieve if teachers' jobs depended on this (Rosenfeld: 103).

It is clear that there are some parallels between the relationship of the school and teachers to the pupils and community in minority populations in the United States and the like relationship that has developed in many of the modernizing nations. Although there are profound differences in the two situations, the similarity is that the educational institutions in both cases are intrusive. These institutions stem from a conceptual and cultural context that is different from that of the people whose children are in the schools. This tends to be true whether "natives" or aliens are utilized as teachers and administrators for the schools. In the modernizing populations, as among the Sisala, the teacher, even though Sisala himself, is alien by virtue of his having been educated, removed from his community, socialized to norms, values, competencies, and purposes that are not a part of his community's culture. He is a member of a different class, for which there is as yet no clear place in the Sisala cultural system. He feels isolated from the community, and this isolation is reinforced by the character of the school in which he teaches. In Harlem School, or its prototypes, the teacher tends to be an alien whether he is white or black. Only some black teachers can maintain or acquire an identification with the people and community in which the school exists. The same processes of socialization and alienation that have taken place for the Sisala teacher have taken place for the black teacher in the United States. This is particularly true for the black teacher who comes from a middle-class background to begin with, then goes on to the university for advanced training. This teacher may be as far removed from the black community in a slum school as any white teacher. Of course not all black communities are in slums, but the slum school is the one we have been talking about.

At Rosepoint?

The interactions we are describing between school and culture occur elsewhere in the urban slum. Martha Ward describes a community in what she calls Rosepoint, near New Orleans (1971). Rosepoint is a very small rural community, a former plantation occupied now by some of the people who worked on it, plus others. Rosepoint has its own culture—that of the Negro south together with a heavy French influence characteristic of the area as a whole, and the unique ecological characteristics of a community built along a levee of the Mississippi River. Martha Ward was particularly concerned with language learning and linguistic features. She found that there were many substantial differences in speech and learning to speak between Rosepoint adults and children and white people. These differences contribute to the separation between community and school, which is the focus of our attention, since the school is taught mostly by whites, although they are by no means the sole cause of this separation.

Rosepoint parents believe that most of the teachers in the schools their children attend—black or white—are authoritarian and punitive. They also see that their children attending white schools for the first time are subjected to discriminatory practices, sometimes subtle, sometimes very obvious. There is little communication between the home and the school, whether primary or high school. Parents have little notion how the school is run, what their children are taught, or how to cooperate with the school or teachers. And the schools show no understanding of the social problems or cultural characteristics of Rosepoint. The conflicts are profound. The irrelevancy of the school for most Rosepoint children is measured by a high dropout rate and low rates of literacy. From about eleven years of age on, states Martha Ward, staying in school is a touch-and-go proposition, especially for males. She describes certain characteristics of the school environment and expectations that are at odds with those of the Rosepoint children.

> The school creates for the Rosepoint child an environment not as much unpleasant as unnatural. For years he has been determining his own schedule for eating, sleeping, and playing. The content of his play is unsupervised and depends on the child's imagination. His yard does not contain sand boxes,

swings, clay, paints, nor personnel obliged to supervise his play. At school, however, play is supervised, scheduled, and centers around objects deemed suitable for young minds. There are firm schedules for playing, napping, eating, and "learning and studying" (with the implication that learning will occur only during the time allotted for it). The authority buttressing even minimal schedules is impersonal and inflexible with an origin not in face-to-face social relationships but in an invisible bureaucracy.

Moreover, the Rosepoint home relies on verbal communication rather than on the written word as a medium. Adults do not read to children nor encourage writing. Extraverbal communication such as body movements or verbal communication such as storytelling or gossip are preferred to the printed page. The lack of money to purchase books, magazines, and newspapers partly explains this. . . . [sentence omitted] . . . for children of a culture rich in in-group lore and oral traditions the written word is a pallid substitute.

Another conflict arising out of the home-school discrepancy is language—specifically, "bad" language. Remember, the Rosepoint child is rewarded for linguistic creativity . . . [three sentences omitted]

In the classroom such language has an entirely different interpretation on it. Some educators discretely refer to it as "the M-F problem."[3] [sentence omitted] A nine-year-old girl was given a two-week suspension from classes for saying a four-letter word. This was her first recorded transgression of the language barrier. The second offense may be punished by expulsion . . . [two sentences omitted to end of paragraph] (Ward 1971:91–92).

The problems of Rosepoint and the schools that are intended to serve it are probably less overtly intense than those of Harlem School, its staff, and the community, but they are closely related to each other, and in turn to the problems of education among the Sisala, the Kanuri, and in Malitbog. The school in all of these situations is intrusive and the teachers are aliens. Resentment, conflict, and failures are present in communication from all sides.

We should be very careful here to realize that what we have been describing is not a problem of black minority populations alone. To some extent the disarticulation described between the school and community will be characteristic in any situation where the teachers and school stem from a different culture or subculture than that of the pupils and their parents. There is disarticulation between any formal school and the community, even where the school and community are not culturally divergent. Conflicts ensue when the school and teachers are charged with responsibility for assimilating or acculturating their pupils to a set of norms for behavior and thought that are different from those learned at home and in the community.

Education for minorities in North America is complicated by a variety of hazards. Harlem School operates in a depressing slum environment. No

---

[3] Refers to the use of obscenities in the school, including "Motherfucker."

one wants to go there and the people there would like to get out. The conflicts and disarticulation germane to the school-community situation we have described are made more acute and destructive because of this. Rosepoint and its schools have their special circumstances also. The Rosepoint population has inherited the culture and outlook of a former plantation slave population. They are close to the bottom of the social structure. The teachers, particularly if they are white, have inherited attitudes toward black people from the south's past. Let us look for a moment at a quite different place and people, the Indians of the Yukon Territory of Canada and the Mopass Residential School.

In the Mopass Residential School?

The children who come to this school represent several different tribes from quite a wide area of northwestern Canada. Many of these tribal societies adapted quickly to the fur trade economy that developed soon after the first white men arrived and many became heavily acculturated to the other aspects of European culture. One could not say that on the whole the native Americans of this area resisted the alien culture. In fact, they welcomed many of its technological and material advantages. As the northern territories have been opened for rapid development during the past decade, however, the native Americans already there have found it increasingly difficult to find a useful and rewarding place in this expanding economy. The reasons for this are altogether the fault of neither the white Canadians nor the Indians, but certainly prejudice has played a role. One of the serious problems of the Indians, however, has been that, on the whole, they have had neither the skills that could be used in the expanding economy nor the basic education upon which to build these skills. The task of the school would seem to be that of preparing young Native Americans[4] to take a productive and rewarding role in the economy and society now emerging in the Northwest Territories. This is what it is like at Mopass Residential School, according to Richard King, who taught there for a year and did anthropological observations during that period.

> For the children, the residential school constitutes a social enclave almost totally insulated from the community within which it functions; yet Mopass School reflects in a microcosmic, but dismayingly faithful, manner the social processes of the larger society. Two distinct domains of social interaction exist independently: Whiteman society and Indian society. Where these domains overlap, they do so with common purposes shared at the highest level of abstraction—but with minimal congruence of purposes, values, and perceptions, at the operating levels of interaction. The Whiteman maintains his social order according to his own perceptions of reality. The Indian bears the burden of adaptation to a social order that he may perceive more realis-

[4] The term *Native Americans* is preferred by many American Indians. We use Indian and Native American interchangeably in recognition of this preference.

tically—and surely he perceives it with a different ordering of reality—than does the Whiteman. From his perceptions the Indian finds it impossible to accept the social order and, at the same time, impossible to reject it completely. He therefore creates an artificial self to cope with the unique interactive situations.

In the residential school, the Whiteman staff and teachers are the end men of huge bureaucratic organizations (church and national government) that are so organized as to provide no reflection of the local communities. These employees derive their social, economic, and psychological identity from the organizations of which they are members. . . . [four sentences omitted]

. . . The children of the school are little more than components to be manipulated in the course of the day's work. . . . No job at school is defined in terms of *outcomes*, expected, or observable, in children (King 1967:89–90).

King goes on to describe the factionalism among the adult faculty and staff in the school. He suggests that many of the people who take teaching jobs in the residential school are deviant or marginal personalities, and that the isolation of the school, and its nature as a closed system, tend to create a tense interpersonal situation. The children have to adjust to this as well as to the alien character of the institution itself.

The school children become uniquely adept at personality analysis, since their major task is to cope with the demands of shifting adult personalities. But this analysis is limited to their needs as the children perceive them in specific situations (p. 88).

An artificial self is developed by the Indian child to cope with the total situation in which he finds himself. King says that the children sustain themselves with the conviction that their "real self" is not this person in the school at all. Through this, and other processes, the barriers between Whiteman and Indian are firmly developed:

. . . not so much by a conscious rejection on the part of the Whiteman as by a conscious rejection on the part of the Indian child. The sterile shallowness of the adult model presented by the school Whitemen serves only to enhance—and probably to romanticise—memories of attachments in the child's primary family group, and to affirm a conviction prevalent among the present adult Indian generation that Indians must strive to maintain an identity separate from Whitemen (p. 88).

There is much more we could say about the social and learning environment that this school provided[5] the Indian children who attended it. King's

---

[5] The school was closed in 1969. The "ethnographic present" is used in this description since it was in operation so recently and to be consistent with the other analyses.

case study should be read in order to understand it more thoroughly, for it is a startling example of miseducation—and with the best of intentions on the part of the sponsoring organizations and the teaching and administrative personnel of the school itself. All the features of disarticulation, isolation and nonrelatedness we have ascribed to the other schools discussed are present, but in a special and distorted form because the school is a closed residential institution even more removed from the community that it is intended to serve than the other schools. It is also a church school, run by the Episcopalian church for the Canadian government. Its curriculum is even less relevant to the native American children who attend it than the curriculum of the Sisala school was to the Sisala children, for it is the same curriculum that is used in other Canadian schools at the same grade level. It appears that the Mopass Residential School intends to recruit children into the white culture and a religious faith (since religious observances and education are a regular part of the school life). It fails in these purposes and, in fact, creates new barriers to this recruitment and reinforces old ones. More serious by far is the fact that it does not prepare the children who attend it to cope with the new economy and society emerging in the north. The children leave the school without necessary basic skills, alienated from what they see as white culture, alienated from themselves, and nonrelated to their own communities. This kind of schooling creates marginal people.[6]

Is There a Way Out of the Dilemma?

In the discussion so far we have dealt only with formerly colonized, now modernizing, tribal societies or minority peoples who have had to operate in what some would describe as an essentially colonial situation. That is, they may have the theoretical rights of self-determination and self-regulation, but, in fact, do not and could not exercise these rights. There are now strong movements underway toward self-determination. Some are very militant, separatistic, and nationalistic. Others are more accommodative. But all share in striving for self-determination, and regulation of the schools is an important aspect of this determination. These people recognize, perhaps in different terms, what we have said—that education is a process of recruitment and maintenance for the cultural system. For minority people the schools have been experienced as damaging attempts to recruit their children into an alien culture. Their self-images and identities were ignored, or actively attacked.

There are some minority communities that have successfully resolved the problem. They have done so by creating and maintaining a closed cultural system that maintains a more or less defensive relationship toward the rest of the society. The Old Order Amish and the Hutterites are good

---

[6] Mopass Residential School is neither better nor worse than other residential schools for Native Americans because it is Episcopalian, and certainly not because it is Canadian. Most of the same conditions exist in residential schools in both the United States and Canada, in Protestant, Catholic, and non-denominational schools.

examples of this solution. Both are nonaggressive pacifistic peoples, communal in orientation, and socioreligious in ideology and charter.

Amish communities are distributed principally throughout Pennsylvania, Ohio, and Indiana but are also found in several other states. The total Old Order Amish population is estimated at about 60,000. They are agrarian, use horsepower for agricultural work and transportation, and wear rather somber but distinctive dress. They strive to cultivate humility and simple living. Their basic values include the following: separation from the world; voluntary acceptance of high social obligations symbolized by adult baptism; the maintenance of a disciplined church-community; excommunication and shunning as a means of dealing with erring members and of keeping the church pure; and a life of harmony with the soil and nature—it is believed that nature is a garden and man was made to be a caretaker, not an exploiter. The goals of education are to instill the above values in every Amish child and maintain, therefore, the Amish way of life. John Hostetler and Gertrude Huntington describe the concept of a true education from the Amish point of view.

True education, according to the Amish, is "the cultivation of humility, simple living, and resignation to the will of God." For generations the group has centered its instruction in reading, writing, arithmetic, and the moral teachings of the Bible. They stress training for life participation (here and for eternity) and warn of the perils of "pagan" philosophy and the intellectual enterprises of "fallen man," as did their forefathers. Historically, the Anabaptist avoided all training associated with self-exaltation, pride of position, enjoyment of power, and the arts of war and violence. Memorization, recitation, and personal relationships between teacher and pupil were part of a system of education that was supremely social and communal (1971:9).

Realizing that state consolidation of schools constituted a severe threat to the continuity of their way of life and basic values, the Amish built the first specifically Amish School in 1925. By 1970 there were over three hundred such schools with an estimated enrollment of ten thousand pupils. When the population of the United States was predominantly rural and the major occupation was farming, the Amish people had no serious objections to public schooling. In the rural school of fifty years ago in most of the United States a curriculum much like that of the present Amish school was followed, the teacher was a part of the community, and the school was governed locally. Consolidation of schools in order to achieve higher educational standards shifted control away from the local area and the educational innovations that followed were unacceptable to the Amish. The Amish insist that their children attend schools near their homes so that they can participate in the life of the community and learn to become farmers. They also want qualified teachers committed to Amish values. Teachers who are merely qualified by state standards may be quite incapable of teaching the Amish way of life or providing an example of this way of life by the way they themselves live. The Amish also want to have their children educated in the basic skills of reading, writing, and arithmetic but training beyond that, they feel, should be related directly to the Amish religion and way of life. They do not agree with what they perceive to be the goals of the public schools, ". . . to impart worldly knowledge, to insure earthly success, and to make good citizens for the state." Ideally, from the Amish point of view, formal schooling should stop at about age fourteen, though learning continues throughout life. They feel that further schooling is not only unnecessary but detrimental to the successful performance of adult Amish work roles. The Amish pay for and manage their own schools in order to attain these goals (Hostetler and Huntington 1971·35–38).

Naturally there have been serious conflicts with state authorities about the schools. Forcible removal of the children from Amish communities has been attempted in some cases, and harassment in legal and interpersonal forms has characterized the relationship of state authority to the Amish in respect to the problem of education. The Amish have doggedly but nonviolently resisted all attempts to make them give up their own schools, for they realize that these schools are essential to the continuance of their cultural system. They have made accommodations where they could, as for instance in providing "vocational" schooling beyond elementary school to meet state educational age requirements concerning duration of schooling.

The Amish story is one that anyone interested in the processes and consequences of separatism should know about. Hostetler and Huntington's study is a good up-to-date overview that presents the case for the community-relevant school clearly and objectively and with a sympathetic understanding of the Amish point of view and lifeway.

The Hutterite culture is similar in many ways to that of the Old Order Amish, as seen from the outside, although the Hutterites are more communal in their economic organization and they use advanced agricultural machinery as well as trucks and occasionally cars. Hutterites are Anabaptists, like the Amish and the Mennonites, originating during the Protestant Reformation in the sixteenth century in the Austrian Tyrol and Moravia. They arrived in South Dakota in 1874 and have prospered since. There are about 18,000 Hutterites living on more than 170 colonies in the western United States and Canada. They are noted for their successful large-scale farming, large families, and effective training of the young.

Hutterites are protected from the outside world by an organized belief system which offers a solution to their every need, although they, like the Amish, have been subjected to persecution and harassment from the outside. The community minimizes aggression and dissension of any kind. Colony members strive to lose their self-identity by surrendering themselves to the communal will and attempt to live each day in preparation for death, and, hopefully, heaven. The principle of order is the key concept underlying Hutterite life. Order is synonymous with eternity and godliness; even the orientation of colony buildings conforms to directions measured with the precision of a compass. There is a proper order for every activity, and time is neatly divided into the sacred and the secular. In the divine hierarchy of the community each individual member has a place—male over female, husband over wife, older over younger, and parent over child. The outsider asks, "Why does this order work? How can it be maintained?" The implicit Hutterite answer is that "Hutterite society is a school, and the school is a society." The Hutterites, like the Old Amish, do not value education as a means toward self-improvement but as a means of "planting" in children "the knowledge and fear of God" (Hostetler and Huntington 1967).

We will not go into detail concerning Hutterite schools. Although they differ somewhat from the Amish schools in curriculum and style, particularly in being more strict and "authoritarian," the basic principles are the same. The Hutterites also understand that they must retain control of their schools and teachers if they are to retain their separatistic and particularly their communal and socioreligious way of life. They do this by retaining a "German school" that is, in effect, superimposed upon the "English school" required by state or provincial law. The two schools have rather different curricula and teachers and of the two the former is clearly the one that carries the burden of cultural transmission that recruits youngsters into the Hutterite cultural system and helps maintain that system most directly. The Hutteries will be encountered again in the chapter on culture change when the persistence of cultures is discussed.

Here they serve as another example of how to solve the problem faced by the Sisala, the people of Malitbog, the Kanuri, the children of Harlem School and their parents, the people of Rosepoint, and the children in the Mopass Residential School.

The problem all of these people face is how to relate a culture transmitting institution that is attempting to recruit their children to a cultural system different from that of the community, class, area, or minority from which the children come. The school and teacher are alien in all of these cases, and they are charged, by governments or the dominant population, with the responsibility of changing the way of life by changing the children. Understandably the consequences are at least disruptive, and at worst tragic.

The Hutterites and Amish have done exactly what is logical according to the anthropologist viewing the relationship between education and culture. Realizing the threat to the continuity of their way of life from the outside world, particularly from schooling and transmission of concepts and views alien to their fundamental principles, they have taken control of their schools to whatever extent they can, given the exigencies of survival in contemporary North America. The schools are so ordered as to recruit and help maintain the traditional cultural system. They are successful. The way of life, beleaguered though it is in both cases, survives, in fact, flourishes.

It is important to understand, however, that, from another point of view, the cost of this success is too great. The result of success is a closed cultural system in a defensive relationship to the rest of society. That there are restrictions on personal behavior, sharp limits on self-expression, and confinement in the very thought processes and world view in both cases, is undeniable. The values of spontaneity, individual creativity, discovery and invention, pursuit of knowledge, and innovation, that are important to men elsewhere, are not values in these or any other closed cultural systems. There is also a kind of self-created disadvantage imposed by the Hutterites and Amish upon themselves. Since they lack higher education, in fact are opposed to it, and control as vigorously as possible the context of primary education, they cannot participate fully in the give and take of our dynamic society. True, they do not want to, but it is a hard choice, and one that could be very disadvantageous to any minority group. Somehow the modernizing peoples of the world emerging from a tribal and then colonial past, and the minority peoples in vast societies like the United States and Canada, must balance the consequences of a closed system and the educational institutions to support it, and an open system and the educational institutions to support it. It is clear, however, that it is necessary for all peoples to exercise and develop the rights of self-determination and self-regulation in education, as well as in other areas of life. It may be that this can be done without creating closed, defensive, and confining cultural systems. It may help for us all to realize that we actually have little control over what happens in our schools, no matter who we are. The educational bureaucracy in a complex urban system functions in some ways like an alien cultural system in relation to the local community, the children in school, and their parents, whether these parents and children are members of minority or majority groups. We all have this problem in common. In this age of cultural pluralism in the United States it is difficult to discern what else we all have in common. Perhaps it is possible to agree that there are some competencies all children should acquire, such as functional literacy, concepts of mathematical processes, and so forth, that are necessary if they are not to be severely handicapped in later life in a complex society. But in the area of specific values, ideologies, and world views we cannot repeat the mistakes of the past, when we assumed that the melting pot would melt all ethnic differences down to the same blendable elements. The cultures of the American Indians, Afro-Americans, Mexican Americans, and Asian-Americans did not disappear as our ideology said they would. The challenge is to recognize and accept the differences without creating disadvantageous separatism or segregation, whether self-imposed or imposed from the dominant group. There are many paradoxes in the relationships we are discussing, and they are not easily resolved.

Summary

In this chapter we started with the question, What are some of the ways culture is transmitted? We answered this question by examining cultural systems where a wide variety of teaching and learning techniques are utilized. One of the most important processes, we found, was the management of discontinuity. Discontinuity occurs at any point in the life cycle when there is an abrupt transition from one mode of being and behaving to another, as for example at weaning and at adolescence. Many cultural systems manage the latter period of discontinuity with dramatic staging and initiation ceremonies, some of which are painful or emotionally disturbing to the initiates. They are public announcements of changes in status. They are also periods of intense cultural compression during which teaching and learning are accelerated. This managed cultural compression and discontinuity functions to enlist new members in the community and maintains the cultural system. Education, whether characterized by sharp discontinuities and culturally compressive periods, or by a relatively smooth progression of accumulating experience and status change, functions in established cultural systems to recruit new members and maintain the existing system. We then turned to a discussion of situations where alien or future-oriented cultural systems are introduced through formal schooling. Schools among the Sisala of Ghana, a modernizing African nation, and a Philippine barrio were used as examples of this relationship and its consequences. The disarticulation of school and community was emphasized. The point was made that children in these situations are intentionally recruited to a cultural system other than the one they originated from, and that the school does not maintain the existing social order, but, in effect, destroys it. This is a kind of discontinuity very different than the one we discussed previously, and produces severe dislocations in life patterns and interpersonal relations. We turned then to a discussion of parallels between the situation among the Sisala and in the Philippine barrio and the relationship between minorities in North America and their schools. A ghetto school in a slum area in New York City, the school and community at Rosepoint in Louisiana, and the Mopass Residential School in the Yukon Territory were used as examples. In each case it was clear that the school and community were disarticulated, and that the school represented an essentially alien cultural system. An alternative relationship between school and community represented by the Hutterites and the Old Order Amish was described. These communal groups maintain a defensive relationship with the dominant society and successfully recruit their children into their cultural system, and maintain the system. It was pointed out that this solution has certain costs. The chapter ends on a normative note, reminding the reader that this is the age of pluralism and that the melting pot ideology has not worked for a number of minorities, but that in the working out of our difficulties we would do well to avoid either self- or other-imposed segregation or the creation of closed, defensive cultural systems, as solutions.

Further readings

For a meaningful and broad perspective on cultural transmission, placed in the context of long-term cultural continuity, change, and evolution, see Part I of Margaret Mead's *Continuities in Cultural Evolution* (1964). For anthropological treatments of schools and schooling in a wide variety of cultural systems, see the series, *Case Studies in Education and Culture,* including books on a Japanese school (Singleton 1967), a Kwakiutl Indian school on an island in British Columbia (Wolcott 1967), a school in a rural German village (Warren 1967), teaching the new mathematics in an old culture, the Kpelle of Liberia (Gay and Cole 1967), education in Amish

Society (Hostetler and Huntington 1971), enculturation in Dusun society, Borneo (Williams 1970), the way of life and schooling in a Philippine barrio (Jocano 1969), the study of a slum school (Rosenfeld 1971), a problem of identity in an Indian residential school (King 1967), a study of language learning at Rosepoint (Ward 1971), Indian education in the Chiapas highlands, Mexico (Modiano 1973), education and modernization among the Sisala of Northern Ghana (Grindal 1972), education and modernization among the Kanuri of Bornu, Nigeria (Peshkin 1972), a study of traditional education among the Ngoni of Malawi (Read 1968), and a study of socialization in an Ijaw Village, Nigeria (Leis 1972). Two of the best case studies about the consequences of introducing educational systems representing the dominant society into established minority communities are *Indian Education in the Chiapas Highlands*, by Nancy Modiano (1973), and *Alaskan Eskimo Education*, by John Collier, Jr. (1973).

For further understanding of how schools operate as culture transmitting systems you might want to read Margaret Mead's *The School in American Culture* (1950), Jules Henry's *Culture against Man* (1963), George Spindler's *The Transmission of American Culture* (1959), and some parts of *Education and Cultural Process*, edited by G. Spindler (1974), and H. Wolcott's *The Man in the Principal's Office* (1973).

No single cultural system and its process of transmission has been given thorough treatment. To get a more complete picture of single cultures and their transmission, you could read Margaret Mead's *Growing up in New Guinea* (1930), her *Coming of Age in Samoa* (1928), Melford Spiro's *Children of the Kibbutz* (1958), *Child Rearing in Six Cultures*, edited by Beatrice Whiting (1963), and Francis Deng's *The Dinka of the Sudan* (1972).

There is still more that one should know if interested in cultural transmission. *A Cross-Cultural Outline of Education* by Jules Henry (1960) lists many of the processes.

Problems and questions

1. Read any two good descriptions of growing up in another culture. Identify and compare periods of discontinuity and compression in cultural transmission. In what way do you think these discontinuities interfere with or reinforce cultural transmission in these cases?
2. Observe initiation proceedings in a group or organization to which you have access, such as a fraternity or sorority, a military unit, a musical group, a gang, a religious organization. Look for parallels to the cases discussed in this chapter. What purposes do these initiation proceedings serve? How do they transmit culture? What culture?

3. Examine collections of children's toys displayed in a large store, in sales catalogues, in magazine advertisements. Which of these toys encourage children to imitate adult activities? What activities?

4. Collect a brief life history from a classmate. Identify periods of discontinuity and compression, experience with models, encounters with initiation proceedings, and other processes deemed significant in learning to participate in a cultural system. (You may find L. Langness' booklet [1965] on the life history method useful.)

5. Do an ethnography of some adolescent group and its cultural system. How does the group deviate from adult norms? How do new members of the group learn the cultural system? How do old members try to teach it to them?

6. Examine children's books of the present, for some particular age level, to similar books from another period in our history, such as the 1920s or 1890s. What moral themes appear to be present in each period? How are they similar and different? What possible implications does this have for changes in our culture over this period of time? Do a comparable analysis of TV seen most frequently by children under 12. Are the TV programs consistent with the story book themes of the older literature? The more recent?

7. Watch parents try to teach a child how to do some specific thing, like talking, walking, throwing a ball, drawing, dressing himself, or riding a bike. What techniques do they use? How do you think these techniques might differ from those used by the Alaskan Eskimo, the people of Guadalcanal, the Ulithians, the village of Demirciler?

8. Ask ten or more adults what a "spoiled" child is and how one is created. Are children in Guadalcanal, Palau, Sensuron, Ulithi, among the Eskimo, "spoiled"?

9. Visit a school, preferably an elementary school, that a significant number of children from some minority group attend. Talk to some of the children to discover what their attitudes towards the school and teachers are. If possible, talk to some of the teachers to find out how they perceive the children from this group with respect to probable success in school, learning capacity, and special educational needs. Look into the books and other materials used in classrooms. Are any special concessions made to the presence of the minority children? What forms do they take?

10. Examine at least three cases reported in the literature of the role of the school in situations where the school is an alien influence, or is charged with responsibility for recruiting children into a cultural system or subsystem that is different than that from which they come. Develop hypothetical solutions, taking into account the factors discussed in this chapter, for the problems that emerge.

10

Control of behavior

Processes of cultural transmission prepare the individual for the part that he is to play in the operation of the cultural system of which he is a member. The best trained of individuals in the most organized of cultural systems may nevertheless encounter situations in which correct behavior is ill-defined or fails to lead to the expected result. This chapter concerns the forces that cause individuals to break rules or do the wrong thing and the means by which other members of cultural systems heal the breaches resulting from misbehavior.

What are the rules and can you follow them?

If cultural systems exist in perfectly predictable environments where members have succeeded in developing a cultural tradition which predicts all that will happen, they reflect a utopian state where meals are always served on time, where cross-cousins are always available for marriage, where brides are always beautiful and grooms always handsome, where enemies are always defeated after just the right amount of conflict, where children never cry, where criminals do not exist, and where nothing ever happens except what already happened. In Utopia, all families contain precisely the same number of children, and all children have precisely the same number of playmates, siblings, mother's brothers, and father's sisters. Every 104 years, one of the young men suggests an expedition to the faraway hills, but each time he does so, an official known as the Expedition-quasher says, "Let's go another day." There is no real change in Utopia; all is as it was when the state of perfect predictability and environmental equilibrium was first achieved.

On the other side of the faraway hills lies the equally imaginary community of Hillside. For years Hillsiders have been attempting to study themselves and nature with a view toward establishing the same degree of predictability enjoyed by their neighbors, the Utopians. At present, the only predictable thing in their lives is that on November 23 when they make their traditional attack on the Utopians they get defeated. Some years ago, a brilliant Hillsider scientist, R. B. Branaslaski, concluded that predictability should start in the home. If, he reasoned, rules were written governing the behavior of each kinsman toward every other kinsman, there would be at least one area of life that was perfectly predictable. Branaslaski proposed two simple rules for the control of family interaction: (1) men have authority over women; and (2) older people have authority over younger people. Branaslaski felt that this would prevent quarrels within the family and, since everybody would obey the oldest male, help to make family behavior predictable.

As soon as Branaslaski's rule had been passed, a series of violent quarrels developed between mothers and sons. Mothers claimed that since they were older they had authority over their sons; sons claimed that since they were male they had authority over their mothers. Branaslaski solved this problem by decreeing that the older men should hold an initiation ceremony for the younger men and that, after the initiation ceremony, the young men would be permitted to give orders to their mothers instead of the other way around. A number of young men were promptly initiated. As soon as the initiation had taken place, these young men entered into conflict with their fathers because the young men and their fathers both wanted to give orders to their mothers at the same time. Bruised and battered youths and parents appealed to Branaslaski for relief. Branaslaski decreed that all young men, immediately after their initiation ceremonies, should leave home and live in a young adult residence on the outskirts of the village. This solution worked well for several weeks before complaints began coming in from neighboring villages. The young men were stealing women and cattle, misbehaving, picketing, rioting, and making noises in the night. Again the problem was brought before Branaslaski, but by this time he had achieved true wisdom and merely remarked, "Think how dull things would be if everything were predictable."

Although men have authority over women in most cultures, most men spend their early years under the domination of their mothers. Branaslaski's use of an initiation ceremony to create an abrupt transition between boyhood

and adulthood disregards the knowledge that boys mature gradually over several years and at different rates. In every culture, different sets of rules must govern the behavior of children and adults, yet there are long periods during which individuals are neither children nor adults. The contrast between Utopia and Hillside is a contrast between what people expect from their cultural traditions and what they get. In effect, a cultural tradition is a set of earnest policies designed (insofar as it is designed at all) to control and render predictable the forces of nature and the vagaries of human behavior. If the forces of nature are predictable, they do not seem *easily* predictable and the same can be said for human behavior. Despite a universal human diligence in the conscious and unconscious formulation of written and unwritten rules to cover every conceivable situation, cases often arise in which human beings do not do what other human beings expect them to do. Every cultural system, then, must contain processes designed to cope with the unexpected perversities, contrariness, and unpredictability of the human animal.

Young men have a tendency to emulate their fathers, but, as the following example taken from the Makah Indians of the Northwest Coast of the United States indicates, they may emulate the wrong behavior at the wrong time:

> This happened in Ozette. This chief fixed up his son to catch a whale. He built a canoe for him, make harpoon, and blow up the hair seal for floater. About dozen of them. So when he got everything, he told his son, "You must bathe every night. You must bathe every night if you want to be clean, if you want to catch a whale. Go in the salt water and bathe every night and pray. Ask for a whale." So this young man went off every night. And he didn't bathe at all. He went round look for sweetheart. Well, about a month, pretty soon this young man brought his sweetheart home to his father's house. Well, this old man got up. They used to have a flat roof, all flat roof, loose cedar timber on top. So this old man shoved that board one side. "You always sleep late in the morning!" And he goes with the light in the house to his son's bed. And two heads laying there. One woman head and one man. He went to his wife and said, "That young man! After I had hard time making things, he spoil the things. He got a woman now instead of a whale." He go around, go around. They used to have five, six family in the house, big house. He went around there pouring out all the slops, put them in his square bucket made of cedar. He open his son's face and throw that on his son's head. He said, "I didn't want you to catch woman! I want you to catch whale, not woman. You spoil yourself!" (Colson 1953:183–184).

Although the inexplicable failure of human plans can often be attributed to the fact, noted even in ancient Babylon, that each successive generation of human beings is markedly inferior to the one before, trouble in this world and unpredicability cannot be blamed entirely upon the generation gap. Consider the Lugbara of Uganda in Africa:

When the bride becomes pregnant the marriage becomes more settled, and when she is a mother of a son it is complete. If she does not become pregnant it is said that the blessing which her father gave her on her marriage day, by spitting on her forehead, was not given with a good heart, and visits are made to persuade him to bless her properly. If she does not conceive within six months or so there is usually quarreling and the wife is sent home and the bride-wealth demanded back, or a sister may be sent in her place. Although her own lineage will try to blame the matter on the husband's lineage, usually by accusing them of witchcraft, it is generally accepted that barrenness of the wife is the cause (Middleton 1965:56).

Here, again, all human efforts, all the careful marriage arrangements, are unavailing. Among the Hillsiders, the Makah, the Lugbara, among all of the peoples of the world, the perversities of nature and humanity result in rule breaking and in the defeat of expectations. Even the good man who does all the "right" things may find himself in difficulties. The following section deals with good intentions and difficult problems.

What Is the Solution?

He (Miguel) had boasted to his age mates that he would "conquer" Margarita at a forthcoming dance. It was important for him to carry out his plan to prove his *machismo*. Retreat from his open declaration of intent would have "reduced" Miguel in the eyes of his friends. A few days later, he was stunned to discover that his elder brother had become interested in the same girl. For Miguel to proceed with his plan of seduction would be a serious affront to his brother. Caught in this dilemma, Miguel brooded. He could see no out from the hopeless situation. When illness struck him, it seemed like a blessing rather than a misfortune. The day before the dance, Miguel noticed stiffness and pain in his left leg. As the pain increased, he mentioned it to his parents. His mother examined Miguel and announced that he had *aire*. He was ordered to bed for twenty-four hours with a poultice of ground tomatoes and herbs over the stiff leg. Before the dance, his elder brother came to Miguel's bedside to wish him a rapid recovery (Madsen 1964:98).

Here, in an example from South Texas, the young man avoids conflict and loss of face by consciously or unconsciously making use of a culturally sanctioned process which permits graceful withdrawal from an impossible situation.

In most of the cultures and communities of the modern world, processes of rapid cultural change multiply the unpredictabilities of human life creating problems only gifted innovators can solve.

Before he had finished the first year at the mission school, he had to do something about his steady girl. She was now of age when suitors were clustering around her and she could hardly avoid marriage to someone else if Sulli delayed any longer. Not that she would be forced by her parents, but rather that she would very likely become pregnant—given the usual proclivities of a young Kota woman—and then she would have to get a father for the child. Many a man would be only too eager to get an attractive young wife, with a child on the way to boot.

She came to Sulli and clasped his feet, he tells, in the gesture of entreaty. "She was 16 and her breasts were so big and she was very beautiful. But the teacher had told me that the boys who get married leave their studies, they don't care for the lessons. . . . So that night I thought hard which was best. If I married, I would have a few days happy and then all the rest of my life I would have to dig the earth and sweat. If I worked hard for about four years, then all the rest of the time I would be a teacher or a government servant."

He put her off temporarily with an excuse and disposed of her entreaties permanently with a stratagem. Among her suitors was a gay youth who sang very well and had a persuasive way with the girls. Sulli arranged with this lad to stay the night in a house where the unmarried young men and women of the village often came to sing and then to sleep. Sulli and his girl were there that night. He acted coldly toward her. When the lamp was put out and she came to sleep at his side, he did not cover her with his cloth as usual but straightaway turned his back to her and pretended to fall asleep.

Rebuffed and angered, she made little resistance to the singer when he crept over and induced her to move to the other side of the room to lie intimately with him. Then the singer coughed, a signal prearranged; Sulli struck a match and saw her there in the singer's arms. At once she came over to beg his forgiveness but he was adamant and would have nothing more to do with her (Mandelbaum 1960:291–292).

Where men are less wise in the manipulation of the rules of their traditional cultures, the cleavage between culturally induced expectations and the realities of life may widen dangerously. Consider the case of Biboi, a member of a Brazilian Indian tribe.

Biboi was the son of a Mundurucú chief who had been educated by a Brazilian trader and thus felt himself to be superior to his fellows. He was installed as the chieftain of Cabitutú by his trader patron in the expectation that he would relay to the group information about the trader's needs for wild rubber. Biboi had no kinsmen in Cabitutú and was younger and less prestigious than many of the men of the village. In an attempt to strengthen his position, Biboi contracted a marriage with a widow several years older than himself. Finding the older woman unattractive, he brought home a second wife. The first wife expressed her displeasure violently and her brothers ordered Biboi to remove his second wife from the village. Biboi sent her to his father's village of Cabruá.

Having left his pretty bride in the safe confines of his father's house, Biboi returned to Cabitutú to set matters right and quiet the discontent. But he continued in his arrogant and demanding ways and the sentiments of the villagers became further inflamed, with no small assistance from his first wife and her family. There grew among them a firm determination to kill him. . . .

In the meantime, the person of the young wife was not as secure as Biboi thought it would be. Her husband was away and she was a rather wayward girl; whatever rectitude she possessed was certainly no match for the insistent attempts upon her body by the men of Cabruá. Soon, all of the men of the village except those prohibited by incest regulations—and there were some exceptions even to this—were enjoying the favors of Biboi's young wife in the underbrush surrounding the village, at the stream, in the forest, in the gardens, or whenever they might find her alone. . . .

The balance of power and of moral correctness lay with Biboi's opponents, and the task of his supporters was made most difficult by virtue of the fact that Biboi had almost ceased to be a social person—the rules no longer applied to him. We left the field before the curtain fell on our little drama, but one could already predict the conclusion. This was seen most clearly when, shortly before our departure, Caetano fell from a palm tree and lay seriously injured for several days. Knowing that the people of Cabitutú would kill him as soon as they were assured of his father's death, Biboi came immediately to Cabruá and remained there until the old man's recovery was certain. During this period, Biboi approached me and said, "You know, if my father dies, I will leave this land and go to live on the banks of the Tapajós River." I asked him why, and, in fine Biboi style, he answered, "Because it is so beautiful there." Biboi knew that his life as a Mundurucú was finished (Murphy 1961:60).

In the Kota example, Sulli approximated what Malcolm McFee calls a 150 percent man—a man who knows his own culture and a newly introduced culture as well and can therefore manipulate both to his advantage. Biboi, by contrast, was a 75 percent man—at home in no culture. He did not know the rules for getting along in Mundurucú society and was far too superior to consider them worth learning. Even if he had been more sophisticated in coping with the realities of his two different cultural situations, he would probably have encountered difficulties. As it was he found himself forced to choose between death and exile.

In the above cases, Miguel and Sulli extricated themselves from difficult situations by manipulating available cultural resources in such a way that their behavior appeared to be above reproach. In the other cases, among the Makah, the Lugbara, and the Mundurucú, conflict arose over the question of the appropriateness of the behavior of the different individuals involved. Because individuals may always choose to break rules or to do things in improper ways, processes of social control are often designed to attach punishments or disadvantages to rulebreaking behavior. How do the Bush Negroes of Dutch Guiana encourage conformity to the rules?

What happens when you break the rules?

Why is it, Bayo, that Sadefo lost his food in the still water? Was it because he felt safe and didn't take care in such small rapids?

"No," he said promptly, "that's how kunu works. A man travels on the river all his life. He goes over small rapids and large rapids. He carries loads and returns to his own village. But then something happens. His boat is good. He walks *koni*—carefully—but he loses his food, or his entire load, or his boat, or even his life. Something is working against him. It might be *wisi*—bad magic, it might be kunu. If you have kunu then your enemies can make their bad magic work against you. So it is" (Herskovits 1934:65–66).

When men break rules, they are afflicted with *kunu,* a kind of weakness which renders the individual powerless against the attacks of his ever-present enemies. If a man breaks numerous or important rules, ancestors or gods can be counted upon to bring death to one member after another of the rulebreaker's family.

Such automatic punishments may also afflict the evil-doer after his death. South Indian evil-doers receive the following punishments in the afterworld:

1. A man who always sees the young and beautiful girls and describes her dress and her shape, that fellow will be nailed to the wall with sharp nails and then thrown into melting limestone and limewater poured into his eyes.
2. The man who loves another man's wife and makes false to his own teacher will be beaten with a hammer to reduce his pride and asked to walk on a stick. His teeth will be removed and he will be cut into pieces and cooked on the fire and branded with hot iron bars.
3. A man who abuses others will have dirty things poured into his mouth.
4. The man who loves his friend's wife or his brothers' wives or if he loves others often will be asked to embrace a heated steel pillar.
5. The man who wishes to love a woman of good character has a mixture of sand and lime poured into his eyes.

6. The man who puts up cases and quarrels for the property of others will be asked to put his hands in the fire.
7. The man who causes others to be sinful and jealous is put into a stone mill and ground up.
8. The man who kills sheep, goats, and buffaloes will have his head cut off and played with like a ball.
9. People who cheat their own brothers or steal property will be cut to pieces and thrown to the crows.

The concept of automatic punishment implies that something or someone, ordinarily a supernatural figure or mechanism, keeps track of the individual's sins and follows up with inevitable retribution. Such a device is likely to be effective only when the individual has a direct experience of swift and effective punishment and so experiences fear and guilt whenever he commits a misdemeanor. Another process of social control is illustrated in the following examples:

"*Verguenza* is the regard for the moral values of society, for the rules whereby social intercourse takes place, for the opinion which others have of one. But this, not purely out of calculation. True verguenza is a mode of feeling which makes one sensitive to one's reputation and thereby causes one to accept the sanctions of public opinion."

Thus a *sin verguenza* is a person who either does not accept or who abuses those rules. And this may be either through a lack of understanding or through a lack of sensitivity. One can perceive these two aspects of it.

First as the result of understanding, upbringing, education. "Lack of education" is a polite way of saying "lack of verguenza." It is admitted that if the child is not taught how to behave it cannot have verguenza. It is sometimes necessary to beat a child "to give him verguenza," and it is the only justifiable excuse for doing so. Failure to inculcate verguenza into one's children brings doubt to bear upon one's own verguenza.

But in its second aspect of sensitivity, it is truly hereditary. A person of bad heredity cannot have it since he has not been endowed with it. He can only behave out of calculation as though he had it, simulating what to others comes naturally. A normal child has it in the form of shyness, before education has developed it. When a two-year-old hides its face from a visitor it is because of its verguenza. Girls who refuse to dance in front of an assembled company do so because of their verguenza. Verguenza takes into consideration the personalities present. It is verguenza which forbids a boy to smoke in the presence of his father. In olden times people had much more verguenza than today, it is said (Pitt-Rivers 1961:113–114).

A contrast from Africa:

The all-embracing virtue to the Nyakyusa is wisdom (*amahala*). It includes the enjoyment of company and the practice of hospitality, for no man is wise who is surly, or aloof, or stingy; it includes neighborly behavior, dignity, respect for law and convention, but it does not include display. The wise may dance, but they do not need to dance in order to be wise, and those who commit adultery, or are boastful, or quarrelsome show foolishness (*ubukonyofu*) and sinful pride (*amatingo*), the opposite of wisdom. Wisdom is expressed in all relationships, not only in village relationships, but it is *learned* in the village; pagan Nyakyusa insist that "it is by conversing with our friends that we gain wisdom" (Wilson 1963:89–90).

And again, in North America:

542. Gangs and clubs. This is the age for the blossoming of clubs and gangs. A number of kids who are already friends decide to form a secret club. They work like beavers making membership buttons, fixing up a meeting place (preferably hidden), drawing up a list of rules. They may never figure out what the secret is. But the secrecy idea probably represents the need to prove they can govern themselves, unmolested by grownups, unhampered by other more dependent children.

It seems to help the child, when he's trying to be grownup, to get together with others who feel the same way. Then the group tries to bring outsiders into line by making them feel left out or by picking on them (Spock 1957: 389–390).

In many human cultures those who lack verguenza or amahala, or those who are labeled "dumb guys," are brought into line through gossip, ridicule, and other forms of verbal attack. The fear of losing "face," of losing the regard of valued others, is a major device for the control of behavior which operates in every known culture. The phenomena labeled ridicule, shame, teasing, gossip, and so on involve a real or threatened withdrawal of psychological support on the part of the other members of the cultural system. With the withdrawal of affection and approval, there is often a suggestion that the individual really belongs in some other group: In Spain, gypsies and (playfully) infants are sin verguenza; in Plainville (West 1945), there are "the people who live like animals." Such "untouchable" groups are also found in India and Japan. Sometimes the implication that the rulebreaker is not a proper member of the group is carried even further.

Who Is Responsible for This?
The B-29 crew were distributed throughout the airplane in the following manner:

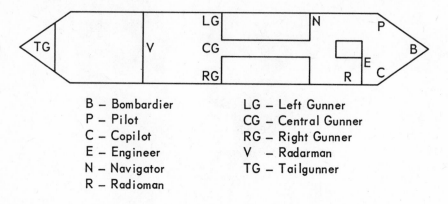

B – Bombardier   LG – Left Gunner
P – Pilot   CG – Central Gunner
C – Copilot   RG – Right Gunner
E – Engineer   V   – Radarman
N – Navigator   TG – Tailgunner
R – Radioman

FIGURE 1.   *Positions of B-29 crew members.*

Studies conducted during the 1950s of the behavior and attitudes of the members of such crews indicated that almost every crew possessed a *foul-up*. A foul-up is a person who through stupidity and sometimes malign intent is responsible for practically everything that goes wrong on the airplane. The person most often named as a foul-up was the tailgunner, with the radioman a close second. Although the tailgunner was the lowest ranking member of the crew, this did not ordinarily apply to the radioman. Thus it cannot be argued that the lowest ranking or least trained member of the crew was automatically assigned the status of foul-up. The tasks assigned to the radioman and to the tailgunner were not vital to the actual flying of the airplane, and thus the status of foul-up cannot be attributed to anxiety over the performance of important tasks. Similarly, there are other men who have equally unimportant roles in the flying of the airplane, so it is not a matter of picking out the least important members of the crew as targets of hostility.

The selection of tailgunners and radiomen as foul-ups seems to be connected to their degree of interaction with members of the plane crew when it is in flight. The tailgunner sits alone in a small compartment. He has few duties beyond looking out of the window. He can't move around much. If he smokes, he is likely to start a small fire and suffocate. Deprived of stimulation, the tailgunner has a tendency to fall asleep. Because of the fire hazard, the pilot is required to communicate with the tailgunner periodically to see if he is still conscious. Because the tailgunner is usually asleep, the crew spends many anxious moments buzzing him on the intercommunications system and hoping that he will respond.

Although the radioman is located in the front compartment of the plane, he is visually accessible only to the navigator. Even here, the navigator must turn around in order to see him and can only see the radioman's back. Because the radioman must maintain communication with ground stations, he is also inaccessible through the intercommunication system. The duties assigned to the tailgunner and the radioman are such that they cannot participate freely in crew patterns of communication and their activities are consequently somewhat mysterious. One of the consequences of the relative isolation of the tailgunner and radioman is that, should the crew parachute from the airplane, there is always a chance that they will do so without informing anyone. Thus, the tailgunner and the radioman can inflict a kind of ultimate disgrace upon the crew and its pilot. We can hypothesize, then, that a foul-up is a person about whom other members of the crew are anxious because he tends to violate notions of proper behavior, can inflict a grave loss of status upon the crew, and cannot be subjected to continuous observation or control.

Is It the Same in Africa?

A somewhat similar situation exists among the Nupe, a tribe in Nigeria. Nupe territory consists of strips of forest alternating with parkland. In 1931, 300,000 Nupe lived in cities and villages, most earning their living through agriculture. Traditionally men perform all of the agricultural work, while the women refine the harvested crops and sell them in the marketplace. Because the Nupe environment is hot and humid, there is a relatively high incidence of disease, and illness is one of the central problems of life. Illness is quite frequently caused by witchcraft, and witches are always women. In particular, they are believed to be women who do not laugh, never play or joke, get angry easily, and have no friendly words for others. The witch is an enemy of male authority who attempts to dominate family relationships through malignant attacks upon her husband and his relatives.

In fact, Nupe women are often away from home for long periods. While the husband is slaving away in the fields, the wife may set up a business empire, perhaps in modern times acquiring a fleet of motorbuses. Women have been known to place their husbands in debt and to take over the father's role of providing financial assistance to male children. The real power and actual dominance of the Nupe woman is countered by the possibility that she will be accused of witchcraft (Nadel 1954).

For the B-29 crew and the Nupe, those whose behaviors are hard to control and whose activities are mysterious are likely to be made into scapegoats when misfortune strikes. Among both groups, fear of being identified as a foul-up or a witch provides a powerful incentive toward correct behavior. In both cases, the normal fear of gossip and ridicule is powerfully supported by the danger of direct accusation and subsequent punishment. A foul-up may be beaten or transferred, while a witch may be killed. A scapegoat or witch spoils things for others mainly by means of a malevolent and/or inexplicable desire to do the wrong things. The logic of scapegoating is "I am good or my people are good, and therefore this trouble is being caused by somebody bad." Such logic leads to conflict, violence, and mistrust, and anthropologists often wonder whether the price of this kind of social control is not too high. If you can't blame others for your misfortunes, then you are left with no recourse but to blame yourself.

What Did You Do That Was Wrong?

Among the Iglulik Eskimo a village may be haunted by evil spirits that cause all game to vanish from the district. When this happens, shamans instruct community members to gather together in a single overcrowded room where they can be suitably purified. The shamans themselves go outside, returning shortly to report that numbers of angry spirits have appeared in the village. People in the room now begin to reflect upon their misdeeds and especially upon the various *tabus* or rules of life that they have violated. People confess their sins to the assembled community and ask forgiveness. As they confess more and more spirits appear outside. The people are terrified and beg the shamans to help them. The shamans leave the room and do battle with the spirits, returning covered with blood and with their clothing in rags.

The next day there is no hunting. All gather before breakfast and once again confess to their various breaches of the rules. The shamans finish purifying the community and go outside. The men follow them and return with one of the shamans attached to a dog's harness. He acts like a madman, lashing out on every side. When the harness is removed, the shaman returns to his normal manner. He sings a spirit song and there is a grand feast composed of the best food available. After the meal each person lays out objects of value he possesses and these are exchanged without regard for their actual worth. All are happy and there is no more fear (Rasmussen 1929:120ff).

The guilty man is punished by the anxious fear, often a certainty, that he will be caught and punished. For him, confession and punishment or forgiveness is a relief. The Eskimo exploit this psychological principle by creating a host of "rules of life," rules which often seem to make no sense and are therefore often broken. The process of confession and forgiveness creates solidarity at times when solidarity is most needed. The process is akin to those forms of psychotherapy in which the individual may cure himself by reporting his transgressions and innermost thoughts to a forgiving outsider. These examples of automatic punishment, scapegoating, and guilt and confession all emphasize the consequences of misbehavior. Social control may also be achieved in more positive ways. From the Ngoju of South Borneo:

Use your hard bones, stiffen your soft muscles. Cultivate the large field, work the wide clearing.

So that you can show each other the heaps of golden cloud-flowers (rice) and measure the quantity of golden blossoms of the dew-clouds (rice).

Use part of the abundance of the golden cloud-flowers, employ the rest of the blossoms of the dew-clouds for the purpose of the wrought gold-work, the acquisition of the golden scales of the Watersnake (gold or gold ornaments).

From the remainder of the gold-work buy roots from the trunk of the tree; with the balance of the golden scales of the Watersnake cut through the chains of the gongs. (The roots of the Tree of Life, which are referred to here, consist of gongs. Gongs are thus to be bought with the gold.)

If you act so, your renown will gradually increase and will spread to the surrounding villages and people will begin to speak about you on neighboring rivers.

Keep in mind that large stones are worked with a small knife (Schärer 1963:127–128).

In effect, do the right thing and you will be richly rewarded. But all of the subtle and not so subtle systems of reward and punishment and of the giving and withdrawing of social approval involve the existence of rules that may be easily understood and followed. In the course of everyday life, human beings in all cultures encounter situations in which, regardless of the possible consequences, they find it necessary to break the rules or to behave in ways which others interpret as violations of the rules. Conflict then arises and the problem becomes one of restoring the social fabric torn by disagreement. How do the Ibo of Nigeria cool such conflicts?

Conflict: who was right?

In the course of a quarrel about the cutting of some palm nuts a man, K., . . . and the widow, G., of his dead father, fell to abusing one another. She said that he and the other sons of his father were talking against her to the family of the girl she was trying to marry to her son and were telling them that she had not enough money to pay the bride price. The man, K., retorted by asking if that was why she was trying to kill them by supernatural means, by magic that is to say, or by making sacrifices to a spirit to kill them. The widow then made the provocative remark . . . "Why don't you die and let us mourn for you?" (Green 1964:116).

Later G. went to one of her kinsmen and asked him to interview K.; K. admitted accusing G.; and G. paid a fee to a member of the court, who held an informal inquiry and judged the case in her favor. K. appealed by taking a drum and beating it in various parts of the village. The elders convened and decided that both G. and K. should furnish funds to buy a goat for a feast. At the feast, the dispute would be settled. There were further discussions, but the ethnographer concludes:

> When I returned to the village a year later the case had not been retried nor had the decision been carried out. Also G.'s opponents had tried to make her refund the money they spent on the case but she had refused (Green: 124).

Particularly in larger and more complicated cultural systems, when two individuals or subgroups disagree, there is often some outside source of moral authority to which the dispute may be appealed. At times the moral authority, in this case a court and a council of elders, may settle the dispute by providing authoritative decisions concerning who did wrong. In this case, where both parties appear to have knowingly committed breaches of proper behavior, legal procedures had the effect of drawing out and delaying any settlement and at the same time increasing the cost of settlement. Ultimately the contending parties have no choice but to forget the whole thing.

Because legal procedures involving recourse to third parties are often costly, difficult, and time consuming, it can be argued that those who appeal to third parties generally have in mind some rule that their opponents have violated. Very commonly, in the spirit of "if you can break a rule, I can break a rule," both parties to the dispute have broken a rule and both parties feel entitled to a judgment in their favor. Particularly in small groups, the third party, faced with the necessity of continuing to live with both disputants, cannot bear the risk of a decision in favor of either party and therefore tends to delay decision while gradually increasing the cost of arbitration. In other cases, the opposed parties are genuinely confused about the nature of the rules that apply to their situation or the rules themselves are inconsistent or inapplicable.

How Big a Share?

For example, South Indian rules concerning the inheritance of land seem crystal clear. When a group of brothers live together in the same household, each is entitled to an equal share of the family property when the household is divided. When two brothers live together, each is entitled to half of the family property. Suppose, however, that one of the brothers dies before claiming his share and the surviving brother undertakes the responsibility of raising his brother's children to maturity. Suppose that the surviving brother has one son and the deceased brother has two sons. Inevitably when the two adopted children reach maturity, they will tend to claim two thirds of the family property. The surviving brother will tend to claim that they are only entitled to a 50 percent share; namely, the share which would have been claimed by their father had he survived. Because the rules do not spell out what should be done in a case of this kind, such cases almost always involve bitter conflict and end up as legal cases to be settled by the village elders. Such cases arise frequently enough to cause a great deal of trouble, but not frequently enough to merit the formulation of a more precise rule of inheritance. A cultural tradition, viewed as a body of law, cannot be sufficiently specific to cover every conceivable source of disagreement. This is one of the reasons why conflict can be assumed to be universal in human society and why processes for the resolution and settlement of conflict must be present.

Can You Win?

Consider, now, the following case from Bulgaria. Here two definite rules are listed in order of importance: (1) peasants should defer to the power and prestige of urban men; and (2) business contracts must be honored. In this case it seems likely that both men knew the rules, and it is fair to argue that Trayko Danev was well aware that he would lose his case. Why, then, did he bring the case?

> After these two men went out, Trayko Danev, whom the reader knows by now as one of the richest peasants in the village, brought charges against a Sofia merchant for breach of contract in a financial transaction involving hay. Trayko apparently had justice on his side and was ready to prove his case by the use of two witnesses, one of whom was to testify regarding the agreement made and a second to testify regarding the partial fulfillment of the agreement. The first witness testified:
>
> "As I recall the incident, I was at the table with this merchant and Trayko Danev and heard them make an agreement whereby Trayko said he would give 780 leva for hay. He went away and that is all I remember."
>
> Trayko then asked for the testimony of the second witness, whose name had been written on the brief as Nikola.
>
> *The Judge* (Mayor): "Nikola. Nikola. But the last name is not written."
>
> *The Merchant* (Defendant): "Your Honor, I object. This man has not indicated the last name of his second witness and God knows how many Nikolas there are in Bulgaria. Furthermore, the second witness was present in the courtroom while the first witness was testifying. Therefore, the second witness, according to law, cannot testify, no matter what his last name is."
>
> *Trayko:* "I didn't tell him to come in here. It's not my fault."
>
> *Judge:* "The defendant's objection sustained. We cannot accept the testimony of the second witness unless the defendant agrees."
>
> *Defendant:* "I do not agree."
>
> *Judge:* "In that case, the plantiff loses, since he cannot use the second witness and cannot prove his charge" (Sanders 1949:164–165).

One possible interpretation is that Trayko Danev thought that a rich peasant enjoyed the same privileges as a rich merchant. If so, he was rudely disabused of his misinterpretation of the rules. More probably, because a man does not become a rich peasant by being an idiot, Trayko Danev saw this as a situation in which he might get his money back, but in which, win or lose, the cupidity of the merchant would be exposed to public view. After

the public trial, it seems unlikely that the Sophia merchant would have many more opportunities to violate his agreements. From this case, it can be suggested that one reason that people break rules, such as the rule that peasants should stay away from law courts, is that they wish to call attention to intolerable situations. To make a dispute public is to expose both parties to the threat of ridicule and punishment and to call into being all of those subtle forces by means of which the members of a group compel their fellows to conform to the cultural tradition.

The above point is made again in the following case, but, here, conflict can also be seen as an exchange of ritualistic and symbolic actions which carry a clear and definite meaning. The case of Fantan the Interpreter, from the island of Alor in Indonesia, also opens the question of universal characteristics of husband/wife conflict.

Can This Marriage Be Saved?

About a month ago Fantan's wife gambled and lost her dance necklace and anklets. Fantan said he gave her money to try to win them back, but she only lost that too. He was angry, and in telling me about it he put his anger on the moral basis that women should not play cards though it was all right for men. . . .

On Friday (November 18) Fantan was wandering about and joined a game in a remote garden house where some unmarried girls were gambling. . . .

Early Sunday morning (November 20) while he was away two of the girls present at the gambling told his wife about the episode. When he returned from an early market where he had been with me, his wife berated him for returning the jewelery to Fungata where she herself had none, and for not winning hers back for her. She asked if Fungata were his sister or maybe his wife and implied that he had had intercourse with her. She boxed his ears, and he picked up a rattan switch and hit her twice across the thigh. She took her field knife and hit his shoulder with the flat of the blade. He was terrorized and told me he had a large wound. This was patently untrue; he had not even a scratch. . . .

His wife then ran off to Karieta and fought with Fungata. They came to blows, and in ripping off Fungata's necklace, Tilamau broke it. She then came back to the house, but Fantan had meanwhile hidden himself in the servants' quarters behind my house. . . .

Meanwhile Fungata had already made a litigation with the chief of Dikimpe because of her broken necklace. The chief said Tilamau would have to pay a fine; but neither Tilamau, her parents, nor Fantan would pay. So the chief of Dikimpe was angry and brought the oath stone (*namoling*) from Karieta and swore an oath, saying that they could not come to him any more to try cases. . . .

So early Monday morning (November 21) Fungata brought her case to the tumukum. Involved at first were only Fantan, Fungata, and Tilamau. The older and more responsible people did not appear. Fantan, meanwhile, was avoiding his wife. . . . He returned to his own house in the early morning to discover that his wife had burned his rattan switch with a leprosy curse. . . .

When Fantan ran to me in the morning after discovering that his wife had cursed him, he said that this morning at the litigation he was going to divorce his wife and then marry Fungata. . . .

Both Fantan and Tilamau insisted, when asked by the tumukum, that they wanted to separate. The tumukum then had Tilamau's parents called. This she didn't want. Her excuse was that they would talk loudly and vulgarly. . . .
November 23, 1938

Fantan still insisted that his own divorce proceedings must go through and that if he didn't separate from his wife he would surely die of leprosy. . . .
November 24, 1938

There was still no indication that Fantan's divorce proceedings would be continued. . . .
November 25, 1938

At about seven-thirty in the morning I was told that Fantan's parents-in-law had instituted litigation in Karieta.

Tilamau's backers kept insisting on a divorce. Fantan told me before the litigation began that he was angry at its being called, that it was his right to litigate. (This was not true, since either side could sue for divorce.)

Then the tumukum spoke to Fantan's sister and her husband, who had come after being summoned, and told them if Fantan and Tilamau fought again to take them next door to the mandur of Dikimpe and see that they each got a lashing. . . .
December 3, 1938

On November 30 Fantan went to Kalabahi. He traveled with his father-in-law, with whom he was now on perfectly good terms. He had still not spoken to his mother-in-law. "She is still making a sour face at me." Then he told with evident self-satisfaction that he had slept at home the night of December 1, after his return from Kalabahi. He said that he and his wife were happy together again (DuBois 1961:372–380).

Despite the violence of this dispute and the apparently irrevocable actions by both parties, Fantan and Tilamau refused to exhibit actions which would have symbolized a desire for divorce. Tilamau continued to cultivate her husband's garden and resisted the suggestion that her parents be involved in the dispute. Fantan on his side refused to take steps that might have led to the return of the bride-price that he had paid at the time of his marriage. Through his violent actions, Fantan loudly and publicly exclaimed, "See how my wife is extravagantly wasting family resources." Tilamau for her part was exclaiming, "See how my husband over-reacts every time I make a small mistake." Although both acted angrily and "without thinking," neither went so far as to commit breaches which would have led to punishment. By the time the tumukum reached his verdict, "Settle down or you will both get a lashing," pressures from relatives and friends had apparently brought both parties to a state of mind where they were prepared to make concessions.

In terms of cultural universals, it seems probable that a husband and wife who are unable to agree concerning each other's proper conduct will inevitably seek to involve relatives and third party arbitrators in the dispute. In the United States, a husband whose wife repeatedly lost large sums of money at the bridge table might also have vengefully sought a Fungata, thus exposing his wife to a very real threat of divorce. Although the general tactic of solving "irreconcilable" disputes by involving additional persons in the dispute can be regarded as universal, a comparison of the United States and Alor shows that most of the specific actions whereby the dispute is widened and brought to the attention of the authorities are quite different. Leprosy curses and rattan switches have fairly precise symbolic meanings on Alor even though the use of physical aggression by men and verbal aggression by women may have to do with fairly widespread biological differences in the size, weight, and physical strength of men and women.

Social control, getting people to do the right thing, inevitably involves conflict and dispute and formal and public means for resolving such conflicts and disputes. Very often, the breaking of a rule is a symbolic gesture which is met by other symbolic gestures. A poet or lunatic may break rules in a meaningless or unintelligible way, but such people are often unpredictable, unresponsive to punishment and reward, and beyond understanding in terms of cultural regularities. The ordinary person involved in ordinary conflicts plays a cultural game, a kind of ritual in which the individual exhibits behaviors which are grammatical and meaningful as performances of processes of conflict and resolution.

Because, even more than in the case of ritual, the proper conduct of a dispute involves great freedom in the choice of individual actions, the study of conflict and social control involves the study of a great many cases before the rules of the game or the meaning of the various behaviors involved can be established.

Where Have You Been?
In the South Indian village of Namhalli, husbands and wives appear to define the initiation of severe marital conflict as any behavior which can be construed as a denial of the marital relationship. About half the time such a denial is concretely expressed in the form of a direct rumor or visible evidence that the wife has committed adultery. More rarely, it is evidence that the husband has done so. In addition to direct rumors or messages on the order of "what was your wife doing with so and so," the wife may reveal her adulterous nature by gazing boldly at strange men, by stealing from the family grain supply, or by the possession of candy or other goods. The commencement of a marital dispute may also be signaled by chronic illness, sexual impotence, or improper performance of household duties.

Once the existence of a marital dispute is established, couples may move quickly or slowly toward divorce or reconciliation; they may involve few or many outsiders; or they may use much or little physical violence and verbal aggression. The endpoint of a marital conflict is, of course, either divorce or reconciliation. Completed conflicts tend to move through five stages: beginning, physical violence, flight, arbitration or third party intervention, and divorce or reconciliation.

The movement from beginning to physical violence may involve warnings, demands for explanations, mild or salutary beatings, or scolding. At this stage, both husband and wife may express dissatisfaction by means of little misdeeds and noncompliances which are of great symbolic significance. The wife may serve cold food, forget salt or chilis, slight important relatives, or address fellow villagers as "potential spouse." The husband is likely to deliver a mild or salutary beating, but he may also fail to purchase new clothing at festival time, spend his earnings on the cinema, patronize prostitutes, or leave town. The spouse's response to these signals of dissatisfaction is of great importance to the outcome of the dispute. If the husband contents himself with demanding an explanation or giving a warning, divorce is almost inevitable. If the husband delivers a salutary beating, divorce practically never occurs. If the spouses scold each other in public, people intervene and divorce is avoided.

In roughly two thirds of recorded marital conflicts, the conflict escalates to the stage of physical violence. Here, the most common happening is that the husband beats the wife with a stick or in some other violent way. At this stage, he has "eyes like a tiger." Although, as indicated in Figure 2, the wife may beat a third party or attempt to injure herself, the wife's strategy is evidently to provoke an outburst of violence. In a few cases, not represented in Figure 2, the wife's tears and recriminations may have the effect of physical violence. In any case, the home situation is now unbearable and the victim, almost always the wife, flees or is driven out. Here, the further the wife flees, the lower the likelihood of reconciliation. If she flees starving into the fields surrounding the village or runs weeping down the village streets, she is sure to be discovered by neighbors or officials and returned to her husband. If she flees to her natal village, her mother and father are likely to support her against her husband and divorce is inevitable.

Where the wife flees in an appropriate manner it symbolizes a plea for intervention and arbitration. Sometimes a single distinguished elder will take the wife back to the house and urge the husband to mend his ways; at other times a formal council of elders intervenes until divorce or reconciliation has taken place. Figure 2 presents the network of alternatives used in a number of actual cases of conflict. The headings, 1A, 1B, and so on, represent the stage of the conflict and the different major alternatives available at each stage. The lines connecting the different stages represent the patterns followed by actual cases of conflict. Such a diagram is a means of arriving at the set of rules that govern participation in marital conflict.

Although Figure 2 is only a first attempt at an explanation of marital conflict, it serves to illustrate the general nature of cultural processes. Traditionally, anthropologists and sociologists have described human behavior in terms of usual or customary practices. Those who break rules have been described as "abnormal," "deviant," or "nonconformist." Such a "normative" view of human behavior is useful for certain purposes, but it does not provide a fair view of the complexity of human life. Human beings conform in a variety of ways. Thus, even though Figure 2 represents only the essential parts of the conflict process, it still provides each husband and wife with a variety of ways of conforming to the proper method of carrying out a

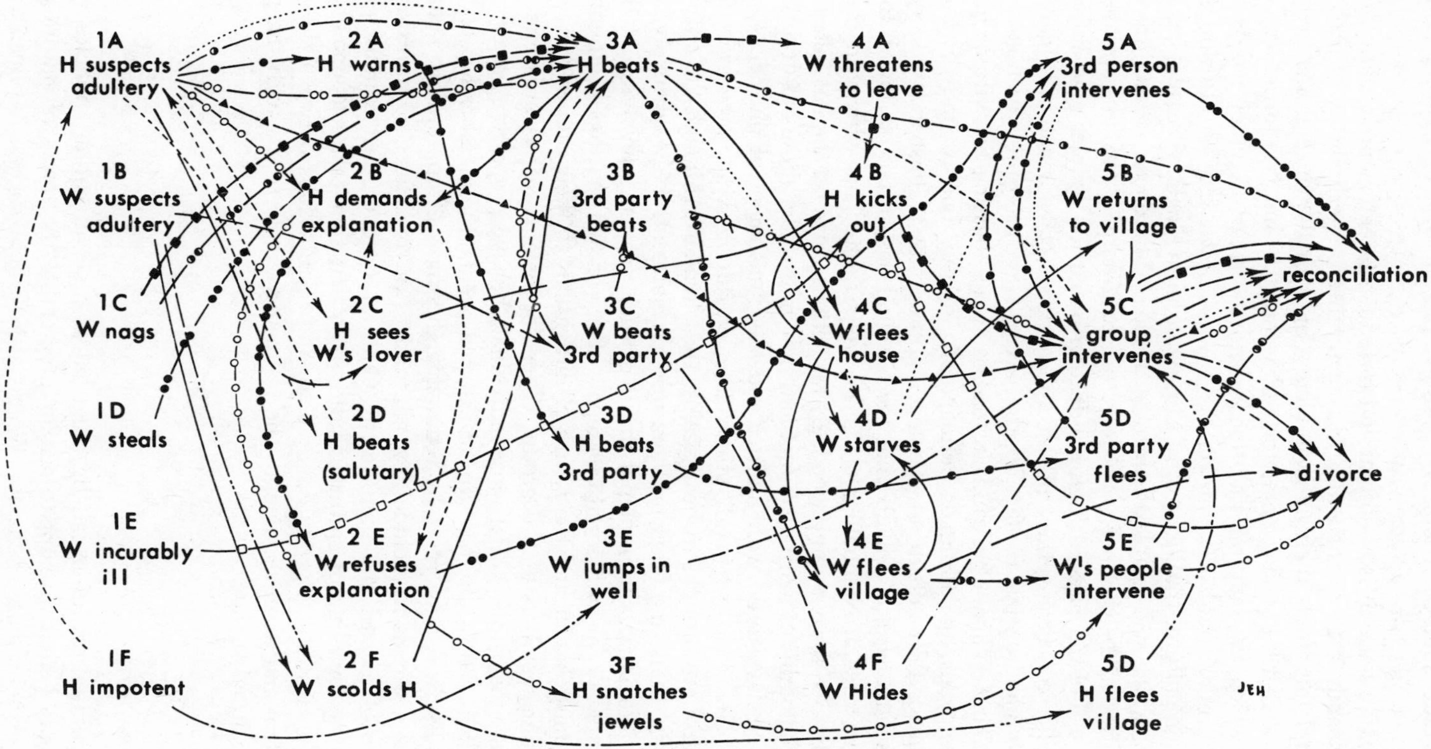
1A
H suspects adultery
1B
W suspects adultery
1C
W nags
1D
W steals
1E
W incurably ill
1F
H impotent
2 A
H warns
2 B
H demands explanation
2 C
H sees W's lover
2 D
H beats (salutary)
2 E
W refuses explanation
2 F
W scolds H
3A
H beats
3B
3rd party beats
3C
W beats 3rd party
3D
H beats 3rd party
3E
W jumps in well
3F
H snatches jewels
4 A
W threatens to leave
4 B
H kicks out
4C
W flees house
4D
W starves
4E
W flees village
4F
W Hides
5 A
3rd person intervenes
5 B
W returns to village
5C
group intervenes
5D
3rd party flees
5 E
W's people intervene
5D
H flees village
reconciliation
divorce
JEH

FIGURE 2. *Alternatives in marital conflict, South India.*

domestic conflict. There is no single proper way of fighting with one's spouse; there are a variety of proper ways.

In a sense, it is abnormal and forbidden to enter into a marital dispute. Husbands and wives should treat each other properly, listen to each other's complaints, solve their own problems. Individuals who become involved in public marital conflict enter forbidden territory, but it is forbidden territory for which the cultural tradition provides a map. In other words, marital conflict, although disapproved, is a well-known fact of life and for this reason cultural traditions tend to provide individuals with rules and guidelines which will enable them to settle their differences, to seek third party arbitration, or in other ways to return to a normal and appropriate status.

All of the cases in Figure 2 deal with married couples who entered into conflict concerning the rules of appropriate behavior and who carried out their inappropriate conflict appropriately. There are rules which govern rulebreaking. When a husband, instead of merely beating his wife or his wife's lover, ends up killing or permanently injuring one or both of them, his behavior falls outside of "behavior appropriate to husband/wife conflict." In such a case, it is likely that the husband has, in fact, followed the norm for murder in Namhalli; that is, he has assaulted his wife with the heavy knife used for chopping wood. By his actions, however, he has fallen outside of the norms of marital conflict and now falls under those cultural processes which have to do with murder and the punishment of murder.

Here, too, as in all other cases of rulebreaking, processes of social control are brought to bear against the offender. Although gossip, ridicule, formal trials, and other mechanisms of social control always involve costs to the individual, the principal thrust of such processes involves not the punishment of the individual but repair of the breach that has been created by the misbehavior and the return of individuals to their proper roles as functioning members of the group. When the balance of rewards and punishments that ensures that most individuals behave properly most of the time is disrupted by the pressure of external events, the membership of the cultural system must react by redrawing the maps of appropriate behavior in such a way as to include new alternatives or to restore the preexisting balance of reward and punishment. Cultural systems must contain processes for the rewriting of cultural traditions so that they take account of stresses or new problems produced by changing relationships between the cultural system and its environment. The following chapter deals with the problem of cultural change.

Summary

A cultural tradition can be regarded as a set of earnest policies whereby human beings attempt to render predictable the forces of nature and the vagaries of human behavior. Where, as in Utopia, success has been achieved, there is no problem of misbehavior and no need for mechanisms designed to cope with improper and unexpected human behaviors. In Hillside, which serves as the prototype for all nonimaginary human communities, it turns out that it is impossible to write rules which deal precisely with reality or which cover every conceivable situation.

Although the case of the Makah shows that rule breaking and conflict can sometimes be attributed to the faulty transmission of culture known as the "generation gap," the case of the Lugbara illustrates the fact that trouble can also be traced to the failure to predict such "minor" events as a woman's barrenness. From South Texas, the case of Miguel provides evidence that even when a human being scrupulously obeys the rules, he may still encounter difficulties and conflicting situations. The problems of behaving appropriately are magnified when new and changing circumstances produce situations unforeseen within the cultural tradition. Thus, Sulli confronts the problem of delaying his marriage by means of brilliant improvisation upon the rules of his culture. Biboi, unfamiliar with his own cultural tradition, is trapped in the yawning chasm between new and old.

When rules are broken, processes of social control act to return the rulebreaker to social conformity. In Dutch Guiana and South India, the conscious rulebreaker is threatened with automatic and supernatural punishment. In other cultures, gossip and ridicule confront the individual with the loss of his "face" or social identity, and the individual acts to avoid being labeled a sucker, a dumb guy, or a sin verguenza. Complex societies often contain untouchable groups and social control may then capitalize on the individual's fear of being labeled, as in Plainville, one of the "people who live like animals." Scapegoating is the practice of attributing the misfortunes of the many to the misdeeds of a few. The examples of the B-29 crew and the Nupe are evidence of the manner in which the individual's fear of being labeled a foul-up or witch may be used to enforce conformity. Processes of confession, in which the individual confesses his mistakes and receives appropriate punishment or forgiveness, are illustrated by the case of the Eskimo.

When individuals disagree concerning whether rules have been broken or not, the task of healing the breach and applying processes of social control tends to fall to a third party who possesses the moral authority required for convincing arbitration or judgment. Because even a properly endowed moral authority such as a court or council often finds it difficult to rule in favor of either party, some courts, such as those of the Ibo, may act by prolonging the dispute and increasing its cost to the participants. An example from South India shows why convincing resolution of disputes is often impossible and therefore why processes of arbitration and adjudication are necessary. The case of Trayko Danev suggests that, even where rules are clear and definite, they may still be broken as a means of calling public attention to intolerable situations.

The use of rule breaking, conflict, and public litigation to call attention to insolvable interpersonal problems is also illustrated by the case of Fantan and Tilamau. This dispute raises questions concerning the meaning of the various behaviors interchanged in the course of a dispute. Thus, although there might be some universal attributes of husband/wife disputes, marital disputes as well as other kinds of conflict can be interpreted as exchanges of culturally meaningful behaviors. The problem of establishing the nature of the rules governing marital disputes and interpreting the meaning of the behaviors exchanged is discussed in terms of an analysis of South Indian marital disputes. Processes of conflict, like many other cultural processes, are seen as involving not so much conformity to a norm as selection from a variety of acceptable alternatives.

Further readings

A variety of recent works deals with aspects of politics, law conflict, and government. These include *Political Anthropology* (Swartz, Tuden, and Turner 1966), *Law and Warfare* (Bohannan 1967), *Political Anthropology* (Balandier 1970), *Divisiveness and Social Conflict* (Beals and Siegel 1966), *Law in Culture and Society* (Nader 1969).

Most of the Case Studies deal with problems of social control, especially Lessa's *Ulithi* (1966), Hudson's *Padju Epat* (1972), Beals' *Gopalpur* (1962), the Spindlers' *Dreamers without Power* (1971), Jones' *Sanapian* (1972), and Bascom's *The Yoruba* (1969).

Problems and questions

1. Examine some portrayals of conflict situations on television or elsewhere. What sorts of behavior are presented as being likely to trigger violent responses?
2. What seem to be some of the more important techniques of social control used in an organization or cultural system familiar to you?
3. Interview some representatives of a particular cultural system concerning their definitions of proper behavior in some particular type of situation. To what extent are there norms to which everyone conforms and to what extent are there alternative ways of behaving which are considered proper?
4. Examine a number of ethnographic sources and comment on the various techniques of social control that seem to be employed.
5. Carefully avoiding sensitive or private topics, collect a number of case histories of minor arguments or disputes. Is there any pattern in the way such disputes are carried out or ultimately resolved?

11

Culture change and related processes

Cultural systems are never static. They are influenced by external conditions and environmental forces. Their internal structure is in a constant state of flux, due to changes in the status of individuals and repetitive changes in the status of the community. This chapter stresses the adaptation of cultural systems to changing conditions of survival both within the system and external to it. Processes of urbanization and modernization, technological change, diffusion, reinterpretation of borrowed or introduced elements, innovation, synthesis of old and new, and acculturation are demonstrated by examples taken from many cultures around the world. The persistence of cultural systems, or aspects of them, is also considered. Relationships between rural and urban populations are discussed. Examples of culture change range from situations where single introduced elements have caused repercussions throughout the cultural system, to situations where the external conditions of survival have shifted so

287

massively that the cultural system has undergone almost total collapse, as among some American Indian groups. Nativistic, reaffirmative, and revitalization movements are seen as reponses to external threat, and a number of cases are explored. The boundary-maintaining mechanisms of cultural systems and their influence on receptivity to change are demonstrated. Discussion of the psychological consequences of changes in the cultural system, with special reference to the Menomini and Blood Indians, is included. Contemporary changes among American youth, affecting the whole society, are analyzed in the same framework of concepts applied to other cultural systems.

The new wind in Gopalpur

The new wind blows in Gopalpur, however fitfully, and its effects are sometimes surprising. The government officials, charged with bringing the new wind to Gopalpur, work honestly and efficiently, insofar as it is possible for them to do so. At the same time, many changes which could be made are not being made. Government officials tend to lay the blame for lack of progress upon the people of such villages as Gopalpur, who in turn tend to lay the blame upon the government officials. Both groups feel helpless and apathetic. The new wind blows in an unchanneled and undisciplined way, stirring up new problems for every one solved. The source of the difficulty seems to lie in the government officials' failure to perceive the interrelationships among the things they are trying to change. The culture of Gopalpur is an organic whole; its religion and its social organization are adapted to the economic tasks traditionally carried out in the village. The reform programs stimulated by the new wind are not organic wholes. The new wind offers some hopeful and some frightening prospects, but it does not offer a way of life (Beals 1962: 83).

The new wind, "Navira" as the people of Gopalpur call it, is being felt in small villages throughout the world in much the same manner as it is in this small South Indian village. It is born of new scientific and technical knowledge—advances in medicine and experimental agriculture, for example—and is nourished in the urban environment. The initial reactions to its force are for the most part disruptive. So often the agents of change are unaware of the importance of viewing a culture as a system.

After many centuries of coping with and adapting to the environment, consisting of people and of natural forces, Gopalpur has attained a state of equilibrium, where the checks and balances are finely equilibrated:

The traditional culture of Gopalpur contained the answer to every problem. The fathers and forefathers of people in Gopalpur weathered flood, famine, pestilence, and war and built great cities on the fertile plain. As the new wind blows, feelings of pride and greatness are replaced by feelings of poverty and helplessness (Beals 1962:76).

If a Gopalpur farmer decides to adopt new agricultural practices, he does so at the risk of threatening significant social and economic relationships.

To purchase improved agricultural equipment, the farmer must sever his traditional relationship with the Blacksmith and Carpenter. This is more than an economic relationship. Not only are the Carpenter and Blacksmith neighbors and friends, but they have religious functions that make their presence essential on such occasions as birth, marriage, and death. The Carpenter and Blacksmith offer an integrated set of tools and guarantee repairs. Under these circumstances, the purchase of a moldboard plow, or any improved equipment, becomes a tricky and difficult business. On their side, the Carpenter and Blacksmith receive a fixed quantity or grain at harvest time. If they were to improve their product, they would find it difficult to raise their prices to cover its greater cost. The benefits of improved agricultural techniques have not been demonstrated, and their use is attended by great economic and social risk. In refusing to adopt new methods, the farmer of Gopalpur shows common sense, not conservatism (Beals 1962:79).

Other changes proposed by government officials in village religion and social organization threaten the basic patterns of cooperation and competition necessary for the economic life of the village. Government officials and missionaries are opposed to such practices as human or animal sacrifice, institutionalized prostitution, arranged marriages, gambling, meat eating, drinking, concubinage, divorce, quarreling, landlords, and time "wasted" on rituals and ceremonies. The condemning of these practices reveals a lack of understanding of the system as a finely balanced, functionally related whole, for the patterns of cooperation and competition that make the economic life of the village possible are interlocked, within the system, with the condemned practices. Each of the two opposing groups believes itself to be more moral than the other, but this is not the problem. The real problem is finding substitutes for these condemned practices. As Beals writes, "People in Gopalpur do not know what to do *instead* of meat eating, animal sacrifice, and ceremonies, nor do they know of any advantages to be gained by renouncing them" (Beals 1962:82). But while the government officials and merchants of the nearby town are debating among themselves the desirability of change, it is pressing in from every side.

Cultural systems are in a constant state of change and adaptation. Changes can be slow and almost imperceptible or they can be revolutionary. Paradoxically, some changes are a result of members of cultural systems attempting to reject outside stimuli, as represented by nativistic and revivalistic movements (see pp. 325–328). The members of some cultural systems are able to minimize change by utilizing various boundary-maintaining devices (for example, the Hutterites, pp. 311–313).

Changes are effected when: (1) new ideas or material paraphernalia are accepted within cultures from elsewhere; this process is termed *diffusion*; (2) when a person or persons introduce new ways of thinking or behaving which are accepted within a culture; this process is called *innovation*; or (3) when the members of a cultural system have first-hand contacts with members of one or more cultural systems that result in changes in the systems of both groups; this process is known as *acculturation*. It is important to remember that it is the actual individuals and groups of individuals that are readjusting to the new stimuli and not an "abstract system." The acculturative process is extremely complicated and accounts for the greater mass of change phenomena. Factors such as the size of the populations that meet, who dominates and who submits, the adaptability or flexibility exhibited by the cultures involved, the number and kinds of compatible and understandable behaviors and ideas which the people of one system present to another are all important considerations in the process of acculturation.

Modernization or urbanization processes may be considered either as independent processes or as acculturative phenomena. Folk peoples, like those in Gopalpur, are continually being affected by the modern world or transformed into urban peoples. Modernization processes, begun millennia ago, have never ceased. They continue today on the Western-managed tropical plantation, in the African kraal, on the American Indian reservation, and in the Ozark mountain valley. These populations, neither primitive nor modern, form the majority of mankind (Wolf 1966:vii). The prescientific cultures must perforce give way to the sheer rationalized efficiency manifested by the scientific cultures of the twentieth century. The situation in Gopalpur is more typical than not—one in which the members of the system experience confusion during the first phases of modernization, when the basic equilibrium of their system is threatened.

What happens when the ecological system changes?

The majority of processes subsumed under the heading of culture change—borrowing, urbanization, diffusion, acculturation, forced acculturation—have their origin in people. But now and then the *natural environment* plays the primary role in changing a system. The natural environment must always be taken into account as an aspect of the external condition in which a cultural system operates. As stated in Chaper 2, the natural environment, interacting with the artificial and social entities, constitutes the *ecology* of the system.

The Tanala of Madagascar were forced to adapt to a new type of natural environment. When land was no longer available for the traditional dry rice type of cultivation, the people either had to face starvation or adopt the new technique of wet rice cultivation. By transporting water for irrigation, large new areas of land were made available for agriculture. But how could anyone predict that this relatively small change could so radically alter the social system and the personalities of the people living in it? The democratic and individualistic Tanala who moved their villages informally from one area to the other as the land was depleted under the old system, were transformed into a class-structured society with a king, a system of warfare, settled villages, and a change in family life from permissive to authoritarian types of control. Some of the many changes are described in the following passage:

> Thus there gradually emerged a group of landowners, and with the process came a breakdown in the joint family organization. The cohesiveness of this older unit was maintained by economic interdependence and the need for cooperation. But an irrigated rice field could be tended by a single family, and its head need not recognize any claim to share it with anyone who had not contributed to its produce.
>
> This group of permanent rice sites formed the nucleus of a permanent village, because the land could not be exhausted as was the land exploited by the dry method. As land suitable for wet rice near the village was presently all taken up, the landless households had to move farther and farther away into the jungle. So far away would they be that they could not return the same day. These distant fields also became household rather than joint family affairs.
>
> The moving of the older unit from one land site to another had kept the joint family intact. But now single landless households were forced to move, while there were in the same unit landowners who had a capital investment and no incentive to move. The migrant groups were thus cross-sections of the original lineages. Each original village had a group of descendant villages, each one surrounded by irrigated fields and private ownership.
>
> The mobile villages had been self-contained and endogamous. The settled villages were much less so. The joint family retained its religious importance, based on the worship of a common ancestor, even after its component households had been scattered. Family members would be called together on ceremonial occasions, and thus the old village isolation broke down. Intermarriages became common. In this way, the transformation from independent villages to a tribal organization took place.
>
> The process brought further changes in the patterns of native warfare. The old village had to be defended; but not at so great a cost nor with the necessity for permanent upkeep. When the village became permanent the defenses had to be of a powerful kind, involving big investments and permanent upkeep.
>
> Slaves, who were of no economic significance in the old system, now acquired economic importance. This gave rise to new techniques of ransom. Thus the tribal organization grew in solidity, and with the change the old tribal democracy disappeared. The next step was a king at the head who exercised control over the settled elements but not over the mobile ones. The kingdom came to an end before any adequate machinery of government could be established. This king built himself an individual tomb, thus breaking an ancient custom.
>
> The changes were therefore, a king at the head, settled subjects, rudimentary social classes based on economic differences, and lineages of nothing but ceremonial importance (Linton 1939:282–283).

The adaptation of the Tanala to changes in the natural environment serves as an illustration for the statement made earlier (Chapter 4) that "an adaptation can be successful only if it works simultaneously within the natural, artificial, and social environments." (See Chapter 2 for elaboration of types of environment.)

Who are the innovators?

A Cheyenne Creator

The first lodge of modern shape is said to have been suggested by a man who was handling a large poplar leaf, and quite by accident bent it into the shape of a cone—that is to say, of a lodge, such as are used today. As he looked at the leaf it flashed into his mind that a shelter like it would be better than those they then had. He showed it to the people and they made lodges in the shape of this leaf, and have used them ever since (Grinnell 1923:50, quoted in Hoebel 1949:471).

Was this Cheyenne Indian an innovator? If a Cheyenne man ever went through a process such as that described above by another Cheyenne—of combining the idea of the cone formed by the leaf and the idea of a lodge—he was truly an innovator. Innovation is a matter of creatively reorganizing and recombining ideas provided by one's culture. Homer Barnett (1953) views people as highly innovative creatures, organizing and reorganizing their field of experience at every moment.

Innovation is an important means through which cultures undergo change, changes both large and small in scope—ranging from the introduction of a new religious cult to a new type of hair styling. But when is a change an innovation? Most anthropologists would agree that there is no innovation until it is accepted by a group or society and integrated into its ongoing culture.

The Marquesas: How Many Ways To Skin a Cat?

In about the year 1900 a Gilbert Islander settled in the island of Hiva Oa in the Marquesas group. He took a native wife and began to earn his living as a fisherman. Even twenty years before, his fishing activities would have been resented as poaching. Under the old Marquesan patterns this was carried on as a semi-communal activity. There was a sacred place at the shore where the fishing canoes were kept, and the men of the community served as fishermen in rotation, with a formal division of the catch. In each fishing place there was a resident priest who directed the activities and, incidentally, watched the canoes. By the time our hero arrived all this had broken down and fishing had become individual. All canoes had always been personal property, but under the old conditions this meant little. The owner always gave his permission for the canoe's use and, probably, received a little more of the proceeds in return. Under the new conditions the idea of individual ownership was strengthened, but canoe-stealing became endemic and was a great nuisance to the more industrious members of the community. The canoe watcher had passed with the fisher-priest, and the complete breakdown of the old religion had destroyed the efficacy of magically supported taboos. Many a man who came down to the beach for a night's fishing would find his canoe gone and would only recover it several days later when someone stumbled on it abandoned in some neighboring cove. We may imagine that the Gilbert Islander, being a stranger, was subjected to more annoyance in this respect than the local fishermen. The Marquesans combine with their light-fingered tendencies an almost sophomoric delight in practical jokes and hazing.

Whatever the reason, the visiting fisherman invented a new type of detachable outrigger. This contrivance was quite different from the outrigger of the home islands and, as far as I know, from that used in any other part of the Pacific. The float was indirectly attached to the crosspieces which held it to the canoe. The uprights which connected the float with the crosspieces were made from staves of European casks and were fitted solidly into the float at the bottom. They were pierced with holes a few inches below the top and through these holes the ends of the crosspieces passed. Both uprights were lashed to the crosspieces, and the crosspiece in turn lashed to the canoe, with a single continuous piece of rope. When the owner beached his canoe, he undid the lashings, laid the float and crosspieces side by side, wound the rope around them and carried the whole up to his house on his shoulder. Since the canoe could not be used without an outrigger, it was quite safe from theft, while when he wanted to use it himself he could put on the outrigger in five minutes (Linton 1936:313–314).

It is not difficult to understand why this simple, yet ingenious, device was quickly accepted by the community. A real need had existed for this innovative act. It is probably not coincidental that the innovator was a foreigner, who saw the situation in a fresh manner, unencumbered by the weight of past customs. Innovators are often "marginal men," who are, for a variety of reasons, somewhat divorced from the core of their culture and thus more free to create.

A Man with a Cause

Wovoka, or Jack Wilson, was a Paiute Indian living in Nevada in the 1890s. The Nevada Indians, with their hunting and gathering routes broken up by White infiltration, were in bad shape. They were forced to modify their old patterns, hunting and gathering only part-time and working for Whites part-time. Their culture was being extinguished, and no one cared (Underhill 1953: Chap. 11). When things became unbearable Wovoka, as his father had done in 1870, had a trance and "saw God." As a result of this, he encouraged his people to return to the old ways and to love each other. He told his people to dance in a circle five nights in succession, and he reintroduced the old Basin dance with the old songs about wind, cloud, and animals sung in the old monotonous tones typical of the Basin groups. Wovoka claimed that if his advice were followed, the Whites would disappear and the dead Indians return. This became the famous Ghost Dance and swept Indian country. It spread eastward through the Plains Indian tribes, with tragic results among the Sioux in the famous battle of Wounded Knee. The message of the Ghost Dance was enthusiastically welcomed by oppressed Indians. It even spread to some eastern Woodlands tribes, becoming modified to fit local cultural circumstances.

Wovoka, the Gilbert Islander, and the Cheyenne Indian comprise only a very small sample of the many kinds of innovators cultures throughout the world produce. They represent some of the creative processes which are a part of the human potential.

How do new ideas spread?

The American Case

Our solid American citizen awakens in a bed built on a pattern which originated in the Near East but which was modified in Northern Europe before it was transmitted to America. He throws back covers made from cotton, domesticated in India, or linen, domesticated in the Near East, or wool from sheep, also domesticated in the Near East, or silk, the use of which was discovered in China. All of these materials have been spun and woven by processes invented in the Near East. He slips into his moccasins, invented by the Indians of the Eastern Woodlands, and goes to the bathroom, whose fixtures are a mixture of European and American inventions, both of recent date. He takes off his pajamas, a garment invented in India, and washes with soap invented by the ancient Gauls. He then shaves, a masochistic rite which seems to have been derived from either Sumer or ancient Egypt.

Returning to the bedroom, he removes his clothes from a chair of southern European type and proceeds to dress. He puts on garments whose form originally derived from the skin clothing of the nomads of the Asiatic steppes, puts on shoes made from skins tanned by a process invented in ancient Egypt and cut to a pattern derived from the classical civilizations of the Mediterranean, and ties around his neck a strip of bright-colored cloth which is a vestigial survival of the shoulder shawls worn by the seventeenth-century Croatians. Before going out for breakfast he glances through the window, made of glass invented in Egypt, and if it is raining puts on overshoes made of rubber discovered by the Central American Indians and takes an umbrella, invented in Southeastern Asia. Upon his head he puts a hat made of felt, a material invented in the Asiatic steppes.

On his way to breakfast he stops to buy a paper, paying for it with coins, an ancient Lydian invention. At the restaurant a whole new series of borrowed elements confronts him. His plate is made of a form of pottery invented in China. His knife is of steel, an alloy first made in southern India, his fork a medieval Italian invention, and his spoon a derivative of a Roman original. He begins breakfast with an orange, from the eastern Mediterranean, a cantaloupe from Persia, or perhaps a piece of African watermelon. With this he has coffee, an Abyssinian plant, with cream and sugar. Both the domestication of cows and the idea of milking them originated in the Near East, while sugar was first made in India. After his fruit and first coffee he goes on to waffles, cakes made by a Scandinavian technique from wheat domesticated in Asia Minor. Over these he pours maple syrup, invented by the Indians of the Eastern Woodlands. As a side dish he may have the egg of a species of bird domesticated in Indo-China, or thin strips of the flesh of an animal domesticated in Eastern Asia which have been salted and smoked by a process developed in northern Europe.

When our friend has finished eating he settles back to smoke, an American Indian habit, consuming a plant domesticated in Brazil in either a pipe, derived from the Indians of Virginia, or a cigarette, derived from Mexico. If he is hardy enough he may even attempt a cigar, transmitted to us from the Antilles by way of Spain. While smoking he reads the news of the day, imprinted in characters invented by the ancient Semites upon a material invented in China by a process invented in Germany. As he absorbs the accounts of foreign troubles he will, if he is a good conservative citizen, thank a Hebrew deity in an Indo-European language that he is 100 percent American (Linton 1936:326–327).

One of the most powerful incentives for change comes when one culture borrows from another (*diffusion*). The complexity of our modern civilization is due in large part to the receptivity of our ancestors who saw advantages in the ideas and material artifacts of other peoples. And since World War II, Americans have become even more receptive, as can be noted by the flood of German and Japanese goods on our market. Of special interest is the fact that most recent items have been added without requiring basic changes in our culture.

The Brazilian Negroes

Other cases of relatively uncomplicated borrowing occur when new elements are borrowed and old meanings are ascribed to them. Herskovits terms this process *reinterpretation* (Herskovits 1950:553). *Syncretism,* one form of reinterpretation, is well illustrated in the identification of African deities with the saints of the Catholic church by Brazilian Negroes:

As in other New World Catholic countries, ancestral African beliefs have been reconciled with Christianity, as a result of the forced conversion of slavery times. Today, the descendants of these Africans, who worship the African gods, are professing and practising Catholics as well as members of African cult-groups. It has been described, how, due to the process of reinterpretation through syncretism, they identify their African gods with the saints of the Church. The process, however, goes much farther. A hollow-log drum that has not been "baptized" will not call the proper deities to the dance, since it does not have the disciplined spiritual control that goes with baptism. In Salvador, Bahia, a novitiate, after a long period of initiation into cult-practices in the cult-house of her group, will immediately on emerging from her training make one pilgrimage to the shrine of the principal saint of the city, and another to worship at the altar of the saint that is identified with the African god to whose worship she is vowed . . . even in a single city, one cannot flatly say that a given African deity is always identified with a given Catholic saint. In Recife, for example, though the African water-goddess named Yemanja was identified by the members of four cult-centers with Our Lady of the Immaculate Conception, Shango, the African thunder-god was held by one group to be the same as St. Jerome, by another as St. Anthony, and by a third as St. John the Baptist (Herskovits 1950:570–571).

An Australian Case

In contrast to these examples of borrowing where no serious disturbances occurred is the example of the Yir Yiront, "stone age" people, who substituted our steel axes for their stone axes, an act which affected their entire cultural system, according to L. Sharp (1952). It is obvious why this introduced artifact was so disruptive if we examine the role which the stone axe played in the old Yir Yiront culture.

> The production of a stone axe required a number of simple skills. With the idea of the axe in its various details well in mind, the adult men—and only the adult men—could set about producing it, a task not considered appropriate for women or children. First of all, a man had to know the location and properties of several natural resources found in his immediate environment: pliable wood, which could be doubled or bent over the axe head and bound tightly to form a handle; bark, which could be rolled into cord for the binding; and gum, with which the stone head could be firmly fixed in the shaft. These materials had to be correctly gathered, stored, prepared, cut to size, and applied or manipulated (Sharp 1952:73).

The variety of uses of the stone axe indicate its importance in Yir Yiront subsistence:

> Anyone—man, woman, or child—could use the axe; indeed, it was used more by women, for theirs was the onerous, daily task of obtaining sufficient wood to keep the campfire of each family burning all day for cooking or other purposes and all night against mosquitoes and cold. . . . The stone axe was essential in making the wet-season domed huts, which keep out some rain and some insects; or platforms, which provide dry storage; or shelters, which give shade when days are bright and hot. In hunting and fishing and in gathering vegetable or animal food the axe was also a necessary tool; and

in this tropical culture without preservatives or other means of storage, the native spends more time obtaining food than in any other occupation except sleeping (Sharp 1952:74).

The stone axe also played a prominent role in interpersonal behavior:

> Yir Yiront men were dependent upon interpersonal relations for their stone axe heads, since the flat, geologically recent alluvial country over which they range, provides no stone from which axe heads can be made. The stone they used comes from known quarries four hundred miles to the south. It reached the Yir Yiront through long lines of male trading partners, some of these chains terminating with the Yir Yiront men, while others extended on farther north to other groups, having utilized Yir Yiront men as links. Almost every older adult man had one or more regular trading partners, some to the north and some to the south. His partner or partners in the south he provided with surplus spears, and particularly fighting spears tipped with the barbed spines of sting ray which snap into vicious fragments when they penetrate human flesh. . . . While many other objects may move along these chains of trading partners, they are still characterized by both bush and station aboriginals as lines along which spears move south and axes move north (Sharp 1952:75).

Most of the trading took place during the dry season when the great corroborees occur, centering about initiation rites or totemic ceremonials.

The stone axe played an important role in other kinds of interpersonal relationships. It was only adult men who made and retained the stone axes. Women and children were continually forced to borrow them, use them promptly, and return them to the men in good condition. The borrowing was done according to regular patterns of kinship behavior:

> A woman on good terms with her husband would expect to use his axe unless he were using it; a husband on good terms with his wives would let any one of them use his axe without question. If a woman was unmarried or her husband was absent, she would go first to her older brother or to her father for an axe. Only in extraordinary circumstances would she seek a stone axe from a mother's brother or certain other male kin with whom she had to be most circumspect. A girl, a boy, or a young man would look to a father or an older brother to provide an axe for her or his use, but would never approach a mother's brother, who would be at the same time a potential father-in-law, with such a request. Older men, too, would follow similar rules if they had to borrow an axe (Sharp 1952:76).

Of further importance is the fact that the knowledge of how to produce the axe is a part of the Yir Yiront adult masculine role. With an understanding of the functions which the stone axe played in Yir Yiront culture, the result of the availability of steel axes to young men and women who won the favor of the mission staff, could be predicted. The undermining of the dependency upon older males had important repercussions for the authority structure of the community, for male-female role definitions, for the structure of interpersonal behavior, and for the patterns of kinship behavior. A man who wanted a stone axe could depend upon established relationships with other men and with nature to get one. A man wanting a steel axe could not be self-reliant; he had to assume a dependent relationship with a missionary who gave them out erratically (from the native point of view) to "better" aboriginals or to those who did odd jobs for the mission. Dependency was substituted for self-reliance. Even women and young boys would get steel axes from the missionaries occasionally, which they considered their "own" in a new concept of possession, while some older men would be left with only stone axes. These older men would then borrow steel axes from their women and sons in a drastic reversal of roles and consequent loss of dominance and respect. Most disturbingly, the new steel axe had no origin myth, or mythical ancestors associated with it (and none was invented). So suspicions began to be directed at the whole complex of belief about the origin of the world and of the creatures (including man) and objects in it. As Lauriston Sharp writes: "The steel axe . . . is not only replacing the stone axe physically, but is hacking at the supports of the entire cultural system" (Sharp 1952:80). The effects of this item may be somewhat overstated, but the case is a good example of the interrelatedness of the parts of a cultural system.

Two-Way Borrowing

Is it necessary to continue the study of the American Indian? He is more than an exhibit in a museum, more than a vendor of trinkets, more than an extra in a Hollywood western. The Amercian Indian has left an indelible mark upon the culture of America, upon its customs, its habits, its language, and even upon its mode of thought . . . there are more ways to study the Indian than to botanize on the grave of his dead past: History and literature have too long done no more than that. To discover his ever-living impact on the society that we call modern is the function of anthropologists, ethnologists, sociologists and folklorists. Add to these the social psychologist and the instrumentalist and we get a half dozen intellectual disciplines with which to study the totality of American culture, a culture in which the Indian has had and still has a very significant part (Williams 1956:ix–x).

We in the United States, viewing the small minority of Indians, whose cultures have for the most part been broken for several decades, naturally assume that borrowing has been a relatively one-way process: from us by them. But this is not so. Our borrowings from the American Indian have been numerous and can be found in many different areas and segments of our culture, and, perhaps, even in our personalities. A glance at the various types of things and ideas that have been borrowed is rather startling. For instance, plants domesticated by American Indians furnish almost half of the world's food supply today (Driver 1961:584). A few of the better known plants include "Irish" potatoes, corn, beans, squash, and sweet potatoes. Among drugs and stimulants, tobacco is the most widely diffused of the plants borrowed from the American Indian. Of the many native American drugs which are found in modern pharmacology, the best known are coca in cocaine and novocaine, curare in anesthetics, cinchona bark as the source of quinine, ephedra in ephedrine for clearing sinuses and nasal passages, datura in pain-relievers, and cascara in laxatives (Driver 1961:587).

We acquired the woolen poncho, the parka, and moccasins from Indian cultures. The commercial cottons used today are derived principally from the species cultivated by American Indians, and thus native American varieties of cotton supply much, if not most, of the world's clothing needs at the present time (Driver 1961:589).

American Indian music had a decisive influence on some American composers. In 1939 one composer commented, "Many devices of the ultramodern composers of the present day have long been employed by Indians—unusual intervals, arbitrary scales, changing tune, conflicting rhythm, polychoral effects, hypnotic monotony" (Skilton 1939). The composers turned to the Indians. Edward McDowell composed the famous *Indian Suite* in 1891–1892. And in the early 1900s a number of composers visited Western reservations, gathering and arranging melodies and borrowing themes (Hallowell 1957:207).

Literature in the United States also reflects the influence of the Indian. Most readers are familiar with Longfellow's *Hiawatha* and James Fenimore Cooper's *Leather-Stocking Tales*. The hero of Cooper's novels, Natty Bumppo, became the epitome of pioneer character, combining the best personality traits of both Indians and Whites (Driver 1961:610). Cooper was the first novelist to dramatize the psychological consequences of the acculturation process (Jones 1952).

It is obvious today that the present-day Indian has taken over large areas of the Euro-American culture. But we can see from this brief sketch of the contributions of Indians to modern life that parts of their culture are alive today in the American way of life. The borrowing has been a two-way process.

How are new ideas resisted?

Germany: How Does Tradition Persist?

The Bauern ("peasants") of Bürgbach, Germany are a class segment of a larger population that contains an urban center—actually a metropolitan capital. They are tradition-oriented and rural, though they have accepted many technological changes. They produce through cultivation most of their own food, but produce also for a market. Land is largely inherited rather than purchased and the people have strong ties of sentiment to it. The community is subordinately dependent upon a wider polity. Therefore that segment of Bürgbach to which I will devote major attention fits the criteria of "peasant" proposed by many who have written on the subject (Spindler 1961:2).

In spite of the new influences and pressures for change introduced by the many refugees from former German areas, by commuters from the city, and by the introduction of factories, the traditional way of life of the grape-growing German peasant persists. The traditional patterns coexist with those of modern urban, industrial, Western Germany.

Bürgbach today is a village of contrasts. The most important structure in the village, as seen from the rim of the valley above, is the ancient Stiffskirche, the Evangelical church, built in 1533 on the site occupied by a chapel probably built in the 7th century. Scattered among the lesser houses are the Grossenhäuser (great houses) of the tradition-oriented Bürgbachers—116 of them—occupied on the average by eight people, four milk cows, 15 chickens, three pigs, and one rabbit. In the center of town, in the old market area, are new stores with large plate glass windows and attractive displays. On the side of the village opposite the Stiffskirche is the new ultra-modern rectangular-spired and triangular-shaped Catholic church. Mercedes-Benz, Volkswagens, and lesser automobiles, most of them quite new and all of them shiny, course the narrow streets. Small, noisy, diesel tractors growl along, hauling ancient wagons loaded with manure from the heaping, neat piles in front of the Grossenhäuser. Occasionally a huge oxlike cow does the pulling urged along by a husky Bauer (farmer or "peasant") or his Frau. A walk down the center street will take one past a row of attractive, colorful and very modern apartment houses, a dozen or so Grossenhäuser and as many manure piles, a modern gas station and garage, with an Opel display room . . . [several] high class Gastätte catering largely to the commuters and Stuttgarters, and next to them the butcher, working on the carcass of a huge pig.

The forces for change seem overwhelming, and yet many people make their living predominantly or in substantial part from the soil, and live a way of life with marked continuity to the traditional past.

Let us look inside one of the Grossenhäuser. In the first story are the animals—the pigs, chickens, cows—behind large double doors that open to the street. An electric turnip chopper, electric apple masher, wine press, fodder cutter, electrically operated water dishes, all indicate that technical progress has arrived. The diesel tractor, rototiller, and mowing machine, confirm this observation further.

In back of this section is the door of the root cellar. Here are stored the canned fruits, the vegetables, potatoes, turnips, apples, eggs in large crocks, that the family consumes. The Bauern supply virtually all of their own food. They raise all their fruit and vegetables, grind their own wheat for bread and Küchen, press their own wine grapes, and mash their own apples for Äpfel-saft. The cows furnish milk, the chickens—eggs, the pigs—the ingredients for Würst, about the only form of meat the Bauern eat. The Bauern raise all their feed for animals—oats, barley, wheat, corn, turnips, alfalfa and timothy hay—everything excepting a protein feed concentrate fed as a supplement for higher milk production.

The Grossenhäuser are mostly quite old. Many of them were built in the 16th and 17th centuries. Their remodeling, and the electrical equipment installed in them, is not necessarily symptomatic of the destruction of a way of life, but rather may indicate a reaffirmation of its validity as it adapts to contemporary conditions (Spindler 1961:4–6).

The traditional Bürgbacher way of life persists in part due to a very tight-knit set of functional relationships existing among the various segments of the socioeconomic-cultural system. For example, the traditional, large extended family of the "Bauern" is required for the growing of wine grapes, since it is the familial, wage-free labor of this large family that makes the operation feasible. Manure is essential for fertilizing the vineyards and the only source of manure is the livestock kept in the lower part of the "Great House" of the large family, so this traditional form of house has another function. Baking bread in the bake house is only possible if a person has the necessary bundles of grapevine prunings or twigs from the vineyard land.

This traditional way of life in Bürgbach has persisted until the present (1972) partly because the changes that took place were substitutive in nature. Electric motors substitute for human power in pressing fruit for juices and milking machines substitute for the milk maid; a tractor substitutes for the ox pulling the wagon, and so forth. At present, however, major changes are occurring that are affecting the core values of the culture. An example is the process of recontouring the vineyards to combine family plots into large plots (*Flurbereinigung*). Ownership tends to concentrate in fewer and fewer hands and almost total mechanization becomes inevitable. This is part of an over all rationalization of agriculture designed to increase production at the same time that costs are lowered. This program calls for elimination of the traditional practices connected with cultivating the small family plots. These old, ritualized ways of doing things afforded great satisfaction for the Bauern, including the utilization of extended familial relationships as a source of labor, and contributed to the maintenance of the finely equilibrated system described above. One elderly woman remarked:

Where our forefathers painfully labored to build terraces to hold the soil and drainage channels to carry off the water during storms, and where they carried the earth washed down the slope back up again on their backs, now all that is gone forever. . . . and what is to keep the soil on the hillsides with the terraces gone? (G. Spindler 1973).

These traditional practices connected with growing wine grapes have been a part of her and her ancestors' way of life for centuries and there is nothing to replace them.

The situation in Bürgbach illustrates a possible paradox in the process of economic rationalization. This process may create the conditions for a new rationality that can be dangerous for successful long-term adaptation. The rationalization process occurring in Bürgbach is creating a situation where men and women tend to be alienated from the products of their labor, from each other, and from themselves—a situation where impersonal units are substituted for people. Under these conditions social and personal disorganization often occur. This process may apply to many other comparable situations where people are being forced by new circumstances to rationalize their economic systems and eliminate established, satisfying ways of doing things.

Zinacantecos: Why Does the System Still Thrive?

The modern Mayan Zinacantecos of Mexico are another example of a peasant group which has been able to maintain its special identity in spite of the effects of modernization. The highly ceremonialized religious system of the Zinacantecos has persisted despite the change from independence before the European invasion to status as a conquered people. It has survived Christian Catholic proselytizing and, in fact, has been enriched by it, for example, by borrowing religious figures and fiesta days. As Evon Vogt (1970) reports, this belief system defines, explains, and defends everything about the world for the Zinacantecos. It serves as a philosophy, cosmology, theology, code of values, and science. Thus, as long as the individual remains within this belief system and his external conditions do not change too drastically, nothing else need be "known."

Why has the Zinacantecos' belief system persisted with so many odds against it? The system requires a great deal of money. There are thirty-four religious fiesta days and each requires extensive funding. Each time a man assumes a new position in the hierarchy of religious statuses (*cargos*), he must raise money (up to 14,000 pesos). And each time a curing ceremony is needed, money is necessary. Thus the economic values of the Zinacantecos converge rather neatly with those of the Ladinos and urbanites, perforce. The Zinacantecos leased land from Ladinos and became entrepreneur-type maize farmers. They also became money lenders. The one important difference, however, between the economic behaviors of the Ladinos and those of the Zinacantecos is that the Zinacantecos do not use their surplus money for personal reasons. They pour most of their money into the ritual system. The needs of the system supersede those of the individual, and the system continues to thrive (Vogt 1970).

How do cultures influence each other?

When cultural systems come into first-hand contact with each other, the changes that occur are termed *acculturation*. As mentioned earlier (See pp. 289–290), this is a complex process and the results are not really predictable. The rate of change, acceptance, rejection, and the particular areas vulnerable to change are dependent upon a wide variety of factors. Following are some examples of situations where acculturation is taking place, with different consequences in each.

Why Do They Change?

The Greek Case The people of the village of Vasilika in modern Greece find many of the material items acquired from the city to be very convenient. When a modern and a rural group come in contact with each other, the practical appeal of convenience often plays a less important role than the appeal of prestige. The saying that "man does not live by bread alone" applies to all peoples of all times.

> For example, most of the wells in the village have no windlasses to ease the labor of bringing up the pails full of water. Women simply keep a rope attached to a pail, lower the pail into the well, and use the rope to lift it out again, hand over hand. The water level in many of the wells is low, so that drawing a pail of water is hard physical labor which must be done at least twice a day, but the women did not agitate for windlasses in the way they did for cement basins, for obviously, windlasses have no urban cachet about them. They do want running water in the homes—an urbanism—and it will, incidentally, relieve them of the drudgery of drawing so much well-water, but for a generation, the presence of a few windlasses in the village did not inspire other families to acquire them (Friedl 1962:46).

The cement basins were relatively meaningless without the windlasses but they had great prestige value. If something stands for progress and sophistication, its utilitarian value fades into the background. Another example, one man who lived in one of the poorest houses in the village had one naked light bulb hanging in the center of his small room. But he did have electricity. When he returned from a village that did not have electricity he said, "I couldn't stay there more than a day. They had no electric light, and I cannot live like that any more. I have become European" (Friedl 1962:46).

Another reason for the acceptance of new items from the city is the rivalry that exists among Vasilika's families. "If one family with urban connections has something new, other families make an effort to get the same thing. One of the effects of the process is that some families whose incomes barely enable them to subsist sometimes use their meager cash resources on plastic tablecloths or new clothes, as a token of their participation in the battle for prestige" (Friedl 1962:46–47).

In Palau   When the Palauans came in contact with the Americans on their islands after World War II, they had no built-in antagonisms toward accepting change. Throughout their entire history they had welcomed economically efficient innovations introduced from the outside world, even though they feared making changes originating from within the culture. They seemed to lack confidence unless they had a good working model to copy. The Palauan views the foreigner as having great prestige and power and has been quick to adopt many customs of diverse origins. Palauan culture is a compound of Trukese, Yapese, English, Spanish, German, Japanese, and American and has been influenced by New Guinea and India (Barnett 1960:16).

The receptivity of the Palauans has been costly. In large measure the result is a deep sense of inferiority. Most foreigners have contributed to this sense of inferiority, but the Japanese were the most systematic in reinforcing it during their administration, when they pursued a policy of forced acculturation:

> They taught school children that they were congenitally inferior to the Japanese and could never hope to match them in spirit or intelligence. True, Palauans are powerful and cunning, but so are animals. The children had no reason to question this doctrine and they were witnesses to its social consequences. Except for the few taken into Japanese homes as servants, they and their parents were treated with contempt. They were not allowed to enter Japanese homes unless, in the exceptional case, they were seated at the threshold on a mat to protect the floor. In mixed groups in public places the Japanese held their noses, objecting to the odor of coconut oil. On boats and buses they were segregated (Barnett 1960:16).

District rivalry has been intense in Palau with a continuous threat of a flare-up over some political or prestige issue. The Americans had an idea that a central club house, built cooperatively by the Palauans, would inspire a feeling of unity and pride that would override the limits of district, village, and family loyalties. The idea had first to be sold to the Palauans in such a way that it would seem to have been their own. The Palauan system still functions at its best under the drive of pride and the excitement of competition (Barnett 1960:35). In engineering the acculturative process, the Americans stimulated, advised, and encouraged, with an understanding of the Palauan compulsion to succeed and excel. Thus the community center was completed in a little over two months, which astonished the Palauans and Americans alike. When Palauans saw the project as a contest, their enthusiasm was unbounded:

> Few Palauans grasped this lofty design, but many of them wanted a building of their own in the town of Koror, the hub of economic and political action; and the rest could not afford to let themselves be excluded. When several contenders for American patronage leaped at the chance to support the project, their adversaries did likewise. Planning committees were formed and their meetings well attended out of fear of losing influence or a chance to propose something. Craftsmen who carved and painted the thematic panels on the gables of the club house vied for public praise of their skill and at the same time selected episodes and heroic acts for portrayal that proclaimed the glory of their clans and districts. Even ordinary people, old and young, claimed the right to contribute some special material or service and receive credit for it. Some villages took pride in supplying a specialty, such as a kind of timber or a thatching material, for which their localities are famous. Old men, reviving their ability, braided the coconut fiber used throughout the building to hold its parts together and made thousands of fathoms of cordage and rope. They also made many of the hundreds of strips of thatch necessary to cover the immense roof of the building. Women and children were kept busy with the specialties reserved for them—feeding the men and cleaning up (Barnett 1960:36).

Twenty-five Years Later The people of Manus, who live in the Admiralty Islands of the South Pacific, were restudied by Margaret Mead after twenty-five years. When she first studied the group over twenty-five years ago she lived in and studied a community built on stilts out in the shallow salt lagoons and between the islands—a community constituted of a people who had no comprehension of the world outside, knew no writing, handled the problem of social interaction and reciprocal obligation in terms of kinship, who wore G-string and grass skirts, and whose economic system Margaret Mead described as a "treadmill." When Dr. Mead returned, twenty-five years later, she was ". . . greeted by a man in carefully ironed white clothes, wearing a tie and shoes, who explained that he was the 'council,' one of the elected officials of the community" (Mead 1956:22). She was handed a letter, signed by the locally chosen school teacher, a man who had been a babe in arms when she was there before, that asked her if she would help him teach the children. A few days after her arrival she was asked by another elected official to help work out a list of rules for modern child care—feeding, discipline, sleeping, and so forth. When she explained that her comments would be based on the latest thinking of the International Seminar on Mental Health and Infant Development, held at Chichester, England, in 1952, under the auspices of the United Nations, this man, who was born into what was then a primitive "stone age" society, *understood what she was saying.*

The anthropologist had left an isolated, nonliterate people twenty-five years earlier. She returned to find them moving rapidly and purposefully into the stream of modern world culture. She found them searching for education that would permit them and their children to participate more fully in the modern world. And this occurred in one lifetime!

Why did this happen? Over a million American men poured through the Admiralty Islands during World War II. They set up sawmills in the bush to make lumber to build barracks. They knocked down mountains, blasted channels, leveled airstrips. And they treated the Manus men who worked for and with them more like individuals than they had been treated by other contacts. The American men furnished a special kind of model for the Manus, and, for whatever the reasons, they were generous. The Americans also brought with them a special and powerful version of our highly technological material culture.

In using Americans for their model, the Manus literally threw away their old culture and attempted to recreate a way of life modeled after the American way as they interpreted it. Anthropologists had long thought that rapid change was inevitably disruptive. Dr. Mead suggests the opposite: if change is desired by an entire group and if it affects all of the culture and its parts simultaneously, there may be less social disorganization and personal maladjustment than if changes occur segmentally over a long period of time.

There is, however, one great danger in this rapid change for the Manus. They believe that by modeling themselves in the image of American society they can participate fully in a world dominated by the Western way of doing things and receive benefits from this participation. If they find that this is not the case, as so many other peoples have discovered in the last century, they too will become discouraged and demoralized. As George Spindler stated it:

> Successful reformulation in the adaptation to the impact of industrial-urban civilization on the part of the "backward" peoples of the world can only occur when the fruits of participation are made freely and fully available to them. This is not merely a sanctimonious generalization. It is a conclusion based on good evidence (G. Spindler 1958:129).

Why Don't They Change?

Ethnocentrism and Boundary-Maintaining Devices   Americans and Germans and others with super efficient technology are not the only ones who consider themselves superior, possessing the only "right" way of thinking about the world and of coping with their environment. Likewise most primitive peoples, before extensive contact with the Western world, were extremely ethnocentric, thinking that they were *the* people and their ways the only correct ones for dealing with the environment. These feelings make people unreceptive to the ideas and methods used in other cultures to solve problems. Extreme ethnocentrism is a boundary-maintaining mechanism which protects the group from outside influences. A Latin high school teacher summed up the ethnocentric attitude of Anglo-Americans in south Texas:

> The Anglo-American sees himself as the most important being that ever lived in our universe. To him the rest of humanity is somewhat backward. He believes his ways are better, his standard of living is better, and his ethical code is better although it is of minor importance. In fact, he is appalled to find people on the face of the earth who are unable or unwilling to admit that the American way of life is the only way (Madsen 1964:7).

The term for Eskimo (*Innuit*) means "the people," as does the word *Denè* used by the Navajo to describe themselves. Hart and Pilling describe the ethnocentrism of the Tiwi:

> Thus, the word "Tiwi" did not mean "people" in the sense of all human beings, but rather "we, the only people," or the chosen people who live on and own the islands, as distinct from any other alleged human beings who might show up from time to time on the beaches. This exclusion of outsiders from real "us-ness" and hence from real "human-ness" was continued when

the Europeans began to arrive in the early nineteenth century, and certainly as late as 1930 the Tiwi continued to call and think of themselves as Tiwi, *the* people, and to use other words for all non-Tiwi, whether they were mainland aborigines, Malay fisherman, Japanese pearl-divers, French priests, or British officials, who penetrated into their exclusive little cosmos (Hart and Pilling 1960:10).

Ethnocentrism coupled with geographic isolation makes a rather effective barrier to change.

The Nilgiri Tribes   The tribes of the Nilgiri Hills in South India furnish examples of the kinds of barriers to change that can occur as a result of boundary-maintaining devices. The tribes live in constant and close contact with each other and yet have little or no effect on each other's culture.

How can this be? The tribes themselves were isolated for centuries from the Hindus of the lowlands due to the steepness of the hills and the climate of the plateau. So the Nilgiri folk, made up of four separate tribes, formed an isolated group living in economic and social symbiosis. The Todas were a pastoral people, the Badagas agriculturalists, the Kotas artisans, and the Kurumbas food gatherers and sorcerers. David Mandelbaum, who lived with and observed the interaction of the groups, offers several reasons why so little mutual acculturation went on among these people. For one thing, he writes, ". . . all of Toda life had to do with the buffalo herds. Kota religion and interest centered about the smithy. Badaga life was engrossed with the welfare of the crop. Each group had a different focus of interest to which the other societies could contribute little" (Mandelbaum 1941:12–20). But it is the nature of the social intercourse, he continues, that forms a strong barrier to acculturation and borrowing between members of the separate tribes:

Perhaps more important is the nature of social intercourse. Kurumbas are often called from their jungle homes to minister to Kotas and Badagas. Their magical services are indispensable. In the practice of their profession, Kurumbas may have occasion to call on their Kota clients several times a week. Yet whenever a Kurumba comes into view, the word flashes through the village, women and children run for the safety of home, cower inside until the Kurumbas have gone. All transactions between Kota and Kurumba take place outside the village limits, rarely is a Kurumba allowed within the home confines of another tribe.

In like manner, Kota musicians have to be present at all major Toda ceremonials; yet if the band comes too close to a dairy, the place is polluted and can only be resanctified by elaborate purificatory rituals. So it goes for the relations among all the tribes. Although contact was frequent, social intercourse was confined to a fixed number of narrowly defined activities. Any intimate contact, of a kind which would allow members of one group to mingle freely with another, was stringently tabooed.

A third bar to intertribal diffusion is the matter of prestige symbolism. A unique tribal trait tends to be interpreted as a symbol of group status. Any attempt to imitate it by another group is violently resisted. For example, Badagas wear turbans, Kotas do not. When a few Kotas once took to wearing turbans, the Badagas felt that the Kotas were getting above themselves. Some of the Badagas ambushed and beat up the Kota offenders, tore off their head-gear, and effectively blocked the borrowing of this trait (Mandelbaum 1941:20.)

The boundary-maintaining devices used by these tribes were unique and effective: the spreading of fear of the sorcerer (a member of the out-group); the emphasis on symbols of prestige for each group with controls exercised against the "imitator"; calling upon the canons of religion to keep the outsider from "polluting" the sacred dairy.

Minority Groups: Shall We Remain Apart?

Some groups self-consciously decide to remain apart from the larger soci-eties in which they live. They use some of the boundary-maintaining processes described. Two of these groups, the Gypsies of Spain and the Hutterites of the United States and Canada, are good examples. They have been so successful in maintaining their identities that they (especially the Hutterites) are often used as models for others, including some modern youth who are attempting to set up alternative societies.

The Gypsies The Gypsies have been able to survive as a cohesive group, flouting the laws of their host country and accepting only new ideas or artifacts which serve their interests. After being banished by state authorities and excommunicated by the clergy of central Europe, France, and Italy by 1447, they migrated to Spain. Their antireligious attitudes, petty thievery, and methods of duping the non-Gypsy brought them into disfavor with the general populace. Harsh laws were enacted against them in Spain but:

> Throughout the long history of sixteenth, seventeenth, and eighteenth cen-tury law in Spain, it appears that the Gypsies' response to all laws directed at their control was marked by characteristic indifference or, at best, by short-lived, superficial adaptation to their conditions; the need to outwit the hunter becoming no more nor less than part and parcel of the whole round of Gypsy life. Cut off, then, from other European countries which had legis-lated against them, protected by influential friends and the bribable state of Spanish justice, sheltered by wild terrain, and developing to the highest degree their own capacity for resistance, the Gypsy had yet to be tamed or made captive by Spanish law (Quoted in Quintana and Floyd 1972:21).

The basic values of a people, which are expressions of how they view themselves, offer clues to their propensity for survival as a distinct group. One of the basic values held by the Gypsies is their strong belief in their ethnic superiority to non-Gypsies. In their origin myths, Gypsies claim to be descendants of kings and dukes (originally from Egypt). Gypsies consider themselves separate from peasants and, like the noble, believe that to work for the sake of work is to be unworthy of the dignity of man (Quintana and Floyd 1972:45).

> Through his belief in Gypsy superiority—the individual comes to view *himself* as hero. Although he lives on the fringes of history, he lives there as a hero in his own eyes, proud and aloof (Quintana and Floyd 1972:114).

Another strong value held by the Gypsies is the importance of obeying Gypsy law, and these laws are all aimed at maintaining the Gypsy culture in a hostile environment.

> Close examination of these dictates (Gypsy laws) revealed that they stressed, in the main, the maintenance of Gypsy separateness from non-Gypsy populations. The first, for example, enjoined the Gypsy not to live with non-Gypsies, as well as to conform to all aspects of the Gypsy way of life. The second, directed primarily at Gypsy women, discouraged marriage with non-Gypsies, and underlined the marital responsibilities of Gypsy women, complete faithfulness to their husbands being the foremost among them (Quintana and Floyd 1972:34).

Gypsies who break laws (for example, stealing from another Gypsy, violating a Gypsy woman, or revealing tribal secrets) are summoned to appear before the tribunals for judgment of their crimes. The ultimate and most dreaded punishment for breaking a law is temporary or permanent banishment from the tribe.

The Gypsies have self-consciously created an "image" that would affront non-Gypsies in the dominant Western cultures. It includes elements such as petty thievery, begging, claims to occult powers and superiority, plus unconventional dress and life styles. An anthropologist and an ethnopsychologist, who spent parts of many years with the Gypsies of southern Spain, sum up some of the dynamics involved in retaining the Gypsy identity:

> Rejecting values of the urban, technological world (thrift, serious attitudes toward work and responsibility, cooperation, science) he clings tenaciously to his concept of freedom, "alegría" fatalism. . . . Confined as he is to his own closely knit group, he holds the values of the *payo* (non-Gypsy) in contempt and, therefore, is not significantly affected by them. The cohesiveness of Gypsy society facilitates self-acceptance and a strong sense of identity. . . . Highly perceptive, his survival dependent upon accuracy in judgment, the Gypsy has come to excel at sizing up the *payo* in the service of his own interests. Fearful of solitude, he has clung to the society of which he is a product (Quintana and Floyd 1972:114).

And, regarding the Gypsies' attitude toward changes taking place around him, the same authors write:

> Plugged into the changing world, the Gypsy with few exceptions remains traditionally *not* future oriented, looking instead to the present or past for directionality. He rarely asks, "Where am I going?" in the sense of transforming his life style. In many ways he wants to "stay put," borrowing from those around him only those things which he perceives as relevant to the Gypsy way. His materialistic bent tends to be misleading; the television set does not replace face-to-face communication in his society, his world of things remains subordinated to his world of persons (109).

> *The Hutterites* Hutterites view the world dualistically. The carnal nature is temporal and passing and brings death to man. By contrast, all who are "born of Christ" are ruled by the spiritual nature, which is eternal. . . . The two kingdoms are separate and each must go its separate way. It follows that Hutterites aim to live separate from the (carnal) world with their loyalties rooted in the spiritual. Separation is ordained by God, says Rideman (quoted in Hostetler and Huntington 1967:8).

The Hutterites, unlike the Gypsies, separated from the "carnal" world and the medieval Protestant church in the sixteenth century for religious purposes. They were an Anabaptist group, founded in Moravia, which wished to establish a Christian type community where private property would be abolished. They, like the Gypsies, are visibly distinct in their pattern of dress and way of life.

Two researchers who lived with the Hutterites (see Hostetler and Huntington 1967:95) describe their religious doctrine of separation from the world as a most effective means for maintaining the group's identity. Concerning their attitude towards those around them, one colony spokesman said: "A good neighbor is one we never see, talk with or help back and forth, or that never comes on the place." Further, the Hutterite colonies are self-sufficient economically, with strong ethnocentric attitudes concerning their way of life. The Hutterites' segregation is viewed as intolerable by the larger society. It aids in the spreading of myths and falsehoods about their communal life but "the persecution and dislikes expressed by outsiders tend to strengthen the internal cohesion of the colony" (Hostetler and Huntington 1967:96).

Aside from disliking their segregation, neighboring farmers fear their seemingly unfair economic competition and rapid expansion in an area. In some areas, these fears have led to restrictive laws regulating the acreage and location of the colonies. In one area a control board must decide whether or not it is in the public interest to permit the sale of land to Hutterites.

Throughout history, persecutions of the Hutterites, like those of the Gypsies, have been long and continuous. In 1557 Hans Kral, an imprisoned Hutterite preacher, placed in the stocks for 37 weeks in Tyrol, wrote:

> My shirt decayed on my body. There was not a single thread left of it except for the collar. I did not see the sun for one and a half years. In the dark and awful dungeon I no longer knew the difference between day and night. All of my clothes rotted so that I was stark naked. The insects and the worms ate my food as soon as they smelled it (Hostetler and Huntington 1967:8).

When Kral later escaped he became a leader and, after his death, a martyr.

Persecutions in 1918 of a group of young Hutterites in South Dakota who were conscientious objectors, were just as barbaric as those described in 1557. The young men were chained in a "dungeon" on Alcatraz with the warning from the guard: "There you will stay until you give up the ghost—just like the last four that we carried out yesterday" (Hostetler and Huntington 1967:9). After many beatings, standing nine hours a day with hands tied and stretched through the prison bars with their feet barely touching the floor, they were taken out dead. The Hutterites had been uncompromisingly loyal to their community and faith. Death to them was a release from the "Valley of Tears." This basic philosophy is intimately related to the ceaseless hostility directed at them from the outside world. As Hostetler and Huntington wrote (p. 95):

> Hostile acts from outsiders are taken for granted and are built into the world view. When acts of hostility do occur, they tend to function as a cohesive force, thereby integrating the structural relations of the society. When there is no "persecution" or anti-Hutterite sentiment, Hutterite leaders acknowledge a tendency toward internal disruptive patterns.

One might ask at this point, "How does this system work?" "Why do the members find martyrdom simple as a way of coping with hostility?" Partial answers lie in the strong commitment to particular religious beliefs and the socializing process which each member experiences from birth until death. It begins with the infant:

> In infancy the child learns to enjoy people and to respond positively to many persons. After age 3 he is weaned away from his nuclear family and learns to accept authority in virtually any form. He learns that aloneness is associated with unpleasant experiences and that being with others is rewarded with pleasant experiences. During the school year he is further weaned from his family, learns more about authority, and acquires a verbal knowledge of his religion. He acquires the ability to relate positively to his peer group and to respond to its demands. As a small child his universe is unpredictable, but as he matures in his peer group and takes part in colony life his universe becomes highly predictable. He learns to minimize self-assertion and self-confidence and to establish dependence on the group. As a member of a categorically defined age set the young child learns explicitly when and whom to obey (Hostetler and Huntington 1967:112).

The "community" in a sense becomes reified:

> The community is more important than the individual and governs the activity of the individual, and the corporate group has the power to exclude and to punish, to forgive and to readmit. . . . self-assertion by the individual against the group is not permitted (Hostetler and Huntington 1967:12).

What happens if an individual balks or questions the system?

> Disobedience to the community means forsaking the commandment of God, and sin must be punished in proportion to its severity. Unconfessed sins will be held against the individual on the day of judgment and punishment will be meted out in the afterlife (Hostetler and Huntington 1967:12).

The fear of becoming excluded from the protective group and of being given some unknown punishment in the afterlife prohibits most from committing the sin of disobedience. And the group continues intact.

Some minority populations within larger, dominant societies resemble the Gypsies and Hutterites in their desire to retain a recognizable identity and a certain degree of separateness. Few are as successful in maintaining their boundaries, and are subject to changes in some areas of life while retaining their traditional character in others.

A Contrast

The Navajo and the Zuni Indians, neighbors in the southwest area of the United States, contrast sharply in their tolerance potential in treating the new things and ideas introduced by contact with the Western world. Both groups had veterans returning from World War II. Each reacted differently to the innovations brought back by them, and the problems faced by each group of veterans in reintegrating were strikingly different.

The Zuni, in attempting to restrict the influence of the outside world upon their system, requested large numbers of deferments for men in religious offices when the draft began; and when the draft board asked that deferments be requested only for men who held these offices for life, the Zuni filled lifetime offices that had not been occupied for years and revived ceremonials that had become defunct. When the Zuni veterans returned, they were met with a solid front of conservatism and strong pressures were used by the priests and others to make veterans conform to the traditional Zuni norms and reintegrate into the traditional statuses and roles provided by the Zuni system. The veterans who could not conform left the community. The anthropologists John Adair and Evon Vogt, who did the research on this problem, write:

Some of the processes whereby the Zuni veterans were reintegrated into the social framework were gossip, rumor, and ridicule. An older veteran who belongs to one of the most acculturated families wanted to establish a branch of the American Legion in Zuni. It was not long before gossip to the effect that he was going to use the money collected in dues for his own ends grew into a rumor campaign. After a few meetings, indifferently attended, the project was dropped. Terminal leave pay which could be collected upon application to the War Department was rumored by some of the elders to be a method of getting Zuni men into debt to the government, and would have to be paid off by more military service. One of the veterans was seen in the village dressed in a double breasted suit. Members of the community ridiculed him and accused him of "trying to be a big shot, trying to act like a white man."

The most dreaded of all rumors is to be labeled as a witch. Peculiar behavior and aggressive action which makes the individual stand out from the community may elicit this rumor. In Zuni belief conspicuous conduct is also to be avoided because it attracts the attention of witches and their malevolent action. Witches are believed to be jealous of those with wealth. An informant said that he had considered opening a store in the village but had not done so because he was afraid of those "jealous people" (1949:550–551).

We can see the use of boundary-maintaining mechanisms in the form of social control—the effective use of gossip, rumor, ridicule, and of the dreaded label "witch."

In contrast to the Zuni, hundreds of Navajo males enlisted, few deferments were requested, and there was no increase in ritual activity to keep newly made religious functionaries at home. Drs. Clyde Kluckhohn and Dorothea Leighton, who did extensive field work among the Navajo, commented that the Navajo did not exhibit the same reluctance to go to war as did the Hopi and that there was interest on the part of the Navajos in the events in Europe and Asia even before the United States actively entered the war. Navajos, who read no newspapers and spoke no English, would constantly ask: "What is happening in the war?" "Who is winning, the Germans or the English?" (Leighton and Kluckhohn 1947:103).

When the Navajo veterans returned, they were greeted with interested curiosity. Pressures on them to conform were not intense, and some have become active innovators in their culture since then. One of the conservative Navajo leaders remarked: "The way I feel about these soldier boys is that most of them can already speak English and write. It looks like they should go on with the white people and learn more and more and then lead their people" (Leighton and Kluckhohn 1947:104).

Whenever the social scientist is attempting to explain why a group of people do or do not change when they come in contact with another independent group, he must take into account the type of cultural system of each group as a variable of extreme importance. The Zuni have resisted change for centuries. Their system is tightly organized, inflexible, and with strong emphasis on cooperation, the community presents a united front. The Navajo, in contrast, have adapted to new environments and peoples in their history of migration from the north to the southwest. Their system is more flexible, more loosely organized. And the individuals are individu-

alists, with each household living separate and with considerable distance
between it and the household of its nearest neighbor. Clyde Kluckhohn,
in analyzing Navajo values and themes, integrating principles underlying
the cultural system, has described Navajo social relations as being premised
upon a "familistic individualism" which permits a relatively large area of
freedom for the expression of individuality in Navajo society (Kluckhohn
1949:367). By contrast, Benedict describes Zuni culture as one with strong
communal orientations which demand a high degree of social and cultural
conformity on the part of the individual (Benedict 1934). It becomes rather
clear that a better understanding of the cultural system of a people and of
the personalities in the system could enable one to predict what the attitudes
towards innovations might be.

How Do You Introduce Change?

With Their Support Change agents sent out by a country that is interested for one reason or another in helping to shape the future course of
events for people in another land have learned by bitter experience that the
only kinds of introduced changes that become effectively incorporated into
a culture are those that have the support of the people themselves or their
recognized representative. The use of the King of Swaziland (Sobhuza) is
an example of how changes can be more easily introduced by using recognized channels of communication and control.

> . . . the position of the Swazi king *cum* paramount chief has long been the
> focus of opposing systems. In the first period of contact the whites exag-

gerated his rights and powers to obtain concessions for themselves; later, they curtailed the substance of traditional authority but used the king indirectly to act as the primary agent in bringing about his people's acceptance of innovations. At present, Sobhuza is still expected to be the first to improve his stock, use new agricultural techniques, employ demonstrators, encourage creameries and dairies, patronize schools and hospitals, and so forth. Until the early forties, he alone had regular and formal contacts with senior members of the white administration; these gave him a greater semblance of power than he actually wielded, with the result that his subjects tended to blame him for legislation for which he was in no way responsible and about which he was sometimes not even consulted. He and his mother were the only two members of the traditional hierarchy who were paid by the administration. He received 1250 pounds sterling (approximately 3000 dollars) per annum and she 500 pounds sterling (approximately 1200 dollars), which amounts were obviously inadequate for any national undertaking but described by some Swazi as an attempt to "buy the kings" (Kuper 1963:40).

As can be seen in this example, even when administrators seek the support of the people in introducing change, many complex problems can arise. In this case the administrators, in working through a figure of high status such as the Swazi king, inherited a myriad of problems inherent in the system itself. Many people who had long been dissatisfied with the system now had the courage to criticize the king who had lost some of his power.

Another example of the importance of co-opting a people into the administration of their own affairs is the case of a Guadalcanal society. The administration (British) experimented at first by appointing an ex-police officer as the representative in each series of villages. But some of these men, relying upon official backing, degenerated into petty despots. Ian Hogbin, who studied this group, states:

At length, towards the end of the war, a determined step was taken to return to the past and give the natives a greater say in the running of their affairs. Recognition was given to the principal men of the smaller social units such as the hamlets or subclans, and in each administrative subdistrict patrol officers encouraged them to set up a council and a court. Today the councils consist of those elders recommended for appointment by the Government representatives. He presides over the meetings, which he calls regularly at intervals of about a month, when matters of common policy are discussed and principles established for transmission to the European district commissioner.

The Government representative also sits as president of the court, a body consisting of himself, a clerk, and six elders nominated by the council. It deals with criminal, civil, and native customary cases. Serious crimes (such as murder, rape, and incest) must be brought before a magistrate or judge, but the villagers have jurisdiction in matters where adequate punishment does not exceed a fine of 14 dollars (5 pounds sterling) or imprisonment for one month. Similarly, in civil disputes the property in question must have a maximum value of 28 dollars (10 pounds sterling). From decisions in customary cases there is no appeal, but persons found guilty of a crime or a civil offense, if dissatisfied with the verdict, can appeal to the district commissioner for a new trial (1964:96).

The intelligent use of the established native system proved to be successful.

Getting There First   There are many ways of working through a system to introduce change. Father Gsell, who was a Catholic priest among the Tiwi of northern Australia, thought of a truly ingenious method of saving female infants from the barter system. The currency in Tiwi society is women. Men compete for prestige and influence through their control over women. Old, wealthy men buy newborn female infants and speak for female infants before they are born. Thus in most cases a man is unable to have a wife until he is past middle age and has acquired enough material wealth to buy one. Father Gsell, realizing that many of the aspects of the old pattern of Tiwi life had to be abandoned before he could make the Tiwi into Christians, decided to enter the system, observing the rules of the game, and "acquire wives" for himself. The following is the account of what happened:

> To the missionaries, polygamy was sinful and could not be part of the new Tiwi life. Prenatal and infant bestowal had to be abolished. Marriages should be between agemates and should be arranged freely and solely by the couple involved. Such changes were the crux of Father Gsell's program, and the story of how he went about it has run in many a Sunday supplement in the cities of Australia under the title "The Bishop With 150 Wives." Father Gsell did not try to convert or drastically change the behavior of the older Tiwi; he believed that they were too set in their ways. Rather, he built toward a distant day by working among the younger generation. When infant girls became widows, he purchased them from their fathers. Men with young widowed daughters and those with spare young wives sold such girls for axes, flour, tobacco, cloth, and trinkets. Such "Blackies," as they became affectionately called, lived in the convent with the French (and later Australian) sisters. When such a girl reached the age of 18, she was asked to choose one of the young single men for her husband. For his part in this excellent deal which provided him with a wife long before he would get one under the old tribal system, the young man had only to promise that he would never take another wife. Such a wedding was not a Mass, for neither party was Catholic. However, the children born of this new union were baptized and reared as Catholics. Later, a few of the girls who had been sold to Father Gsell before they were ten went through confirmation as did their youthful fiances. The first nuptial Mass between two such Tiwi took place in 1928 (Hart and Pilling 1960:102).

Unlike the introduction of the steel axe to the Yir Yiront of Australia, described earlier in this chapter, this innovation was not abruptly disruptive.

The New People   "The New People" of the Lugbara of Uganda illustrate another method of introducing change by working in and through the

system itself. Government officials and missionaries have made it possible
for young men to attend schools, live in Western houses and adopt a Western way of life. And yet these men still retain their strong ties with Lugbara
society.

> Labor migration and cash-crop growing, together with the appearance of
> chiefs and traders, have led to the last development, that of an incipient new
> class of people who gain their livelihood by earning wages or selling produce
> instead of by traditional subsistence farming. These are the "New People"
> (*'ba odiru*). The more important New People are the educated and semi-
> educated protégés of the government and the missions, and the wealthier
> traders. They are men who come into contact with Europeans and other
> foreigners. They attend the same schools; they live in brick houses and adopt
> a Western way of life; their families intermarry and many of them have ties
> with similar people outside Lugbaraland. These men are Lugbara and there-
> fore have intimate ties with Lugbara society, but as New People their loyal-
> ties are to members of their class, as well as to members of their own line-
> ages and families. The leaders of this class provide a new example for the
> aspiring younger men who can earn money from labor migration or cash-
> cropping. The traditional ideal of slowly becoming a respected elder by
> merely growing old and acquiring lineage seniority, a necessarily slow proc-
> ess, is giving way to that of acquiring power and position outside the lineage
> system. To achieve this a man needs wealth, education, perhaps a job with
> the government or missions, and a willingness to deny many of the tradi-
> tional ties with lineage and family. Many—perhaps most—of these men
> have seen southern Uganda as labor migrants, and the elder among them
> were soldiers in the second world war and saw countries outside East Africa.
> They consider themselves to be the vanguard of social and political progress.
> The older people who see modern developments in a different light—as
> stages in the progressive and regrettable destruction of Lugbara culture—
> call them *Mundu* and bewail their growing importance. But the older people
> are dying out and the New People are clearly the men of the future (Middle-
> ton 1965:91–92).

By furnishing models for the young Lugbara males, these New People are
paving the way for a simpler transition from old to new. They have successfully bridged the gap between Lugbara society and the new Western-type
social order and have *realized the rewards* of the new society. Thus they
furnish a most ideal kind of example for the Lugbara youth.

What Happens to the Systems in Contact?

The Sequence Despite the Manus case, cultures adapting to each
other do not often suddenly change and turn into new, unrecognizable systems. The process of adapting is usually long and slow and occurs through
complex processes of syncretizing, selecting, reinterpreting, and rejecting. In
some cases this process of progressive adjustment results in a rather unique
third culture. This happened in Mexico after hundreds of years of adjusting
between the Indians and the Spaniards, so that a common culture synthesizing elements from both has emerged.

Occasionally the cultures in contact just do not adapt to each other and each retains its traditional autonomous system (Social Science Research Council Summer Seminar on Acculturation 1954). Examples of this type of adjustment would be the caste system of India, or the Nilgiri Hill tribes in India described previously.

Some interesting and sometimes creative forms of synthesizing often occur. One example of syncretism—the Afro-Brazilian religion—was described earlier in this chapter. Another instance of syncretism concerning a mixture of Swazi (South African) and Christian elements occurred when the sister of the deceased Queen Mother *had* to secure the "tickets across Jordan" before the traditional funeral service could proceed:

Largely because of tribal status and a vested interest in polygyny, Swazi male aristocrats have tended to resist conversion from the ancestral cult, but their mothers and wives have been more responsive. The Methodists were the first to establish a mission in Swaziland. The late Indlovukati Lomawa was a recognized supporter of the church, though the National Council ruled that full conversion—including the clothing in which it could be demonstrated— was incompatible with the ritual duties of her position. She was particularly sympathetic to the Zionist Separatist church, whose charismatic local leader had converted close members of her natal family, and, at the same time, had acknowledged the claims of hereditary kingship exercised by her son, the Ingwenyama. When she died, she was buried according to custom away from the capital in a former royal village, so that her son would not be weakened by contact with death or the dead. At her funeral—which her son was not permitted to attend—various church officials paid their respects. Despite the fact that leading councilors tried to follow traditional practices, the entire mortuary procedure was interrupted for a few hours when her sister, who later succeeded to the position of queen mother, found that the church membership cards of the deceased (described as her "tickets across the Jordan") had been left behind at the capital. These were fetched and placed beside the dead woman in a wooden coffin that had been specially shaped to hold her body which was bound in fetal position and wrapped in a shroud of black cowhide (Kuper 1963:67).

The sermons of the Christian minister had far more effect upon the Swazi ladies than the traditional Swazi councilors could have predicted.

Sometimes substituting and equating new but similar ideas and practices for the old does not work. An example of this occurred when the missionaries in Swaziland did their own interpreting:

At the same time 90 percent of the schools in Swaziland are mission controlled, and mission institutions are by definition opposed to traditionalist values. The conflict between Christian churches and the Swazi state is producing a cleavage in the Swazi people between Christians and traditionalists, a cleavage that does not necessarily coincide with the division between the educated and uneducated. In 1936 Sobhuza attempted to bridge the gulf by suggesting the introduction of a modified age-class system in all the schools. The idea, investigated by anthropologists, met with the approval of the (unorthodox) head of the local administration, but the missionaries, who obviously could not support a system directed by a polygynous king, head of a tribal religion, offered the Pathfinder Movement (Black Boy Scouts) instead. Sobhuza's scheme was finally applied in three schools and maintained and financed by the Swazi nation itself. For various reasons, however, it failed to achieve a unity—which the Swazi state itself no longer represented (Kuper 1963:56).

The introduction of the Pathfinder Movement could not be equated with the plan of Sobhuza, the chief. It lacked the necessary "binding quality" since it did not originate from the people themselves.

When Systems Are in Conflict

What do present-day Europeans and Nyoro expect of chiefs? As elsewhere in Africa, the European officials tend to look for efficiency in tax collection, expeditious handling of court work, quick despatch of correspondence and other business. Irregularities in the handling of cash are especially con-demned, as are drunkenness and idleness. A bright and willing manner with Europeans is expected. The qualities that most Nyoro peasants look for are quite different. The traditional basis for their respect is the fact that the chiefs are the king's nominees, "the Mukama's spears." There must be chiefs, they say, for how otherwise could the country be ruled? Chiefs should be calm, dignified, and polite; they should not shout at their people or abuse them angrily. They should know their subjects and visit them often; people do not like a chief who sits in his office all day. Chiefs should be strong but not "fierce," and they should be generous and give frequent feasts and beer drinks (Beattie 1960:45–46).

The Bunyoro system is in conflict with Western culture. Even in confining the analysis to the administrative level, there is a conflict of purpose inher-ent in the two orders. And this East African kingdom is representative of many groups today who are in contact with the Western world.

The American Indian, as a small conquered minority group, has had a particularly difficult time adjusting to the conflict-laden situation. The prob-lem of adjusting and adapting to American culture has been met in a some-what different manner by each tribe. Some have fared better than others. The pueblo peoples of the Southwest have resisted influence from the out-side since the first Spanish invasions. As we saw earlier in their attitude toward the draft and their reception of the returning veteran, they have until now been fairly successful. The pueblo peoples have always (histori-cally) maintained a precarious existence within a hostile world by means of close integration of the individual into the group. All tendencies toward individuation were made subservient in favor of group conformity and a united front. Whereas superficial changes have occurred (in material cul-ture, subsistence), the ancestral modal group-designed behavior patterns still prevail. When a person from the pueblo groups does move into a non-Indian town or village, he is overwhelmed by the problem of orienting him-self to a number of unrelated institutions without the backing of his extended family (Hawley 1948:623).

A Tewa Indian, however, who is also a member of a pueblo group, fares better in adapting to the patterns found in non-Indian villages, accord-ing to Florence Hawley (1948:623). He has been more directly related to a larger and more impersonal central institution—the moiety—than to the small extended family and clans of the Hopi. Thus the depersonalized institutional structure of the American town does not contain unsurmountable psycho-logical barriers for him as it does for the people from the western pueblos.

The Navajo from the Southwest react differently to the pressures from the outside world. Their flexible, receptive cultural system has more readily ingested both ideas and material equipment from the outside. At the same time, their loosely knit social organization was more easily disrupted by outside contacts than was that of the Hopi. Their method of coping with the situation was to place a greater emphasis on the smaller social units, with an increased emphasis on individualism (Reichard 1949).

In spite of their positive attitude toward change, the Navajo have rigorously rejected the American middle-class value system. These values, expressed in the Protestant Ethic, are in direct conflict with Navajo values. The conservative Navajo are mainly interested in the here and now rather than in the future. The Navajo enjoy the religious experience and their rituals furnish a vehicle for expression of pleasurable emotions. Thus it is difficult for a Navajo to accept the austere Christian attitudes of reverence and repression of pleasurable feelings in the religious situation. To a Navajo, man is the greatest thing in the universal scheme. Thus, the idea that he is conceived in sin and must sacrifice and do penance is incomprehensible (Reichard 1949).

The Basin groups, such as the Ute, have not fared well in the acculturative situation. Living at a basic subsistence level is precarious in the old culture. When they migrate to towns, they segregate into small groups and remain apathetic. The people in the surrounding towns believe that the Indians are incompletely evolved and biologically incapable of successful participation in American culture, partly because of their marginal subsistence level and partly because of their lack of adaptation to town life. These beliefs place insurmountable barriers in the path of the Indian (Stewart 1952).

On the other hand, some groups, such as the Washo Indians of California and Nevada, made a unique kind of temporary adjustment to the impact of another culture. Unlike the Paiute raiders, the Washo had no escape. They were surrounded by ranchers and trading posts. The invading whiteman provided opportunities for the Washo who wished to take advantage, and the constant scarcity of food for the Basin groups made them ready to seize any advantage available. The farmers of western Nevada needed the Indians to harvest crops and help around the farm. A symbiotic relationship developed between individual Washo families and bunches and individual farmers. James Downs describes this relationship:

> . . . few white ranchers would let Indians starve if he knew them. Individual families and bunches began to develop close relationships with individual farmers. In the spring, the Indians drifted into the mountains to fish and hunt, but as the summer wore on, they came back into the valleys to gather what wild food was still available and to work in the harvests, hold a "gumsaba," pick pine nuts, and then set up a winter camp near a ranch or farm. If their food ran short, they could depend on the farmer to contribute a few sacks of potatoes or flour or even a side of beef for their survival. During this period many Washo began to adopt the last names of their rancher benefactors. Because Indian girls often bore the children of early ranchers, the names were often deserved. These Indian-white relationships were the basis on which many Indian families recognized their kinship to a white family. The whites, more inhibited about the sexual adventures of their ancestors, are less willing to openly recognize the relationship. But nonetheless, there is a curious unspoken recognition even today between Indian and white descendants of the same pioneer forefathers (Downs 1966:87).

But this adaptation lasted only as long as the family-run pioneering ranches were in operation. And today Washo men must compete with transient workers of all races for the agricultural work available.

The Plains Indians, likewise, found it extremely difficult to adapt to American culture. Our society could not offer compatible roles or opportunities for these socially mobile, highly competitive, and status-oriented Plainsmen. With the disappearance of buffalo hunting and warfare, the basic values of bravery, generosity, fortitude, and moral integrity were no longer operative. With the channels for securing prestige closed to them, the Plains Indians have no anticipation of manhood (Macgregor 1946).

One group, the Blackfoot Indians of Montana, have made a special kind of adjustment to the impact of American culture. After 230 years of adaptation and adjustment to change, a bicultural community has evolved, held together by special bonds. The white-oriented group is organized around basic values such as work, self-dependence, individuality, acquisitiveness, and work toward future goals. The major goal of the Indian-oriented group is to retain its ethnic identity. As the anthropologist Malcolm McFee writes of this group:

> Traditional definitions of the good person, and particularly the value placed upon generosity, persist and serve as both symbols of being Indian, and a check against the achievement necessary for full economic integration with the dominant society. This goal tends to make the Indian-oriented Blackfeet present rather than future oriented (1972).

McFee describes the bicultural community, with two distinct groups sharing a common reservation social structure:

> The past events have not resulted in tribal disorganization, but in a reorganization that accommodates the simultaneous persistence of many traditional social and cultural characteristics from both interacting societies. A large part of the tribe has adopted the culture of the dominant society and aspires to assimilate. A smaller number, for reasons already mentioned, retains more from the Blackfeet past and resists further change. The reservation social structure has changed to accommodate these contrasting points of view. The structure of a non-reservation community tends to be unilinear, with one general set of values, and one status hierarchy. But the physical and social boundaries of the reservation and the tribe incorporate two societies, and make possible a linear structure that offers a choice of alternative limitations and possibilities for adaptation. An individual, consciously or otherwise, can choose, and possibly choose again, which pattern he wishes to follow. His choice, and his acceptance and class assignment, depend upon what he brings to the situation in the way of aspirations, experiences, and capabilities (1972:76).

McFee believes that the Blackfoot example of cultural pluralism could serve as a model for American society as a whole.

The Blood Indians of Alberta, Canada, formerly a part of the Blackfoot Nation, have been able to adjust to the demands of white society rather easily in some areas, due to striking similarities in their personalities (see p. 335).

And so it goes. For each group there is a different story to be told. One of the most significant responses to the deprivation and threat to cultural continuity represented by alien dominant cultures is the *reactive movement*. Such movements take many forms. The following section includes several examples of *revitalization movements*, which are one of several forms of reactive movements.

What Are Some Ways of Coping?

The tepee meeting begins with an opening prayer outside the tepee at sundown on Saturday and ends in the early hours of Sunday morning. It is usually called by one of the members for a declared purpose. In one instance it was for collective prayer for the host's son, who had been in prison several years. In another instance it was to cure the chairman, who had suffered shock and some internal injury in an automobile accident. The family giving the meeting furnishes a prepared tepee ground, puts up the tepee and arranges cedar boughs, splits four-foot lengths of ash firewood, and provides a substantial portion of the food consumed the next day. The head of the family may or may not act as the ceremonial leader.

After the opening prayer, the leader enters first, then the rest of the assemblage. The men sit in the circle of the tepee on cedar boughs and blankets. Their wives, if present, sit in back of them, half crouched against the sloping tepee poles. The meeting is then opened by the leader, who asks the person giving it to explain its purpose. When he is finished, the leader makes appointments to the place of drum chief, cedar man, and fire tender, gives the first prayer, and explains the procedure for the night. Then the peyote is passed, first in ground and moistened form, then in solid button form. Each person may take as many as he wishes the second time, but only four the first. With this, the singing and drumming begin, each man taking the staff and gourd rattle as he sings. He is accompanied by the rapid beat of the Peyote drum—a small kettle with a head of tautly drawn tanned buckskin and an inch or two of water in the bottom. The drum is played either by a regular partner or by the man next to the singer. The drum, staff, and rattle are passed from man to man, clockwise, as each sings four songs.

In the center of the tepee ground is the carefully laid fire of clean split staves, the ashes of which are swept at dawn into the form of a dove or "waterbird." There is a half-moon altar of sand between the leader's place and the heart, with a small pedestal for the "Master" peyote, and a line drawn along the top of the half-moon's ridge to symbolize the difficult and narrow path the Peyote member must follow through life.

Christian symbols are apparent in the material structure and paraphernalia, as well as in the prayers and speeches. The tepee's poles represent Jesus Christ and the disciples. The staff is carved with crosses. The prayers and many of the songs are directed to Christ by name. The leader sometimes crosses his breast with his hand before lifting the blessed water to his lips.

The basic conception, promises, and procedure, however, are native North American, if not specifically Menomini, warped to fit the peculiar needs of the members and penetrated here and there with Christian ideas (G. Spindler 1955:83–85).

Why are these people doing this? This is a meeting of the Peyote Cult of the Menomini Indians of Wisconsin who are, in their own unique way, coping with the threat of losing their "way of life." The Peyotists have combined, in a creative fashion, Indian and Christian elements such as the cross and the drum with the "master peyote." The Peyote Cult is one of the more successful and realistic revitalization movements, which may be defined as *deliberate,* organized, conscious efforts by members of a society to construct a more satisfying culture (Wallace 1956:265). There are no spectacular miracles promised at a set time by the leaders of the cult. There is an escape from anxiety and tension offered to members of the group. The consuming of the peyote, which induces visions, while listening to the monotonous beat of the drum throughout the night, gives to the members a spirit of "oneness" with the powerful "master peyote" and each other, cleanses them of sin, and cures them of illness. It is not uncommon for a grown man to share his problems with the other members in a long speech, with tears flowing down his cheeks. This has therapeutic value for him. Of greatest importance here is the fact that each member has the group behind him, sharing, supporting, understanding.

Revitalization movements can be found in many places throughout the world—in Asia, Africa, the Pacific Islands, America. They are the reactions of peoples to stress and disillusionment resulting from contact with a dominant culture. They are successful or unsuccessful, depending upon the "realism" of the doctrine and the active opposition exerted against the group by opponents in the dominant culture (Wallace 1956:278–279).

Some of the more unrealistic and less adaptive forms of revitalization movements occurred in Africa and Melanesia. In 1856 one such movement occurred among the Xhosa of South Africa which had tragic results for the people:

The Xhosa first showed their opposition to Europeans and their culture by fighting. There were a series of "Kafir Wars." In 1856–57 came the cattle-killing. Nongqawuse, a girl of 15 or 16, reported to her uncle (a diviner) visions of men who told her that people must consume their corn, cease to plant, and kill their cattle, and then, on a certain day the ancestors would rise armed with guns and spears, and with the help of a whirlwind, Europeans would be swept into the sea. At the same time kraals would be full of cattle, and store-huts piled high with grain. Several other women and girls in different parts of the country reported similar visions. The people were also urged to destroy any material of sorcery they possessed. Many Xhosa, and a few Thembu, killed their cattle and refrained from planting. When the day first named passed without anything unusual happening excuses were made—the ancestors were waiting for those who had not yet killed. Several times the day was deferred. Eventually vast numbers died from starvation, and others, weak and emaciated, entered the Colony in search of food and work (Hunter 1936:159).

The largest number of revitalization movements in the twentieth century have arisen in Melanesia, in reaction to the pressures created by contact with a dominant Western culture. One of the most spectacular of these movements was the Vailala Madness which broke out in the Gulf of Papua after World War I. As Piddington describes this:

> This movement involved a kind of mass hysteria, in which numbers of natives were affected by giddiness and reeled about the villages. So infectious was it that almost the whole population of a village might be affected at one time. The leaders of the movement poured forth utterances in "djaman" ("German"), which were in fact a mixture of nonsense syllables and pidgin English. Sometimes these were incomprehensible, but sometimes the leaders gave intelligible utterance to prophesies and injunctions. The central theme of the former was that the ancestors would soon return to the gulf in a ship, bringing with them a cargo of good things. The leaders of the movement communed with them by means of flag-poles, down which messages were transmitted to the base where they were received by those who had ears to hear—an obvious adaptation of the idea of a wireless mast. Elaborate preparations were made to receive the ancestors, and offerings of food for them were placed in special houses under the control of the leaders (1957:739).

The prophets of the movement claimed that they were told by the ancestors to have the people abandon the old ceremonial customs, burning their bull-roarers (noise makers) and masks. The Vailala Madness, in its intense form, lasted only about three years. It was unrealistic and, therefore, ineffective in coping with the stressful situation in which the people found themselves.

In New Guinea another "Cargo" cult (the term used for cults prophesying the delivery of great wealth as part of a ship's *cargo*) resulted in unanticipated consequences. The disciples of the cult went to the mission station and presented the missionary with their myth, asking him what he thought of it. As Ward Goodenough describes the transaction:

> He did not sneer, but expressed approval of its obvious Biblical content, of the aspirations it revealed, and what it was they were trying to conceptualize within the outwardly fantastic myth. Finding that he was not hostile, they asked him if he could show them the road by which they might achieve their aspirations. By agreeing to teach them the way, he came to occupy the position of "prophet" for the revitalization movement, at least in the people's eyes. In this way he acquired considerable control over its adaptation and transformation phases. He succeeded, accordingly, in getting the several villages in the movement to revise a number of their marriage and family customs in the direction endorsed by his religious denomination (1963:314–315).

The missionary had found a way of working from the "inside" to the "out," introducing many changes in the pattern of village life which were in keeping with the aims of his mission.

What Happens to the People in These Systems?

Different Ways of Reacting So far the emphasis has been on the directly observable, manifest aspects of cultural adaptation. There is also a psychological dimension that does not change in quite the same way as these manifest cultural aspects. As traditional patterns of belief erode or break down during culture change, the personality characteristics of the people become more important, since the automatic guides to appropriate behavior and the standard solutions to problems no longer work. The people are thrown on their psychological resources to a greater extent than when the culture is stable. It will be useful to direct some attention to this dimension.

Some individuals with weakened cultural guidelines, and particularly those living in economically deprived situations, react apathetically to the changing outside world. William Friedland and Dorothy Nelkin found this to be the case among migrant workers in northeast America. The migrant worker, hostile and resentful like his deprived urban counterpart, is more dependent and, therefore, more afraid to express his needs. Thus, the authors write:

> Where participation and individual effort are required for social change, the migrant, in his position of impotence, has learned to withdraw and avoid problems, or to depend completely on others. These are the contradictions and dilemmas that confront and frustrate the efforts from within and without the system to "do something" to change migrant labor. Indeed, the norms that make life viable in the camp are useless and, in fact, disreputable from the viewpoint of the larger society: the very accommodations necessary and adaptive to the migrant labor system limit the potentiality of social change (1971:143).

The migrant laborer may be more "apathetic" than the urban ghetto dweller. Most migrants are apathetic about the war and do not initiate discussion about this or other world events. When they hear, on television programs, about riots taking place throughout the nation, the authors report, many leave the room or go to sleep (Friedland and Nelkin 1971:212).

The Spindlers have generalized about types of adaptation generated in the melee of culture change and culture conflict among American Indians, and their observations also seem to fit other situations (G. and L. Spindler 1957). One type, the native-oriented, includes the people who were raised as Indians and had only marginal contacts with the dominant American culture. They think and act Indian and speak as such in both the figurative and literal sense. They maintain the old culture in its most coherent form. There are many people living on the Hopi and other Western pueblos who fit this category. They are quite misunderstood by the average modern American. Headlines in a prominent journal recently read: "Lo, The Poor Indian: Past Blocks Path To Modern Life" (*Milwaukee Journal,* 1965:4). The columnist had no understanding of why an Indian might wish to cling to his old way of life and expressed shock at the idea of his refusing electricity.

> *Help on the Way.* The Indian's world—an impoverished, underdeveloped country in the midst of the richest nation in history—will receive 210 million dollars in aid this year from the United States Bureau of Indian Affairs, triple the bureau's budget 10 years ago. The Indian war now is against unemployment and poor education, health and housing. Some may feel that help is almost as belated as reinforcements were to Custer. But it is coming.
>
> Paradoxically, it is not always welcome.
>
> "The Indian is the only group in the country that is not trying to jump into the melting pot," said Graham Holmes, assistant commissioner of the Indian bureau.
>
> The Negro's objectives as a minority group are heard daily. The Indian does not seem to feel the Negro's goals of parity are his, but he isn't sure what his are.
>
> *Some Refuse Electricity.* Many want to be left alone with their "people"— a word one often hears in talking with Indians—with their culture, with what land they have left. In the Taos pueblo in New Mexico, tribal elders have refused to have electricity in their ancient homes.

The *reaffirmative native type* is a reactive adaptation closely related to the first. People of this type were raised Indian but experienced intensive contact with non-Indian children through years of boarding school and with off-reservation employment. For one reason or another their adaptation to American culture was blocked, and they sought refuge in the reservation to escape their punishing experiences. They have really not learned either culture fully, but often outdo the native-oriented at being "real Indians." It is from this group that the "prophets" such as the Paiute, Wovoka, arise. The largest portion of most native-oriented groups existing in contemporary reservation communities is drawn from this type.

Then there is the *transitional* type—these individuals are suspended between the modern American and Indian ways of life. They are not accepted by the dominant whites or the conservative native-oriented. They are marginal men and women, characterized by a breakdown in emotional controls which makes their behavior unpredictable. They are capable of great generosity and hospitality but are also capable of dangerous violence, particularly when drinking. Since they constitute a sizable portion of most tribes today, their psychology must be taken into account. In tribal decision making they may shift abruptly from one stance to another in an unpredictable fashion. The following statement of a transitional Menomini Indian woman expresses the confusion and the "press" arising as a result of the conflict between two cultures:

I can't go to church now. If I should die I suppose I would be buried out in that Potter's field. It always seemed kinda funny that my mother liked all those things—Indian dances and medicine—when my grandmother was a good Catholic. I don't know where I belong. I don't go to church and I use Indian cures for different things (L. Spindler 1962:80).

Some transitionals among the Comanche Indians react to the confusion and tension inherent in the transitional status by developing what they refer to as "ghost sickness," a paralysis of voluntary muscles believed to be inflicted by a ghost. E. Jones, who studied this phenomenon among the Comanche, found that the victims were individuals who had failed to adapt to white society and, finding cultural marginality unendurable, wished to reintegrate with the traditional group. Jones believes that the sickness is comparable to a hysterical conversion (Jones 1972:85–86). This is an efficient and effective disorder for the victim as he becomes visibly "Indian" and can only be cured by a native doctor. By becoming the patient of the native doctor, he indicates his faith in the ancient Comanche curing ritual and, when cured, will have his faith substantiated. In this condition, the individual is pitied by other Comanche who, in ideal Comanche form, show him generosity and kindness. And, usually, the victim has found a way out of his intolerable emotional state (Jones 1972).

Is It Always So Difficult?

There are some who find this in-between situation advantageous and feel quite comfortable in it. One Menomini woman, for example, was born of Catholic parents but chose to identify with her great-grandmother, who had a widespread reputation as a curing doctor and a witch. The woman herself soon became known as the witch. Her longing for power was a chief motivating force in her life, and she is proud of her reputation. She says:

I can cure anyone of sickness. When she (great-grandmother) died, she said, "Here's a seed, eat it and dream of medicine I know." When someone's sick, I know what's wrong. Then I go out and pick it. She said I would know what she knowed (L. Spindler 1962:80).

Many people on and off the reservation came to her for cures. With outsiders she would sometimes use a crystal ball for looking into the future and could sometimes charge large fees.

This type of adjustment to two cultures at once is not by any means unique to American Indians. Hilda Kuper describes a Swazi ruler, Sobhuza II, who is so adept at adjusting that he can readily change roles as he walks from one section of his house to another:

Very few Swazi attempt deliberately to live in both worlds at the same time. The exception to this general rule is the present *Ingwenyama*, Sobhuza II, an educated conservative, with a deep pride as well as a vested interest in the traditional culture of his people. Applying the crude cultural indices of building and clothing, we find that he is the head of the most conservative homestead in Swaziland, but that he has also bought two of the most modern houses in the country. He retains the heavy drapes and solid furniture of the original white owners in the front rooms, where he serves hard liquor, and tea from bone-china cups. The rooms at the back have acquired a more traditional atmosphere; here one sits on mats on the floor with Sobhuza's wives and drinks beer from the common bowl. Sobhuza's clothing, like his housing, mirrors a conflict of cultures. When he interviews white officials in their own offices, he wears a tailored suit and polished shoes, and when he goes visiting, he usually carries a cane and a hat. But in his own homes he dresses in cloth and loinskin and walks barefoot and bare headed with conscious majesty. Sobhuza typifies the dilemma of many a hereditary African ruler. He is a king at the crossroads—and for him there is no green light. The clash of cultures is part of a more basic conflict between two social systems: one, a small scale monarchy with a rather feudal economy, the other a colonial structure based on expanding capitalism (1963:4).

In describing the Mexican-Americans of Texas, caught in a conflict situation, William Madsen writes:

Mexican-Americans caught in the middle of the conflict between two cultures may react in one of several ways. Some retreat to the security of the conservative Mexican-American world. Some seek geographical escape by migrating to the larger cities of Texas or to California, Michigan, or Illinois. Some escape into the twilight zone of alcoholism. Some rebel and commit crimes or engage in antisocial behavior. As their numbers increase, more and more acculturated Mexican-Americans are trying to create for themselves a respected place embracing the best of both worlds (1964:109).

The reactions to the threat posed by powerful alien or dominant cultures to the continuity and integrity of less powerful cultural systems described above are adaptive or accommodative. They are attempts to somehow get along with the situation, however threatening it may be. Retreats to cultural traditions of the past, attempts to synthesize elements of the native and alien cultures, and even apathy and alcoholism are accommodations to a reality over which the adapting people have no control. During the past decade or so we have seen a new spirit of rebellion on the part of submerged minorities all over the world. The new militant power movements are assertive, not accommodative. They demand rather than adjust. Red Power, for example, in its various forms, organizes Native Americans for social, economic, and political action on their own behalf. Protest marches and delegations to the state and provincial legislatures of the United States and Canada, as well as to the federal governments in these countries, have a very different tone than did those of a decade ago. The power movements are nationalistic and, in varying degrees, separatistic. They are assertions of a separate identity and demand equal treatment and opportunity. They often involve a selective revitalization of lapsed customs in dress, food, even language, as an aspect of the assertion of identity and difference. This revitalization is not intended, however, as an escape from or avoidance of confrontation with the dominant cultural system. It is a call for recognition. Peyotism, in its accommodative form, is not likely to appeal to new generations of Native Americans, for it was never and is not now mainly directed at changing things. Movements and organizations directed at change favorable to the particular minority group are more attractive.

What If Your Personality Doesn't Fit the New System?

It seems logical to hypothesize that before an Indian (or a Mexican-American or Filipino) can become "successful" in middle-class American terms, his personality will have to match his psychological resources to the demands placed upon him by the new socioeconomic system (G. & L. Spindler 1971). We can turn to the Menomini again for some case data.

The old Menomini personality pattern "fit" the native Menomini culture with which it evolved through time. The native-oriented Menomini was passive and fatalistic, accepting whatever the Powers meted out. He was inward-oriented, cautious in his approach to the outside world. His aspiration level was low and his reaction to intellective stimuli measured and slow. The native-oriented group still lives today in the heart of the country they inhabited when first encountered by the white man—about 400 square miles of heavily timbered land in northern Wisconsin. Until very recently, the majority of the native-oriented lived by hunting and gathering and a little gardening. This group still retains the beliefs, customs, and values of the old culture—belief in the predictive value of the dream and visions, the power of the elders, the rebirth of ancestors in newborn babies in Menomini cosmology, the efficacy of Menomini medicines, the destructive effects of menstrual blood, the retaliative powers of the witch, and so forth.

Today the native-oriented group comprises only a small minority of the Menomini population,. During the process of adapting to Western culture over the past three centuries, several kinds of adaptations similar to the type just discussed have become stabilized and are represented today as actual groups in the Menomini population. There are today, besides the native-oriented group, a Peyote Cult (discussed under revitalization movements); a transitional category of marginal people who have participated in both Catholic and native-oriented religious activities; a lower-status acculturated group made up of persons who had been born Catholic and maintain this identification but participate only intermittently in services and are not members of the elite Catholic societies; and finally, the elite acculturated, composed of members who participate regularly in Catholic services and are members of the prestigeful Catholic societies which include middle-class persons from the surrounding area. All of these groups, *except the acculturated*, exhibit a recognizable Menomini psychological structure, showing signs of breakdown among Peyotists and transitionals, to be sure, but still recognizable (G. & L. Spindler 1971). The acculturated Menomini exhibit a personality structure that is radically un-Menomini and thoroughly American middle class in broad outline. Aggressive, individualistic, achievement motivated, the elite acculturated Menomini are like the other successful people in the towns surrounding the Menomini community. This personality adaptation is the antithesis of nearly everything that could be called native-oriented.

It was assumed that the same personality reformulation would be made by other American Indians in comparable situations. With this in mind, the Spindlers began research on the Blood Indian reservation in Alberta, Canada. Certain important dimensions were comparable: the Blood Indians, like the Menomini, are Algonkian speaking peoples; both groups have successful, economically well-to-do members, very poor members, and many members in between; native beliefs and customs persist among some groups in both communities. The same research techniques were used, including projective tests, life histories, and direct observation. And yet, after the initial period of fieldwork, it became obvious from the data that the successful and seemingly most acculturated Blood Indians were not very different psychologically from their less acculturated and usually less economically successful Blood brother. Why?

Certain things were comparable in the two groups, but the answer to the question as to why the hypothesis was not supported among the Blood Indians lies in the differences. Although both groups are Algonkians, one culture developed to its present form in the Plains and the other (Menomini) in the Woodlands. The Blood Indians spent a great deal of time in warfare—capturing the enemy's horses, counting "coup" (a system of points accumulated by things such as touching or capturing an enemy), and performing other deeds of bravery. Other times they were out buffalo-hunting on their spirited horses. They were aggressive, outgoing, competitive people who took delight in material achievement and, later, in trading situations.

Today most members of the Blood tribe still speak their own language—in the home, at social occasions, on the street in town, and many other traditional aspects of Blood culture survive. The Sun Dance (minus the original self-torture elements) is still performed, with the carefully guarded secrets of the men's Horn Society and the women's Mohwtokay Society. There are still medicine bundles on the reserve which are opened privately at specified times of the year with only a few relatives of the owners present, and native medicine men still covertly practice on the reserve. The "give-away" still plays a very important role in Blood society. At most important social functions (social dances, marriage ceremonies, name-taking, age-grade functions and meetings) the group involved "gives away" quantities of food, blankets, and money to persons in the assembled crowd. The more valuable gifts are given by one specified person to another, but food is distributed by the society to all present. This ritual validates the existence of the particular group. It makes public the meaning of the group. It is also a form of banking, since each donor expects the recipient to reciprocate in the future. A form of "give-away" is present at a more informal, personal level when relatives come, usually unexpectedly, to visit.

Among other traditional institutions surviving in the Blood community today are the age-grade societies. All but a few young men belong to a society with other men of their same age range who sponsor Indian-oriented social dances and "give-aways." Only a few years ago a new society was formed, called at first the "Baggy Underwear Society," as there had been a pair of heavy winter underwear on the clothesline near the house where the initial meeting was held. This name was soon changed to "Warriors." The members said that "Baggy Underwear" did not sound too good when translated into English, and, further, the men couldn't use that term in front of their in-laws. The Blood Indians still play the hand game, a traditional Indian gambling game, and still bestow Indian names upon members to signify some special event in their lives or some relationship to an animal.

The young modern Blood Indians have found a satisfying substitute for the war party of the old days in the rodeo termed the "stampede" in Alberta. Here, instead of counting coup and stealing horses, they ride bucking horses and bull-dog steers, taking great risks to win prize money. The Blood admire masculinity, and the aggressive, exhibitionistic rodeo hand becomes a model for the young Blood male, as the cattlemen and cowboys had been for the older men.

It is clear that much traditional (though modified) Blood Indian culture survives today in spite of the fact that contemporary Blood culture appears adapted to certain conditions (such as living on a reservation) that result from the impact of the white man. This cultural continuity is accompanied by the persistence of a Blood Indian personality structure that even the most successful and most acculturated Blood Indians share. The consequences of adaptation for the Blood and the Menomini are therefore very different. The latter have already lost their cultural identity, and are losing their psychological identity. The former are keeping both, to a surprising degree. Why should this be the case?

We know there are similarities and differences in the conditions to which the Blood and the Menomini had to adapt, but these factors do not seem by themselves to account for the observed outcome. The answer may lie in part in the difference between Menomini and Blood personality. The aggressive, competitive Blood personality structure is more like that of the Canadians and Americans to whom they had to adjust than that of the aggression-limiting, passive, nonachievement-oriented Menomini. The Blood, we can hypothesize, keep their identity and yet can adapt to the modern Canadian-American world without a psychological reorganization in depth because they are much like the people who live in that world. The Menomini cannot make this adaptation with the psychological resources that worked well in their traditional cultural setting so they must change more.

The Menomini and Blood cases do not in themselves permit us to generalize about the extent to which psychological restructuring is necessary or inevitable as adaptation to the demands of a dominant cultural system takes place. It appears that the answer lies in a complex set of interrelationships between the cultural system and the people involved. Among the important factors are the ways in which the psychological characteristics of the groups involved are convergent, or divergent, and the attitudes of the people toward each other.

It is also important to recognize that the new assertive power move-ments call for different psychological characteristics than many of the movements and adaptations described. It is probably easier for peoples whose personality orientations are convergent in some way, like the Blood Indians. The new Blood Indian of the generation now coming into power, is aggressive like previous ones. He has also rejected the inferior status and marks of inferiority inflicted by the colonialism, however benign, of the Canadian and provincial governments, and by the prejudice of neighboring whites. The new generation seeks to solve its own problems in its own manner, although it is secure enough to accept help. The new generation of Menomini is more militant, perhaps as a compensation for the relative mildness and nonassertive character of the older generation still affected by traditional Menomini culture.

It is not only minority groups who are adapting to changes in the world about them, and to new demands placed upon them. Young people today find themselves in much the same situation as minority groups whose original cultures were different from those of the dominant cultural system within which they had to survive.

How does the modern world change today?

Modernization and Urbanization

The anthropologist Robert Redfield posited a *continuum of change,* which was a short-cut description of the transformation of folk into urban peoples. He distinguished the folk society, at one end of the continuum, by charac-teristics such as personal, familial relationships and contrasted it to urban populations at the other end of the continuum. For the urban groups he posited a breakdown of kinship organization where social relationships be-come impersonal and superficial (Redfield 1947). The sharp delineation between what is rural and what is urban provided a useful model for ana-lyzing changing peasant societies until anthropologists found that there were many situations the model did not fit.

In using the rural-urban dichotomy, Redfield and others assumed that peasants must have established relationships with the city. However, as Eric Wolf points out, in some societies the rulers "camped" among the peas-antry, spending brief periods in the country interspersed with other periods in cities or courts. In some cases, they lived at religious centers to which the peasants brought their produce. In other areas, as in Wales and Norway, many functions of the city are dispersed over the countryside and the development of cities is weak (see Wolf 1966: 10,11).

Many terms are used to describe this complex process of change. *Urban-ization,* as commonly used, usually implies the influence of Western technol-ogy, but it need not be so limited. *Modernization* is a more general term that includes the less disruptive types of change. Some contemporary authors see rural-urban distinctions disappearing. Joel Halpern describes a "rural revolution" (1967:43).

> One of the characteristics of the modern political state appears to be the attempt to eliminate the distinction between urban and rural life. One apparent consequence is the last exodus from rural areas and the entry of technology into the countryside.
>
> It is possible to conceive of the export of trained technicians, skills, and products to villages and the incorporation of rural people into town life as resulting in the simultaneous peasantization of cities and the urbanization of villagers. The inconclusive results of present programs seem to indicate that what is actually taking place is the creation of totally new kinds of units, which are neither urban nor rural in the old meaning of the term (1967:2).

Halpern describes an example of this peasantization of the town:

> . . . initial peasantization of the towns is to a degree reflected in the partial replication of the village in the town or more frequently a part of the village in a part of the town. This situation is clearly reflected in a major modern metropolitan area such as New York City, where once in various areas the white-washed stone houses of rural Southern Italy, complete with grape arbor and small truck garden, could be seen, with perhaps a goat in a nearby lot, although most have now been modernized or obliterated by apartment houses (1967:39).

Many anthropologists studying current changes taking place in peasant villages confirm Halpern's generalizations. They do not observe a dichotomy between rural and urban phenomena. The Buechlers, in studying an Aymaran peasant community in Bolivia, viewed the rural-urban relationships as a part of a complex system in a broader spatial framework. They focused on the network of relationships existing between the village and city dwellers. The villagers who migrated to the city remain in constant contact with villagers who stayed at home. They go to local village affairs and fiestas or to help cultivate plots of land, while the village peasants stay at their relatives' homes in the city, where they sell their produce (H. & J. Buechler 1971:107). These kinds of interrelationships are common phenomena and take many forms.

Is Modernization Always Painful?

The Japanese

Aki had never visited Takashima and Jiro (a young man from the village of Takashima) had not been there for several years. When Jiro's parents expressed a wish to see their new grandchild, Aki (his city-born wife) said that it was their duty to take the child to Takashima and added, honestly enough, that she would like to make the trip. The visit was brief, and none too comfortable. Aki and Emi were well received, and Aki in her usual way was friendly and gracious. But there was an atmosphere of reserve that was especially evident when they met Jiro's more distant relatives and former neighbors. Beyond greetings, expressed in the vocabulary of country courtesy, those outside Jiro's family had found nothing to say to the visitors. The trip was Aki's first close contact with country people other than acquaintance with various maids from the country in the employ of her family and the families of friends. Like most urban Japanese, she had thought of rural residents as people apart. She found the scenery beautiful, the houses and farm plots picturesque, the food coarse, and the people quaint and timid but worthy. Jiro's ideas had become much the same, and both returned to Osaka with the secret feeling of a duty performed (Norbeck 1965:77).

Jiro had been born in the small fishing village of Takashima, yet, by the time he had finished college in the city, he could be considered urbanized. His ideas were then "much the same" as those of his city-bred wife, Aki. Nevertheless, both shared a commitment to the value of duty to one's parents, a basic Japanese value common to peasant and urban dwellers alike for many centuries.

Why has the transition characteristically been swift and nonrevolutionary for the Japanese? "A century ago Japan was a nation composed principally of peasants whose way of life conformed in general outlines with that of folk societies elsewhere in the world" (Norbeck 1965:9). Edward Norbeck, an anthropologist who has studied both folk and urban Japanese, continues:

In 1941, at the time Japan entered into war with the United States and Europe, profound changes had taken place peacefully in almost all sectors of life. No other nation of the modern world had undergone such drastic and self-sought cultural changes under conditions of internal peace in an equally short period of time (1965:10).

One of many partial explanations for this peaceful transition lies in the fact that Japanese culture is receptive and flexible. Japan has been ingesting innovations from other cultures for many centuries. Chinese culture had previously brought a flood of new ideas, behaviors, and material items to Japan. Norbeck writes:

> The mode of reception of Chinese and the later Western culture was the same, one of selective adaptation rather than wholesale borrowing, adaptation that permitted innovations to become assimilated without suddenly obliterating the old ways and causing violent social upheaval. Foreign culture that conflicted seriously with established ways was rejected. The Confucian idea that an inadequate ruler should be deposed, for example, was anathema to the Japanese, to whom the continuity of family lines in fixed positions of status was a value of prime importance. When individual members of any social group were incompetent, means other than frank disbarment were preferred, means that preserved social forms and individual and group honor. Throughout, the acceptance of Western as well as Chinese culture resulted in assimilations that had a distinctively Japanese cast (1965:9, 10).

The relatively easy transition on the part of the Japanese to urban patterns of living does not mean that change, and rather dramatic change, was not imperative. A few of these necessary changes are touched upon in the following:

> In the city, a sentiment has grown against living with one's parents, parents-in-law, or mature children, and the idea is not a total stranger to rural residents. Father's voice had lost a good deal of authority and mother's has gained. Younger sons are often at no disadvantage as compared with the eldest son, and sisters and new brides have lost some of their meekness. To prepare them for an adult life that is likely to take them away from farming, younger sons and even daughters of rural families may receive more formal education than eldest sons, who are ordinarily expected to remain on the farm. The mother-in-law who attempts to dominate her son's bride is in danger of being branded as "feudal," a demeaning word. A common postwar saying is that two things have grown in strength since the war, stockings—now of tough nylon—and women (Norbeck 1965:13).

Another explanation of the peaceful transition accomplished by the Japanese lies in the fact that many of their traditional values are compatible with those of Western urban dwellers. High value was placed upon education, and great sacrifices are often made by the entire family to educate a son. Success, competition, and cleanliness were all important. The practice of thrift and industry was commonplace. The ethic of achievement was an integral part of Japanese culture. As Norbeck comments, "Whatever the origin of this ideal, the modern Japanese 'naturally' values industriousness and 'naturally' wishes to succeed" (1965:20).

In Taiwan   Groups other than the Japanese have special traditional values that converge with those of the industrializing society. K-un Shen, a Taiwan village, is a good example. The people are receptive to new ideas and respect "science." Dr. Norma Diamond, who lived with these villagers for a long period, reports:

> The proverbial conservatism of the Chinese peasantry appears to be absent from K-un Shen, with little in over all ideology to block change and modernization. In many ways, the values held by most people in the community are already in line with the demands of an industrializing society. . . .
>
> Long and hard hours of work are not perceived as something to be avoided . . . and the work ethic is closely related to the individualism evident among the villagers. Life is a constant and often difficult struggle to maintain a small household. Rarely is cooperation extended automatically among kinsmen. The values of the community hold that a man's first responsibilities are to his wife and children and to aged parents without means of support, but his grown brothers should be able to fend for themselves, and feelings of responsibility are even weaker to more remote collateral kin. Values such as these make mobility possible. And as new industries develop in the urban centers, we would expect a relatively painless change in occupation . . .
>
> The transition to the modern world is also eased by the villagers' view of the natural world and man's place within it, particularly the view that man does have some control over nature and can better his life through improved knowledge and skills. The religious beliefs current in the community do not present a serious barrier to acceptance of change. In the area of health, the system has proved flexible enough to allow the incorporation of new methods of curing and preventing of disease. More generally, scientific knowledge introduced from the Western World is seen as an increment to knowledge rather than a blanket refutation of traditional beliefs (1969:108–109).

> There is a strong respect for "science" in K-un Shen which is undoubtedly the result of recent culture change as far as content is concerned, but the ease with which "science" has been accepted suggests an earlier pragmatism and openness to new methods which prove workable. People speak often of looking into "new ways" of doing things as well as learning the customary ways of doing things. "Newness," in itself, is neither good nor bad . . . (1969:28).

Although dramatic changes have not yet occurred within the village, there is an eagerness for certain kinds of change such as improvements in the standard of living, the taking on of new occupations (particularly among the young people), and the learning of ideas that will make the village "modern" or "progressive" when viewed by the rest of Taiwanese society. The word "change," like "science," has also acquired a positive connotation (1969: 109).

In spite of great potential for change, it has occurred rather slowly in K-un Shen, largely because economic assistance and opportunities have been less available to the villagers than they have been in other similar situations.

In Malta   The villagers of Hal-Farrug in Malta, like those of Taka-shima, Japan, experienced a simple and gradual period of transition from agriculturalists to industrial laborers between 1871 and 1960. During that period the number of full-time farmers decreased from 77 percent to 15 percent (Boissevain 1969:10). One of the reasons for the relatively painless transition was that, like the Japanese villagers, the Maltans had been adapting to outside cultures (both Christian and Moslem) for many centuries. Until Malta achieved independence from Britain in 1964, the island had been essentially a fortress in the hands of the British naval forces, and before that, except for a brief interlude, had long been the seat of the famed Knights of Malta. As a bastion between the Christian and Moslem worlds, it had been strongly influenced by the cultures of both. Another factor conducive to change among the villagers of Hal-Farrug in particular and Malta in general was that there is a high literacy rate among Maltans. Also, rather than simply supply their conquerors with agricultural products, the villagers had provided special services to foreign garrisons for many centuries.

The networks of personal and familial relationships furnished innumerable contacts with urban dwellers and others villagers, comparable to those found among Bolivian Aymara. Jeremy Boissevain describes these:

> . . . contacts exist between Farrug and other social and geographical areas of Maltese society in each major activity field. The part is in contact with the whole through economic, kinship, religious and political relations. Villagers work outside Farrug, and outsiders work in the village . . . today 219 of the 296 workingmen travel outside the village daily. Most work in the conurbation surrounding the capital. There, they meet persons from many other villages and towns. They are invited to attend special family celebrations and annual fiestas in other villages. At work, they are in touch with persons from all over the island. They exchange news, stories, and notice slight differences between villages. This is a forum where men, and in ever-increasing numbers, women from all over the island meet one another and exchange information (1969:93).

It is apparent that there is no straight line, or continuum, from folk to urban, and no single form of influence emanating from the city and transforming the countryside. There is a complex of interrelated processes that result in change, but not change in a single direction. Persistence of established values and patterns of behavior occurs along with transformation.

How Did the Sumatrans and Vasilikans Modernize?

The Toba Batak of Sumatra   One anthropologist field worker in Sumatra found that none of the theories developed by sociologists and anthropologists from Maine (1861) to Redfield (1947) applied in the transition of
the Toba Batak from rural to urban living. The predicted isolation of the
individual, breakdown of kinship organization, and the development of
impersonal, superficial social relationships did not occur there. As Edward
Bruner describes the situation:

> The kinship and ceremonial practices of the government official in Medan
> (the city to which the villagers had migrated) were found to be basically
> similar to those performed by his uncle in the village. Batak urbanities have
> become increasingly sophisticated and cosmopolitan, but the traditional basis
> of their social life has not been undermined. Kinship has remained the major
> nexus of interpersonal relationships in the urban Batak community, the
> patrilineal descent group is intact and flourishing, and the village life crisis
> ceremonies are performed in the city with relatively little modification. Of
> course, Batak culture today is not the same as it was a century ago, but
> comparison of the social and ceremonial organization in *contemporary* rural
> and urban environments indicated that no major differences existed. . . .
> The people themselves are well aware of the retention of village ways
> within the urban center and say that all Batak, wherever they may reside,
> follow essentially the same "adat" (custom) (1961:508–509).

Bruner makes some suggestions as to why the Toba Batak social and ceremonial organization has been maintained in an urban environment. One
explanation lies in the fact that the urban Batak do not assimilate the national Indonesian superculture since a national Indonesian culture does not
yet exist. Indonesia is a nation of 90 million people fragmented into many
diverse ethnic groups. Since the Japanese occupation and the creation of
the New Republic of Indonesia, it is no longer necessary for any Toba Batak
to renounce his ethnic identity. In this diverse urban center "no superordi-
nate colonial administration is armed with a program of directed culture
change and the power to enforce it. . . ." (Bruner 1961:520). Another explanation for these persistences is that "the rural and urban Batak are linked
through a complex communication network in which Western goods and
ideas do flow from city to village, but the flow of people and of the moral
support and vitality of the *adat* is primarily in the other direction" (Bruner
1961:515). A brief description of a modern Batak wedding among the urban
elite illustrates the persistence of traditional forms:

> In the morning a Christian service is conducted by a Batak minister in the
> Batak language. In the afternoon adult Batak men participate in a ritual
> which symbolizes the kinship organization and the relationship between the
> patrilineal descent groups, and they discuss, in Batak, the meaning of the
> adat [traditional] ceremony. In the evening brief congratulatory speeches are

given in Indonesian by business associates, women's organizations, and youth groups (Bruner 1961:517).

The important point to note here is that the wealthy city dweller has not modified his village *adat;* he has merely added on the Western reception.

A Greek Village Ernestine Friedl describes *lagging emulation* in the Greek village of Vasilika which she studied. She writes:

> The emulation in question is the process whereby social groups of lower prestige, upon the acquisition of new wealth or other forms of opportunity, imitate and often successfully acquire what they conceive to be the behavior of those with greater prestige; the emulation "lags" in that the behavior imitated is that which reached its acme as a prestige symbol for the higher social group at an earlier period in its history, and is now obsolescent. Lagging emulation occurs, then, under conditions in which the groups which constitute the traditional elites or which are otherwise considered worthy of emulation are themselves acquiring new ways at the same time that the traditionally less advanced groups are enabled to alter their previous patterns of life (1964:569).

The kinds of situations referred to are those where the people are never quite able to catch up. Friedl gives an example of lagging emulation related to attitudes towards time:

> Most business or official transactions are preceded by the drinking of a cup of Turkish-style coffee and some extended general conversation. The postman on his rounds of the village often stops at the coffee house to accept the sweet or drink offered him by the village host. Such uses of time, including a much wider latitude for the keeping of appointments, are entirely expectable in any rural community. But the leisurely pace, with time always available for amenities, even as part of what are otherwise exclusively business or official transactions, was part of the pattern of the relations between people of influence in the Athens of several decades ago (1964:577).

Vasilika is thus really out of step with modern urban industrial society. It is more congruent with the atmosphere of contemporary Athens than with New York City, to be sure, but even Athens is adopting the rigid schedule and clock-bound routine of the city, "with more brusqueness and what Americans would call a more business-like attention to the matter in hand" (Friedl 1964:577–578).

Dr. Friedl poses the question: Why should rural populations imitate outmoded upper-class behavior rather than strive to acquire the newly emerging forms with which those in the forefront of national development identify? Her answer to this question is related to the models available to the villages. The immediate contacts of the villagers are usually with persons from the city who are not themselves at the forefront of change. The city relatives of the villagers—members of the civil service and the local professionals—are not of upper or even upper-middle rank in power or culture. The villagers who are attempting to better their lot find that following the outmoded urban models of high position gives them the prestige they seek in their local community. And so life goes on in a relaxed manner for them, and their emulation continues to lag.

Robert Redfield (1953) in "The Primitive World and Its Transformation" emphasizes the creative aspects of the processes of modernization and urbanization. He dwells on the changes that have taken place in men's minds as a result of the technological revolution rather than on the technological changes themselves. In the folk society, the technical order is subordinate to the moral order. During the urbanization process, the old moral orders are shaken or destroyed. But there is a rebuilding of moral orders on new levels which results from the thinking of many different kinds of peoples. The kinds of men found in the city—the administrative elite, the literate jurist with opportunities for reflection and cultivation of esoteric knowledge, the specialized artisan—are different from the peasant. They can spend time reflecting and looking inwards; they have a new world view and style of life. In civilization the technical order becomes great but the moral order does not become small; it is simply of a different level. *It is at a level marked by self-consciousness and by conscious creativeness* (Redfield 1953). It is in the city environment that intellectuals can construct new and contradictory theories about the social order, that psychiatrists can aid people to become ultra self-conscious—conscious of their motives and the reasons for them. A member of a primitive society rarely has to analyze his thoughts and feelings in this fashion. The traditional formulae for behavior are usually sufficient for his adjustment to his social and natural world. Dangerous, potentially destructive ideas are born in the city but so also are ideas such as the concept of human dignity, freedom from slavery, equality of mankind, permanent peace, and so on.

A contemporary writer comments on what he believes to be coming changes for all of mankind as the world's population becomes industrialized and the technological revolution to which Redfield refers is more complete:

> The super-industrial revolution can erase hunger, disease, ignorance, and brutality. Moreover, despite the pessimistic prophecies of the straight line thinkers, super-industrialism will not restrict man, will not crush him into bleak and painful uniformity. In contrast, it will radiate new opportunities for personal growth, adventure and delight. It will be vividly colorful and amazingly open to individuality (Toffler 1970:187).

Today, it is the same self-consciousness referred to by Redfield, born of the effects of the urbanization and industrialization processes, that is causing youth to examine and criticize the world about them, where the demands of elaborate technology are in conflict with their concept of a "moral order." It is paradoxical that without the elaborate technology, man would not be conscious of his relationship to nature and the moral order. And some interpreters of the modern scene believe that this special self-consciousness may lead men to ultimately find means for surviving (See Reich 1971:82–83).

How is American youth coping?

There is a revolution coming. It will not be like revolutions of the past. It will originate with the individual and with culture, and it will change the political structure only as its final act. It will not require violence to succeed, and it cannot be successfully resisted by violence. This is the revolution of the new generation (Reich 1971: front cover).

Many people in responsible positions in American society, as well as other social scientists, would not call contemporary changes revolutionary, whereas others, such as Justice William Douglas and Senator George McGovern, find Reich's statements challenging and penetrating. We must admit that we are in a period of rapid change, but, at the same time, in view of what we have already discussed about change and persistence, Reich's assertions can be viewed as overly dramatic.

In this picture of social change, many American youth are playing the important roles of challenger and innovator. They face the same personal problems in adjusting to what they perceive as an incompatible system as did many American Indian and African peoples when they were temporarily overwhelmed by the impact of European culture and colonialism. Traditional patterns in American and European cultures are breaking down Standard solutions to problems no longer work for many of the young. They view the older system as threatening both physically, due to fear of destruction of the environment by pollution and a nuclear holocaust, and psychologically, due to fear of the uncontrolled power exercised over them in an age of machines.

One of the most common techniques used in adjusting to the conflict situation is represented by the appearance of a seemingly limitless number of cults. These cults represent a way used by youth for coping while seeking for a personal identity or a release from hostilities bred from frustration, or while simply searching for a "different" American dream.

The techno-societies, far from being drab and homogenized, are honeycombed with . . . colorful groupings—theosophists and flying-saucer fans, skin divers and sky divers, homosexuals, computerniks, vegetarians, body builders and Black Muslims.

. . . The same destandardizing forces that make for great individual choice with respect to products and cultural wares, are also destandardizing our social structures. This is why, seemingly overnight, new sub-cults like the Hippies, burst into being. We are, in fact, living through a "sub-cult explosion" (A. Toffler 1970:285).

The Cults Come and Go

The term *cult* is used here for most of the new groupings rather than sub-culture because the turnover rate is extremely rapid. For example, many LSD advocates in specialized drug cults are, after a few years, calling "acid a bad scene" and underground newspapers warn followers against getting too involved with "tripsters" (Toffler 1970:296). The original Hippie Haight-Ashbury subcult in San Francisco, known as the "flower children," ended

after a brief period because it became too large and had to diversify. Many Hippies later formed tribes and lived in communes; some lived near Indian tribes or in simulated "Indian" style; others established specialized non-violent subgroups, using various models offered by established groups such as the Hutterites and Amish. Some groups dedicated to violence developed as the original Hippie Movement waned. Their ideology, focusing on affronting behaviors, converged in many respects with that of the Hell's Angels, a motorcycle subcult originating in Southern California. The earlier street gangs that had engaged in warfare disappeared in the early 1960s. (See Keiser 1969 for a study of a Chicago gang.) The aggressive passions, however, given stimulus from the oppressive conditions of ghetto life, are represented by new subcults emerging in the ghetto, cults directed at the social system itself rather than at rivalry between street gangs.

> What we sense, therefore, is a process by which sub-cults multiply at an ever-accelerating rate, and in turn die off and make room for still more and newer sub-cults. A kind of metabolic process is taking place in the blood stream of the society, and it is speeding up exactly as other aspects of social interaction are quickening (Toffler 1970:298).

What are the implications of these new stimuli for American society? Let us examine one of the groups, a Hippie ghetto, in greater detail.

> What is a "hippie?" The answer is not very clear if one tries to dissect the strange conglomeration of Christian Mysticism, Vedic teachings, revolutionary tracts, Madison Avenue pop psychology, American Indian religions, hedonism, and the particularly American virtues of Horatio Alger, such as individualism, independence, and frontier courage (Partridge, 1973:9–10).

William Partridge spent a year as an anthropological participant-observer in a Hippie ghetto. He was able to trace, step by step, the means by which a new member becomes initiated into the society. The Elders of the group play the important role of acting as models and counselors for the neophytes. Some of the core values of the group, such as transience and mobility, isolation (from the "straight" culture), experimentation with alternatives, intimacy in social relations, and communal intoxication, are expressions of patterns of interaction which have developed among Hippies in their attempt to survive. These values represent the group's methods for solving the problems of group living, sex, subsistence, housing, entertainment, and other human problems. The residents (of the Ghetto) are in a process of "experimentation with and exploration of another person's potential as a possible friend, lover and spouse. This is what has been called promiscuity, but one might call it opportunity as well as a conscious exploration of mutuality" (Partridge 1973:35).

Communal intoxication, the sharing of the sacrament (marihuana), is a prerequisite in this particular group for communication. The communication takes the form of a "rap" session and occurs frequently for the purpose of establishing rapport. Members claim the session is for open and honest communication with one another. Since newspapers and media from the "straight" society are to be mistrusted, the emphasis is upon personal experiences. The rap session includes tales relating "groovy" (in this case implicitly or explicitly "confronting") behavior toward straight society, the dangers of living in straight society, or projected alternatives to living in straight society.

Females sometimes find themselves uninvolved with the important "instrumental" roles (see Zelditch 1955) of the group. The associational groups in the Hippie ghetto are often male-oriented, with females appended on as such alliances shift. The males handle the drug traffic and the females don't fit the needs of a tight associational network existing for finding jobs or buyers for drugs (Partridge 1973:33).

Some interpreters of the modern scene (Roszak 1968) regard the Hippie cult as a counterculture. On the other hand, Partridge, with his first-hand knowledge of the subcult, described the movement as a "part and product of American society" (Partridge 1973:xiii). Hippie ideology—with emphasis on the quest for self-knowledge, self-discovery, and spiritual growth—converges with the cultural tradition of American adolescence.

Anthony Wallace (1969:121–122) traces core Hippie values to the cultural values of Western Civilization and Judeo-Christian mythology. The Hippie Movement may indeed represent the lost spirit of the Crusaders. The emphasis in Western mythology is on the individual, not the society, which is considered immoral. It is the self that must be examined and altered to achieve happiness in Western mythology. And it is the fervent seeking for self-expression and identity that furnishes a common link between many grouped and ungrouped youth of the present.

The particular Hippie ghetto described above has probably had an almost complete turnover in membership and may not even exist at the time of this writing. But, doubtless, some of the old members have joined other cults in other areas with similar ideologies.

Can Religion Help in Searching for an Identity?

The following is an account of an experience of a member of a religious cult, seeking an identity through finding "Salvation":

> It is the third day of our quest for enlightenment. We are wandering through leaves, in a birch grove, solitary figures, not speaking, asking silently, intoning repeatedly until we are dizzy and numb: "Who am I?" We have suffered through desire and despair, weakness and exhilaration, doubt and calm disinterest. And now we are waiting.
>
> What has kept us here is the wish, the hope for and the need to seek inner

peace. We are sweating, and the men have three-day growths of stubble.
We have eaten millet and swallowed great handfuls of vitamins and slept
on the floor, head to toe. We have screamed and cried and hugged and stared
into space. What has carried us is the power of what we are promised: a
sudden crack in the consciousness, a splitting open of the soul when you are
flooded with joyous certainty. A direct experience of who exactly we are.
Salvation (Account in Davidson 1971:40).

And religions of variegated types in the form of cults seem to offer
a formula for many young people for making their lives more livable
immediately.

The Three H (Happy, Healthy, Holy) Organization, founded by Yogi
Bhajan, and all schools of yoga, have had wild bursts of growth, as have
groups dedicated to Zen, Krishna Consciousness, Jewish Mysticism, Scien-
tology, Abilatism, Gurdjieff, light radiation, macrobiotics, Jesus Freaks,
Sufism, Buddhism, Taoism, Naturalism, and Astral Projection (Davidson
1971:40).

Much of the ideology of the Hippies is shared by these religious groups,
but each religious subcult tends to be specialized. A striking difference between many of the religious cults and the Hippie cult, however, is that
religion does not necessarily require withdrawal from the world or rejection
of straight society, and many members of the religious cults remain a part
of the traditional culture. The Jesus Movement includes subcults of this type.
Although the adherents to the movement are critical of the traditional modes
of worship, many attempt to work through the existing structure of the
Church. They are met with antagonism for the most part. The movement
includes a great variety of young people with a range of hair styles and
dress. But they are all seeking the same goal—individual salvation and a
personal relationship with God.

While the majority of the religious subcults are dedicated to the ideals of a better understanding of the self and the creation of a "better world," some are dedicated to "Satan" and Evil. These subcults, which center in Southern California, practice various forms of Black Magic or enact the "Black Masses," according to decriptions recovered from early writings of the Church (see *Esquire*, March, 1970). But the life span of most of these subcults is even shorter than that of others.

Has the larger society been affected?

Among today's youth, the phenomenon of "conversions" is increasingly common . . . What happens is simply this: In a brief span of months, a student, seemingly conventional in every way, changes his haircut, his clothes, his habits, his interests, his political attitudes, his way of relating to other people, in short, his whole way of life. He has "converted" to a new consciousness. The contrast between well-groomed freshman pictures and the same individuals in person a year later tells the tale. The clean-cut, hardworking, model young man who despises radicals and Hippies can become one himself with breath-taking suddenness (Reich 1971:240).

The many "conversions" of this type are the direct result of diffusion of the life style and values of the Hippie Movement.

Its direction may be unpredictable, but change is occurring and Hippie values are being diffused. Less dramatic than a conversion are the special aspects of the Hippie cults that are being widely accepted by straight society—clothing, special phrases (for example, "do your own thing"), and sexual mores.

The institutions it (the Hippie Movement) is competing with have been entrenched for centuries. Yet, they are reacting to the innovations spinning out of Hip communities.

Clothing manufacturers mass produce Hippie clothes, complete with embroidered patches that mock the very real poverty of the Alternative Society. Advertising copy is laced with Alternative Society phrases "right on" and "groovy." Sexual mores are imitated; so is the right of marijuana smoking, already as acceptable among some junior executives as a double martini before lunch (*Palo Alto Times*, April 16, 1971).

Advertising agents, realizing the business potential of the Hippie and religious movements, have jumped on the bandwagon: "Numerous . . . travel agents advertise round-trip tickets to Nirvana or to wherever else a tourist believes he might find God-consciousness" (Davidson 1971:40).

The growth of specialized institutions of the contemporary Alternative Society (representative of the Hippie Movement), such as free clinics, free universities, and free stores, is still dependent upon the support of straight society; these institutions serve a large number of Americans and their influence cannot be wholly assessed at present. Referring to the number of doctors who are planning to devote their careers to free medicine, Dr. Julius R. Krevans, Dean of the University of California Medical Center in San Francisco, said it is too early to tell just how significant that number will be.

"But," he said, "there is no question that social awareness is quickening among other students and faculty members in the nation's medical schools.

"You won't be able to judge how much is discussion and how much is performance until one sees where these people go when they become physicians" (*Palo Alto Times*, April 27, 1971:17).

And Jerry Billow, a member of a legal collective in Cambridge, Massachusetts, predicted: "These alternatives will snowball." "Already," he said, "there are at least 15 similar groups of young activist lawyers scattered throughout the nation's cities."

Many people living in the contemporary system have been inspired by values of the Alternative Society and are playing the role of infiltrator. And it is impossible to estimate the number of individuals who are transmitting the new values to the larger society.

New values have been diffused to the social elite and even to the international jet set. An article in the *San Francisco Examiner* reports:

> . . . the Beautiful People—only yesterday magnets for the masses of nobodies yearning to be somebodies—are no more" (Sunday, November 14, 1971:1).

What has happened to these people? The article goes on to report:

> Perhaps most revolutionary of all, the custom-tailored scions of the leisure class are going to work. Mrs. ———, loaded with———money (her stepfather heads the———Broadcasting System)and a veteran of the Best Dressed List by the time she was in her mid-twenties, has been teaching in a Harlem elementary school.
> ———and——— ——— are two more drop outs from the Beautiful Scene. ———, whose grandfather founded ———, and whose father is a retired Episcopal bishop, left the banking business and now teaches in a suburban school. ——— spends much of her time helping former addicts at Reality House, a Manhattan rehabilitation center for drug users. Young Roosevelts and Rockefellers are working for Vista.

And the "influence," immeasurable, continues to grow.

At Stanford University, where a total of seven hundred college students had been given the same values-eliciting technique intermittently since 1952, a marked shift was observed in the students' values during the last few years (beginning in 1968). The results of the technique consist of verbal expressions of the belief systems of the respondents concerning pivotal areas of American ideology (See G. Spindler, 1955, for a description of the technique). The new values of these college students are convergent with some of the values represented by the Hippie Movement and the contemporary Alternative Society. Some of the value shifts include an attitude of "uncertainty and anxiety" about the future; a "positive" attitude towards nudity and sexual liberation; a definition of the most successful people as those who have an interest in others and enjoy their work, instead of the earlier "trying to get ahead" type responses; a preponderance of responses such as "be considerate," and "be good to others," rather than the typical earlier response of "achieve"; and a strong positive orientation toward communal rather than individual responsibility.

It must be added here that other values elicited by the technique remained constant over the years and might be viewed as core values in a patterned belief system which is representative of a large number of people in American society. Some examples of this type are: the value placed on equality, honesty, time, and effort, and the belief that it is futile to lament what happened in the past.

The expressed values that have remained constant, however, are *not* discrepant with those that have undergone change. These core values represent the tenacity of some cultural experiences and, at the same time, the flexibility and creativity of American youth in selecting and reworking old elements into a new pattern.

The effects and influences of changes related to the reactions of many youth to American society are not all apparent. And it may be that only the historian or anthropologist of the future can give them proper weighting.

Summary

In discussing the complex problems related to how cultural systems change or resist change, many specific processes were dealt with—urbanization and modernization, technological change, diffusion, reinterpretation of borrowed or introduced elements, innovation, synthesis of old and new, and acculturation—with extensive case materials used to illustrate them. Special cases of nativistic, reaffirmative, and revitalization movements were described as special and important types of responses to the threat of annihilation of cultural systems.

Attention was given to the psychological dimension, which is of particular significance in that it does not change in quite the same way as the manifest, overt cultural aspects of a system do. When a culture becomes disorganized, the personality characteristics and psychological resources of the people become more important, since the built-in automatic guides for behavior are no longer operative.

Changes in the modern world (modernization and urbanization) were described, with special focus on modern youth, who are coping in many innovative and creative ways in striving for a separate identity.

Further readings

The literature in culture change is vast. The following selections will be useful in gaining further understanding of the field. *Culture and Experience* (Hallowell 1955): See Part IV, The Psychological Dimensions in Culture Change, where the author deals with the personal reactions to culture change. *New Lives for Old* (Mead 1956): A description of a unique situation where a people transformed their entire culture in a twenty-five year time span.

The following two books give insights into the possible applications of anthropology for community development and technological change. *Traditional Cultures and the Impact of Technological Change* (Foster 1962); *Cooperation in Change* (Goodenough 1963).

For useful bibliographic review of the culture change and acculturation literature, see the relevant chapters in the *Biennial Review of Anthropology*, Bernard Siegel (ed.), for 1959, 1961, 1963, and 1965.

Case studies with useful materials on culture change include *The Eskimo of North Alaska* (Chance 1966); *The Two Worlds of the Washo* (Downs 1966); *Hano: A Tewa Indian Community in Arizona* (Dozier 1966); *Fishermen of South Thailand* (Fraser 1966); *The Qemant, a Pagan-Hebraic Peasantry of Ethiopia* (Gamst 1969); *Modern Blackfeet* (McFee 1972); *Changinig Japan* (Norbeck 1965); *Dreamers without Power: The Menomini Indians* (G. and L. Spindler 1971); *Burgbach: Urbanization and Identity in a German Village* (G. Spindler 1973); *The Zinacantecos of Mexico: A Modern Maya Way of Life* (Vogt 1970). The *Case Studies in Education and Culture* (Wolcott 1967; Warren 1967; Singleton 1967; Gay and Cole 1967; Grindal 1972; Modiano 1973; Jocano 1969; Peshkin 1972) all give attention to the role of the school in culture change.

Problems and questions

1. Interview a person from your grandparents' generation. What kinds of values does he or she express which are not held by you and your peer group?
2. What kinds of innovations are you able to observe during a one-day period (new ways of dressing, cooking, speaking, decorating, and so forth)?
3. Describe a person, with whom you have had first-hand contact, who lives in two subcultures at the same time. What problems can you discover in his or her adaptation? What positive aspects are there in his or her adjustment?
4. Using any one of the Case Studies in Cultural Anthropology, such as the Qemant (Gamst 1969), what are some of the questions you would want answered before you would attempt to introduce a new form of housing, medical care, or agricultural techniques?

5. Interview a member of a subcultural group (Orthodox Jew, Mexican-American, for example) or religious cult to discover how he is able to maintain his culturally deviant behavior (as viewed in the dominant culture) against strong pressures to conform?

6. Select any one culture from the Case Studies in Cultural Anthropology and outline particular values, customs, and beliefs that you would expect to cause the greatest conflict for the members if they were to attempt to adjust to Western-Euro-American culture. Which ones would be most likely to cause the least conflict?

12

Questions and processes

What has been accomplished?

In Utopia the successful young person is captain of his team, hotly pursued by members of the opposite sex, plays all of the works of Grunebaum on the computerized bazoo, holds a straight A average, prepares a superb almond duck, and manufactures psychedelic drugs in the garage in his spare time. At the age of eighteen or so, those who have failed to accomplish these things look back upon their wasted lives and pronounce themselves failures. In the same vein, anthropologists and their critics, looking back upon the recent progress in their field, incline toward hopelessness and despair. Where are the laws of anthropology? Where is our Newton or Darwin? Where is our grand theory? What have we done to save the world?

Actually, the first Ph.D. in anthropology was granted less than one hundred years ago. It may be that anthropology has made false starts or involved itself in silly games and infantile diversions, but it is also true that it has been a slum-child of the sciences bereft of manpower and living on the table scraps of the more prosperous disciplines. From the beginning the efforts of anthropology have been scattered across the cultures of the earth and the several million years of human history. Instead of a massive assault on some single human problem, anthropologists have skirmished against a host of questions claiming few victories and accepting few defeats.

The rise of anthropology vaguely corresponds with the colonization and development of the "underdeveloped" nations. It corresponds with the rape and destruction of the archaeological record and the deliberate destruction of countless peoples and their ways of life. At the moment of its founding anthropology faced the problem of a disappearing subject matter. Early in this century, Franz Boas said to Robert Lowie, "Here is a hundred dollars, go study the Navajo." Lowie set out knowing only that the Navajo lived somewhere to the west of New York. Here was no chance to formulate significant theoretical questions or to develop methodology. Here was only a chance to find some old people and say, "What was it like when you were young?" So it went and so it goes today. Archaeologists snatch their data from the teeth of bulldozers; cultural anthropologists work with remnants of peoples not yet destroyed.

Out of the frantic attempts of these ethnographers have come written records concerning hundreds of cultures that no longer exist or exist in altered form. At this very moment, Brazilian soldiers and frontiersmen are completing the extermination of unstudied Indian tribes of the Amazon Basin, the mountain peoples of Southeast Asia are perishing in wars they never sought and do not understand, and in California a bulldozer is destroying the last fragile records of a vanished tribe. In a few unthinking moments of history many of the cultures and works of man constructed over centuries have been destroyed. But much has been saved, and the laden bookshelves of almost any library bear testimony to the hero's task the ethnographers performed. So long as there are human beings, so long as they care about others, this monumental contribution of an infant science will remain one of the great treasures of humanity. There are still cultures to be studied and archaeological sites to be excavated, but will we get to them in time?

The ethnographic record, the books and articles written by anthropologists, missionaries, and explorers, contains much information about our own and other people's cultures. Out of the comparison of these materials, out of an awareness of the similarities and differences among the peoples of the world, the concept of culture has gradually emerged. If there is some great discovery in anthropolgy, some great contribution to human wisdom, then it is the discovery of culture. Of course, human beings have always been aware of culture, but they have often attributed a sacred quality to their own. One's own way of life has always seemed right and proper, perhaps a gift from the creator to be preserved as a sacred trust. Even where men have not been convinced of their superiority to other men, they have

seen their own cultures as right for them and other cultures as right for other people.

Brought up in a culture regarded by its members as god-given, biologically inherited, and infinitely superior to all others, the early anthropologists struggled slowly toward the truth: Cultures are invented by ordinary men and passed on to others by means of processes of cultural transmission. Cultures may be sacred because they are beautiful or because they represent sincere, triumphant, human work. Beyond that, they are no more sacred than an eggbeater, a telephone, or any other human work. Historically, anthropologists did not begin to use the term *social heredity* in definitions of culture until the 1920s, and *learning* appeared frequently in definitions of culture in the late thirties and early forties.

In the abstract, the idea that ways of life are simply the product of messages handed down across the generations seems innocuous enough. In fact, the view of culture as natural, rather than supernatural, is as revolutionary and as hard to believe as the idea that the earth is round and circles the sun or the idea that human beings evolved by natural processes from other animals. In our daily life we act as though the earth were flat, we speak of sunrise and sunset, and we separate the artificial from the natural. When an ethnographic film shows us Bushmen hunting, warfare in New Guinea, or an Australian aboriginal initiation, we snicker in the back rows. Here are people who do not know how to act properly, crazy people doing crazy things. Do we not recognize that we are equally crazy and that our own customs are equally absurd or, if you like, equally rational? Perhaps we do know it in a way, but we are not prepared to act upon it. The idea that everything we think of as right or wrong was just an idea thought up by some wise man or fool several centuries ago is as repugnant as it is revolutionary and subversive.

Imagine that it is Sunday in Cicero Falls. The minister, a recent convert to anthropology, has decided to express his respect for God in the manner of the ancient Sumerians. He strips off his ornaments and clothing and delivers his sermon in the nude. As anthropologists we are inclined to say, "so what," but as citizens of Cicero Falls we are outraged. Who decided that it was good to wear clothing in a church with the thermostat set at eighty? Who decided that it is wrong to eat dog meat, that cultural transmission can occur in a lecture hall, that "shit" is a dirty word, that only women wear skirts, that you should sleep with the same woman all of your life, or that it is uncomfortable to sit on the floor? Anthropology tells us that these are all arbitrary conventions constructed by men and quite likely to change. Such conventions may, of course, be useful and adaptive in one way or another, but should we not examine them? Perhaps, after all, the Sumerians were right.

We have opened a Pandora's book of questions. Why should a man who collects garbage, surely a difficult and unpleasant job, receive less money than a man who has inherited several hundred shares of stock in the United States Steel Company? Are women properly regarded as inferior to men? Is alcohol really so different from marihuana? Is it really a crime to drive a car that no one else is using? Do prisons reduce crime or do they cause it? Is justice blind or are law courts instruments of oppression? Must children be forced to attend school or might they learn willingly under certain conditions? But suppose our customs are silly, what will we have left if we throw them out?

Why Is It So?

Anthropology, the study of other cultures and the explanation of similarities and differences, leads to the asking of questions that most people, perhaps wisely, prefer not to hear. This is especially true when the only possible answer is "es costombre," it is the custom, we have always done so. A part of the concept of culture is that it is insidious. It affects people in deep ways. It affects the unconscious positioning of their bodies and the sudden flashes of their eyebrows. Much of culture is transmitted and received unconsciously and comes to form a vital but unrecognized part of the individual personality. What does the physicist see when he looks at the tracks made by elementary particles; what does a biologist see when he looks through his microscope? Can it be that he sees what he has unconsciously learned to see? Is science, in fact, a religion or a world view no different in kind from that of the Saora? Anthropologists tend to believe that the world is round, that diseases are often caused by bacteria, that reinforcement contributes to learning, and so on; but at the same time they tend to recognize that most "knowledge" is mythological rather than scientific. People believe what they believe because they want to and because it was passed down from ancestors. In all of the sciences, even the so-called hard sciences, the instrument of observation is a human being brought up in some particular cultural tradition and committed to blind faith in its mythology. Under these circumstances, systematic or even unsystematic explorations in other cultures would seem to be fundamental in separating the truths and myths in any science.

After studying visual perception in a variety of cultures, Segall, Campbell, and Herskovits (1966:213) conclude:

> Perception is an aspect of human behavior, and as such it is subject to many of the same influences that shape other aspects of behavior. In particular, each individual's experiences combine in a complex fashion to determine his reaction to a given stimulus situation. To the extent that certain classes of experiences are more likely to occur in some cultures than in others, differences in behavior across cultures, including differences in perceptual tendencies, can be great enough even to surpass the ever-present individual differences within cultural groupings.

In a way, then, one of the functions of anthropological research has become that of playing a spoiler role in regard to the findings of other sciences. One hears the cry, "The Hopi don't think that way," or "It's not so in my village."

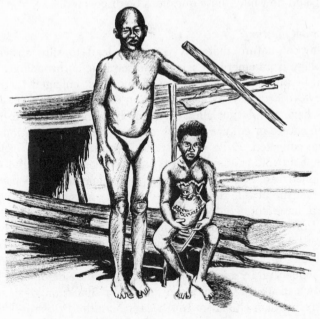

In Freudian psychology the Oedipus complex is conceived as reflecting a *natural* rivalry between a male child and his father. Malinowski (1927) presented evidence that in the Trobriand Islands, where children are disciplined by the mother's brother, the same sort of rivalry develops, not between the child and his father, but between the child and his mother's brother. The locus of the child's rivalries appears to be determined not by biology but by culture. In the same vein, studies of adolescents in the United States have shown the period of adolescence to be a time of great psychological turmoil. Mead (1953) found that adolescents in Samoa did not experience such problems. Far from being of biological origin, adolescent turmoil appears to be no more necessary and inevitable than the Hopi initiation ceremony.

The existence of these small, and not always undisputed, triumphs says more about the promise of anthropology than about its achievements. Cross-cultural research, not by itself but in association with other kinds of research, can contribute to the solution of many of the problems of our society and the human species. If it is accepted that we can "see" our own culture only in the light of contrast with other cultures, then anthropology is vital to the answering of all scientific questions and to the solution of all problems. But if anthropology is to be of use, if it is to pursue the earth-shaking implications of the concept of culture, it must put away childish things. It must become a mature science with a well-defined set of questions or body of theory and a well-designed set of research methods or strategies for the discovery of truth. What kinds of questions should anthropologists be asking and how may those questions be discovered?

What Is the Question?

It is a law of nature that silly questions lead to silly answers. Because anthropology is an emergent scientific discipline, anthropologists have often asked the wrong kinds of questions. Sometimes, engaged in frantic efforts to preserve records of a rapidly changing or fast vanishing culture, anthropologists have simply not allowed themselves enough time to think deeply about the nature of culture or the broad theoretical implications of the data they have collected. Even where, as is often necessary in order to obtain funds for fieldwork, anthropologists have worked out careful theories and well-designed research questions and methodologies, they have often discovered that the people they intended to study never did what they thought they did or have stopped doing it or refuse to discuss it.

Very often research in anthropology has been directed by the short-term practical interests of foundations or government agencies. In the United States, studies of acculturation (What happens when one cultural system is strongly influenced by another?) often seemed to be dominated by the question, "How can we make American Indians or Blacks or Mexican-Americans into good American citizens?" In Africa, where the British followed a policy of ruling indirectly through established leadership, anthropological research questions often had to do with the nature and structure of that leadership. In the early years of anthropology, research concerning the historical origins and development of human cultures often seemed to justify a kind of caretaker relationship in which the "advanced" nations "helped" their "backward" brethren along the rocky road to civilization.

Because any realistic understanding of the nature of culture almost requires that an anthropologist have some detailed understanding of a culture different from his own, the early experience of most anthropologists is an ethnographic experience. Thus, the attention of the anthropologist is directed toward the understanding of some particular group of people and the ethnocentrism which might otherwise have been devoted to the supreme and unique virtues of his own culture comes to be focused upon the supreme and unique virtues of the people he studies. Confronted with almost any kind of broad explanation of human behavior, the standard response of the anthropologist has often been, "It's not that way in my village." Of course no two things in nature—no two molecules, no two cells, no two individuals—are exactly alike. To the poetic imagination it is precisely the marvelous uniqueness of things that is important. To the scientific imagination what is important are the fundamental uniformities that lie concealed within apparent diversity. Although a good ethnographer must be both poet and scientist, the attempt to be both things at once has often precluded the asking of such questions as, "How is my village like all other villages?"

Of course, the central problem in the understanding of cultural systems lies in the fact that they are wondrously complicated but not too systematically organized. There are many different kinds of cultural systems and innumerable ways of arranging and classifying them. The parts of different cultural systems are often quite different and they are arranged differently within the system. The complexity of cultural systems makes it impossible to compare entire systems and this means that comparisons must be made in terms of the isolation of some part from the whole. Ideally the comparison of cultural systems should be made in terms of a uniform set of system-defining variables characteristic of all cultural systems. Meteorologists, for example, define storm systems in terms of measurements of wind velocity, wind direction, temperature, and so on. But what are the defining variables for cultural systems and how can they be measured?

Because a cultural system is the result of a relationship among a set of people, a cultural tradition, and a setting, the system variables that would explain a cultural system have to be found in those three things. There is no problem in measuring the number of people of different ages and sexes who form the membership of a cultural system, but what parts of the cultural tradition and the setting should be measured and how may the measurements be carried out? It is easy to think up an almost infinite series of things to be measured and ways of measuring them, but it is not easy to think of measurements that could be applied to any cultural system. Annual rainfall might be extremely important in defining the setting of one cultural system, but it might be totally unimportant in defining the setting of another.

One research strategy for estimating the importance of particular measurements, first suggested by Franz Boas at the turn of the century, is to study groups of cultures so closely related that most of the variables affecting them have the same value. For example, the study of neighboring communities of different population sizes has given indications of the importance of size to the nature of cultural systems. Insights concerning witchcraft have been achieved through the comparison of neighboring groups some of which possess it and some of which do not. The study of villages at increasing distances from urban centers has been used as a means of estimating the effects of urban influence upon villages. Attempts to measure the general influence of environment on culture have been based upon the study of different cultures located within the same general environment or within similar environments. Although most studies that have attempted to control particular variables have produced interesting results, they have rarely been followed up in a systematic way. Thus, we still know very little about the effect of variations in size upon cultural systems even though the question is clearly of great practical significance.

Although there are many ways to skin a cat, most anthropologists suspect that those ways are not infinite. One procedure for the development of research questions involves the investigation of some human attribute that appears to be widespread or universal. Most frequently this approach involves assembling a large number of ethnographies of hopefully unrelated cultures and investigating the factors affecting the nature or the presence of the attribute. The major problem in this sort of investigation centers about the definition and identification of the attribute to be studied. To study witchcraft, for example, it is necessary to know what witchcraft is and then to be able to decide whether it is present or absent. How would one determine, for example, whether witchcraft is present or absent in the modern United States? If it is present, is it really the same thing as witchcraft somewhere else? Unless witchcraft can be very sharply defined, there is always the possibility that superficial resemblances might lead to the lumping together of two quite different things. If something that looks like witchcraft can have different origins or causes in different cultural systems, then it is impossible to find any general explanation of the thing that was labeled witchcraft. Still, the principle of limited possibilities (the ways of skinning a cat are not infinite) would suggest that there would not be too many kinds of things that looked like witchcraft and that they would not have very many different kinds of causes.

On the whole, even though it is not possible to point to any very dramatic discoveries or any undisputed "laws" of anthropology, the field as a whole has made good progress in developing adequate definitions of cultural systems and perhaps more progress than is readily apparent in identifying important system variables and in working out ways of comparing cultural systems in terms of separated attributes or parts. Although one of the points made in this book is that fruitful comparisons of cultural systems might well be based upon a consideration of fundamental processes necessary to the operation of all cultural systems, other approaches based upon sometimes quite arbitrary definitions of the parts of culture have also proven fruitful. It would appear that the central problem for anthropology at the moment is not so much that of developing new theory or finding new research methods as that of refining old theory and collecting the data necessary to test it. There is still a lag of at least a generation between the development of new research questions and the collection of ethnographic data adequate to provide answers to them. Anthropologists are still engaged in the collection of the data required for the refinement of the urbanization theory first proposed by Park and Burgess in the 1920s and based upon their understandings of urbanization in Chicago.

What happens next?

The growth of any science is a slow process. At the beginning, time is required for the exploration of possibilities. The field of interest must be defined; appropriate methodologies must be sought. Early research in any field is impressionistic and anecdotal—the bird must be glimpsed before its wingspread can be measured. Simple explanations must be tested and found wanting before more complicated explanations can be attempted. Anthropologists first sought to explain similarities and differences among cultures in terms of single factors such as climate, environment, race, economics, the combination and recombination of a few basic inventions, "divine plan," and techniques of child rearing. The discovery that anthropology, besides being romantic and a lot of fun, involves a lot of hard work is as unappealing to the professional as it is to the beginner. Even when anthropologists accepted the idea that cultural systems represented complex wholes, they were reluctant to throw out the idea of simple causation in favor of the idea of complex interactions among numerous variables each of which exerted complex causal influences upon the others. Anthropologists hoped that their materials could be reduced to a few simple formulas like those of classical mechanics in physics, and only reluctantly accepted the idea that anthropology was much more like meteorology.

The great and meaningful problems in anthropology have to do with the ways in which cultural systems hang together, adapt, and proceed. Questions concerning the manner in which human beings identify and solve the problems that face them remain to be solved. We do not know very much about describing the environment or the environmental stresses that constitute the problems that people in cultural systems must solve if their cultural systems are to adapt. Problems that arise as a result of interaction between cultural systems may be quite different from other sorts of environmental problems, but we have not begun to describe the differences. We know that the members of different cultural systems react to stress in very different ways. Some flee, some fight, some talk, and some pray. We do not know how or why these choices are made or even if they are adaptive or how they are adaptive.

We do not know very much about the relationships between environmental stresses and cultural traditions. Do the ideas that form cultural traditions develop out of reactions to environmental problems or are the environmental problems often created by the kinds of ideas and interpretations that form the cultural tradition? We know that people in all cultural systems, even those regarded as relatively stable, are constantly modifying their cultural traditions and the techniques by means of which they cope with their environments. New ideas develop somehow and are transmitted from person to person, but we are not really sure how such ideas develop or who develops them. Even if we could explain why particular persons become inventors or innovators, we still lack firm explanations of why the innovation was proposed at a particular time or why other persons accepted it. We have many accounts of inventions, of social movements, and of other changes in culture, but we have little systematic or satisfactory theory concerning these matters.

As anthropologists survey the several million years of biological evolution and the several hundred thousand years of cultural evolution that fall within the domain of their investigations, they cannot fail to be aware of the extraordinary and rapid change that has taken place within the last few hundred years. Before our eyes there is an explosive reproduction of people, ideas, artifacts, and weapons. Because Nature, the earth goddess about whom so many anthropologists have written, abhors anything that increases at an increasing rate, the long view of human history tells us that the modern age of change and revolution cannot continue for more than another generation or two. Human populations must stabilize; human consumption of energy and resources must level off; the production of new ideas must slow. There cannot be a situation in which infinite numbers of people consume infinite amounts of energy and resources or produce infinite numbers of new inventions and ideas. As we examine the course of human history and observe that almost everything human is increasing at an increasing rate, we are led to the conclusion that the human species must reach an equilibrium with the environment and with itself or quickly perish from the earth.

In the past, the human species has survived similar periods of explosive cultural change. Ten thousand years ago with the invention of agriculture there was a period of rapidly increasing population, energy consumption, and invention. We can take some comfort in the fact that the agricultural revolution turned out to be self-limiting once the potentials inherent in agriculture and irrigated agriculture were worked out. There is less comfort in the fact that numerous agricultural peoples destroyed their environments and experienced rapid declines in population. If an agricultural civilization like that of Mohenjo Daro could destroy the little world its peoples knew, might not a worldwide civilization destroy the earth?

Whether the current cultural explosion proves to be self-limiting or not, the cultural systems caught up in it must adapt within the next few generations to a totally different and unprecedented set of environmental circumstances. If this adaptation is to be planned and systematic it must make use of the experience and wisdom preserved in the existing variety of human cultural systems. The problem of unlimited population growth can be solved technologically through the development of new techniques of contraception and abortion; but it also needs to be solved culturally through the introduction of new traditions, new forms of marriage, and new social arrangements.

The population explosion itself is merely a reflex of the explosive development of new ideas and ways of doing things. It would hardly have been possible without an explosive increase in the production of food and other requirements for human existence. The explosive development in technology has inevitably led to an explosive increase in man's capacity to exterminate himself or to alter the face of the earth. The threats of atomic warfare, bacteriological warfare, or chemical warfare are obvious and visible. Less visible are the threats posed by the introduction of new chemicals or by slow but massive changes in the seas, land masses, and atmospheres of earth. Does a slight increase in the temperature of the ocean make a difference? As the plastic doodads floating in the Sargasso Sea disintegrate and release the subtle poisons they contain, will the oceans die and will we become extinct? Are we already extinct? Some of these problems of technological explosion are problems for physicists or marine biologists, but the technological explosion also has to do with human cultural traditions and human social arrangements.

The technological explosion is the product of new discoveries and new information. There has been an almost infinite increase in the length and complexity of the cultural message, an information explosion. Because a single human being can "know" only a limited amount, cultural systems have always contained information economies. Some people know some things; others know other things. A cultural system works because the information available to different people is somehow assembled at the proper time and used in the solution of outstanding problems. At the present time we know very little about how information is stored and retrieved in human beings or in cultural systems. Is it possible for a cultural tradition to contain so much information and to become so complicated that it simply fails to function? Are children in the United States or in other complex modern societies learning their cultural traditions through processes of cultural transmission or are they learning uncoordinated bits and pieces of a cultural tradition so large that it cannot be comprehended?

The technological and information explosions have made it possible to transport human beings and ideas from one place to another with great rapidity and in great numbers. Formerly independent cultural systems have been brought into contact with others. Cultural systems which once served a multiplicity of functions have come to serve relatively few functions. Vast increases in population have multiplied the number of existing cultural systems. The cultural differences between New York and Pukapuka are declining while the differences between fishermen and physicists are increasing. It is not known whether this implies a net gain or net loss in cultural diversity, but the worldwide spread of anything, whether it is DDT or a new idea, should be viewed with alarm. The fact that human beings and human cultural systems are different is the most exciting thing about them, yet the destruction of diversity is implicit in the worldwide spread of rock and roll, communism, capitalism, or anything else. When a song is forgotten or a ceremony ceases to be performed, a part of the human heritage is destroyed forever.

As cultural traditions and cultural systems have become larger and more all encompassing, the little traditions of neighborhood, community, and tribe have lost their uniqueness and their coherence. One hundred years ago most of the people of the earth lived in small communities in intimate relationship to their neighbors. Because the small community has been so general and pervasive for so many years, anthropologists have often drawn the conclusion that communities are essential to the preservation of human identity and well-being. Looking at the modern world, it almost seems as if the small group and the small community have been declared enemies of the state. It is believed to be more efficient to have one large university with ten thousand students than ten small universities. The same principle holds true for factories and farms and all the other contexts within which people work or play or live.

In many modern societies the life of the individual is governed, not by his neighbors, but by faceless bureaucracies. In modern states and cities such bureaucracies contend against each other for resources and seek to increase their size and influence. Whether seeking to grow or to control their clients, bureaucracies formulate new rules and employ more persons to enforce them. The individual is governed now, not by the cultural tradition of his community, but by the countless and inexplicable rules of the innumerable bureaucracies with which he must deal in order to survive. With the evolution of larger and larger cultural systems and the increasing inclusion of all mankind within a single world order, perhaps all this is necessary, but perhaps it is time to consider what has been sacrificed upon the twin altars of modernity and efficiency.

At any event, the decline of the small community appears to have gone hand in hand with a kind of normlessness and alienation represented in the United States by such code phrases as "the drug problem," "the generation gap," "dropping out," or the "rising crime rate." On an even wider scale most modern nations are witnessing the formation of countercultural groups of people of all ages and degrees of political persuasion. In part these groups appear to represent a conscious effort to revive and perpetuate the lost community of the past in the form of retirement colonies, mobile home parks, or communes. One of the characteristics of such groups is their rejection of all or some aspects of officially endorsed reality. The larger countercultural groups possess their own newspapers, television programs, and trained scientists. In the United States in particular, but in other countries as well, the outstanding problems of society can no longer be approached in terms of established fact or, if you like, establishment fact. Scientists as well as ordinary people disagree concerning the dangers of marihuana, the extent of the Russian menace, the degree of environmental pollution, the causes of poverty, the safety of fluoridation, the effect of capital punishment, the dangers of atomic war, or the consequences of population growth. Although much of the world's population might be brought to agree that humanity faces the greatest crisis in its history, neither scientists nor laymen agree concerning its nature.

If good fiction depends upon the voluntary suspension of disbelief, so do cultural traditions. Modern traditions have been founded upon an information explosion triggered through the use of the scientific method. Although the nineteenth- and early twentieth-century faith in Science as a solver of all problems now seems naive and childish, the alternative to a worldwide scientific establishment enjoying some protection from political and self-serving influences is a return to the more traditional pattern when people made up "truths" to suit themselves. Perhaps it is the case that in times of trouble people tend to return to the mythological truths that comforted them as children.

Perhaps it is time for some Quetzalcoatl, some mythological savior, to appear and lead us to the light. Certainly, in its underdeveloped state the field of anthropology cannot propose itself as an instant source of significant solutions to human problems. The systematic comparison of cultural systems and the achievement of an understanding of ourselves is a formidable task requiring the cooperation of many men, women, and disciplines. The science of stones and bones, the quaint and remote, offers no quick solutions. It offers, instead, two million years of change, conflict, exploration, music, kindness, and cruelty. It offers the first fumbling attempts at an understanding. Above all, it offers an image of man—always the same, always different:

My lovely moon, my sister; I feel now that I want to marry you, I should like to unite with you, O my sister, that is the way I feel.

I have no objection, O my brother, and I agree that you shall marry me and that we shall be united, but there is something that I must say to you, O hornbill, O my brother Manyamei Limut Garing Balua Unggom Tingang. Do not be angry in your heart, do not be furious within, O my brother, when you hear my words, when you learn what I have to say to you.

What is your desire, O my sister, and what are the words that you have to speak to me?

Indeed, hornbill, my brother Manyamei Limut Garing, I do not oppose you if you want to marry me, I do not resist your desires if you want to unite your body with mine, I do not refuse you, but you must first carry out my request, you must grant my wish.

My wish is not so wide as the branches of a tree, it is not so big as the boughs of trees. My wish is this, O hornbill, O my brother: seek an island, find a small piece of earth as landing place for our boats, and when you have found it then you may marry the moon, then you can tenderly cling to me, the woman, then I shall permit you to unite with me, the wife.

What you say is too hard, and what you demand is too great, it is more extensive than the branches of a tree, it is bigger than the boughs of trees.

Indeed, Putir Kuhukup Bungking Garing, here now is the land that you desired of me.

Yes, my brother, O my brother, there is some land now and I shall marry you, I shall surrender myself to you—when you have erected a large house, when you have built a tall dwelling.

(Manyamei Limut Garing shakes his head so that his golden ear-rings joggle, he looks hither and thither and he scratches audibly at his face) (Schärer 1963:175–179).

Bibliography

Adair, John, and Evon Vogt, 1949, Navaho and Zuni veterans: a study of contrasting modes of culture change. *American Anthropologist*, 51:547–561.

Adams, J. Stacy, and A. Kimball Romney, 1959, A functional analysis of authority. *Psychological Review*, 66:234–251.

Alland, Alexander, Jr., 1971, *Human Diversity*. New York: Columbia University Press.

————, 1972, *The Human Imperative*. New York: Columbia University Press.

Arensberg, Conrad M., and Solon T. Kimball, 1948, *Family and Community in Ireland*, 2d ed. Cambridge, Mass.: Harvard University Press.

Balandier, Georges, 1970, *Political Anthropology*. Trans. by A. M. Sheridan Smith. New York: Random House, Inc. (First published in French, 1967.)

Barker, Roger G., and Herbert F. Wright, 1955, *Midwest and Its Children: the Psychological Ecology of an American Town*. New York: Harper & Row, Publishers.

Barnett, Homer G., 1953, *Innovation: the Basis of Cultural Change*. New York: McGraw-Hill, Inc.

————, 1960, *Being a Palauan*. New York: Holt, Rinehart and Winston, Inc.

Barrow, Sir John, 1846, *Voyages of Discovery and Research within the Arctic Regions from the Year 1818 to the Present Time*. New York: Harper & Brothers.

Bascom, William, 1969, *The Yoruba of Southwestern Nigeria*. New York: Holt, Rinehart and Winston, Inc.

Basso, Keith H., 1970, *The Cibecue Apache*. New York: Holt, Rinehart and Winston, Inc.

Bates, Marston, 1958, *Gluttons and Libertines: Human Problems of Being Natural*. New York: Vintage Books.

————, 1960, *The Forest and the Sea: a Look at the Economy of Nature and the Ecology of Man.* New York: Random House, Inc.

Beals, Alan R., 1962, *Gopalpur: a South Indian Village.* New York: Holt, Rinehart and Winston, Inc.

————, and Bernard J. Siegel, 1966, *Divisiveness and Social Conflict: an Anthropological Approach.* Stanford, Calif.: Stanford University Press.

Beals, Ralph L., and Harry Hoijer, 1971, *An Introduction to Anthropology,* 4th ed., New York: Crowell-Collier and Macmillan, Inc.

Beattie, John, 1960, *Bunyoro: an African Kingdom.* New York: Holt, Rinehart and Winston, Inc.

Beidelman, T. O., 1971, *The Kaguru: a Matrilineal People of East Africa.* New York: Holt, Rinehart and Winston, Inc.

Bennett, John W., 1969, *Northern Plainsmen: Adaptive Strategy and Agrarian Life.* Chicago: Aldine Publishing Co.

Berry, Brewton, 1969, *Almost White.* London: Collier-Macmillan, Ltd.

Bettelheim, Bruno, 1954, *Symbolic Wounds: Puberty Rites and the Envious Male.* New York: The Free Press of Glencoe.

Birdsell, Joseph, 1968, Some predictions for the Pleistocene based on equilibrium systems among recent hunter-gatherers, in *Man the Hunter,* Richard B. Lee and Irven DeVore, eds. Chicago: Aldine Publishing Co.

————, 1972, *Human Evolution: an Introduction to the New Physical Anthropology.* Skokie, Ill.: Rand McNally & Company.

Bloomfield, Leonard, 1933, *Language.* New York: Henry Holt and Company, Inc.

Boas, Franz, 1948, The limitations of the comparative method of anthropology, in *Race, Language, and Culture.* New York: Crowell-Collier and Macmillan, Inc. (Paper read at meeting of AAAS at Buffalo, first printed in *Science,* N.S. Vol. 4, 1896, 901–908).

Bodmer, Walter F., and Luigi Luca Cavalli-Sforza, 1970, Intelligence and race, *Scientific American,* October 1970, Pp. 19–29.

Bohannan, Paul, 1963, *Social Anthropology.* New York: Holt, Rinehart and Winston, Inc.

————, ed., 1967, *Law and Warfare.* Garden City, N.Y.: The Natural History Press.

Boissevain, Jeremy F., 1969, *Hal-Farrug: A Village in Malta.* New York: Holt, Rinehart and Winston, Inc.

Bordes, Francois, 1968, *The Old Stone Age.* New York: McGraw-Hill, Inc.

Bowen, Elenore Smith, 1954, *Return to Laughter.* New York: Harper & Row, Publishers.

Brace, C. Loring, 1967, *The Stages of Human Evolution: Human and Cultural Origins.* Englewood Cliffs, N.J.: Prentice-Hall, Inc.

Braidwood, Robert J., 1967, *Prehistoric Men.* Glenview, Ill.: Scott-Foresman and Company.

Bressler, Jack Barry, ed., 1966. *Human Ecology: Collected Readings.* Reading, Mass.: Addison-Wesley Publishing Company, Inc.

Brown, Judith K., 1963, A cross-cultural study of female initiation rites. *American Anthropologist* 65:837–853.

Bruner, Edward, 1961, Urbanization and ethnic identity in North Sumatra. *American Anthropologist,* 63:508–521.

Buchler, Ira R., and Henry A. Selby, 1968, *Kinship and Social Organization.* New York: Crowell-Collier and Macmillan, Inc.

Buechler, Hans C., and Judith-Maria Buechler, 1971, *The Bolivian Aymara.* New York: Holt, Rinehart and Winston, Inc.

Casagrande, Joseph B., ed., 1960, *In the Company of Man, Twenty Portraits of Anthropological Informants.* New York: Harper & Row, Publishers.

Chagnon, Napoleon A., 1968, *Yanomamö: The Fierce People.* New York: Holt, Rinehart and Winston, Inc.

Chance, Norman A., 1966, *The Eskimo of North Alaska.* New York: Holt, Rinehart and Winston, Inc.

Chomsky, Noam, 1966, *Syntactic Structures.* Paris: Mouton and Co.

Clark, Grahame, 1967, *The Stone Age Hunters.* New York: McGraw-Hill, Inc.

————, 1969, *World Prehistory: A New Outline, Being the Second Edition of "World Prehistory."* Cambridge: Cambridge University Press.

Cohen, Ronald, and John Middleton, eds., 1967, *Comparative Political Systems.* Garden City, N.Y.: The Natural History Press.

Cohen, Yehudi, 1964, *The Transition from Childhood to Adolescence.* Chicago: Aldine Publishing Co.

Collier, John, Jr., 1967, *Visual Anthropology: Photography as Research Method.* New York: Holt, Rinehart and Winston, Inc.

————, 1973, *Alaskan Eskimo Education: Analysis of Cultural Confrontation in the Schools.* New York: Holt, Rinehart and Winston, Inc.

Colson, Elizabeth, 1953, *The Makah Indians: a Study of an Indian Tribe in Modern American Society.* Minneapolis: University of Minnesota Press.

CRM Books, 1971, *Anthropology Today.* Del Mar, Calif.: Communications Research Machines, Inc.

Davidson, Sara, 1971, The rush for instant salvation. *Harper's Magazine,* July, pp. 46–54.

Deng, Francis M., 1972, *The Dinka of the Sudan.* New York: Holt, Rinehart and Winston, Inc.

Dennis, Wayne, 1940, *The Hopi Child.* New York: Appleton-Century-Crofts. (For the Institute for Research in the Social Sciences, University of Virginia, Institute Monograph No. 26.)

Dentan, Robert Knox, 1968, *The Semai: A Nonviolent People of Malaya.* New York: Holt, Rinehart and Winston, Inc.

De Vore, Irven, ed., 1965, *Primate Behavior: Field Studies of Monkeys and Apes.* New York: Holt, Rinehart and Winston, Inc.

Diamond, Norma, 1969, *K'un Shen: a Taiwan Village.* New York: Holt, Rinehart and Winston, Inc.

Dorn, Harold F., 1962, World population growth: an international dilemma. *Science,* 135:283–290.

Doughty, Charles M., 1937, *Travels in Arabia Deserta,* 2 vols. New York: Random House, Inc. (First published in 1888; English ed., 1 vol., 1926.)

Downs, James F., 1966, *The Two Worlds of the Washo: an Indian Tribe of California and Nevada.* New York: Holt, Rinehart and Winston, Inc.

————, 1972, *The Navajo.* New York: Holt, Rinehart and Winston, Inc.

————, and Hermann K. Bleibtreu, 1969, *Human Variation: an Introduction to Physical Anthropology.* Beverly Hills, Calif.: Glencoe Press.

Dozier, Edward P., 1966, *Hano: a Tewa Indian Community in Arizona.* New York: Holt, Rinehart and Winston, Inc.

Driver, Harold E., 1961, *Indians of North America*. Chicago: University of Chicago Press.

Dubois, Abbé J. A., 1947, *Hindu Manners, Customs and Ceremonies*, 3d ed. by Henry K. Beauchamp. Oxford: Clarendon Press. (First published in 1897.)

DuBois, Cora, 1961, *The People of Alor, a Social-Psychological Study of an East Indian Island*. New York: Harper Torchbooks. (First published in 1944.)

Durkheim, Émile, 1961, *The Elementary Forms of the Religious Life*. Trans. by Joseph Ward Swain. New York: Crowell-Collier and Macmillan, Inc.

————, 1912, *Les Formes Élémentaire de la Vie Religieuse*. Paris: Librairie Felix Alcan.

————, and Marcel Mauss, 1963, *Primitive Classification*. Trans. by Rodney Needham. Chicago: University of Chicago Press. (First published in French, 1903.)

Dyk, Walter, 1967, *Son of Old Man Hat: A Navajo Autobiography*. Lincoln: University of Nebraska Press. (First published in 1938.)

Dyson-Hudson, Rada, and Neville Dyson-Hudson, 1969, Subsistence herding in Uganda. *Scientific American*, February 1969, Pp. 76–89.

Eggan, Dorothy, 1956, Instruction and affect in Hopi cultural continuity. *Southwestern Journal of Anthropology*, 12(4):347–370. (Reprinted in *Education and Culture*, G. Spindler, ed. New York: Holt, Rinehart and Winston, Inc., 1963.)

Ehrlich, Paul R., and Anne H. Ehrlich, 1972, *Population, Resources, Environment: Issues in Human Ecology*, 2nd ed. San Francisco: W. H. Freeman and Company.

Eibl-Eibesfeldt, Irenaus, 1970, *Ethology: The Biology of Behavior*. Trans. by Erich Klinghammer. New York: Holt, Rinehart and Winston, Inc.

Eiseley, Loren, 1969, *The Unexpected Universe*. New York: Harcourt Brace Jovanovich.

Ekvall, Robert B., 1968, *Fields on the Hoof: Nexus of Tibetan Nomadic Pastoralism*. New York: Holt, Rinehart and Winston, Inc.

Ellsworth, John S. Jr., 1952, *Factory Folkways: a Study of Institutional Structure and Change*. New Haven, Conn.: Yale University Press.

Elwin, Verrier,1950, *Bondo Highlander: Bombay*. London: Oxford University Press.

————, 1955, *The Religion of an Indian Tribe*. London: Oxford University Press.

Erikson, Erik H., 1950, *Childhood and Society*. New York: W. W. Norton & Company, Inc.

Esquire, March 1970, California evil. Vol. LXX, pp. 90–123.

Evans-Pritchard, E. E., 1969, *The Nuer: A Description of the Modes of Livelihood and Political Institutions of a Nilotic People*. New York: Oxford University Press. (First published in 1940.)

Fichter, Joseph H., S.J., 1964, *Parochial School: a Sociological Study*. New York: Anchor Books.

Firth, Raymond, 1963, *We, the Tikopia: a Sociological Study of Kinship in Primitive Polynesia*. Abridged by the author with a new introduction. Boston: The Beacon Press. (First published in 1936 by George Allen & Unwin Ltd., 2d ed., 1957.)

Foerster, Heinz von, Patricia M. Mora, and L. W. Amiot, 1960, Doomsday: Friday 13 November, A.D. 2026, *Science*, 132:1291–1295.

Foster, George, 1962, *Traditional Cultures and the Impact of Technological Change*. New York: Harper & Row, Publishers.

————, 1972, The anatomy of envy: a study in symbolic behavior, *Current Anthropology*, 13(2):165–186.

Fox, Robin, 1967, *Kinship and Marriage*. Baltimore: Penguin Books, Inc.

Frake, Charles O., 1964. Notes on queries in ethnography, in *Transcultural Studies in Cognition*. American Anthropological Association special publication, A. Kimball Romney and Roy G. D'Andrade, eds. *American Anthropologist*, 66 (6, Pt. 2): 132–145.

Frantz, Charles, 1972, *The Student Anthropologist's Handbook*. Cambridge, Mass.: Schenkman Publishing Co.

Freilich, Morris, 1970, *Marginal Natives: Anthropologists at Work*. New York: Harper & Row, Publishers.

Fried, Morton H., 1972, *The Study of Anthropology*. New York: Thomas Y. Crowell Company.

Friedl, Ernestine, 1962, *Vasilika, a Village in Modern Greece*. New York: Holt, Rinehart and Winston, Inc.

————, 1964, Lagging emulation in post-peasant society. *American Anthropologist*, 66:564–586.

Fürer-Haimendorf, Christoph von, 1956, *Himalayan Barbary*. New York: Abelard-Schuman Ltd.

————, 1969, *The Konyak Nagas: an Indian Frontier Tribe*. New York: Holt, Rinehart and Winston, Inc.

Gaeng, Paul A., 1971, *Introduction to the Principles of Language*. New York: Harper & Row, Publishers.

Gamst, Frederick, 1969, *The Qemant, a Pagan-Hebraic Peasantry of Ethiopia*. New York: Holt, Rinehart and Winston, Inc.

Gay, John, and Michael Cole, 1967, *The New Mathematics and an Old Culture*. New York: Holt, Rinehart and Winston, Inc.

Gleason, Henry Allan, 1961, *An Introduction to Descriptive Linguistics*, rev. ed. New York: Holt, Rinehart and Winston, Inc.

Gluckman, Max, 1965, *Politics, Law and Ritual in Tribal Society*. Chicago: Aldine Publishing Co.

Goffman, Erving, 1967, *Interaction Ritual*. Chicago: Aldine Publishing Co.

Golde, Peggy, ed., 1970, *Women in the Field*. Chicago: Aldine Publishing Co.

Goodenough, Ward Hunt, 1963, *Cooperation in Change*. New York: Russell Sage Foundation.

Green, M. M., 1964, *Ibo Village Affairs*. New York: Frederick A. Praeger, Inc. (First published in 1947.)

Greenberg, Joseph H., 1968, *Anthropological Linguistics: an Introduction*. New York: Random House, Inc.

Grindal, Bruce, 1972, *Growing Up in Two Worlds: Education and Transition among the Sisala of Northern Ghana*. New York: Holt, Rinehart and Winston, Inc.

Grinnell, G. B., 1923, *The Cheyenne Indians*, Vol. I. New Haven, Conn.: Yale University Press.

Gudschinsky, Sarah C., 1967, *How To Learn an Unwritten Language*. New York: Holt, Rinehart and Winston, Inc.

Gumperz, John J., and Dell Hymes, eds., 1964, *The Ethnography of Communication*. American Anthropological Association special publication. *American Anthropologist* 66 (6, Pt. 2.).

Hall, Edward T., 1961, *The Silent Language*. New York: Fawcett Publishing Co. (First published in 1959.)

Hallowell, A. Irving, 1955, *Culture and Experience*. Philadelphia: University of Pennsylvania Press.

————, 1957, The impact of the American Indian on American culture. *American Anthropologist*, 59:201–217.

Halpern, Joel M., 1967, *The Changing Village Community*. Englewood Cliffs, N.J.: Prentice-Hall, Inc.

————, and Barbara Kerewsky Halpern, 1972, *A Serbian Village in Historical Perspective*. New York: Holt, Rinehart and Winston, Inc.

Hammel, E. A., ed., 1965, *Formal Semantic Analysis*. American Anthropological Association special publication. *American Anthropologist*, Vol. 67, No. 5, Pt. 2.

Hanks, Lucien M., 1972, *Rice and Man: Agricultural Ecology in Southeast Asia*. Chicago: Aldine Publishing Co.

Harris, Marvin, 1971, *Culture, Man and Nature*. New York: Thomas Y. Crowell Company.

Hart, C. W. M., 1955, Contrasts between perpubertal and postpubertal education, in *Education and Anthropology*, G. Spindler, ed. Stanford, Calif.: Stanford University Press. (Reprinted in *Education and Culture*, G. Spindler, ed., New York: Holt, Rinehart and Winston, Inc., 1963.)

————, and Arnold R. Pilling, 1960, *The Tiwi of North Australia*. New York: Holt, Rinehart and Winston, Inc.

Hawley, Florence, 1948, An examination of problems basic to acculturation in the Rio Grande pueblos. *American Anthropologist*, 50:612–624.

Hays, H. R., 1964, *From Ape to Angel*. New York: Capricorn Books. (First published in 1958.)

Heider, Karl G., 1970, *The Dugum Dani: a Papuan Culture in the Highlands of West New Guinea*. New York: Wenner-Gren Foundation for Anthropological Research, Inc.

Henry, Jules, 1960. A cross-cultural outline of education. *Current Anthropology*, 4: 267–305.

————, 1963, *Culture against Man*. New York: Random House, Inc.

Henry, William E., 1947, The thematic apperception technique in the study of culture-personality relations. *Genetic Psychology Monographs*, Vol. 35, 1st half. Provincetown, Mass.: The Journal Press.

Herskovits, Melville J., 1950, *Man and His Works*. New York: Alfred A. Knopf, Inc.

————, and Francis S. Herskovits, 1934, *Rebel Destiny: Among the Bush Negroes of Dutch Guiana*. New York: McGraw-Hill, Inc.

Hitchcock, John T., 1965, *The Magars of Banyan Hill*. New York: Holt, Rinehart and Winston, Inc.

Hockett, Charles F., 1962, *A Course in Modern Linguistics*. New York: Crowell-Collier and Macmillan, Inc.

————, and Robert Asher, 1964, The human revolution. *Current Anthropology*, 5:135.

Hoebel, Edward Adamson, 1949, *Man in the Primitive World*. New York: McGraw-Hill, Inc.

————, 1960, *The Cheyennes: Indians of the Great Plains*. New York: Holt, Rinehart and Winston, Inc.

————, 1972, *Anthropology: the Study of Man*, 4th ed. New York: McGraw-Hill, Inc.

Hogbin, Ian, 1964, *A Guadalcanal Society: the Kaoka Speakers*. New York: Holt, Rinehart and Winston, Inc.

Horowitz, Michael M., 1967, *Morne-Paysan: Peasant Village in Martinique*. New York: Holt, Rinehart and Winston, Inc.

Hostetler, John A., and Gertrude E. Huntington, 1967, *The Hutterites in North America*. New York: Holt, Rinehart and Winston, Inc.

————, 1971, *Children in Amish Society: Socialization and Community Education*. New York: Holt, Rinehart and Winston, Inc.

Hudson, A. B., 1972, *Padju Epat: the Ma'anyan of Indonesian Borneo*. New York: Holt, Rinehart and Winston, Inc.

Hulse, Frederick S., 1971, *The Human Species: an Introduction to Physical Anthropology*, 2d. ed. New York: Random House, Inc.

Hunter, Monica (*See also* Monica Wilson), 1936, *Reaction to Conquest*. London: International Institute of African Languages and Cultures, Oxford University Press.

Jay, Phyllis C., ed., 1968, *Primates: Studies in Adaptation and Variability*. New York: Holt, Rinehart and Winston, Inc.

Jocano, F. Landa, 1969, *Growing Up in a Philippine Barrio*. New York: Holt, Rinehart and Winston, Inc.

Jones, D. E., 1972, *Sanapia: Comanche Medicine Woman*. New York: Holt, Rinehart and Winston, Inc.

Jones, Howard Mumford, 1952, Prose and pictures: James Fenimore Cooper. *Tulane Studies in English*, 3:126–137.

Kaberry, Phyllis M., 1950, *Aboriginal Woman, Sacred and Profane*. New York: The Humanities Press.

Kardiner, Abram, and Edward Preble, 1961, *They Studied Man*. Cleveland: The World Publishing Company.

Kawai M., 1965, Newly-acquired pre-cultural behavior of the natural troop of Japanese monkeys on Koshima Island. *Primates*, 6(1):1–30.

Kearney, Michael, 1972, *The Winds of Ixtepeji: World View and Society in a Zapotec Town*. New York: Holt, Rinehart and Winston, Inc.

Keesing, Roger M., and Felix M. Keesing, 1971, *New Perspectives in Cultural Anthropology*. New York: Holt, Rinehart and Winston, Inc.

Keiser, R. Lincoln, 1969, *Vice Lords: Warriors of the Streets*. New York: Holt, Rinehart and Winston, Inc.

Kelso, A. J., 1970, *Physical Anthropology: an Introduction*. Philadelphia: J. B. Lippincott Company.

Kennard, E. A., 1937, Hopi reactions to death. *American Anthropologist*, 39:491–496.

King, A. Richard, 1967, *The School at Mopass: a Problem of Identity*. New York: Holt, Rinehart and Winston, Inc.

Klima, George J., 1970, *The Barabaig: East African Cattle-Herders*. New York: Holt, Rinehart and Winston, Inc.

Kluckhohn, Clyde, 1949, The philosophy of the Navaho Indians, in *Ideological Differences and World Orders*, F. S. C. Northrop, ed. New Haven, Conn.: Published for the Viking Fund by Yale University Press.

Kochman, Thomas, 1971, "Rapping" in the black ghetto, in *Conformity and Conflict*, James P. Spradley and David W. McGurdy, eds. Boston: Little, Brown & Company.

Kroeber, A. L., and Clyde Kluckhohn, 1963, *Culture: a Critical Review of Concepts and Definitions*. New York: Vintage Books. (First published in 1952.)

Kummer, Hans, 1968, *Social Organization of Hamadryas Baboons*. Chicago: University of Chicago Press.

————, 1971, *Primate Societies: Group Techniques of Ecological Adaptation*. Chicago: Aldine-Atherton Press.

Kuper, Hilda, 1963, *The Swazi: a South African Kingdom*. New York: Holt, Rinehart and Winston, Inc.

Lamb, Sidney M., 1964. The sememic approach to structural semantics, in *Transcultural Studies in Cognition*. American Anthropological Association special publication. A. Kimball Romney and Roy Goodwin D'Andrade, eds. *American Anthropologist*, 66 (Pt. 2):57–78.

Langness, L. L., 1965, *The Life History in Anthropological Science*. New York: Holt, Rinehart and Winston, Inc.

Lantis, Margaret, 1960, Eskimo childhood and interpersonal relationships, Nunivak biographies and genealogies. The American Ethnological Society, Verne F. Ray, ed. Seattle: University of Washington Press.

Lee, Richard B., and Irven DeVore, eds., 1969, *Man the Hunter*. Chicago: Aldine Publishing Co.

Leighton, Dorothea, and Clyde Kluckhohn, 1947, *Children of the People*. Cambridge, Mass.: Harvard University Press.

Leis, Philip, 1972, *Enculturation and Socialization in an Ijaw Society*. New York: Holt, Rinehart and Winston, Inc.

Lerner, I. Michael, 1968, *Heredity, Evolution and Society*. San Francisco: W. H. Freeman and Company.

Lessa, William, 1966, *Ulithi: a Micronesian Design for Living*. New York: Holt, Rinehart and Winston, Inc.

————, and Evon Z. Vogt, 1965, *Reader in Comparative Religion: an Anthropological Approach*, 2d ed. New York: Harper & Row, Publishers.

Lewis, Oscar, 1951, *Life in a Mexican Village: Tepoztlán Restudied*. Urbana: University of Illinois Press.

————, 1960, *Tepoztlán: Village in Mexico*. New York: Holt, Rinehart and Winston, Inc.

Linton, Ralph, 1936, *The Study of Man, an Introduction*. New York: Appleton-Century-Crofts, Inc.

————, 1939, The Tanala of Madagascar, in *The Individual and His Society*, Abram Kardiner, ed. New York: Columbia University Press.

Lorimer, Frank, 1954, *Culture and Human Fertility*. (With special contributions by Meyer Fortes, K. A. Busia, Audrey I. Richards, Priscilla Reining, and Giorgio Mortara.) Paris: UNESCO.

Lowie, Robert H., 1956, *The Crow Indians*. New York: Holt, Rinehart and Winston, Inc. (First published in 1935.)

McFee, Malcolm, 1972, *Modern Blackfeet Montanans on a Reservation*. New York: Holt, Rinehart and Winston, Inc.

MacGregor, Gordon, 1946, *Warriors without Weapons*. Chicago: University of Chicago Press.

Madsen, William, 1964, *The Mexican-Americans of South Texas*. New York: Holt, Rinehart and Winston, Inc.

Maine, Sir Henry, 1861, *Ancient Law*. London: John Murray.

Malinowski, Bronislaw, 1927, *The Father in Primitive Psychology*. London: Kegan Paul, Trench Trubner & Company.

————, 1955, *Magic, Science and Religion and Other Essays*. New York: Anchor Books. (First published in 1925.)

————, 1961, *Argonauts of the Western Pacific: an Account of Native Enterprise and Adventure in the Archipelagoes of Melanesian New Guinea*. New York: E. P. Dutton & Co., Inc. (First published in 1922.)

————, 1967, *A Diary in the Strict Sense of the Term*. New York: Harcourt Brace Jovanovich.

Malthus, Thomas Robert, 1965, *First Essay on Population, 1798*. New York: A. M. Kelley. (First published in 1798.)

Mandelbaum, David G., 1941, Culture change among the Nilgiri tribes. *American Anthropologist*, 43:19–26.

————, 1960, A reformer of his people (South India), in *In the Company of Man, Twenty Portraits of Anthropological Informants*. New York: Harper & Row, Publishers.

Maranda, Pierre, 1972, *Introduction to Anthropology: a Self-Guide*. Englewood Cliffs, N.J.: Prentice-Hall, Inc.

Masters, John, 1958, *Bugles and a Tiger*. New York: Bantam Books, Inc. (First published in 1956.)

Mead, Margaret, 1949, *Coming of Age in Samoa: a Psychological Study of Primitive Youth for Western Civilization*. New York: Mentor Books. (First published in 1928.)

————, 1950, *The School in American Culture*. Cambridge, Mass.: Harvard University Press.

————, 1953, *Growing Up in New Guinea*. New York: Mentor Books. (First published in 1930.)

————, 1956, *New Lives for Old*. New York: William Morrow & Company, Inc.

————, 1964, *Continuities in Cultural Evolution*. New Haven, Conn.: Yale University Press.

Meggers, Betty J., 1971, *Amazonia: Man and Culture in a Counterfeit Paradise*. Chicago: Aldine-Atherton Press.

Messenger, John Cowan, 1969, *Inis Beag: Isle of Ireland*. New York: Holt, Rinehart and Winston, Inc.

Metzger, Duane, and Gerald E. Williams, 1963, A formal ethnographic analysis of Tenejapa ladino weddings. *American Anthropologist*, 65: 1076–1101.

Middleton, John, 1965, *The Lugbara of Uganda*. New York: Holt, Rinehart and Winston, Inc.

Milwaukee Journal, 1965, Lo, the poor Indian: past blocks path to modern life. Sept. 5.

Modiano, Nancy, 1973, *Indian Education in the Chiapas Highlands*. New York: Holt, Rinehart and Winston, Inc.

Murphy, Robert, 1961, Deviancy and social control I: What makes Biboi run? *The Kroeber Anthropological Society Papers*, 24: 55–61.

————, and Julian Steward, 1956, Tappers and trappers: parallel process in acculturation, in *Economic Development and Culture Change*, Vol. 4, No. 4, 335–355. (Research Center in Economic Development and Culture Change, University of Chicago.)

Myrdal, Gunnar, 1944, *An American Dilemma: the Negro Problem and Modern Democracy*. New York: Harper & Row, Publishers.

Nadel, Siegried F., 1954, *Nupe Religion*. New York: The Free Press of Glencoe.

Nader, Laura, ed., 1965, *The Ethnography of Law*. American Anthropological Association special publication. *American Anthropologist*, Vol. 67, No. 6, Pt. 2.

Netting, Robert M., 1968, *Hill Farmers of Nigeria: Cultural Ecology of the Kofyar of the Jos Plateau*. Seattle: University of Washington Press.

Newman, Philip L., 1965, *Knowing the Gururumba*. New York: Holt, Rinehart and Winston, Inc.

Norbeck, Edward, 1965, *Changing Japan*. New York: Holt, Rinehart and Winston, Inc.

Palo Alto Times, 1971a, Free people still dependent on the straights. April 27.

————, 1971b, Untold thousands pursue a different American dream. April 26.

Parkman, Francis, 1950, *The Oregon Trail*. New York: Signet Classic, New American Library. (First published in 1849.)

Parrington, Vernon Louis, 1927, *Main Currents in American Thought: an Interpretation of American Literature from the Beginnings to 1920*, Vol. I. New York: Harcourt, Brace and Company, Inc.

Partridge, William L., 1973, *The Hippie Ghetto: the Natural History of a Subculture*. New York: Holt, Rinehart and Winston, Inc.

Pelto, Pertti J., 1970, *Anthropological Research: the Structure of Inquiry*. New York: Harper & Row, Publishers.

Peshkin, Alan, 1972, *Kanuri Schoolchildren: Education and Social Mobilization in Nigeria*. New York: Holt, Rinehart and Winston, Inc.

Pettit, George A., 1946, *Primitive Education in North America*. Publications in American Archeology and Ethnology, Vol. XLIII. Berkeley: University of California Press.

Pfeiffer, John E., 1969, *The Emergence of Man*. New York: Harper & Row, Publishers.

Piddington, Ralph, 1957, *An Introduction to Social Anthropology*, Vol. II. London: Oliver and Boyd, Ltd.

Pierce, Joe E., 1964, *Life in a Turkish Village*. New York: Holt, Rinehart and Winston, Inc.

Pitt-Rivers, J. A., 1961, *The People of the Sierra*. Chicago: Phoenix Books, University of Chicago Press.

Pospisil, Leopold, 1963, *The Kapauku Papuans of West New Guinea*. New York: Holt, Rinehart and Winston, Inc.

Quintana, Bertha B., and Lois Gray Floyd, 1972, *Que Gitano! Gypsies of Southern Spain*. New York: Holt, Rinehart and Winston, Inc.

Rappaport, Roy A., 1967, *Pigs for the Ancestors: Ritual in the Ecology of a New Guinea People*. New Haven, Conn.: Yale University Press.

Rasmussen, Knud, 1921, *Greenland by the Polar Sea: the Story of the Thule Expedition from Melville Bay to Cape Morris Jesup*. Trans. by Asta and Rowland Kenney. London: William Heinemann, Ltd.

————, 1929, *The Intellectual Culture of the Iglulik Eskimos*. (Report of the 5th Thule expedition 1921–24, Vol. VII, No. 1, W. Worster, trans.) Copenhagen: Gyldendal.

Read, Margaret, 1968, *Children of Their Fathers: the Ngoni of Malawi*. New York: Holt, Rinehart and Winston, Inc.

Redfield, Robert, 1930, *Tepoztlán: a Mexican Village*. Chicago: University of Chicago Press.

————, 1947, The folk society. *American Journal of Sociology*, 52:293–308.

————, 1953, *The Primitive World and Its Transformation*. Ithaca, N.Y.: Cornell University Press.

————, 1962, *A Village That Chose Progress: Chan Kom Revisited*. Chicago: Phoenix Books, University of Chicago Press. (First published in 1950.)

Reich, Charles A., 1971, *The Greening of America*. New York: Bantam Books.

Reichard, Gladys A., 1949, The Navaho and Christianity. *American Anthropologist*, 51:66–71.

Reichenbach, Hans, 1959, *The Rise of Scientific Philosophy*. Berkeley: University of California Press.

Rivière, Peter, 1972, *The Forgotten Frontier: Ranchers of North Brazil*. New York: Holt, Rinehart and Winston, Inc.

Rohner, Ronald P., and Evelyn C. Rohner, 1970, *The Kwakiutl Indians of British Columbia*. New York: Holt, Rinehart and Winston, Inc.

Romney, A. Kimball, and Roy Goodwin D'Andrade, 1964, Cognitive aspects of English kin terms, in *Transcultural Studies in Cognition*, American Anthropological Association special publication, A. Kimball Romney and Roy G. D'Andrade, eds. *American Anthropologist*, Vol. 66, No. 3, Pt. 2:253.

Rosenfeld, Gerry, 1971, *"Shut Those Thick Lips": a Study in Slum School Failure*. New York: Holt, Rinehart and Winston, Inc.

Roszak, Theodore, 1968, *The Making of a Counterculture*. Garden City, N.Y.: Doubleday & Company, Inc.

Ross, John, 1819, *A Voyage of Discovery*. London: John Murray.

Sahlins, Marshall D., 1962, *Moala: Culture and Nature on a Fijian Island*. Ann Arbor: University of Michigan Press.

Salaman, R. N., 1952, The social influence of the potato. *Scientific American*, December 1952.

Sanders, Irwin T., 1949, *Balkan Village*. Lexington: University of Kentucky Press.

San Francisco Examiner, 1971, The beautiful people—where did they go? November 14.

Sapir, Edward, 1921, *Language*. New York: Harcourt, Brace and Company, Inc.

Schaller, George B., 1963, *The Mountain Gorilla—Ecology and Behavior*. Chicago: University of Chicago Press.

Schärer, Hans, 1963, *Ngaju Religion, the Conception of God among a South Borneo People*. Trans. by Rodney Needham. The Hague: Martinus Nijhoff.

Schultz, J. W., 1956, *My Life as an Indian*. New York: Fawcett World Library, Premier Books.

Schusky, Ernest L., 1972, *Manual for Kinship Analysis*, 2d ed. New York: Holt, Rinehart and Winston, Inc.

Schwartz, Gary, and Don Merton, 1968, Social identity and expressive symbols: the meaning of an initiation ritual. *American Anthropologist*, 70:1117–1130.

Seeley, J. R., R. A. Sim, and E. W. Loosley, 1963, *Crestwood Heights: a Study of the Culture of Suburban Life*. New York: John Wiley & Sons, Inc.

Segall, Marshall H., Donald T. Campbell, Melville J. Herskovits, 1966, *The Influence of Culture on Visual Perception*. New York: The Bobbs-Merrill Company, Inc.

Service, Elman R., 1971, *Primitive Social Organization*, 2d ed. New York: Random House, Inc.

Shapiro, Harry L., 1962. *The Heritage of the Bounty*, 2d ed., rev. New York: The Natural History Library, Anchor Books.

Sharp, L., 1952, Steel axes for Stone Age Australians, in *Exploring Human Problems in Technological Change: a Casebook*. E. H. Spicer, ed. New York: Russell Sage Foundation.

Siegel, Bernard, 1959, 1961, 1963, 1965, *Biennial Review of Anthropology*. Stanford, Calif.: Stanford University Press.

Simmons, Leo W., 1966, *Sun Chief: the Autobiography of a Hopi Indian*, Leo W. Simmons, ed. New Haven, Conn.: Yale University Press. (First published in 1942.)

Simmons, William S., 1971, *Eyes of the Night: Witchcraft among a Senegalese People*. Boston: Little, Brown & Company.

Singleton, John, 1967, *Nichu: A Japanese School*. New York: Holt, Rinehart and Winston, Inc.

Skilton, Charles S., 1939, American Indian music, in *International Cyclopedia of Music and Musicians*. New York: Dodd, Mead & Company, Inc.

Spindler, George D., 1955a, *Sociocultural and Psychological Processes in Menomini Acculturation*. University of California Publications in Culture and Society, Vol. V. Berkeley, Calif.: University of California Press.

————, 1955b, Education in a transforming American culture. *Harvard Educational Review*, 20 (3):144–156.

————, 1958, New trends and applications in anthropology, in *New Viewpoints in the Social Sciences*, Roy A. Price, ed. Washington, D.C.: Twenty-Eighth Yearbook of the National Council for the Social Studies.

————, 1959, The transmission of American culture, in *Education and Culture*, G. Spindler, ed. Cambridge, Mass.: Harvard University Press.

————, 1961, *Peasants with Tractors*. Paper presented at the Southwestern Anthropological Association meetings, University of California, Santa Barbara, Calif., March 31, 1961.

————, 1963a, *Education and Culture*. New York: Holt, Rinehart and Winston, Inc.

————, 1963b, Personality, sociocultural system and education among the Menomini, in *Education and Culture*, G. Spindler, ed. New York: Holt, Rinehart and Winston, Inc.

————, ed., 1970, Being an anthropologist: fieldwork in eleven cultures. New York: Holt, Rinehart and Winston, Inc.

————, 1972, *Burgbach: Urbanization and Identity in a German Village*. New York: Holt, Rinehart and Winston, Inc.

————, 1974, *Education and Cultural Process*. New York: Holt, Rinehart and Winston.

————, and Louise S. Spindler, 1957, American Indian personality types and their sociocultural roots. *Annals of the American Academy of Political and Social Science*, Vol. 311.

————, and Louise S. Spindler, 1971, *Dreamers without Power: the Menomini Indians.* New York: Holt, Rinehart and Winston, Inc.

Spindler, Louise S., 1962, Menomini women and culture change. *American Anthropologist*, Memoir 91, Vol. 64, No. 1, Pt. 2.

Spiro, Melford, 1958, *Children of the Kibbutz.* Cambridge, Mass.: Harvard University Press.

Spock, Benjamin, 1957. *Baby and Child Care.* New York: Pocket Books, Inc. (First published in 1946.)

Spradley, James P., and David W. McCurdy, 1972, *The Cultural Experience: Ethnography in Complex Society.* Chicago: Science Research Associates, Inc.

Stephens, John L., 1867, *Incidents of Travel in Central America, Chiapas, and Yucatan,* 2 vols. New York: Harper & Row, Publishers. (First published in 1841.)

Steward, Julian H., 1955, The concept and method of cultural ecology, in *Theory of Cultural Change.* Urbana: University of Illinois Press.

Stewart, O. C., 1952, Southern Ute adjustment to modern living. *International Congress of Americanists Proceedings,* 29:80–87.

Sturtevant, William C., 1964, Studies in ethnoscience, in *Transcultural Studies in Cognition,* A. Kimball Romney and Ray Goodwin D'Andrade, eds. *American Anthropologist* Special Publication, 66(3):II,99–131.

Swartz, Marc J., Victor W. Turner, and Arthur Tuden, 1966, *Political Anthropology.* Chicago: Aldine Publishing Co.

Tacitus, 1960. Germania, in *Tacitus on Britain and Germany.* Trans. by H. Mattingly. Baltimore: Penguin Books, Inc. (First published in 1948.)

Tocqueville, Alexis de, 1960, *Democracy in America,* 2 vols. (The Henry Reeve text as revised by Francis Bowen now further corrected and edited with a historical essay, editorial notes, and bibliographies by Phillips Bradley.) New York: Vintage Books. (First published in France, 2 vols., 1835–1840; first English translation published by Henry Reeve, London, 1835–1840.)

Toffler, Alvin, 1970, *Future Shock.* New York: Bantam Books.

Turner, Paul R., 1972, *The Highland Chontal.* New York: Holt, Rinehart and Winston, Inc.

Tyler, Stephen A., ed., 1969, *Cognitive Anthropology.* New York: Holt, Rinehart and Winston, Inc.

Uchendu, Victor C., 1966, *The Igbo of Southeast Nigeria.* New York: Holt, Rinehart and Winston, Inc.

Underhill, Ruth M., 1953, *Red Man's America.* Chicago: University of Chicago Press.

Van Gennep, Arnold, 1960, *The Rites of Passage.* Chicago: University of Chicago Press. (First published in 1909.)

Van Lawick-Goodall, Jane, 1968, The behavior of free-living chimpanzees in the Gombe Stream Reserve. *Animal Behavior Monographs,* 1(3):161–311.

Vayda, Andrew P., 1969, *Environment and Cultural Behavior.* Garden City, N.Y.: The Natural History Press.

Vogt, Evon Z., 1970, *The Zinacantecos of Mexico: a Modern Maya Way of Life.* New York: Holt, Rinehart and Winston, Inc.

Voth, H. R., 1901, *The Oraibi Powamu Ceremony*. Publ. 61, Anthropological Series, III, 2. Chicago: Field Columbian Museum.

Wallace, Anthony F. C., 1956, Revitalization movements. *American Anthropologist*, 58:264–281.

————, 1969, The trip, in *Psychedelic Drugs*. New York: Grune & Stratton.

Ward, Martha, 1971, *Them Children: a Study in Language Learning*. New York: Holt, Rinehart and Winston, Inc.

Warren, Richard, 1967, *Education in Rebhausen: a German Village*. New York: Holt, Rinehart and Winston, Inc.

West, James, 1945. *Plainville, U.S.A.* New York: Columbia University Press.

Whiting, Beatrice B., 1963, *Child Rearing in Six Cultures*. New York: John Wiley & Sons, Inc.

Whiting, John R., R. Kluckhohn, and A. Albert, 1958, The function of male initiation ceremonies at puberty, in *Readings in Social Psychology*, E. Maccoby, T. Newcomb, and E. Hartley, eds. New York: Holt, Rinehart and Winston, Inc.

Whyte, William Foote, 1955, *Street Corner Society: the Social Structure of an Italian Slum*, 2d ed. Chicago: University of Chicago Press.

Williams, Mentor L., ed. 1956, *Schoolcraft's Indian Legends*. East Lansing, Mich.: Michigan State University Press.

Williams, Thomas Rhys, 1965, *The Dusun: a North Borneo Society*. New York: Holt, Rinehart and Winston, Inc.

————, 1969, *A Borneo Childhood: Enculturation in Dusun Society*. New York: Holt, Rinehart and Winston, Inc.

Wilson, Monica (See also Monica Hunter), 1963, *Good Company: a Study of Nyakusa Age-Villages*. (First published in 1951 by the Oxford University Press for the International African Institute.) Boston: The Beacon Press.

Wiser, William H., and Charlotte Viall Wiser, 1963, *Behind Mud Walls, 1930–1960*. Berkeley: University of California Press.

Wolcott, Harry, 1967, *A Kwakiutl Village and School*. New York: Holt, Rinehart and Winston, Inc.

————, 1973, *The Man in the Principal's Office*. New York: Holt, Rinehart and Winston, Inc.

Wolf, Eric R., 1966, *Peasants*. Englewood Cliffs, N.J.: Prentice-Hall, Inc.

Wylie, Laurence, 1964, *Village in the Vaucluse: an Account of Life in a French Village*. New York: Harper & Row, Publishers.

Young, Frank W., 1965, *Initiation Ceremonies: a Cross-cultural Study of Status Dramatization*. Indianapolis: The Bobbs-Merrill Company, Inc.

Zahan, Dominique, 1960, *Sociétés d'initiation Bambara: le n'domo, le Korè*. Paris: Mouton and Co.

Zelditch, M. Jr., 1955, Role differentiation in the nuclear family: a comparative study, in *Family Socialization and Interaction Process*, T. Parsons and R. Bales, eds. Glencoe: The Free Press.

INDEX

To make the index a more efficient tool for use by the student-scholar in cultural anthropology, the authors have prepared one which is classified for specific information: an index of authors and titles, a second section covering cultures and peoples, and one on concepts and topics.

Authors and Titles

Cultures and Peoples

Concepts and Topics

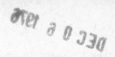

CASE STUDIES IN EDUCATION AND CULTURE

GENERAL EDITORS

George and Louise Spindler

THE NEW MATHEMATICS AND AN OLD CULTURE:
A Study of Learning among the Kpelle of Liberia
John Gay, Cuttington College, Liberia
Michael Cole, University of California, Irvine

GROWING UP IN TWO WORLDS:
Education and Transition among the Sisala of Northern Ghana
Bruce Grindal, Middlebury College

CHILDREN IN AMISH SOCIETY:
Socialization and Community Education
John A. Hostetler, Temple University
Gertrude Enders Huntington

GROWING UP IN A PHILIPPINE BARRIO
F. Landa Jocano, University of the Philippines

THE SCHOOL AT MOPASS: A Problem of Identity
A. Richard King, Teachers College—Columbia

ENCULTURATION AND SOCIALIZATION
IN AN IJAW VILLAGE
Philip E. Leis, Brown University

KANURI SCHOOLCHILDREN:
Education and Social Mobilization in Nigeria
Alan Peshkin, University of Illinois

CHILDREN OF THEIR FATHERS:
Growing up among the Ngoni of Malawi
Margaret Read

"SHUT THOSE THICK LIPS!":
A Study of Slum School Failure
Gerry Rosenfeld, Hofstra University

NICHU: A Japanese School
John Singleton, University of Pittsburgh

THEM CHILDREN: A Study in Language Learning
Martha C. Ward, Louisiana State University, New Orleans

EDUCATION IN REBHAUSEN: A German Village
Richard L. Warren, Stanford University

A BORNEO CHILDHOOD: Enculturation in Dusun Society
Thomas Rhys Williams, The Ohio State University

A KWAKIUTL VILLAGE AND SCHOOL
Harry F. Wolcott, University of Oregon

THE MAN IN THE PRINCIPAL'S OFFICE: An Ethnography
Harry F. Wolcott, University of Oregon

ALASKAN ESKIMO EDUCATION
A Film Analysis of Cultural Confrontation in the Schools
John Collier, Jr., California State University

Related Series Edited by George and Louise Spindler
CASE STUDIES IN CULTURAL ANTHROPOLOGY
STUDIES IN ANTHROPOLOGICAL METHOD

HOLT, RINEHART AND WINSTON, INC.
383 Madison Avenue, New York, N.Y. 10017

CASE STUDIES IN CULTURAL ANTHROPOLOGY
GENERAL EDITORS — George and Louise Spindler

BARNETT, **BEING A PALAUAN**

BASCOM, **THE YORUBA OF SOUTHWESTERN NIGERIA**

BASSO, **THE CIBECUE APACHE**

BASSO, **THE KALAPALO INDIANS OF CENTRAL BRAZIL**

BEALS, **GOPALPUR: A SOUTH INDIAN VILLAGE**

BEATTIE, **BUNYORO: AN AFRICAN KINGDOM**

BEIDELMAN, **THE KAGURU: A MATRILINEAL PEOPLE OF EAST AFRICA**

BOISSEVAIN, **HAL-FARRUG: A VILLAGE IN MALTA**

BUECHLER and BUECHLER, **THE BOLIVIAN AYMARA**

CHAGNON, **YANOMAMÖ: THE FIERCE PEOPLE**

CHANCE, **THE ESKIMO OF NORTH ALASKA**

COHEN, **THE KANURI OF BORNU**

DENG, **THE DINKA OF THE SUDAN**

DENTAN, **THE SEMAI: A NONVIOLENT PEOPLE OF MALAYA**

DIAMOND, **K'UN SHEN: A TAIWAN VILLAGE**

DOWNS, **THE NAVAJO**

DOWNS, **THE TWO WORLDS OF THE WASHO**

DOZIER, **HANO: A TEWA INDIAN COMMUNITY IN ARIZONA**

DOZIER, **THE KALINGA OF NORTHERN LUZON, PHILIPPINES**

DOZIER, **THE PUEBLO INDIANS OF NORTH AMERICA**

DUNN and DUNN, **THE PEASANTS OF CENTRAL RUSSIA**

EKVALL, **FIELDS ON THE HOOF: NEXUS OF TIBETAN NOMADIC PASTORALISM**

FAKHOURI, **KAFR EL-ELOW: AN EGYPTIAN VILLAGE IN TRANSITION**

FARON, **THE MAPUCHE INDIANS OF CHILE**

FRASER, **FISHERMEN OF SOUTH THAILAND: THE MALAY VILLAGERS**

FRIEDL, **VASILIKA: A VILLAGE IN MODERN GREECE**

FRIEDLAND and NELKIN, **MIGRANT: AGRICUL-TURAL WORKERS IN AMERICA'S NORTHEAST**

GAMST, **THE QEMANT: A PAGAN-HEBRAIC PEASANTRY OF ETHIOPIA**

GARBARINO, **BIG CYPRESS: A CHANGING SEMINOLE COMMUNITY**

HALPERN and HALPERN, **A SERBIAN VILLAGE IN HISTORICAL PERSPECTIVE**

HART and PILLING, **THE TIWI OF NORTH AUSTRALIA**

HITCHCOCK, **THE MAGARS OF BANYAN HILL**

HOEBEL, **THE CHEYENNES: INDIANS OF THE GREAT PLAINS**

HOGBIN, **A GUADALCANAL SOCIETY: THE KAOKA SPEAKERS**

HOROWITZ, **MORNE-PAYSAN: PEASANT VILLAGE IN MARTINIQUE**

HOSTETLER and HUNTINGTON, **THE HUTTERITES IN NORTH AMERICA**

HUDSON, **PADJU EPAT: THE MA'ANYAN OF INDONESIAN BORNEO**

JONES, **SANAPIA: COMANCHE MEDICINE WOMAN**

KEARNEY, **THE WINDS OF IXTEPEJI**

KEISER, **THE VICE LORDS: WARRIORS OF THE STREETS**

KIEFER, **THE TAUSUG: VIOLENCE AND LAW IN A PHILIPPINE MOSLEM SOCIETY**

KLIMA, **THE BARABAIG: EAST AFRICAN CATTLE-HERDERS**

KUNKEL AND KENNARD, **SPOUT SPRING: A BLACK COMMUNITY**

KUPER, **THE SWAZI: A SOUTH AFRICAN KINGDOM**

LESSA, **ULITHI: A MICRONESIAN DESIGN FOR LIVING**

LEWIS, **TEPOZTLÁN: VILLAGE IN MEXICO**

McFEE, **MODERN BLACKFEET: MONTANANS ON A RESERVATION**

MADSEN, **THE MEXICAN-AMERICANS OF SOUTH TEXAS**

MESSENGER, **INIS BEAG: ISLE OF IRELAND**

MIDDLETON, **THE LUGBARA OF UGANDA**

NEWMAN, **KNOWING THE GURURUMBA**

NORBECK, **CHANGING JAPAN**

OPLER, **APACHE ODYSSEY: A JOURNEY BETWEEN TWO WORLDS**

O'TOOLE, **WATTS AND WOODSTOCK: IDENTITY AND CULTURE IN THE UNITED STATES AND SOUTH AFRICA**

PARTRIDGE, **THE HIPPIE GHETTO**

PIERCE, **LIFE IN A TURKISH VILLAGE**

PILCHER, **THE PORTLAND LONGSHOREMEN: A DISPERSED URBAN COMMUNITY**

POSPISIL, **THE KAPAUKU PAPUANS OF WEST NEW GUINEA**

QUINTANA and FLOYD, **¡QUÉ GITANO!: GYPSIES OF SOUTHERN SPAIN**

RICHARDSON, **SAN PEDRO, COLOMBIA: SMALL TOWN IN A DEVELOPING SOCIETY**

RIVIÈRE, **THE FORGOTTEN FRONTIER: RANCHERS OF NORTH BRAZIL**

ROHNER and ROHNER, **THE KWAKIUTL: INDIANS OF BRITISH COLUMBIA**

SPINDLER, **BURGBACH: URBANIZATION AND IDENTITY IN A GERMAN VILLAGE**

SPINDLER and SPINDLER, **DREAMERS WITHOUT POWER: THE MENOMINI INDIANS**

TRIGGER, **THE HURON: FARMERS OF THE NORTH**

TURNER, **THE HIGHLAND CHONTAL**

UCHENDU, **THE IGBO OF SOUTHEAST NIGERIA**

VOGT, **THE ZINACANTECOS OF MEXICO: A MODERN MAYA WAY OF LIFE**

VON FÜRER-HAIMENDORF, **THE KONYAK NAGAS: AN INDIAN FRONTIER TRIBE**

WILLIAMS, **THE DUSUN: A NORTH BORNEO SOCIETY**

HOLT, RINEHART AND WINSTON, INC.   383 Madison Avenue, New York 10017